FIRST FUNDAMENTAL RIGHTS DOCUMENTS IN EUROPE

FIRST FUNDAMENTAL RIGHTS DOCUMENTS IN EUROPE

Commemorating 800 Years of Magna Carta

Markku SUKSI
Kalliope AGAPIOU-JOSEPHIDES
Jean-Paul LEHNERS
Manfred NOWAK
(EDS)

intersentia
Cambridge — Antwerp — Portland

Intersentia Ltd
Sheraton House | Castle Park
Cambridge | CB3 0AX | United Kingdom
Tel.: +44 1223 370 170 | Email: mail@intersentia.co.uk

Distribution for the UK:
NBN International
Airport Business Centre, 10 Thornbury Road
Plymouth, PL6 7PP
United Kingdom
Tel.: +44 1752 202 301
Fax: +44 1752 202 331
Email: orders@nbninternational.com

Distribution for Austria:
Neuer Wissenschaflicher Verlag
Argentinierstraße 42/6
1040 Wien
Austria
Tel.: +43 1 535 61 03 24
Email: office@nwv.at

Distribution for the USA and Canada:
International Specialized Book Services
920 NE 58th Ave, Suite 300
Portland, OR 97213
USA
Tel.: +1 800 944 6190 (toll free)
Email: info@isbs.com

Distribution for other countries:
Intersentia Publishers
Groenstraat 31
2640 Mortsel
Belgium
Tel.: +32 3 680 15 50
Email: mail@intersentia.be

First Fundamental Rights Documents in Europe
Markku Suksi, Kalliope Agapiou-Josephides, Jean-Paul Lehners and Manfred Nowak (eds)

ISBN 978–1–78068–360–7
D/2015/7849/146
NUR 828

PREFACE

In 2015, we are celebrating the 800th anniversary of Magna Carta, adopted on 15 June 1215, and the 15th anniversary of the Charter of Fundamental Rights of the European Union, adopted on 7 December 2000. Between 1215 and 2000, and perhaps also before and after that period, various jurisdictions in Europe have adopted documents that are of significance for the protection of fundamental rights and, ultimately, after 1945, of internationally recognised human rights. Historians and others like to commemorate 'round' birthdays: 25 years, 100 years, 800, etc. An event is not important *per se* because of a specific birthday, but it may be worthwhile to take the opportunity to contextualise fundamental rights by studying history and thus at the same time recognise the value of Magna Carta and other fundamental rights documents.

With this book we wish to celebrate 800 years of Magna Carta. At the same time, we congratulate the European Union on the first 15 years of its first fundamental rights document. This volume can be seen as a birthday present to the teenager from the rest of the family, all of whom are older, some very old or even ancient.

But why the *first* fundamental rights document? Do we want to show that some states, regions or cities have been more progressive than others or to imply that there has been no development in some states? Certainly not; this is not a beauty contest. Whenever the first fundamental rights document has been adopted or issued in a jurisdiction, it is likely to have had similar relevance for the individuals living at the material time as a document adopted in some other place at some other point of time, be it earlier or later. Therefore, the topic is fitting for a joint study as part of the cooperation between the universities in the European Master's Programme in Human Rights and Democratisation. Even Magna Carta itself, adopted 800 years ago, is not important *per se*, but it is significant because of the use that has been made of it during the centuries, alongside its strong symbolic value; the same observation is probably true concerning the other fundamental rights documents reviewed here, albeit in most cases to a somewhat lesser extent.

This book takes the reader on a journey across Europe in different times and places within a broad common frame, that of the first signs of emergence of fundamental rights documents. In the beginning of this enterprise, we thought that it would be an excellent result of our project if we could find historical documents to show that the fundamental rights dimension is not limited to England in the thirteenth and France in the eighteenth century but that other peoples in Europe have also managed to secure such rights. We feel that we have achieved this objective and that we have uncovered 'artefacts' that may have previously been known only to a very limited group of people. In doing so, we have mapped out waters previously uncharted and revealed a landscape in the deeper layers of our collective history which has not been generally visible at a European level. We also wanted to make the first fundamental rights documents available to a wider audience by complementing this book with internet access to the documents, provided by the E.MA and EIUC structures in Venice. A selection of the documents is thus available for further study at http://www.eiuc.org/first-fundamental-right-documents.

The idea of compiling this volume was hatched during a relaxed dinner in Venice in September 2014 at which the E.MA professors gathered after a long day of sessions of exam commissions. During the day, E.MA students had defended their Master's Theses on human rights issues of all sorts, so the brains of the professors had been exposed to many interesting and original topics and approaches. As with the previous book produced jointly by the E.MA community, published in 2009 on the reception of the Universal Declaration of Human Rights in Europe,[1] it was again proven that academics can be productive even when not doing anything particular: an innocent question about whether we could carry out a similar joint project immediately received an affirmative reply. Having become aware of the celebrations planned for Magna Carta in 2015, the question was posed whether there were other historical documents of the same kind in other countries. Nobody could give any definite answer, not even necessarily about their own country, but the question sparked the idea that perhaps this uncertainty could be used as a pretext for carrying out a joint inquiry into the roots of rights-thinking in Europe.

The idea was prepared for the meeting of the E.MA Council in December 2014, and the meeting adopted the project plan entitled 'The First Fundamental Rights Document'. The idea was met with enthusiasm by the participants in the E.MA Council, and the participating universities were quick to commit themselves to contributing to this book. It is our belief that the idea has resulted in a truly unique project in which contributors from almost all EU member states have reviewed the historical precursors to their current fundamental rights documents. Every country, old and young, tells a different story about the emergence of fundamental rights in their area. At the same time, they often indicate certain historical links to each other.

The production of this book was only possible on the basis of commitments by the contributing authors who agreed to participate in this endeavour and to submit themselves to a tight production timetable. Therefore, we wish to thank the authors featuring in this volume for their contributions. In addition, we wish to thank the European Inter-University Centre for Human Rights and

[1] V. Jaichand and M. Suksi, *60 Years of the Universal Declaration of Human Rights in Europe*, Intersentia, Antwerp – Oxford – Portland 2009.

Democratisation (EIUC), its Board and its Secretary-General, Professor Florence Benoit-Rohmer for financial support for the editing process. We also wish to thank Ms. Raija Hanski of the Institute for Human Rights at Åbo Akademi University for the technical editing of the entire text and Ms. Anna Barlow of the Department of Law at Åbo Akademi University for correcting the English language of the contributions, most of which are not written by native speakers. Markku Suksi thanks separately Åbo Akademi University and the Pool of Professors for the one-year-long research grant that facilitated research for this volume in August and September 2015. Finally, we wish to thank Intersentia for accepting the book for publication and Mr. Nicola Tonon at EIUC for making the first fundamental rights documents available on the internet.

Nicosia, Luxembourg, Vienna, and Åbo on 15 June 2015

Kalliope Agapiou-Josephides, Jean-Paul Lehners, Manfred Nowak,
and Markku Suksi

CONTENTS

LIST OF AUTHORS

Kalliope Agapiou-Josephides, PhD (Political Science), Assistant Professor of Political Science, University of Cyprus, Cyprus.

Florence Benoit Rohmer, PhD (Law), Professor of Law, University of Strasbourg; Secretary General of the European Inter-University Centre for Human Rights and Democratisation, France.

Louis Berkvens, MA (History); PhD (Law), Endowed Professor of Legal History, Maastricht University, the Netherlands.

Ivett Császár, PhD, Lecturer, International Coordinator, Eötvös Loránd University, Hungary.

Wim Decock, BA, MA, LLB, PhD, Assistant Professor (BOF), Faculty of Law, University of Louvain, Belgium.

Paolo De Stefani, PhD (Law), Aggregate Professor of International Law, University of Padova, Italy.

Tomáš Gábriš, PhD., Associate Professor of Legal History, Comenius University in Bratislava, Slovak Republic.

Felipe Gómez Isa, Dr., Professor of Public International Law, Institute of Human Rights, University of Deusto (Bilbao), Spain.

Agata Hauser, Dr., Assistant Professor of Constitutional Law, Adam Mickiewicz University, Poland.

Jan Holzer, PhD, Associate Professor, Department of Political Science, Faculty of Social Studies, Masaryk University, Czech Republic.

Liana Andreea Ioniță, Dr., Researcher and Teaching Assistant, University of Bucharest, Romania.

Zdzislaw Kedzia, Dr., Professor of Human Rights and Constitutional Law, Adam Mickiewicz University, Poland.

Artūrs Kučs, Dr., Professor of International Public Law, University of Latvia, Latvia.

Eva Maria Lassen, Mag.art., Ph.D., Senior Researcher, Danish Institute for Human Rights, Denmark.

Jean-Paul Lehners, PhD (History), Professor emeritus, UNESCO Chair of Human Rights, University of Luxembourg, Luxembourg.

Koen Lemmens, Dr. (PhD), Associate Professor, KU Leuven, Belgium.

Marelle Leppik, MA iur., theol., PhD student, University of Tartu, Estonia.

Anna-Sara Lind, Dr.iur., Associate Professor of Public Law, Uppsala University, Sweden.

Balázs Majtényi, PhD, Associate Professor, Eötvös Loránd University, Hungary.

Maria Daniella Marouda, PhD (International Law), Assistant Professor of International Law, Panteion University, Greece.

Helena Pereira de Melo, PhD (Law), Assistant Professor, Faculty of Law, New University of Lisbon, Portugal.

Anja Mihr, PhD, Associate Professor, Utrecht University and Humboldt Viadrina Governance Platform, the Netherlands and Germany.

Vygantė Milašiūtė, Dr., Lecturer, Vilnius University, Lithuania.

Nikolay Natov, Dr., Professor of Private International Law, The St Kliment Ohridski University of Sofia, Bulgaria.

Manfred Nowak, Dr, LL.M., Professor of International Law and Human Rights, University of Vienna, Austria.

Michael O'Flaherty, BCL, BPh, STB, MA, MPhil, FRSA, Solicitor, Professor of Human Rights and Director of the Irish Centre for Human Rights, National University of Ireland, Galway, Ireland.

Dawn Oliver, BA, PhD, LL.D., Emeritus Professor of Constitutional Law, University College London, United Kingdom.

Mária Patakyová, JUDr., PhD, Professor of Civil Law, Comenius University in Bratislava, Slovakia.

Stelios Perrakis, Dr. (International Law), Professor of International and European Institutions, Panteion University, Greece.

Teresa Pizarro Beleza, Dr., Professor of Criminal Law, Universidade Nova de Lisboa, Portugal.

Jānis Pleps, Dr.iur., Docent, University of Latvia, Latvia.

Hesi Siimets-Gross, Dr.iur., Associate Professor for Legal History and Roman law, University of Tartu, Estonia.

Hubert Smekal, PhD, Assistant Professor, Masaryk University, Czech Republic.

Markku Suksi, Dr., Professor of Public Law, Åbo Akademi University, Finland.

Brendan Tobin, Dr., Research Fellow, Griffith University, Australia, and Adjunct Lecturer, Irish Centre for Human Rights, National University of Ireland, Galway.

Marija Wakounig, Mag. Dr.MAS, University Professor, Institute of East European History of the University of Vienna, Austria.

Charlotte Wirth, BA (History), Luxembourg.

1. INTRODUCTION

Markku SUKSI
Kalliope AGAPIOU-JOSEPHIDES
Jean-Paul LEHNERS
Manfred NOWAK

In Europe, two famous sets of rights of a fundamental nature exist, the English Magna Carta of 1215 and the French Declaration of the Rights of Man and the Citizen of 1789. Does this mean that no corresponding fundamental rights documents were ever adopted or granted in the territories of the other current Member States of the European Union? This volume proposes to explore Europe's heritage in terms of fundamental rights, while contextualising and tracing their path and impact in the Member States of the European Union.[1]

Until now, there has existed no overall understanding of the historical existence of fundamental rights documents in other parts of Europe than in England and France. The fundamental rights discourse has been so dominated by Magna Carta and the Declaration of 1789 that other possible developments have been overshadowed, if not almost completely sidelined. Yet when asked, persons knowledgeable in the legal history of their own country would often be able to identify at least some precursors to the fundamental rights currently in force on the basis of the constitution of the country, although unbroken lineage between the fundamental rights in force and the early antecedents may be impossible to establish.

By using the term fundamental rights, the intention here is to indicate that the searchlight is on those individual rights that define the position of the individual in a fundamental manner in particular in relation to the public authorities, but perhaps also generally in relation to powers that be. On that view, fundamental rights cover both individual rights established in documents of a constitutional

---

1 It is possible to say that the first elements of fundamental rights of some kind in the history of humanity can be traced back to many centuries BC, but also to some other parts of the world than Europe. Texts like Codex Hammurabi (1754 BC) and Cyrus Cylinder (539 BC) could perhaps be mentioned in this context, although their interpretation in this context is not without problems, and the contributions of Greek philosophers such as Plato, Socrates, Aristotle or Sophocles have been instrumental in formatting the fundamental rights discourse and course over time.

nature and individual rights that appeared in norms of a more general nature. Fundamental rights are, from this perspective, rights that have emerged at the state or sub-state level, even in city-states (although in most cases, the current states did not exist at the time of the adoption of these documents).

Against this background, it can be said that there exists a general interest in and also a need for review of the historical documents concerning fundamental rights that can be found in the current Member States of the European Union. This interest and need is further enhanced by the fact that the fundamental rights that first evolved at a national level, however defined, gave the impetus for international human rights law after World War II. Again, no unbroken lineage, perhaps no lineage at all, between historical fundamental rights and international human rights can be established, but behind both concepts, there is an understanding of individual rights that afford protection from too much interference from the state and that from time to time also require some measures from the state. The terminological point of departure here is, however, that the concept of human rights is used for internationally guaranteed rights. Therefore, the concept of fundamental rights or some similar concept denoting individual rights at the national level is the general terminological framework within which the historical documents are studied. The approach used in this volume thus implies some general application of the first fundamental rights document and an emancipatory aim as well as a politico-legal intention,[2] meaning that the document that is analysed would have a general aim to create rights for individuals, even in cases where those individuals at least initially represent only a segment of the society.

Methodologically, a review of the first fundamental rights documents is best placed in the disciplines of history and legal history, more specifically, the constitutional history of different states. Already at the point when the project idea was first conceived, both the contributors to and the editors of this volume were well aware of the fact that the design of the undertaking might be problematic from a methodological point of view. With a view to the fact that no strict template was imposed on the authors of the different national contributions, the approaches could range from historical to legal and further to politological. Some of the concerns identified early on were the risk of anachronistic interpretations and retrospective teleology, which resulted in a request from the editors to the authors of the chapters that the contributions be context-specific in order to explain the environment in which the first fundamental rights documents emerged. Being context-specific and applying contextualisation may, of course,

[2] Such an approach is pointed out in somewhat different terms in H. Bielefeld, *Menschenrechte in der Einwanderungsgesellschaft: Plädoyer für einen aufgeklärten Multikulturalismus*. Bielefeld, Transcript 2007, pp. 25–26. See also J-P. Lehners, 'Pleading for a New History of Human Rights' in A. Mihr and M. Gibney (eds), *The SAGE Handbook of Human Rights*, SAGE Publications, London 2014, p. 27.

mean that the volume deals with the constitutional history of European states. However, our common feeling is that such a study nonetheless has academic value in the general field of rights of the individual. We understand, however, that anachronisms and retrospective teleology may be difficult to avoid. In any event, being a first overall assessment of the emergence of fundamental rights documents across Europe, this volume may also be seen as a starting-point for further work in this area of fundamental rights documents, creating prospects for deeper analysis of these documents in their proper context. It is therefore hoped that the research featured in this volume will spark further studies, for instance, amongst the contributors to this volume.

Admittedly, the focus on the current Member States of the European Union may, for several reasons, be very controversial. The Member State perhaps did not exist at all at the time when the first fundamental rights document was issued, and it is probably not in most cases possible to give credit to the current nation state for something that perhaps was created a long time ago in a separate jurisdiction with no clear succession to the state that exists today. Such problems would exist, for example, in Italy, Germany, Austria and many other states, although there also exist states where lineage from the creation of the fundamental rights document to its application in modern times can be shown (as in the cases of the United Kingdom and France). Therefore, we are looking for fundamental rights documents that were created within the area of the current state, although not necessarily by the state itself even in any early form of the current state. On that basis, the caveat is issued that although each contribution is connected to a Member State, that particular state is likely to have little to do with the first fundamental rights document adopted or granted in its current territory. In addition to this general caveat, particular points of criticism have, in this respect, been made in a number of contributions in this volume, such as in those of Austria, the Czech Republic, Hungary, and Spain.

To give an example of the complexities from a Finnish perspective, it would be possible to mention the 1766 Freedom of the Press (Constitution) Act (free press, access to government documents) adopted in the Kingdom of Sweden, of which Finland was an integral part until 1809, or to mention some even earlier documents. However, there is only a tenuous lineage to the current constitutional provisions on these issues. Therefore, the Finnish contribution will also be focusing on the 1906 Freedoms of Speech, Assembly and Association (Constitution) Act, which introduced freedoms of association, assembly and the press, and on the 1906 Parliament (Constitution) Act, which introduced universal suffrage (including for women as regards both candidacy and voting) in proportional elections to a unicameral parliament. However, both documents were adopted when Finland was still an autonomous Grand Duchy of the Russian Empire and not an independent state, which it has been only since 1917.

By way of another example, what would the Austrian contribution contain? Only an analysis of the Charter of Tyrol dating back to the fourteenth century or also the first constitutional document of 1848? The authors of the various 'national' contributions were allowed to choose the first approach, but also to explain the later developments, although we have generally wanted to avoid *de lege lata*. Therefore, the authors of the contributions have primarily searched for early documents similar to the Magna Carta of 1215 in the different countries and analysed them in context. However, the scope of the search has been broader than that, covering also the earliest documents of a constitutional nature (sometimes even in codifications as *Bürgerliches Gesetzbuch*) that establish fundamental rights in the respective countries. We are thus actually combining two approaches in order to include also those countries that perhaps do not have any relevant document for analysis from the Middle Ages.

To exemplify this from an Austrian perspective, we find a number of early documents which can, in principle, be compared to Magna Carta. In his well-known book on the history of human rights, Felix Ermacora made, for instance, reference to the freedoms in the Charter of Tyrol of 1406.[3] Others drew our attention to the *Georgenberger Handfeste* of 1186 which enacted specific freedoms for those living in the city.[4] Marija Wakounig, the author of the Austrian contribution to our joint publication, found the Mining Regulation of Assling (Jesenice) of 1381 and the Forest Regulation of Gottschee (Kocevsko) of 1406 as early documents which granted certain freedoms to mining foremen and those who enjoyed forest rights. But all researchers agree that these early documents only granted limited freedoms to a highly specific group of rights holders and, therefore, cannot be regarded as fundamental rights documents of a constitutional nature. The idea of inherent natural rights of all human beings was for the first time expressed in civil codes, such as the *Bürgerliches Gesetzbuch für Westgalizien* of 1796 and the Austrian Civil Code of 1811. These inherent rights included the abolition of slavery and serfdom. But the first constitution with a bill of rights was only enacted during the revolutionary year of 1848 (*Pillersdorf'sche Verfassung*) and was based partly on the Belgian Constitution of 1831.

These revolutionary achievements were, however, reversed during the age of neo-absolutism, and the first lasting Bill of Rights was only proclaimed in 1867 (Basic Law on the General Rights of Citizens). This classical catalogue of civil and political rights has survived as part of the Austrian Constitution despite dramatic political changes, such as the transition from a constitutional monarchy to the Federal Republic of Austria after World War I, an authoritarian period from 1933 to 1938 and the incorporation of Austria into Nazi Germany between 1938 and 1945. Since the European Convention on Human Rights has been adopted as part of Austrian Federal Constitution in 1964, followed by other

---

3 F. ERMACORA, *Menschenrechte in der sich wandelnden Welt*, I. Band. Verlag der Österreichischen Akademie der Wissenschaften. Wien 1974, pp. 73 and 81.

4 See, e.g., K. SPREITZHOFER, *Georgenberger Handfeste. Entstehung und Folgen der ersten Verfassungsurkunde der Steiermark.* Verlag Styria, Graz 1986.

international treaty provisions, the present Austrian Bill of Rights constitutes a synthesis between domestic (primarily historical) and international sources of fundamental and human rights. As for constitutional remedy, Austria was the first state in the world which established a Constitutional Court (first the *Reichsgericht* of 1867, later the *Verfassungsgerichtshof* of 1920) and introduced an individual complaints system for the protection of fundamental rights.

Although the general wish has been to avoid anachronistic conclusions and retrospective teleology, some 'elements of modernity' are present in several contributions. Gender as a theme of fundamental rights is normally considered a relatively late phenomenon, but the authors were encouraged to incorporate a conscious gender perspective and to inquire into whether the first fundamental rights document reflected the position of women alongside that of men and if not, when equality between sexes entered the fundamental rights discourse and documents in each country. The very conceptualisation, publication and, at the end, the sidelining of the legendary 1791 *Déclaration des droits de la femme et de la citoyenne* by Olympe de Gouges mirrors the even longer and harder way to securing women's fundamental rights on an equal footing with those of men in the 1789 *Declaration des droits de l'homme et du citoyen.* The rhetoric inclusiveness of the word universal and the *de facto* exclusion of women as citizens, as rights-bearing individuals in the 1789 Declaration says much. Indeed, the conceptualisation of a universal, abstract, rights-bearing individual as the unit of national sovereignty and embodied as a man, had far-reaching implications for women's fundamental rights.

In addition, although the discussion concerning categories of rights is one attached to modern human rights, it was also felt important to inquire into the nature of the fundamental rights that were granted in the first document(s). Therefore, the authors of the contributions were asked to comment — in suitable ways and from their respective vantage points — on whether the fundamental rights granted were civil, cultural, economic, political or social rights in nature.

By these references to the gender dimension and to the categories of rights, it is hoped that it is possible to indicate something about the profile of the fundamental rights in the first documents against the background of the stereotyped view that women were not featured as beneficiaries of such sets of first fundamental rights and that the first fundamental rights were mainly civil rights, perhaps sometimes political rights. We expect the reader to be surprised.

The different 'national' reports are grouped according to the point of time when a distinction started to be made between constitutional law, on the one hand, and ordinary law, on the other. The relevance of this distinction may be understood from the point of view of the general operation of constitutions, which is that they should, in one way or another, steer the enactment and contents of ordinary legislation. Because this distinction became more commonly a part of the constitutional set-up of different states at some point during the eighteenth century, such fundamental rights documents that are from an earlier date are dealt with in the first part of this volume, while fundamental rights documents adopted from this point of time on are dealt with in the second part of this volume. This means that the contributions from the United Kingdom and from Austria, Belgium, Hungary, Italy, Ireland, Lithuania, Poland, and Spain appear in Part I, while contributions from France and from Bulgaria, the Czech Republic, Denmark, Estonia, Finland, Germany, Greece, Latvia, Luxembourg, the Netherlands, Portugal, Romania, Slovakia, and Sweden appear in Part II.

Within the two parts, states are generally ordered according to the approximate point of time of the adoption of the first fundamental rights document. 'Approximate' is here to be underlined, because a country may be able to report an early collection of norms of a fundamental rights nature, but the main thrust of the documentation is nonetheless of a later date. A case in point is Greece, where a first set of rights of a fundamental nature is reported from Gortyn in Crete, dating back to the beginning of the fifth century BC. In some other countries, the situation might be reversed for the purposes of this volume. The placing of countries in Part I is also partially arbitrary, such as in the cases of Lithuania and Poland, because many countries featured in Part I also have a history of constitutional rights from the nineteenth century and could equally well be placed in Part II.

For various reasons, it was, unfortunately, not possible to secure a contribution from each of the current Member States of the European Union. However, the absence of a country (Croatia, Cyprus, Malta and Slovenia) from this volume should not be taken as evidence of a complete lack of fundamental rights thinking of a historical nature in that country. The number of Member States featured in this volume is, however, more than sufficient for drawing an overall picture of the roots of fundamental rights thinking in Europe and for at least some general conclusions about the historical background of fundamental rights.

None of the documents dealt with in this book are featured as appendices to the book. Instead, with the help of the EMA and the EIUC, a web-site has been started up within the EMA/EIUC web portal where a number of these documents have been stored in electronic form. Therefore, when reading about the fundamental rights document(s) in the various articles, please take into consideration that you might find the text of the original document and perhaps even a translation into English on that web-site, under the address <http://www.eiuc.org/first-fundamental-right-documents>.
As pointed out above, this volume has no intention to indicate an unbroken chain of rights thinking from early documents to current fundamental rights in a certain Member State or, indeed, to international human rights. Instead, what is reviewed is the emergence of fundamental rights in context. This is a study reveals that different countries have different narratives and situations from which fundamental rights discourses begin, but all are equally important and illuminating for the understanding of European fundamental rights thinking and history. Already early on, there was normative action in the area of individual

rights. Later, an evolution of constitutionally entrenched individual rights followed, although not necessarily based on the first set of rights granted.

PART I

2. THE UNITED KINGDOM: FROM MAGNA CARTA 1215 TO THE RULE OF LAW

Dawn OLIVER

1. INTRODUCTION[1]

Magna Carta of June 1215 has been an iconic document in the legal and political histories of England and Wales, on and off, for 800 years. Arlidge and Judge (respectively an eminent criminal practitioner and scholar, and Lord Chief Justice of England and Wales from 2008 to 2013) claim that it 'continues to be a powerful symbol of our liberties' and that 'within its clauses are the germs of constitutional principles which resonate to this day'.[2]

In the document, only later referred to as 'Magna Carta' or 'The Great Charter', the King purported to grant certain 'liberties' to 'all freemen of our Kingdom'. The document also granted certain 'freedoms' and 'rights' to the Church, and to freemen and cities of the Kingdom. These liberties were not, then, regarded by the King — or his predecessors — as inherent or 'natural law' rights. They were privileges to be granted by the monarch to and enjoyed by limited classes of people and institutions, rather than the universal rights and freedoms of today.

The sealing of Magna Carta by the King in 1215 was not however the first time that an English King had granted liberties to his subjects — Henry I had done so in his 1115 Charter of Liberties,[3] for example. In their rebellion in 1215 the barons were seeking, among other things, the restoration of ancient rights and liberties — life, liberty and property — which had been granted in earlier laws and charters and which had been rejected by King John. Quite apart from such

---

1. For authoritative contemporary accounts of Magna Carta and its continuing importance in the English national narrative and legal system see D. CARPENTER, *Magna Carta*, Penguin Classics, London 2015; A. ARLIDGE and J. JUDGE, *Magna Carta Uncovered*, Hart Publishing, Oxford 2015. See also P. LINEBAUGH, *The Magna Carta Manifesto*, University of California Press, London 2008 for discussion of it wider importance, in the USA and in relation to commons; House of Lords Library Note *A Brief History of Magna Carta*, 29 January 2015, LLN 2015/001 <www.parliament.uk/business/publications/research/briefing-papers/LLN-2015-001/a-brief-history-of-the-magna-carta>.
2. ARLIDGE and JUDGE, *supra* note 1, p. 1.
3. See The Laws of Henry I 1115, to which the King's Charter of Liberties was added.

charters, the principle that people enjoyed 'ancient liberties' and that monarchs would be expected to guarantee them had been embedded in the culture of England since the time of Edward the Confessor, King from 1042–1066 (in the *Leges Edwardi*), and in earlier Anglo-Saxon times, well before the Norman conquest of 1066 and the establishment of the feudal system.[4] The grant of rights and liberties came to be part of the deal or contract between the king and his people or 'subjects': he would provide protection, including protection of the law, in exchange for their loyalty and service. As Blackstone put it 'protection and subjecthood are reciprocal'.[5]

The grant in Magna Carta by King John 'to all free men of our kingdom' was 'for us and our heirs forever' of 'all the liberties written out below to have and to keep for them and their heirs'. And it was supposed not only to bind the King, but to have what might nowadays be regarded as a degree of 'horizontal effect' — though in the context of a hierarchical and ordered feudal system: article 60 provides that '[a]ll these customs and liberties that we have granted shall be observed in our kingdom in so far as concerns our own relations with our subjects. Let all men of our kingdom, whether clergy or laymen, observe them similarly in their relations with their own men.'

The Charter, having been granted in June 1215, was repudiated by John and quashed by papal bull by Pope Innocent III at his request in August 1215. Civil war and an invasion by King Louis of France, to whom rebels had offered the Crown, followed. John died in October 1216. In November of that year, William Marshal,[6] regent for the new King, Henry III (aged 9), issued a revised version of the Charter under his own seal (and that of the papal legate). The French invasion was repelled in 1217 and Marshal reissued the charter as regent in November 1217.

Marshal died in 1219. In February 1225 Henry III reissued Magna Carta in return for the provision of tax. It was addressed 'to all our realm' 'in perpetuity': the grants were to all men. The grant was made with Henry's consent. No security clause was included.[7] Successive monarchs thereafter confirmed the reissue. The text of each reissue was updated — in that sense the reissues were iterative and the Charter was a living document. It was not until much later, however, that the Charter came to be recognised as a statute of equivalent legal force as an Act of Parliament.[8] As of 2015 three articles remain part of English

---

4 See CARPENTER, *supra* note 1, chapter 10.

5 Sir W. BLACKSTONE, *Commentaries on the Laws of England*, J. Butterworth, London 1825, Book I, chapter 6.

6 A tombstone effigy of Marshal lies in the Temple Church, London.

7 This clause is discussed in section 4.1. below.

8 The legal status of the Charter is discussed further below.

law,[9] though many others are reflected in later enactments and decisions of the courts.

With each issue and reissue the Charter was copied and distributed to cathedrals and other centres. It was therefore widely known about and became progressively embedded in the culture of the community.[10]

2. MAGNA CARTA: A POLITICAL DOCUMENT

The Charter of 1215 was in many respects a peace treaty between the King and his barons. It is a lengthy document, stretching to 63 articles. Addressed by King John to all his officials and loyal subjects (identifying some office holders), it notes that its provisions are the result of 'the current dispute between us and our barons': its provisions reflect and seek to resolve the issues in that dispute, which had led to rebellion by some of the barons.

Many of the grievances against the King were financial — e.g. his demands for money ('aid' and 'scutage' — a tax to pay for the conduct of war to regain lands in France). The articles also reflect miscellaneous grievances about the operation of the feudal system and the unjust activities of the King and indeed of some barons in recent years. They include matters of international significance: Alexander, King of Scotland, was to be treated in the same way as 'our other barons' in England (article 59);[11] and if any Welshmen had been deprived of their land or liberties without the lawful judgment of their equals, they were at once to be returned to them, in accordance with local law (article 57).

Although some of the provisions of Magna Carta have little relevance in modern conditions, they reflect or foreshadow some fundamental political — and legal — principles which developed later, and are either directly relevant today or can readily be translated or transferred to the here and now.

---

9 These are article 1 (liberties of the English Church), article 13 (rights and customs of London and other cities and towns) and articles 39 and 40, now joined, on access to justice and the rule of law: British Library, *Magna Carta: an Introduction*, accessed 13.01.2015.

10 See CARPENTER, *supra* note 1, chapter 14.

11 Note the implication that Scotland was not an independent country.

3. THE CONTENT OF MAGNA CARTA

3.1. JUSTICE AND THE RULE OF LAW

By the thirteenth century there was already in place a system of royal courts and local courts, and of law — including customary law and the beginnings of the common law across England. Henry II (1154–1189), in Maitland's words 'a great legislator and a great administrator',[12] had reformed the operation of the criminal and civil court systems. But there remained many grievances about the legal system and the scope for its abuse by the King or his barons. Magna Carta included important provisions designed to improve the operation of the justice system, the trial process, and penal policy: the rule of law.

In perhaps the most famous of all the provisions in the Charter, article 40 provided that '[t]o no one will we sell, to no one deny or delay right or justice'. But without the regular holding of courts in accessible places, and expert judges, the promise might be nugatory. Thus articles 17, 18 and 19 required the regular holding of courts in the counties and in other fixed places, with time set aside to complete the business of administration of justice at each session. Article 24 forbad officials other than 'royal judges' from holding certain law suits, thus ensuring that cases were dealt with by appropriate judges. And by article 45 the King agreed to appoint as justices, constables, sheriffs and bailiffs 'only men that know the law of the land and mean to observe it' — the beginning of a professional judiciary. (The separation of the judiciary from the executive, that is, the monarch, was affirmed by Coke CJ in the *Prohibitions del Roy*, 1607, clearly building on article 45 of the Charter.[13])

However, 'The King's Justices' were appointed by the monarch, and were dismissible by him 'at pleasure'. It was not until the Act of Settlement 1700 that they were granted security of tenure, with appointment 'quamdiu se bene gesserint', subject to removal on an address to the monarch by both Houses of Parliament: by that provision a truly independent and professional judiciary was established at last.

As far as the trial process was concerned, the general requirement was for trial by one's equals. This did not necessarily imply jury trial. Article 39 laid down

---

[12] F.W. Maitland, *The Constitutional History of England*, Cambridge University Press, Cambridge 1974, p. 10.

[13] *Prohibitions del Roy* (1607) 12 Co Rep 63, deciding that the King could not sit as a judge because 'His Majesty was not learned in the laws of his realm of England, and causes which concern the life, or inheritance, or goods, or fortunes of his subjects are not to be decided by natural reason, but by the artificial reason and judgment of law, which law is an act which requires long study and experience, before that a man can attain to the cognizance of it: that the law was the golden metwand and measure to try the causes of the subjects; and which protected His Majesty in safety and peace'.

that no free man may be punished 'except by the lawful judgment of his equals or by the law of the land'.[14] This is one of the most enduring of the articles in the Charter.

The law of evidence was also developing: by article 38 credible witnesses were needed in support of the truth of allegations made by an official placing a man on trial. However '[n]o one shall be arrested or imprisoned on the appeal of a woman for the death of any person except her husband' (article 54).

Penal policy was also affected by the Charter: article 20 required that punishments be proportional. By article 55 previous unlawful fines were to be remitted.

3.2. DIFFERENT KINDS OF LIBERTIES AND RIGHTS

The Charter made extensive provision for civil liberties and rights, mostly related to property. These had been the subject of many of the grievances against the King.

- Articles 2–6 granted rights of inheritance for certain subjects in feudal relations with the king.
- Articles 7–8 guaranteed widows' rights of property, and their right not to remarry.
- Articles 9–11 governed the rights of debtors, especially of their heirs and sureties, some of whose rights were to take precedence over creditors.
- Article 27 made provision for the administration of intestate estates.
- Articles 28–31 made provision for the protection of property against seizure without the agreement of the owner.
- Article 52 provided a right to restitution of property unlawfully taken by King John; article 55 provided for the restitution of fines unlawfully levied by him.

The Charter included provisions for 'the general consent of the realm' to be obtained before the King could take action, particularly the raising of tax — one of the main grievances that gave rise to the barons' rebellion. By article 12 'No 'scutage' or 'aid' may be levied in our kingdom without its general consent'.[15] Provisions of this kind could be characterised as political rights and guarantees. Article 14 contained an undertaking from the King to cause the archbishops, bishops, abbots, earls and greater barons to be summoned so that he could obtain the general consent of the realm for an assessment of such taxes.

---

14 See also article 21 – earls and barons to be fined only by their equals.

15 Exceptions were made for the ransom of the King and other royal matters.

This provision is still reflected in the principle that 'redress of grievance comes before supply': Parliament will not agree to the transfer of revenues to the government from the Bank of England (supply) before it has listened to requests for the redress grievances. It was only recently that 'Supply days' in the House of Commons (days when Opposition parties are entitled to choose the topic for debate before the House grants supply to the government) were renamed 'Opposition days'.

The provisions in articles 12 and 14, and the principle of government by the general consent of the realm were precursors of the development of an English Parliament: a 'parliament' was held in Oxford in 1258 (leading to the Provisions of Oxford[16]). And Simon de Montfort's Parliament — the first real Parliament — was held at Westminster in 1265.[17]

Members of fourteenth century parliaments were aware of the link between the Charter and their right to consent (or refuse to consent) to new taxation: the first petition presented to the monarch by the Commons at each new parliament was a request that the Great Charter be firmly kept.[18] The contemporary version of the principle is reflected in the ceremony that takes place when a new Speaker is elected by the Commons: 'Her Majesty does most readily confirm all the rights and privileges which have ever been granted to or conferred upon the Commons by Her Majesty or any of her Royal predecessors.' A similar promise is made to the Lords.[19]

These principles are still reflected in the words of enactment on the face of every Act of the UK Parliament:

> Be it enacted, by the Queen's most Excellent Majesty, by and with the advice and consent of the Lords Spiritual and Temporal, and Commons, in this present Parliament assembled, and by the authority of the same, as follows…

Among the grievances against the King that the Charter sought to resolve a number were commercial: article 35 of the Charter requires consistency of weights and measures throughout the kingdom; article 41 guarantees the freedom of merchants to leave and enter and trade in England; and by article 13 London, other cities, boroughs, towns and ports were to enjoy all their ancient liberties and free customs both by land and by water.

---

16 CARPENTER, *supra* note 1, pp. 437–438, 441–442.
17 *Ibid.*, pp. 426–427, 437–438, 442–443, 459–460.
18 R. TURNER, *Magna Carta Through the Ages*, Harlow 2003, p. 113.
19 See L. LAURENCE SMITH, 'Privilege, Exclusive Cognisance and Law' in A. HORNE, G. DREWRY and D. OLIVER (eds.), *Parliament and the Law*, Hart Publishing, Oxford 2013, p. 6.

Were any of these rights and liberties 'cultural'? The freedom of the Church could be classified thus, but it was an institutional rather than an individual freedom. And of course it was highly political, given the history of conflicts between the Church and successive monarchs and the power of Popes over the kingdom. There was little if any individual freedom of religion at this period, and such freedoms were not mentioned in Magna Carta.

Some of the rights were about the status and security of individuals in society, though it was no part of the duty of the King personally to provide for them (except by the provision of the legal system) so as to constitute social rights of any kind. For instance by article 6 heirs may be given in marriage, but not to someone 'of lower social standing'. And at her husband's death a widow may have her marriage portion and inheritance at once and without trouble (article 7). She is free not to remarry.

The Charter of the Forest of 1217 dealt to a greater extent than Magna Carta with issues of individual security in the sense of access to necessities or primary needs. That Charter was sealed by Henry III under the Regency of William Marshal. It provided for the 'deforestation' or return to common use of much rural land which had been claimed by successive kings with a view to raising revenue from users. These claims had deprived free men of their legal rights of free access to pannage (pasture for their pigs), agistment (grazing), estover (collecting firewood), turbary (cutting of turf for fuel) and other fruits of the land (honey, for instance). These rights, once restored under the Charter, were not however readily enforceable in practice.[20]

Magna Carta is particularly interesting from this gender perspective. Some negative, discriminatory provisions have already been noted, for instance in article 54 about the admissibility in court of evidence from married women. On the other hand guarantees of a widow's inheritance and her freedom not to remarry provide protection in vulnerable situations. Article 10 provides protection for debtors, as noted above, but specifically from Jewish creditors: the heir of a debtor need pay no interest on the debt for so long as he remains under age.

The fact of the matter is that English common law, as it developed, gave very little recognition to the 'rights' of women, especially married women and mothers.[21] Nor did the common law provide protection against racial discrimination. Equality between the sexes and races did not enter the fundamental rights discourse and documents in the UK until after World War II, when the UK helped in the drafting of the European Convention on Human Rights and signed up to it in 1953. The first steps taken by the UK Parliament

---

20 See LINEBAUGH, *supra* note 1, chapter 2; CARPENTER, *supra* note 1, chapters 13 and 14.

21 BLACKSTONE, *supra* note 5, Book 1, chapter 15.

towards equality were the Race Relations Act 1965, the Equal Pay Act 1970 and the Sex Discrimination Act 1975, all primarily concerned with employment rights.

4. MAGNA CARTA AND THE LAW

4.1. THE LAW, THE LEGAL SYSTEM AND THE KING

Whether rules such as those in Magna Carta were to be regarded as 'laws' in the thirteenth century, and the implications of being law, were rather undeveloped. Most of the rules or norms administered by judges were customary or 'common' laws. Statutes in the sense of rules made by a sovereign or legislative authority[22] were also recognised as sources of law.[23] But Magna Carta was not a 'statute' when first sealed in 1215.[24] The text of the 1225 version was copied onto 'the statute roll' with the Charter of the Forest in 1297 and was thus incorporated into the law of the land. It does not follow from this fact that its provisions became justiciable in the way that most Acts of Parliament are today. Many of its terms were breached.[25] Its 'enforceability' and legal bindingness are discussed below.

Although the court system for the administration of justice, and the writ system, were fairly well developed — and were supposed to be improved by the Charter — the machinery for judicial enforcement of writs was not.[26] And there was no provision at all, whether at common law or by other forms of 'hard law', for judicial enforcement of laws against the King.[27]

Kings possessed the quality of perfection: 'The King can do no Wrong'.[28] The monarch was 'fons justitiae' ('the fountain of justice') and it was his duty to provide justice. Monarchs delegated the power to administer justice to royal justices. (Judges of the Senior Courts in England are still referred to as 'Her Majesty's Justices'. The court service is 'Her Majesty's Courts and Tribunals Service'.) Until the Act of Settlement 1700 the monarch not only appointed judges, but could and did dismiss them, at pleasure.

---

22 Shorter Oxford English Dictionary.

23 Nowadays much of the law of England is 'statutory', meaning that it is contained in Acts of Parliament.

24 'Charters' had been issued by kings over many centuries, including in the Anglo-Saxon period, and were widely respected by the people, though lacking legal enforceability by the courts.

25 CARPENTER, *supra* note 1, pp. 443–446.

26 See R.C. VAN CAENEGEM, *The Birth of the English Common Law*, 2nd ed., Cambridge University Press, Cambridge 1988, chapter 2.

27 Indeed the last vestiges of the immunity of the Crown from suit were abolished only in 1948 by the Crown Proceedings Act.

28 BLACKSTONE, *supra* note 5, Book I, chapter 7.

Nowadays effective determination of rights by an independent court or tribunal[29] and effective enforceability (see EU law) are often taken to be essential for a norm to qualify as law: 'ubi jus, ibi remedium'. If that were to be one of the essential ingredients of 'law', then Magna Carta was not 'law', at least as far as its enforceability against the King was concerned.

The system did however allow for actions for private enforcement, for instance between barons in dispute over their 'rights' under the charters.[30] Such actions were rare, and overall the Charter was hardly judicially enforceable.[31]

Many provisions in the Charter appear to subject the King — in modern terms the Executive — to law. Indeed, the Charter is famed for doing so. And it was widely believed in that period that the King should indeed be subject to law. Bracton (a judge, died 1268) asserted that 'The king must not be under man but under God and under the law, because the law makes the king'.[32] It was accepted by then that the King should make laws on the advice of his magnates.[33]

Magna Carta certainly expresses acceptance by King John of a duty to obey its provisions. For instance, the first article provides that 'the English Church shall be free, and shall have its rights undiminished, and its liberties unimpaired'. It continues:

> That we wish this to be so observed, appears from the fact that *of our own free will*, before the outbreak of the present dispute between us and our barons, we granted and confirmed by charter the freedom of the Church's elections .... and caused this to be confirmed by Pope Innocent III. This freedom we observe ourselves, and desire to be observed in good faith by our heirs in perpetuity.[34]

After Magna Carta, John was regarded by the Pope as holding his kingdom as a fief of the Holy See.

Many other articles purport to bind the King to take or refrain from action.

- Article 14 requires the King to cause the archbishops, bishops, abbots, earls, and greater barons to be summoned individually by letter in order

29 See Article 6 of the ECHR.

30 See CARPENTER, *supra* note 1, pp. 435–436.

31 *Ibid.*, pp. 435–449.

32 BRACTON, *On the Law and Custom of England,* Samuel E. Thorn trans, vol. 2, Harvard University Press, Cambridge, Mass. 1968, pp. 305–306.

33 See GLANVILL in C.D.G. HALL (ed.), *The Treatise on the Laws and Customs of England Commonly Called Glanvill,* Oxford University Press, Oxford 1993, p. 21.

34 My italics. This is the only article in the charter expressed to be made 'of our own free will'.

'to obtain the general consent of the realm' for the assessment of tax — an aid or scutage.

- Article 18 commits the King himself to send two justices to each county four times a year to hold the assizes.
- By one of the most famous articles, 40, '[t]o no one will we sell, to no one deny or delay right or justice'.
- By article 45 '[w]e will appoint as justices, constables, sheriffs, or other officials, only men that know the law of the realm and are minded to keep it well'.
- By article 52 the King undertakes to restore properties unlawfully taken by him to their owners.
- By articles 55 and 56 he undertakes that unlawfully taken fines shall be remitted.
- By article 60 '[a]ll these customs and liberties that we have granted shall be observed in our kingdom in so far as concerns our own relations with our subjects'.
- Finally, the security clause in article 61 provided for strong *extra-judicial* enforcement of the King's obligations.

As noted above, the King repudiated the Charter shortly after he gave it his seal. This did not give rise to *judicial* enforcement of its terms, against either the King or his barons. Thus although the Charter is celebrated for subjecting the King to the law, the courts were not in a position to enforce the law against him. 'Subjection to the law' in this context has other connotations.

Although the King was not subject to judicial enforcement of his obligations set out in Magna Carta, the Charter provided extra-judicial ways of enforcing fulfilment of his promises. Article 61 contained a detailed 'security clause'. In summary 'the barons shall choose twenty five of their number to keep, and charge to be observed ...the peace and liberties granted and confirmed to them by this charter'. Further: 'if we, our chief justice, our officials, or any of our other servants offend in any respect against any man, or transgress in any of the articles of the peace or of this security, and the offence is made known to four barons of the ... twenty-five barons' then, if other steps do not secure compliance, the twenty-five barons 'may distrain upon us and assail us in every way possible, with the support of the whole community of the law by seizing our castles, lands, possessions, or anything else...'.

The security clause was humiliating. It is hardly surprising that the King repudiated the charter soon after it was granted, with the support of Pope Innocent III. When the Charter was reissued by William Marshal as Regent for Henry III in 1216 this part of article 61 had been removed.

The security clause was not the only extra-judicial enforcement mechanism available for breach of the charter. Another mechanism – not referred to in the

Charter — was the use of excommunication by or in the name of the Pope. Excommunication was available against not only the King, but barons also.[35]

The Pope excommunicated some barons after Magna Carta, but his Archbishop in England, Stephen Langton, refused to publish the excommunications. However, the 1225 revised version of the Charter issued by Henry III had much greater legitimacy than the 1215 version, and was witnessed by, among others, Langton and other bishops and abbots, together with many earls, magnates and barons; this version of the charter was supported by the Church. Langton pronounced a sentence of excommunication against all who contravened the Charter of 1225.[36] Further sentences were promulgated in 1237 and 1255. They were primarily aimed as deterrents against breaches.

4.2. A CHARTER 'OF FUNDAMENTAL RIGHTS' OR 'OF THE RULE OF LAW'?

It can be seen from the discussion of Magna Carta in this chapter that many of the articles (but by no means all[37]) were about 'fundamental rights'. However, the focus in the development of English law, especially of the common law,[38] has been on the development of civil and political *liberties* rather than specially protected legal rights. If 'fundamental rights' suggests a special *legally*-protected *legal* status, then this is incompatible with the notions first of the sovereignty of the King, based on divine right and then of the sovereignty of Parliament.[39] Nor is it reflected in the machinery for enforcement of Magna Carta in its successive iterations.

Instead of developing what would nowadays be regarded as American style 'constitutional judicial review', the common law courts found other ways of building the rule of law and with it extensive protection for civil and political rights and liberties. They developed the doctrine that the liberties of the King's subjects could not be interfered with by royal proclamation: 'The King hath no prerogative but that which the law of the land allows him'. [40] An Act of Parliament was required, and a remedy was available in the courts for breach of this principle. Liberties cannot be interfered with on the basis of simple assertions by the monarch of public interest: a legal source must be identified for every interference with liberties, and the courts will provide remedies against the

---

35 This collection of essays focuses on 'fundamental rights' of a domestic law nature, rather than internationally enforced 'human rights'. It is of course for discussion whether excommunication by the Pope is properly regarded as falling within this project's discussion of Magna Carta.

36 CARPENTER, *supra* note 1, pp. 422, 446–447.

37 For instance, articles 1, 13, 35, 51.

38 See A.V. DICEY, *Introduction to the Study of the Law of the Constitution*, 1885, 10th ed., ed. E.C.S. Wade, Macmillan, London 1959.

39 See generally DICEY, *supra* note 38.

40 *Case of Proclamations* (1611) 12 Co Rep 74, Per Coke C.J.

King's ministers or servants (but not against the King's person) for breach.[41] At common law, then, liberties are inherent and do not depend upon 'grant' by the monarch, or in modern terms the executive or even Parliament, and they are remediable.

Alongside common law developments of this kind, Parliament of course played a major part in building the rule of law. In the 'Glorious Revolution' of 1688 Roman Catholic King James II was driven out and Protestant William of Orange and his wife Mary were offered the throne. As part of this arrangement, supreme legislative power was transferred from the monarch to Parliament by the Bill of Rights 1689: the monarch — in modern terms the executive — was thus deprived of many powers and made subject in principle to the law.

Procedural requirements for law-making and law-changing processes have thus substituted for substantive limitations on powers to interfere with liberties.

Thus a strong theme in the evolution of the law since Magna Carta in England has been its importance in the development of 'the rule of law' rather than of 'fundamental rights'. The language of fundamental rights developed only relatively recently in the UK. The Charter has been widely regarded as a very early, even the earliest, step in the development of the rule of law in England and Wales. Carpenter concludes that 'Magna Carta ... survived. It did so because it asserted one fundamental and treasured principle, that of the rule of law'.[42]

5. AFTER MAGNA CARTA

Henry V, crowned in 1416, was the last king to confirm the liberties in the Charter to Parliament at the time of his coronation. Magna Carta became less central to constitutional arrangements in England in the fifteenth and sixteenth centuries. However it was kept alive by the development of printing (it was first printed in 1508), and at the Inns of Court where the law was taught and student barristers were trained, and in the courts where it was invoked from time to time by advocates.[43]

Magna Carta revived in importance in the seventeenth century when successive monarchs sought to reassert the divine basis of their rights to rule. It was invoked by Sir Edward Coke, then Chairman of the Parliamentary Commission for Grievances, in the disputes between parliamentarians and King James I over parliamentary privilege: 'Magna Charter is called *Charter Libertatis quia liberos*

---

41 *Entick v Carrington* (1765) 19 State Trials 1029.

42 CARPENTER, *supra* note 1, p. 460.

43 Sir J. BAKER, *Oxford History of the Laws of England*, vol. VI, Oxford University Press, Oxford 2003, pp. 1483–1558. Sir Edward Coke was Chief Justice of the Common Pleas and later of Kings Bench, was dismissed by James I and became a member of the House of Commons in 1621.

facit … The Charter of Liberty … when the King says he cannot allow our liberties of right, this strikes at the root. We serve here for thousands and ten thousands'.[44]

Coke also relied on Magna Carta as the basis of the Petition of Right, the proto-constitution that Parliament forced Charles I to sign in 1628. Coke claimed that Magna Carta amounted to 'a restitution and declaration of the ancient common law'.[45] As Arlidge and Judge observe, 'Magna Carta was not merely a constitutional document, rather it was the foundation for the rights and liberties of the nation represented in Parliament'.[46]

The Habeas Corpus Amendment Act 1679 required that cause be shown to justify detention, drawing on Magna Carta. Blackstone described that Act as 'a second Magna Carta'.

In 1689 the Bill of Rights 'An Act declareing the Rights and Liberties of the Subject and Settleing the Succession of the Crowne' was regarded as 'our second Magna Carta'.[47] It succeeded in shifting legal sovereignty from the monarch to Parliament — in achieving in effect, at last, the subjection of the monarch to law.

Interest in Magna Carta waned in the eighteenth and nineteenth centuries once Kings (and Queens) had become constitutional monarchs, Parliament more democratic, and the common law more developed. By contrast, exported to the USA it became and remains an important and respected source of constitutional principles.

Magna Carta is not by any means the only document providing for protection for 'fundamental rights' in England and Wales: setting aside for the moment the question whether the discussion in this chapter has been about 'fundamental rights' at all, other important documents include the Bill of Rights 1689 and the Human Rights Act 1998. And of course if we are not concerned only with documents which purport to establish rights of general application, anti-discrimination laws would figure in our discussion.

---

44 C. DRINKER BOWEN, *The Lion and the Throne: The Life and Times of Sir Edward Coke*, London 1957, p. 391, quoted in ARLIDGE and JUDGE, *supra* note 1, p. 127.

45 Co. Inst. II, 8. See also Co. Inst. I, 81a 'This statute (nb) of Magna Carta is but a confirmation or restitution of the common law.' Quoted in J. ALLISON, *The English Historical Constitution*, Cambridge University Press, Cambridge 2007, p. 135; see also ARLIDGE and JUDGE, *supra* note 1, chapters 20 and 21.

46 ARLIDGE and JUDGE, *supra* note 1, p. 127.

47 BOLINGBROKE, quoted in A. PALISTER, *Magna Carta: The Heritage of Liberty*, Oxford University Press, Oxford 1971, p. 41.

6. CONCLUDING REMARKS

Despite the difficulties in enforcing Magna Carta and its short first life, Carpenter argues that 1215 marks a 'before' and 'after' moment in English history. Symbolically and textually the Charter subjected the King to the law. It was widely known about. Breaches were widely resented.

In summary, Magna Carta was an important beginning to a lengthy and uneven process which eventually produced an independent judiciary, a strong rule of law, judicial protection for civil and political liberties and 'fundamental rights' and a broadly representative democratic system in England and in the UK. Pollock and Maitland claimed that it remains 'the nearest approach to an irrepealable "fundamental statute" that England has ever had'.[48] This is largely because of its political and cultural importance and its enduring place in the English constitutional narrative.

[48] F. Pollock and F.W. Maitland, *History of English Law*, vol. I, Cambridge University Press, Cambridge 1898, p. 173.

3. IRELAND: INDIVIDUAL AND GROUP RIGHTS IN ANCIENT IRISH LAW

Brendan TOBIN
Michael O'FLAHERTY

1. INTRODUCTION

The historical roots of early Irish law stretch back into antiquity and were passed on in the rich oral history, poetry, sagas, law and wisdom-texts, that have come down to us. The body of law is frequently referred to as Brehon Law, so-called as it was applied by judges named *breitheamhuin* or *brehons,* in the Irish language.[1] The more appropriate term is *fénechas* defined as 'law of the *Féni* [freemen], customary or traditional law, [or] native law'.[2] Promulgated or written law, much of it developed by the church, was known as *Cáin* law.

The primary old Irish law-text is the *Senchas Már* (great tradition).[3] This grounding document constitutes a third of all surviving law-texts. Reputedly originally assembled at the insistence of St. Patrick in the fifth century of the common era (CE), the *Senchas Már* as we now know it was compiled in the seventh century CE and brings together a number of distinct texts, addressing a range of civil and political as well as economic and social matters. An understanding of old Irish law also requires recourse to a wide range of other law-texts, as well as oral tradition captured in the sagas, poems and wisdom-texts. [4] Law-texts on issues as diverse as the law of bee-keeping,[5] the status of poets (who were key to the learning and transmission of the law), the principal remedies for civil and criminal harm, and canon law demonstrate the breadth and depth of old Irish law.

---

1. H.M. WESTROPP, 'On the Tribal System and Land-Tenure in Ireland under the Brehon Laws' (1870) 2 *Journal of the Ethnological Society of London* (1869–1870) No. 3, 343.
2. F. KELLY, *A Guide to Early Irish Law*, Dublin Institute of Advanced Studies, Dublin 1988, p. 311.
3. L. BREATNACH, *On the early Irish law Text* Senchas Már *and the Question of its Date,* 13 E.C. Quiggin Memorial Lectures, Cambridge 2011, p. 42 gives the dates 660–680 AD for the compilation of the *Senchas Már.*
4. L. GINNELL, *The Brehon Laws: A Legal Handbook*, T. Fisher Unwin, London 1894, p. 5.
5. T. CHARLES-EDWARDS and F. KELLY, *Bechbretha*, Dublin Institute for Advanced Studies, Dublin 1983.

Although law in Ireland was not primarily legislative or king-made there was long tradition of national and local assemblies, such as the *Féis* of Tara, which may have served to 'preserve [customary] laws and rules'.[6] While kings could issue ordinances in times of emergency,[7] law was primarily derived from custom and was found and interpreted by the legal class (poets and brehons) with strong clerical influences[8] — an influence probably exercised by druids in earlier times. Though justice was primarily adjudicated by brehons, kings were linked to the process and may have adjudicated certain cases and/or played a role in approving the decision of a brehon.[9] The *Senchas Már* shows the significant influence of the church in revision of the law and may be seen as the end result of a collaborative process to reconcile 'native oral custom with written Christian doctrine'.[10] While codification served to freeze the law in time, glossator commentaries provide evidence of its continuing evolution.

Old Irish law has, on occasion, been eulogised for perceived or projected high standards of justice and equality.[11] In truth, although it has many qualities of merit, it was neither egalitarian nor supremely just. Individual rights were often subordinated to collective familial and tribal rights, capital punishment occurred and slavery was practiced. It did, however, also demonstrate an engagement with issues that today would be termed as fundamental rights. It restrained the power of the ruler and established autonomous spaces for the individual or group that might not be impinged upon by the ruler or society. We will look at three aspects of this proto-fundamental rights aspect of old Irish law: rule of law and guarantees of justice, women's rights and land rights.

2. RULE OF LAW AND GUARANTEES OF JUSTICE

Ireland was traditionally governed by an *Ard-Ri* (High King) and as many as 150 regional and petty kings. Kelly, one of the leading scholars on, what he terms, 'early Irish law', has identified numerous references in the law-texts, wisdom-texts[12] and sagas, to the importance of the king's *fir flathemon* (justice) upon which rest the possibilities of peaceful and prosperous times.[13] A king guilty of injustice, extortion or kin-slaying could be legally overthrown.[14] He could lose his honour-price (the basis of his authority) for kin-slaying, for defaulting on his

6 GINNELL, *supra* note 4, p. 45.
7 KELLY, *supra* note 2, p. 21.
8 *Ibid.*
9 *Ibid.*, p. 24.
10 R. CHAPMAN STACEY, *Dark Speech: The Performance of Law in Early Ireland*, University of Pennsylvania Press, Philadelphia PA 2007, p. 197.
11 GINNELL, *supra* note 4; WESTROPP, *supra* note 1.
12 Texts containing precepts, proverbs and gnomic statements bearing on human behaviors, society, nature and other topics. KELLY, *supra* note 2, p. 284.
13 KELLY, *supra* note 2, p. 18.
14 Triad 186, cited in KELLY, *supra* note 2, p. 18.

oath and for tolerating satire (i.e. not defending the respect his position merited), as well as for a refusal of hospitality, knowingly eating stolen food, or for being defeated in battle, which was considered a sign of the injustice of his rule.[15]

If the king is guilty of *gau flathemon* (injustice), the texts warn, his reign will see the 'soil and elements' rebel against him, bringing 'infertility in women and cattle, crop failure, dearth of fish, defeat in battle, plagues, lightening, etc.'.[16] The link between a just king and social and agricultural harmony as set out in the eighth century text *Audacht Morainn* is mirrored in *De Duodecim Abusiuis Saeculi* (*De XII*) one of the most 'profoundly influential formulations of Christian political obligation in the entire Middle Ages'.[17] The *De XII,* which is accepted as being of Irish provenance, describes in its ninth abuse the unjust king whose rule 'causes not merely his own damnation but cosmological tragedy'.[18] Cross-fertilization between clerical and secular texts of the time was inevitable, and it seems likely that both the foregoing texts reflect both religious and secular notions of kingly justice.[19] Through the dissemination of religious texts and the extensive missionary work of Irish monks during the Middle Ages, precepts of old Irish law may well have influenced notions of kingly justice across Europe. *De XII*, for example, found favour at the Carolingian court,[20] where Charlemagne reputedly 'loved the wandering monks'.[21]

While the King was in theory required to comply with the law like everyone else, in a stratified society like that present in Ireland, imposing equality of the law was likely to have been difficult. These difficulties did not, however, amount to royal immunity. To get around the difficulties associated with enforcing penalties against the King, for example, there arose the custom of appointing an *aithech fortha* (substitute churl) to accept the penalty, thereby avoiding dishonour for the monarch himself.[22]

Like the King, the local *flaith* (chief) was obliged to treat those he ruled justly. Primary responsibility of the *flaith* was toward his *céili* (clients) who were in the

---

15 KELLY, *supra* note 2, p. 19.

16 KELLY, *supra* note 2, p.18 citing Amss 12–21 (and notes).

17 P. WORMALD, 'Celtic and Anglo-Saxon Kingship: Some Further Thoughts' in P.E. SZARMACH and V. DARROW OGGINS (eds.), *Sources of Anglo-Saxon Culture*, Medieval Institute Publications, Kalamazoo, Michigan 1986, p. 160, cited in J. GRIGG, The Just King and De Duodecim Abusiuis Saeculi (2010) 27 *Parergon* 1.

18 GRIGG, *supra* note 17, p. 29.

19 For contrasting opinions on this issue see M.J. ENRIGHT, *Iona, Tara and Soissons: The Origin of the Royal Anointing Ritual*, Walter De Gruyter, Berlin and New York 1985, p. 54, and F. KELLY (ed.), *Audacht Morainn*, Dublin Institute for Advanced Studies, Dublin 1976, pp. xiv–xv. Discussed in GRIGG, *supra* note 17, p. 30.

20 M.L.W. LAISTNER, *Thought and Letters in Western Europe A.D. 500 to 900*, Methuen and Co., London 1957, cited in GRIGG, *supra* note 17, p. 29.

21 On Charlemagne see T. CAHILL, *How the Irish Saved Civilization*, Nan E. Talese/Doubleday, New York 1995, p. 207.

22 KELLY, *supra* note 2, p. 25.

main part likely to be of his own kin. The law imposed stiff penalties for dishonesty on the *flaith* who stood to lose his honour-price for a wide range of infractions. These included refusal of hospitality, failure to fulfil contractual obligations towards his *céili*, eating food known to be stolen, tolerating satire and betraying his honour.[23] When a *flaith* wanted to terminate his agreement with a *céili* who has fulfilled his side of the contract the *flaith* was obliged to pay half the *céili's* honour-price on top of any other monies owed for rent and services already given.[24] Dishonest clerics could also be held liable for their actions and a donor and his kin-group could recover funds donated to the church if they were being misused.[25] Where a cleric was guilty of the murder of a layman he was required, according to the *Penintential of Finnian*,[26] to 'go into exile for ten years, of which seven are to be spent in penance and abstinence'. He must then return and compensate the bereaved kinsmen, and offer himself to the parents of the victim, in the place of their son undertaking to do whatever they tell him.[27]

To avoid the dangers of being responsible for *gau flathemon* (injustice) it was the practice of kings to retain a *brithem tuaithe* (judge of the *túath* or kingdom).[28] Needless to say, a wise king would have sought a wise and learned judge for this position, helping ensure the quality of justice available to those in distress. Brehons also worked as independent arbitrators and might be called upon by contesting parties to adjudicate cases, as such brehonship may be seen as a profession rather than a state appointment.[29] A brehon's training could extend up to 20 years[30] with leading brehons versed in three areas of law, the *Feineachas*, the *Dlighe Filidhecht* or Poetic Law (i.e. the law preserved in poetry), and the *Breith Leighinn* or Canon Law.[31] An unjust judge was seen as one of the 'three ruins of a *tuath*'.[32] Severe penalties including damages, disgrace and physical punishments awaited any brehon who failed to act impartially or who wilfully pronounced an unjust decision.[33] The extent of judges' payments and of support for their sustenance were specifically set out in the law-texts.

23 CIH 15.5-9 +AL v 174.13–9, KELLY, *supra* note 2, p. 27.
24 KELLY, *supra* note 2, p. 31.
25 CIH 4.2–17 AL v 128.13-9, KELLY, *supra* note 2, p. 42.
26 IP 80 § 23.
27 KELLY, *supra* note 2, p. 43.
28 *Ibid.*, p. 24.
29 GINNELL, *supra* note 4, pp. 85–86.
30 *Ibid.*, p. 84.
31 Ancient Law-tract in the book of Ballimote, fol. 181, cited in E. O'REILLY, 'An Essay on the Nature and Influence of the Ancient Irish Institutes, Commonly Called Brehon Laws' (1825) 14 *The Transactions of the Royal Irish Academy* 154.
32 Triad 96, cited in KELLY, *supra* note 2, p. 55.
33 O'REILLY, *supra* note 31, p. 170.

3. WOMEN'S RIGHTS

Old Irish society was patriarchal and early Irish law grouped women with those including children and slaves who were considered *báeth*, 'legally incompetent' or 'senseless'.[34] From this comes the warning, *messam cundarthae cuir ban* — the worst bargains [are] the contracts of women.[35] This derived from the general rule that women lacked capacity to enter into contracts without the authorisation of their guardians. Their guardians included the father in the case of a girl; the prime husband in cases where a woman had a prime husband;[36] the sons in the case of a widow or divorcee; a kinsman when a woman lacked a husband or father; and, the church in the case of women of the church.[37] Women's status as dependents was not, however, immutable and the law recognised their legal rights to contract, to inherit and to divorce, in a wide variety of cases. Binchy, a leading scholar of old Irish law, contends that there was a progressive recognition of women's rights from earliest times, influenced in part by the church, so that by the time the *Senchas Már* was written a woman was entitled to conclude independent contracts; inherit at least a life-estate in the property of her father where there were no surviving sons; make legal 'entry' on her inheritance against a hostile possessor in a procedure varying little from the rights of a man; and, distrain chattels in order to enforce her legal rights.[38] Recognition of this broad range of rights compares favourably with contemporaneous legal regimes of the time.

Women's rights under old Irish law were linked both to their status and to the goods they brought to a marriage. The normal form of marriage was marriage of *lánamnas comthinchuir* in which both parties contributed land, cattle and household items in accordance with their status.[39] In such a marriage the wife, if of equal rank and standing as her husband, was known as *be cuitchernsa*, 'of equal lordship'.[40] In such unions both spouses had a right to annul the contracts of the other if they were considered disadvantageous (a *dochor*) but could not annul the other's contracts which were beneficial to their joint finances (a

---

[34] H-M. ALSOS RAAE, 'The Representation in Old Irish Law Texts of the Legal Position of Women in Early Medieval Ireland as regards the Ownership of Property'. Doctoral Thesis in Celtic Studies, National University of Ireland, Galway 2013, p. 8.

[35] See N. MCLEOD, *Early Irish Contract Law*, Centre for Celtic Studies, Sydney 1992, p. 71 citing the *Díre* text, §§ *37/38*.

[36] Polygyny was practised in old Ireland and the prime or first wife enjoyed a higher and more protected status than subsequent wives.

[37] §§ 38 *Díre* text see translation in MCLEOD, *supra* note 35.

[38] D.A. BINCHY, Legal Capacity of women, in Studies in R. THURNEYSEN, N. POWER, M. DILLON, K. MULCHRONE, D.A. BINCHY, A. KNOCH and J. RYAN, *Early Irish Law*, Royal Irish Academy, Dublin 1936, p. 226.

[39] N. POWER, 'Classes of Women Described in the Senchas Mar' in R. THURNEYSEN, N. POWER, M. DILLON, K. MULCHRONE, D.A. BINCHY, A. KNOCH and J. RYAN, *Early Irish Law*, Royal Irish Academy, Dublin 1936, p. 82.

[40] See glossator *Cáin Lánamna* § 5 cited in POWER, *supra* note 39, p. 82.

sochor).[41] The right to impugn each other's contracts stemmed, according to McLeod, from the close relationship between the partners.[42] As a result, even where a wife was fully dependent upon her husband financially, she was, in certain circumstances, entitled to impugn his contracts that would undermine his ability to maintain her or where disadvantageous to the family well-being.[43] A secondary wife, known since Christian times as *adaltrach*, had less capacity to impugn her husband's contracts. She could still do so, however, if the contract would undermine his capacity to maintain her with 'the necessities essential to their cohabitation'.[44] While the rights of an *adaltrach* with sons to control her husband's contracts approximated those of the dependent primary wife, the right of the *adaltrach* without sons was limited to contracts involving food, clothes, cattle and sheep.[45] In a marriage of *bantinchur* or 'woman-contribution', where capital was provided solely by the wife, it was the husband who lacked contractual capacity.

The role of women in the law is recognised by the appearance in the *Senchas Már* of references to a female jurist Bríg (meaning 'high-status, privilege'), who appears in the text to deliver judgments on women's issues.[46] While women were recognised as having equal rights alongside their brothers to inherit moveable goods, under the Irish custom of gavelkind all the father's sons but not his daughters were entitled to a share of his landed inheritance.[47] Prohibitions of this nature, still found in many customary legal regimes, are increasingly under attack from both a fundamental rights perspective and due to the changing nature of tribal societies in many areas, in particular Africa, where the percentage of women-led families has increased dramatically. In this regard it is noteworthy that old Irish law foresaw an exception to the general rule. This exception, based on the judgement of Bríg, entitled daughters to inherit from their fathers where they had no brothers.[48] In such a case a female heir, *banchomarbae* as she was known, could inherit a life-estate, and presumably, if there was more than one daughter, they shared the land equally as was the case with regard to sons.[49] In the event that the *banchomarbae* married within her kinship group, then her sons were entitled to inherit her lands; otherwise they inherited nothing, the apparent reason being to protect their collective tribal territory.

41 MCLEOD, *supra* note 35, p. 72.
42 *Ibid.*
43 *Ibid.*
44 *Ibid.*
45 POWER, *supra* note 39, pp. 82–85.
46 CHAPMAN STACEY, *supra* note 10, p. 196.
47 O'REILLY, *supra* note 31, p. 206.
48 D.A. BINCHY. 'The Relationship of Mother and son, of Father and Daughter, and the Law of Inheritance with Regard to Women' in R. THURNEYSEN, N. POWER, M. DILLON, K. MULCHRONE, D.A. BINCHY, A. KNOCH and J. RYAN, *Early Irish Law*, Royal Irish Academy, Dublin 1936, p. 174.
49 ALSOS RAAE, *supra* note 34, p. 24.

Irish law gave women rights to divorce that were not always accessible under other European systems of law at the time,[50] and much of the *Cáin Lánamna*, one of the principal texts on women's entitlements, deals with division of property at a divorce.[51] Women could divorce for physical violence leaving a blemish,[52] for adultery,[53] for a husband failing to support her or for spreading false stories or satire about her.[54] She was also entitled to a divorce if he were impotent, homosexual, indiscreet about their sexual relations, if he took holy orders or was so fat he was incapable of intercourse.[55] Where the wife of an infertile man did not wish to divorce him the law allowed her to leave him temporarily to become pregnant by another man, in which case the resultant child was treated as the husband's.[56] The law took a very stern line on women who abandoned the home without due cause and they were to be denied sanctuary.[57] Even in cases of divorce a woman could lose her rights to her own movable goods and chattels if she left her husband before the expiry of a specified period of time.[58]

Improvement of women's rights in ancient Ireland has been linked to the church. With the adoption of the *Cáin Adamnáin* in 697 CE, the church sought to portray itself as the champion of women's rights, doubling the *eric*, or fine, for killing a woman and prohibiting women going into battle. It is interesting to note that half of the increased fine was to go to Adamnan's Church at Iona, making the law a key source of revenue.[59] Although, it is unclear to what extent *Cáin Adamnáin* was successful in improving women's rights, by the eighth century CE, it was listed as one of four principal *Cana* [religious edicts]: 'Patrick's law, not to kill clerics, Adamnan's law not to kill women, Daire's law not to kill cattle, and the Law of Sunday, not to transgress at all thereon.'[60]

---

50 T. MOHR, 'Law in a Gaelic Utopia: Perceptions of Brehon Law in Nineteenth and Early Twentieth Century Ireland' in O. BRUPBACHER et al (eds.), *Remembering and Forgetting: Yearbook of Young Legal History*, Martin Meidenbauer, Munich 2007, p. 264.

51 KELLY, *supra* note 2, p. 73.

52 D.Ó. CRÓINÍN, *Early Medieval Ireland 400–1200*, Longman, London and New York 1995, pp. 129–130.

53 O'REILLY, *supra* note 31, p. 215.

54 KELLY, *supra* note 2, p. 74.

55 *Ibid.*

56 *Ancient Laws of Ireland* Dublin i–vi, 1865–1901, iii 310.16; KELLY, *supra* note 2, p. 75, and fn. 53.

57 O'REILLY, *supra* note 31, p. 194 cites a law-tract regulating the property etc. in Bees (Manuscript Room, Class H. No.34 page 26, and Class H. No. 54. p 398), listing seven fugitives who are not protected by *Neimhid* or either God or man: a lurking thief; deserters from a tribe; a man with blood red arms (a murder); a woman who flies from her matrimonial engagements; a man or woman who fled from the assistance of a mother or father; and one who renders not justice after his theft leaving behind plunder unrestored.

58 KELLY, *supra* note 2, p. 74.

59 J. GRIGG, 'Aspects of the Cáin: Adomnains Lex Innocentium' (2005) 1 *Journal of the Australian early Medieval Association* 41–50, 42.

60 W. STOKES, The Martyology of Oengus the Culdee (ed and trans) Dublin, 1905, (repr 1984) 211, cited in GRIGG, *supra* note 59, p. 47.

With the displacement of old Irish law by the English common law, women's rights took a significant step backwards. Under common law, women had no right to hold property nor to guardianship of their children and had no rights within marriage, with the husband being considered the absolute master of all familial property. It was not until the enactment of the Married Women's Property Act 1882 that married women obtained rights to keep their property — rights old Irish law had recognised centuries before.

4. LAND RIGHTS

In ancient Ireland, the primary unit of society was the *fine* to which all land belonged rather than to any individual.[61] Although private rights over land could be secured they were always circumscribed by the indefeasible nature of *fine* ownership of all land within its jurisdiction. Under this system land appears to have been divided into common land, including land for pasture and tillage, lands subject to private rights and land held for tribal authorities including the *flaith*, the bard, the doctor and the brehon.[62] Demesne-lands of the *fine* were always maintained and passed on to the incoming chief, brehon, etc., and might be added to but could not be reduced.[63] The converse was true with private demesne-lands, which under the custom of gavelkind were distributed equally between all the father's sons including those of his concubines. While gavelkind led to progressive impoverishment of families as land holdings became smaller, it has also been seen as having ensured 'no person could fall into absolute poverty'.[64] Ginnell describes it as giving 'some start in life, however crude, to young men who might otherwise have got none'.[65] Under gavelkind the son who inherited the family house(s), farming implements, etc., was responsible for guardianship of his sisters until their marriage.[66]

A portion of the lands of the *fine* were set aside for the maintenance of the poor and it was the responsibility of the King or *flaith* to look out for all those who lacked guardians. In order to ensure the most worthy person would come to rule and to prevent power struggles upon the death of the King or *flaith* the Irish developed the custom of electing a *Tánaiste* (Second Man) during the reign of the existing King or *flaith*. In practice, disputes did occur, but whether they were more frequent or bloody than the struggle for power under the contemporaneous system of primogeniture under English law (which would later replace it) is unclear. What it did do was to give the *fine* an opportunity to keep unstable,

---

61 GINNELL, *supra* note 4, p. 136.
62 WESTROPP, *supra* note 1, p. 344.
63 GINNELL, *supra* note 4, p. 134.
64 O'REILLY, *supra* note 31, p. 222.
65 GINNELL, *supra* note 4, p. 130.
66 *Ibid.*, p. 132.

incompetent or corrupt individuals out of positions of overriding power. This was important for both individual and collective rights and for ensuring the King's *fir flathemon* — considered fundamental for social and environmental well-being.

Irish lands vested in the *fine* and could not be forfeited or lost due to any 'delinquency in the chief', who only had a life interest in the lands.[67] Ironically, the prohibition of alienation served the interests of the ruling family, fuelling expansion of the *flaith's* lands and progressive reduction of common lands. In the process, some *flaiths* encroached on the 'rights of not alone those below them but of those above them also',[68] undermining the possibility for collective resistance against English colonisation. As part of its colonisation strategy the English offered to grant hereditary titles to those *flaiths* who surrendered their lands and swore allegiance to the Crown. While few *flaiths* did so, in some cases claims were made over whole counties, which effected a conversion of collective lands of the *fine* into private land rights of the *flaith*, with little if any recognition of existing land rights under Irish law.[69]

Irish law placed strict responsibility on families to look after dependents, and one of the seven fugitives of justice who could not be protected by sanctuary by a *Neimhid* of either God or man, was a man or woman who fled from the assistance of a mother or father.[70] Irish law also sought to secure direct rights for all inhabitants of the *túath* to look after their own needs through access to wild foodstuffs and materials as needed to prevent starvation and protect them from the cold and to meet their basic needs. A clear example of this is found in a passage of the law tract *Do fastad 7 dligid* ('On the confirmation of the right and law') cited in the *Erne Fishery Case* (discussed below), where it says:

> How many things have been established as the inherent rights of every territory and of which are equally due to every person? The salmon of every place; wild garlic; the *andach* property of each water; the quick drawing [of a net] from each stream; the sufficiency for a night of faggots of each wood [...]; cooking fuel in each wood; the mast [nuts] of each wood; materials for each carriage; timber for body bearers; a handle for a champions spear; [...] the wild animals of each wood, through which there is passage with necessity; the sea wrack of each strand; the salt-leaf of each rock; the produce of each wave outside the rock; [...]; grinding upon the whet-stone; an acknowledged fair-green; going

67 O'REILLY, *supra* note 31, p. 205.
68 GINNELL, *supra* note 4, p. 96.
69 W.E. MONTGOMERY, *The History of Land Tenure in Ireland: Being the Yorke Prize Essay of The University of Cambridge for the Year 1888*, Cambridge University Press, Cambridge 1889, p. 71.
70 O'REILLY, *supra* note 31, p. 194.

> into a boat; playing chess in the house of a chieftain; [...] the mountain which overtops all; ...[71]

As private property entitlements expanded there was a noticeable reduction in collective property rights. A gloss on the above-cited text, for example, reinterprets the right of inhabitants of the *túath* to *aé áite* or 'the salmon of the place', appearing to limit it to one salmon to meet their needs.[72] Other glosses appear to limit rights to collect nuts to one handful where it is a private wood, to restrict rights to take wild animals to very limited cases and to the use of mountaintops as a commons 'only when not needed'.[73]

During the reign of King James I, the English courts decided two cases which in effect dismantled gavelkind and the tanist system of succession, and in the process displaced the old Irish legal system. The system of gavelkind was declared void in a case which argued that it failed to ensure good use of the land, that it included inheritance rights for illegitimate sons and excluded females, and that as all Irish counties were now to be 'governed by the rules of the common Law of England ... the ... custom of Gavelkind was void in law'.[74] The fate of Tanistry was decided in a case between Cahir O Callaghan, the heir in common law, and Morrough Mac Bryan, the elected Tánaiste. After more than three years of hearings, the King's Bench held that the custom of Tanistry 'was void in itself and abolished when the Common Law of England was established'.[75] Writing in 1888, Montgomery claimed history would decide that as a result of these decisions 'a grave error was committed and substantial injustice done'.[76]

5. CONCLUDING REMARKS: OLD IRISH LAW'S IMPACT IN MODERN IRELAND

A mark of the strength of old Irish law is that despite hundreds of years of colonial rule, it continued to be applied across most of Ireland until the seventeenth century when it was finally displaced by English law. Even then it did not wholly disappear.

In June 1920, insurgents engaged in the war of independence against the United Kingdom established an alternative system of courts, variously referred to as the 'Dáil', 'Sinn Féin', or Republican courts. In this court system parties were

---

71 *Moore v Attorney General* [1929] IR 191, 239. The extract is from Ancient Irish Laws v 482–84 reportedly taken from Dublin, TCD, 1433 olim E.3.5., cited in T. MOHR, 'Salmon of Knowledge' (2002) 16 *Peritia* 360–395; (n 80) 366.

72 MOHR, *supra* note 71, p. 376.

73 *Ibid.*, pp. 377–378.

74 Hill, 3 Jacobi. Davies Reports, cited in MONTGOMERY, *supra* note 69.

75 MONTGOMERY, *supra* note 69, p. 69.

76 *Ibid.*

entitled to refer to old Irish law, Roman law and the *Code Napoleon* as persuasive but not binding.[77] In the manner of customary legal regimes everywhere decisions of the Dáil Courts were made basically on the basis of common sense.

Echoes of old Irish law also resonated for the drafters of Ireland's first post-independence constitution. Those responsible for the drafting of the Constitution of 1922 included a number of influential scholars and lawyers who sought to free Irish law of the elements of colonial rule and in the process recover the perceived high qualities of old Irish law.[78] Their influence was apparent in 'the first optimistic drafts of the constitution', which emphasised popular sovereignty, social equality and a desire to promote the equality of women.[79] Not all of these principles were to find their way into the constitution concluded in a context of increasing national discontent (which would lead to civil war with those that refused to accept the settlement with Britain). Had it not been for the civil war, the Dáil Courts may well have become a central part of a new Irish system of law. It was not to be, and in 1922, the order establishing the Dáil Courts was rescinded and a judicial system firmly rooted in the British common law was validated. In 1937, following a definitive break with Britain (albeit the Republic was only declared in 1949), a new constitution was adopted which is still in force today. The 1937 Constitution retains some of the high aspirations on social equality and the equality of women.[80] It lost, however, the emphasis on popular sovereignty over natural resources.

Following independence, old Irish law underwent a brief resurgence when it was called upon to determine collective rights over water sources in a series of fisheries cases. Three hundred years after its displacement, in what may be seen as an historical irony, the cause of its re-appearance was a provision in *Magna Carta* limiting exclusive fishing rights, the applicability of which required interpretation of old Irish law.[81] In the first of the cases, the *Erne Fishery Case*,[82] the Supreme Court found, on the evidence given by MacNeill and Binchy the leading scholars of old Irish law, that exclusive rights were not recognised in old Irish law and that a 300-year-old grant of exclusive rights on the Erne tidal

---

77 The Republican Dáil Courts: A Revolutionary Irish Legal System, *The Undisciplined* 19 February 2014, available at: <http://theundisciplined.com/2014/02/19/the-republican-dail-courts-a-revolutionary-irish-legal-system/> accessed 22.05.2015.

78 MOHR, *supra* note 50, p. 271, highlights three members of the Constitutional Commission in particular. Darrell Figgis the author of the Gaelic State, Hugh Kennedy who went on to become the first Chief Justice of Ireland, and Eoin McNeill a renowned scholar of old Irish law.

79 See MOHR, *supra* note 50, referring to Eoin McNeill's comments on the draft constitution, National Archives of Ireland, Department of the Taoiseach, § 8953.

80 MOHR, *supra* note 50, p. 273.

81 MOHR, *supra* note 71. The first of these cases, the so-called *Erne Fishery Case*, marked the last time an attempt was made to appeal a case from the Irish Supreme Court to the Privy Council.

82 *Moore v Attorney General* [1929] I.R. 191 and [1934} I.R. 44.

waters was void.[83] This led to a spate of cases challenging similar exclusive fishery grants around the country. By the time of the *Moy Fishery Case*, Binchy had changed his opinion and in this case the judge found that exclusive fishing rights had in fact existed in early Irish law.[84] That decision effectively brought to an early end the use of old Irish law within the modern-day Irish courts, albeit not ruling out its future legal invocation.

Collective rights and customary law still play an important part in the lives of some communities in Ireland, most particularly of the Travellers who are struggling for effective recognition of their rights to their culture and way of life.[85] Other claims by various Irish communities may also be grounded in orally transmitted elements of old Irish law. For example, rights over specific marine areas such as oyster beds and areas for the laying of lobster pots may still be guided by ancient customary rights. Also, rights of way by necessity across the land, which was a part of old Irish law, though disturbed, are remembered and may come to be invoked in the context of the development of public walkways and bicycle paths across the countryside.

Another area of old Irish law with potential significance concerns water rights. These were vested in the *fine* from which the water was drawn[86] and entitled all tribesmen to free access to water for use on their lands. Such provisions are of obvious relevance in the context of the current Irish government policy to privatise the supply of water.

Perhaps of greatest contemporary interest, recalling the King's *fir flathemon*, and the responsibility of *flaiths* and brehons,[87] old Irish law might be invoked to establish a duty of care on state and private sector actors, including corporate bodies, to act with honesty and justice in order to protect individual rights and collective well-being. Indeed, the stipulation in old Irish law that no person should be entitled to sanctuary (i.e. immunity) who has not made good the

---

83 For detailed discussion of the Erne and subsequent fisheries cases see MOHR, *supra* note 71, MOHR, *supra* note 50.

84 *Little v Cooper* [1937] IR 1 at 6. MOHR, *supra* note 71, p. 374 et seq.

85 Travellers' Cultural Rights: The Right to Respect for Traveller Culture and Way of Life, Pavee Point/ Irish human rights Commission, Dublin 2008. See B. TOBIN, *Indigenous Peoples, Customary Law and Human Rights: Why Living Law Matters*, Routledge, London 2014, p. 143 for discussion of the links between customary law and the rights to culture and 'Way of Life'.

86 O'REILLY, *supra* note 31, p. 201.

87 The Navajo Supreme Court in *Re Certified Question II: Navajo Nation v McDonald* 16, ILR 6086 (1989) turned to their own traditional law as set out in the *Hero twins* story to find a customary practice establishing a fiduciary responsibility between tribal leaders and the tribal members, which allowed for the removal of an errant leader. See discussion in TOBIN, *supra* note 85, pp. 78–79.

'plunder [they left] unrestored'[88] is one that would resonate in the Ireland of today.

As Ireland enters into celebrations of the centenary of the event that was the catalyst for its war of independence, the 1916 Rising, there is significant debate on the extent to which the present constitutional order supports the realisation of the objectives of those who achieved Irish freedom or protects the fundamental rights of its people. In this debate it would not be remiss to remember those high principles of community, hospitality, responsibility and justice which old Irish law so clearly espoused and to explore how that ancient body of law might help us better serve the fundamental rights of today's residents of the Irish state.

88 Manuscript Room, Class H. No.34 page 26, and Class H. No. 54. p 398. cited in O'REILLY, *supra* note 31, p. 194.

4. ITALY: THE *LIBER PARADISUS* — A VISION OF GOOD GOVERNANCE

Paolo De Stefani

1. INTRODUCTION

In this chapter it is argued that the 'first document' in Italian history in which 'fundamental rights' were affirmed is an arbitration award issued by the city of Bologna in 1256 and formalised in 1257 proclaiming, within the entire territory of the town, the liberation of slaves (*servi et ancillae*) belonging to local landlords and bonded *de iure* or *de facto* to the masters and their land. The 1257 document was known as *Liber Paradisus* (the Heaven Book), and was complemented by statutes in 1257, 1282 and 1304 extending the measure to serfs (*servi glebae, adsripticii* and other categories of villeins).

In the first section, I provide a very short outline of Italian constitutional history, focusing on two documents of the eighteenth century that marked a remarkable shift in the history of European constitutionalism and codification of individual rights, adopted respectively in Corsica and Tuscany.

In the subsequent sections, however, a discussion of some methodological aspects connected to the topic eventually leads us to another moment in pre-modern history in which the quest for the first Italian document on fundamental rights may prove to be more fruitful. In the long history of Italian civilisation, a crucial transitional epoch can be identified in the decades of the High Middle Ages, when the affluent city-states of Central and Northern Italy fought against the Holy Roman Empire for self-government and independence. In this framework, internal conflicts also erupted within the towns opposing aristocratic and proto-bourgeois factions. The *Liber Paradisus* was drafted in Bologna against this backdrop of political turmoil and class conflict.

The following sections then describe the normative content of the *Liber* and of some of the subsequent acts that complemented it, trying to explain its original character and legal effects. The *Liber* documents the city of Bologna's policy of liberating slaves and granting some liberties to certain groups of people hitherto under the control of aristocratic families. The original aim of such emancipation acts, in Bologna as well as in other towns, was essentially to increase the tax revenues of the municipality. However, in this case, a Preamble to the document, emphatically linking the measure to 'universal' values stemming from the Bible and Roman law, justifies a comparison with modern declarations of rights.

The final sections further discuss and contextualise these parallels and, from this, some conclusions will be drawn.

2. A CONVOLUTED HISTORY AND A DIFFICULT QUEST

The history of Italy as an independent state began in 1861. Its first constitutional charter, the 1848 Albertine Statute, was originally the fundamental law of the Kingdom of Sardinia, the state that championed the political unification of the peninsula, leading a process that came to a conclusion in 1866 and 1918, with the annexation of the Habsburg territories of the North-East (the Istria peninsula went to Yugoslavia — now Croatia — after World War II). An *octroyée*, non-rigid constitution, the Albertine Statute set the basis of the kingdom's legal order until the entry into force of the republican Constitution in 1948. The Statute's moderate liberal principles were challenged and partially replaced during Fascism, which imposed restrictions on individual civil and political rights and set significant exceptions to the rule of law.

However, since the fall of the Roman Empire, Italy had been home to a multitude of political entities, whose histories are entangled with that of the two universalistic powers that have for centuries marked the legal, political, cultural and religious landscape of Europe: the Holy Roman Empire and the Catholic Church. Both were materially or symbolically based in Rome and had the Italian peninsula as their cradle. During the Middle Ages Italian cities, kingdoms, lordships and other political post-feudal autonomous units fought hard to preserve and develop their own ruling systems, but failed to give birth to a unified entity likely to withstand the emerging European monarchies. The Italian territories were therefore governed for centuries as provinces of powerful states or political conglomerates, whose capital and core interests lay outside the country's borders. The fragmented structure of Italian semi-independent states and principalities thus played a relatively marginal role in setting forth the path of modern constitutionalism, whose typical habitat was the modern nation-state.[1] When constitutions and declarations of rights in the modern sense were eventually enacted in Italy, namely in the satellite republics and kingdoms established under Napoleonic rule after the first and second Italian campaigns (1796–97 and 1800), they appeared to be largely inspired by the models that had been elaborated in other European countries and in the United States, and

[1] 'Constitutionalism was born and asserted itself in the context of the forming process of the *modern European State* [to be seen as a] complex historical phenomenon'. M. FIORAVANTI, *Costituzionalismo. Percorsi della storia e tendenze attuali*, Laterza, Roma 2009, p. 5 (my translation).

politically ephemeral, as the respective states were strictly dependent on the French for their very existence.

An interesting exception was the proclamation in 1755 by the General Diet of the island of Corsica, ruled under the Constitution of Corsica. This proclamation was inspired by Pasquale Paoli, the head of the rebellion that separated the island from the Republic of Genoa and granted it a frail independence up to the annexation by France in 1768.[2] The Corsican Constitution combined a genuinely revolutionary 'constituent' approach with more traditional provisions reaffirming the roles of the nobles and of the other classes of the estates society; indeed some elements were borrowed from the confederate republics of Switzerland and of the Seven United Provinces of the Lower Countries.[3] The Corsican experience attracted considerable attention from the *philosophes* and the political activists of the time, including Jean-Jacques Rousseau, who in 1765 was requested by some Corsican republicans to write a *Projet de constitution pour la Corse*. The Corsican Constitution, written in Italian, was conceived as a fixed, stable legal basis for the newly born republic, and a platform to reform the whole traditional legal order, starting from the penal sector — in line with the Enlightenment doctrines that were spreading in Italy around the time of publication in 1764 of the seminal *Dei Delitti e delle Pene* by Cesare Beccaria.

The Corsican Constitution, although vindicated as a revolutionary act that marked a new chapter for the island's community as a political entity, was not particularly innovative in terms of enumeration of fundamental rights. Its aim was rather to set the structure of the republican government of the island, inspired by the division of powers.[4] In particular, by introducing some procedural guarantees for the parties in criminal matters, it followed a trend that in the second half of the eighteenth century mirrored important outcomes in many other parts of Italy, and that culminated with the adoption of 'the first

---

2 Cf. A. TRAMPUS, *Storia del costituzionalismo italiano nell'età dei Lumi*, Laterza, Roma-Bari 2009.

3 The influence of Montesquieu's *Esprit des lois* is evident in the constitutional thought of Pasquale Paoli, who had intellectually grown up in the most advanced Italian enlightened milieu of Naples.

4 The Paoli Constitution is also worth mentioning in that it formulated what a few decades later would become the 'inalienable right to the pursuit of happiness', where is stated that: 'La Dieta Generale del Populo della Corsica ... volendo, riacquistata la sua libertà, dar forma durevole e costante al suo governo riducendoli a costituzione tale che da essa ne derivi la felicità della Nazione, ha decretato e decreta...' ['the General Diet of the People of Corsica ... determined, having re-established its liberty, to give a durable and fixed form to its government in a constitution so that from this may derive the happiness of the Nation, has ordained and ordains that...' (my translation).

modern criminal code'[5] in Europe: the so-called *Codice Leopoldino* or just *Leopoldina*.[6]

The *Leopoldina* was a 'modern' penal code, not because of its structure and position in the system of normative sources of the state, but rather because it formulated for the first time and enunciated in a consistent manner the 'new' principles of criminal legislation that were being elaborated by philosophers and political thinkers of the time. Such principles included the abolition of torture and lessening of the reliance given to confessions as evidence, proportionality of penalties, proscription of some cruel penalties including mutilations and full confiscation of property, and the abolition of the death penalty. Since 2000, the regional government of Tuscany has commemorated 30 November as a special human rights day to celebrate being the first state to have abolished capital punishment.

3. HYPOTHESIS AND COROLLARIES

These eighteenth century documents, however, do not properly respond to the question posed by this chapter. On the one hand, the revolutionary Constitution of Corsica is rather silent on the issue of rights; on the other, the penal code of Tuscany poses no challenge to the *status quo* and responds to an intellectual programme of enlightened reforms, rather than to any socio-political emancipatory claim.[7]

Indeed, the task here is to identify, in complex Italian history, a legal document that — at least *prima facie* — could be the homologue of the modern declarations of rights that have marked the evolution of state constitutionalism and — more recently — of international human rights law. The idea underneath

---

5 G. TARELLO, *Storia della cultura giuridica moderna. Assolutismo e codificazione del diritto*, Il Mulino, Bologna 1976, p. 547.

6 Edict of the Grand Duke of Tuscany for the Reform of the Criminal Law in his Dominions, so named after the Grand Duke Peter Leopold I of Habsburg-Lorraine (who later became the Emperor Leopold II), the enlightened absolutist prince who encouraged its drafting.

7 While the Corsican Constitution has been very scarcely referred to later on in legal and political literature, the achievement of the *Leopoldina* in the area of criminal law and procedure — namely the abolition of torture and capital punishment — has been largely celebrated. It can be maintained that the reject of death penalty — incorporated in the first Italian Zanardelli penal code (1889), suspended during the Fascist rule (1926 and Rocco penal code, 1931), and reinstated with the advent of the Republic (cf. art. 27.4 Italian Constitution, last amended in 2007) — has been a distinctive feature of Italian criminal law tradition. On the international level, this tradition has supported the Italian government's consistent action for the world-wide abolition of the capital punishment and a moratorium of executions (see in particular the series of resolutions adopted since 2006 by the UN General Assembly on the initiative, among others, of Italy, the last being approved by the General Assembly on 18 December 2014, Moratorium on the use of the death penalty, UN doc. A/RES/69/186).

this is that it is possible and meaningful to trace retrospectively a sort of evolutionary lineage that somehow connects contemporary legal manifestations of the principles of legality, rule of law, democracy and human rights — in all their complex and at times controversial and even paradoxical forms — to documents issued in past centuries, in completely different socio-political contexts, that nevertheless contained the genetic blueprint of present-day fundamental rights instruments.

The task at hand can be accomplished, but it requires a short discussion.

First of all, it is clear that there is no intention of looking for anything like 'the first occurrence of human rights in Italian law'. Such a project would be unworkable, considering the shifts the concepts and the practice of 'law', 'rights' and 'fundamental rights' (let alone 'Italy') have had in the country (and in the world) over the centuries, dynamic and changeable links with the religious, economic, and political forces and contexts that have shaped the legal formats in the long term.

Nor is it a realistic programme to explore the depths of history to identify the 'roots' or 'sources' of modern fundamental rights, unless we adopt a rather broad concept of fundamental rights,[8] one that encompasses any civilisation and historical divide and is likely to connect law, religion, philosophy, cultural traditions and anthropological features of any people in any epoch. In such a comprehensive understanding, however, virtually any normative utterances could be associated with some aspects of current fundamental rights issues, making the whole exercise appear little more than a retrospective apology or glorification of the present.

What could be interesting and useful though, in the perspective suggested in the present book, is to search for crucial junctures in the dense history of Italy that resemble, *mutatis mutandis*, the modern and contemporary historical moments whereby fundamental rights declarations have been adopted. Is it possible to find a point in history at which socio-political circumstances generally associated with the enactment of fundamental rights instruments at domestic or international level coincided, leading to the formulation of a normative act that enshrined something that, in that very moment, had the value of what nowadays we call a fundamental rights declaration or the declaration of a fundamental right? This has been the programme of research in this contribution.

8 J-P. LEHNERS, 'Pleading for a new history of human rights' in A. MIHR and M. GIBNEY (eds.), *The SAGE Handbook of Human Rights*, SAGE, London 2014, pp. 22–39, esp. 25–27. The issue is also addressed, in the human rights literature in Italian, by G. GILIBERTI, *Introduzione storica ai diritti umani*, Giappichelli, Torino 2012.

There are two relevant corollaries. First, the 'declaration' we are looking for shall inevitably appear a false start, a turn in the wrong direction compared to the supposed evolutionary lineage leading to the modern configuration of constitutionally based fundamental rights and universally recognised human rights. If a certain document were already recognised as a precursor or an early occurrence of the fundamental rights charters, no doubt it would have already been spotted and included in the 'golden book' of widely recognised fundamental and human rights texts. Its exclusion or just tentative association with the *via regia* of mainstream fundamental and human rights documents could depend either on the very characteristics of the document, or on the way one thinks a fundamental rights declaration ought to look. For example, if one's assumption is that a fundamental rights document should be the outcome of a revolutionary programme as the case was — at least to a certain extent — for the American and French Declarations, a bill of rights graciously conceded by a sovereign to his people, albeit progressive and open-minded, would hardly count as a meaningful precedent, for 'human rights are won'.[9] According to this approach however even the 1948 Universal Declaration should be expunged from the genealogy of fundamental rights documents, as it does not possess all the features of a genuine 'revolutionary' human rights charter 'won' by its proponents and beneficiaries. Similarly, progressive shifts in the interpretation of common law, customs or *ius commune* provisions made by courts and jurisconsults paving the way to the recognition of 'modern' civil rights, can hardly be enlisted as precedents of a fundamental rights document inasmuch as one conceives of it as a legislative act, the punctual manifestation of the will of a political body, rather than the progressive product of jurisprudence, doctrine and wisdom.

In other words, the selection of historical precedents to modern declarations of rights tells us something about the history of fundamental rights, but even more about one's notion of what fundamental rights are today.

Here comes the second preliminary observation. In the search for a 'first document on fundamental rights' this contribution tries to avoid any direct or indirect hagiographic depiction of what a fundamental rights document should be. It is assumed that any legal document is the outcome of a unique, historically determined combination of complex ideological, political, socio-economic and even psychological factors, and that, once enacted, its reception and production of effects in the legal order and in the real world is conditioned by an array of inputs that largely evade the control of any legislator or constitutional father. This is true also for modern fundamental rights charters. Their adoption and the negotiations that led to their drafting cannot be insulated from the socio-political context in which they took place. Whereas the principles they enshrine are

[9] LEHNERS, *supra* note 8, p. 34.

forward-looking and universal, the document encompassing them is the outcome of a distinct political process, and its implementation the result of an even more contingent and unpredictable chain of historical events. Inspired documents may have been ignored by history, or actually used against fundamental rights, while texts that just paid lip service to the principles of justice and human dignity may have resulted in effective progress for the cause of humanity.

4. A POINT IN HISTORY AND A SHIFT IN LAW

After this long premise, it is time to make explicit the working hypothesis of this contribution. It proposes to search for fundamental rights-related documents in Italian history focusing on a particular part of the Middle Ages, namely the period of the rise of Communes and city-states in the twelfth and thirteenth centuries.[10] The communal society, as developed mostly in Central-Northern Italy,[11] marked a paradigmatic moment in Italian history, whose legacy has influenced the socio-political and cultural landscape of the nation to the present day.[12]

This epoch, one of the most dynamic and tumultuous, has been celebrated and idealised, for political reasons, during the Italian *Risorgimento* and early-united Italy. The victorious conflict fought by the Communes, united in the Lombard League, against the German Emperor Frederick I Barbarossa culminated with the 1183 Peace of Constance. The incessant wars conducted by the municipalities against his successor in the Swabia dynasty, Frederick II Hohenstaufen, were

10 On the Italian Communes or city-states cf., among others: P. JONES, *The Italian City-State: From Commune to Signoria*, Clarendon Press, Oxford 1997; G. TABACCO, *The Struggle for Power in Medieval Italy. Structures of Political Rule*, Engl. transl., Cambridge University Press, Cambridge 1989; D. NICOLAS, *The Growth of the Medieval City: From Late Antiquity to the Early Fourteenth Century*, Routledge, London 1997; F. FRANCESCHI and I. TADDEI, *Le città italiane nel Medioevo. Secoli XI–XIV*, Carocci, Roma 2009; M. ASCHERI, *La città-Stato. Le radici del repubblicanesimo e del municipalismo italiani*, Il Mulino, Bologna 2006. For a general introduction to the matter I have used G. PICCINNI, *Il Medioevo*, Paravia Bruno Mondadori, Milano 2004; G. PICCINNI, *I mille anni del Medioevo*, 2nd ed, Pearson Paravia Bruno Mondadori, Milano 2007; in English also C. KLEINHENZ (ed.), *Medieval Italy. An Encyclopedia*, Routledge, New York and Abingdon 2004.

11 Geographic and political-military factors (including the establishment of a Norman kingdom during the twelfth century) prevented cities in Southern Italy from establishing commercial and political ties comparable to those that linked allied towns in Tuscany and in the Po plain.

12 Robert Putnam famously (although very controversially) dates back to this period the socio-cultural divide in Italy between a North, where civic virtues have flourished and with them the conditions for strong civil society and good governance, and a idler South, where civic traditions are weaker and so is the performance of governmental institutions (R. PUTNAM, *Making Democracy Work: Civic Traditions in Modern Italy*, Princeton Univ. Press, Princeton 1993, first published in Italian: R. PUTNAM, R. LEONARDI, R.Y. NANETTI, *La pianta e le radici*, Il Mulino, Bologna 1985. It has been noticed the Putnam's interpretation is strongly indebted to the works of the nineteenth century Italian economist and political thinker Carlo Cattaneo, a proponent of a federal — instead of unitary — political constitution for the new Italian state).

compared in nineteenth and twentieth century Italy to the military campaigns raised against the Austrian-Hungarian Empire to establish a united and independent Italian state. The rhetoric of freedom has been uncritically applied to the medieval scenario to support the claims of Italian nationalism,[13] deeply influencing not only historical research, but also literature, arts, music and popular culture.

The same period of the Italian Middle Ages has attracted the attention of contemporary historians and intellectuals for another reason. The hostility between Guelfs (roughly: pro-Papal factions) and Ghibellines (pro-Empire) was just an incidental aspect of a more substantial conflict taking shape within the social and political body of Italian towns, between the class of landed nobility and the *populus*, that is the order of merchants, bankers and craftsmen, sometimes associated in powerful guilds. The ‘class struggle’ between the orders or estates that dominated the Italian city-states was a powerful paradigm likely to evoke situations and concerns felt as particularly crucial in contemporary Italy, although it never really involved the ‘class’ of salaried workers and the lower ranked guilds (the *popolo minuto,* as opposed to the *popolo grasso* of the better-off). Both the traditional, idealistic historiography, and the materialistic and critical approaches have found in the communal society a particularly suitable area of research.

In conclusion, if the task is to identify in the long history of Italy a turning-point likely to characterise the future development of the nation, this may be symbolically found in the Peace of Constance, whose aftermath witnessed the impetuous rise of Communes and city-states. In 1183 the Italian cities forced Frederick I to recognise their legal personality and political autonomy, including the power to levy all sorts of taxes. Cities were under the fictitious suzerainty of the Empire and the rule of Roman law — the Justinian *Corpus Iuris Civilis* as interpreted by the new class of lawyers educated in the *Studium* of Bologna — but *de facto* the *Pax* granted them complete independence and the cities could run their own politics on an internal and ‘international’ scale. The development of the communal movement in Italy was enormously boosted by the Constance *Pax*, and many city statutes proudly incorporated excerpts from Frederick’s instrument as a solemn confirmation of the Commune’s new status *vis-à-vis* the feudal lords in the countryside.

Within this framework, the Communes consolidated their policies of incorporating the contiguous land — *contado* — under their jurisdiction (i.e. within their *districtus*), including the population living therein that was under the *bannal* lordship (the ‘public’ power to order, compel, punish a freeman) of the

[13] The anti-imperial Lombard League has even inspired in the 1980s and 1990s a separatist Italian political party (the ‘Northern League’), recently turned hyper-nationalistic.

local aristocracy, or just dependent on them as farmers. Farmers, in most of Italian lands in the twelfth and thirteenth centuries, were persons who, as to their legal status, lived in an infinite variety of different conditions, but were fundamentally freemen. This was based on the basic Roman law distinction between *servi* (slaves) — that were considered *res* (things) with no legal personality — and free individuals. The condition of a large category of free peasants, however, the *coloni*, had dramatically worsened through the centuries from Diocletian through Justinian and the Early Middle Ages in Italy and Western Europe. Many of them were annexed to the land they agreed to cultivate (*coloni adscripticii*), becoming, as Irnerio famously said in his *glossae* to the *Digestum*,[14] *servi glebae* — slaves to the land or serfs, a status that progressively extended also to their descendants, and very close to that of a *servus*. When Irnerio and the Glossators framed the definition of *servus glebae*, however, they made reference to a condition described in the Roman *Corpus Iuris*, but that in the meantime had been largely left behind.[15] By the eleventh and twelfth centuries virtually all slaves in Italy had been liberated through manumissions or other measures, and 'serfs' were — at least *de iure* — freemen who farmed the property of their *domini* on the basis of all sorts of real or consensual contracts (of course peasants were also subject to the 'public' powers — the power of *bannum* — the same *Signori* had been given by the Emperors or had usurped by force, but this did not affect their free status).

The general policy of any Commune was to sever the more or less strong ties that linked *contado* peasants to their lords (including ecclesiastic figures: a harsh controversy between the city of Bologna and its bishop led to a temporary excommunication of the Guelf city in 1232) and to attract them to move within the city's *districtum*, or in fortified towns established in areas of strategic interest where fugitive villeins were encouraged to settle, receiving protection against their masters and extensive privileges, including manumission. Such a process inevitably stressed the hiatus, in the city society, between the aristocratic landowners and the bourgeoisie — the *popolo*.

The governance of Italian cities was assured by a complicated set of competing institutions that mirrored the divide between *milites* and *magnati* on the one hand (the traditional aristocracy), and the powerful corporations of merchants,

---

14 'Adsriptitia autem conditio non ea est qua quis alieno principaliter subiiciatur domino, sed glebe servus intelligitur, non principaliter persone, sic et in rerum servitutibus, que prima facie rebus serviunt, et per hoc etiam nobis' (the status of *adscriptio* though is not a form of subjection to a master, rather it should be understood as that of a man who is the slave of the land, not mainly at the service of a person, but of a property, as he first serves a property, and by so doing he also serves us – my translation] (IRNERII, *Summa Institutionum*, a.c. di G.B: Palmieri, in *Scripta Anecdota Glossatorum*, I, 2, Bologna, 1913, p. 6).

15 See, among many others, F. PANERO, *Schiavi, servi e villani nell'Italia medievale*, Paravia, Milano 1999; S. CAVACIOCCHI (ed.), *Schiavitù e servaggio nell'economia europea secc. XI–XVIII. Atti della 'Quarantacinquesima settimana di studi' (14–18 aprile 2013)*, Florence University Press, Florence 2014.

bankers, notaries, butchers, and so forth, on the other. The latter were competing with the aristocratic order in wealth and influence, and even in military power, as the guilds also established armed groups strong enough to counter the *milites*.

In thirteenth century Bologna, for example, the general council of the Commune was under the control of noble families holding castles and large manors populated by slaves, *homines de masnada*, and 'serfs' (*manentes*, *homines*, etc.). The council of the *popolo*, however, and its magistrates (*anziani* and *consoli*) dominated by the guilds, had grown increasingly influential and, quite crucially, was able to appoint its own 'speaker': the *Capitano del popolo*, a top officer of the Commune, hired from the most qualified 'city managers' of other Italian towns and therefore an aristocrat. His power could be compared with that of the *Podestà*, also an outsider, meant to be the highest magistrate of the Municipality and close to the faction of the lords.

In 1256 the *Consiglio del Popolo*, supported by an ingenious *Capitano*, Bonaccorso da Soresina, was determined to intervene to reduce the huge number of persons living either in the countryside or in Bologna, who were dependent on their lords and therefore, among other things, exempted from paying any taxes to the Municipality. The Commune was at that time at the top of its territorial expansion campaign in Emilia and Romagna, after the harsh conflict with the Empire had come to an end with the death of Frederick II in 1250. Bologna was indeed one of the most populated cities in Europe, with almost 80,000 inhabitants in the town and its *contado*. The number of people excluded from the political life of the Municipality, and thus exempted from contributing taxes or other activities to the military and economic efforts of the town, was however disproportionately high. A remarkable number of them were *servi* and *ancillae* 'owned' by a few large aristocratic families, including the *homines de masnada*, i.e. persons strictly pertaining to the manor and the personal service of the *signori* and associated to their militias.

In the past, probably to please the powerful aristocratic families whose support was necessary in the wars Bologna had waged against Frederick II, the Commune had tolerated some contracts and customs that had indeed expanded serfdom in the *contado*.[16] Customs and a generous interpretation of Irnerio's

[16] For example, a statute adopted in 1209 stipulated that, contrary to a certain *favor libertatis* that was present in the work of the *legum doctores* that commented the *Corpus Iuris*, a freeman who had married an *ancilla*, i.e. a non-free woman, lost his status of liberty. Moreover, since according to Roman law the child of a slave woman was a slave (*Digestum* I.5.5 reads: 'Iure gentium servi nostri sunt, qui ab hostibus capiuntur aut qui ex ancillis nostris nascuntur'), the impact of this statute on the composition of the non-free population in the area of Bologna was hardly negligible. The disposition was still in force in 1252 and was among those that the reform of 1256–57 most stigmatised. The text of the statute in A. Antonelli (ed.), *Il 'Liber Paradisus'. Con un'antologia di fonti bolognesi in materia di servitù medievali (942–1304)*, Marsilio, Venezia 2007, p. 129. For a detailed discussion (and partially divergent conclusions) see G.

notion of *servus glebae*, endorsed also by Azo and Accursius,[17] induced landlords to stipulate contracts with free peasants whereby the latter engaged themselves to work in the land of their lord and to dwell there with their descendants 'forever', recognising their bond to the land as a form of homage to the lord and a price for his protection.[18] These *manentes* therefore linked a personal obligation of working for the landlord (and exercising some powers over the estate) with the recognition of a status of bondage to the land extending to future generations. These contracts — which used the terms of Roman law to qualify interests and situations typical of a post-feudal society — were intended, from the lords' side, to assist in stopping the migration of free peasants in search of dwelling and better work from one territory to the other. They were nevertheless a way for both peasants and lords to keep at a distance the hegemonic rule of the city-states, chronically hungry for lands and individuals to tax.

5. THE HEAVEN BOOK OF THE CITY OF BOLOGNA: A MASSIVE MANUMISSION

In 1256, the *popolo* of Bologna and its leader Bonaccorso were committed to putting an end to the situation of an increasing segment of the *contado* population being immune from taxation and being in the hands of the *magnati*. The issue was heatedly discussed for months and was eventually solved using a double strategy: a statute would be enacted to limit recourse to contracts that affected the legal status of individuals, but in the meantime, a measure would be agreed between the Commune and the landlords to liberate the non-free *servi*, *ancillae*, *homines de masnada* and the like. Tumults and tensions accompanied the process that nevertheless reached an historical conclusion 25 August 1256. It is thought that following the advice of some lawyers of Bologna's *Studium*, the *Capitano del Popolo* Bonaccorso da Soresina and the *Podestà* Manfredi da

---

MORELLI, 'Tra diritto comune, normativa locale e dottrina: lo *status* servile fino al *Liber Paradisus*' in A. ANTONELLI and M. GIANSANTE (eds.), *Il* Liber Paradisus *e le liberazioni collettive nel XIII secolo. Cento anni di studi (1906–2006)*, Marsilio, Venezia 2007, pp. 285–350, esp. 312–313.

17 The *Glossa Ordinaria* by Accursius noticed indeed that *coloni abscripticii* (that is 'serfs') could be seen as simultaneously slaves (as regards their relationship with the lord) and free people (as regards all others): 'quoad dominos servi sunt, quoad extraneos liberi'. See MORELLI, *supra* note 16, p. 303.

18 'Le *operae* prestate dal coltivatore erano dovute non in ragione della realizzazione di una volontà contrattuale liberamente espresso dale parti, bensì in quanto attuazione di un più generale dovere di rispetto e obbedienza nei confronti di chi godeva di uno stato sociale superiore' [The *operae* (work) performed by the peasant were owed to the master not to implement an agreement freely expressed by the parties to the contract, rather to implement a broader duty of respect and obedience towards those in a higher social rank – my translation] (C.E. TAVILLA, Homo alterius. *I rapport di dipendenza personale nella dottrina del Decreto. Il trattato* De hominiciis *di Martino da Fano*, ESI, Napoli 1993, p. 82; cf. also MORELLI, *supra* note 16, p. 317.

Marengo were appointed as arbitrators and compiled a list of approximately 5,800 men, women and children, assumed to be either *servi* or *ancillae* of their respective masters. The masters were also specifically identified: noble *magnati* but also several wealthy *popolani* were ranked. The award provided for the manumission of all *servi* by the payment by the city of Bologna to their masters of a sum of 10 lire for any adult man or woman, and 8 lire for any child under the age of 14.[19]

The *Liber Paradisus* was the final version of such a list of liberated 'slaves' and masters thereof, edited during the first half of 1257 by four notaries, one for each gate and respective neighbourhood of the city. There are therefore four lists, and three of them contain also an added Prologue, written by the respective notary, in which the reasons and the motivations of the measure are recalled. The code is a solemn document prepared for the official registry of the municipality where it had to be kept as an official recording (a *memoriale*) of the deal.

This is a segment of the text of the Prologue drafted by the notary Corradino Sclariti of Porta (gate) Procola (indeed, the whole document was named 'Heaven Book' after the incipit of this text):

> A heaven of joy the omnipotent God created in the beginning; there He placed the man He had formed, and adorned his body with a white robe bestowing on him absolute and perennial liberty. But the wretch, forgetful of his own dignity and of God's gift, ate the forbidden fruit breaching the divine commandment and in so doing he dismally drove himself and his entire progeny into this valley and irreparably poisoned humankind, which was bound to the chains of devil's servitude. Hence, from being incorruptible he became corrupted, from being immortal, mortal, subject to the decay of an oppressing servitude.
>
> However, seeing that the whole world was becoming ruined, God had mercy on humankind and sent His only Son, born of the Virgin Mother by the grace of the Holy Ghost, so that, once broken by the glory of his dignity the chains of servitude that held us captive, we have been reinstated to our prior liberty; therefore it is a very appropriate thing that, by a manumission, men are restored to their original freedom, people that at the origins nature

[19] The process that brought to the arbitration and to the subsequent legislation is lively reconstructed in G. De Vergottini, 'La liberazione dei servi della gleba a Bologna' in G. Rossi (ed.), *Giovanni De Vergottini (1900–1972). Scritti di storia del diritto italiano*, Giuffrè, Milano 1977, pp. 853–879, now in Antonelli and Giansante, *supra* note 16, pp. 43–59; see also in the same book the essays by Luigi Simeoni, Antonio I. Pini, Rolando Dondarini, Giovanna Morelli.

> engendered to be free, and the law of nations later subjected to the yoke of servitude.
>
> Considering all this, the noble city of Bologna, which has always fought for liberty, mindful of the past and preparing the future, in honour of our lord Jesus Christ the Redeemer, redeemed for a monetary price all those that, in the city or the diocese of Bologna, it found to be oppressed in servile condition, and after a careful scrutiny decreed to free them, further establishing that in the future no one being constrained in some forms of servitude dares settle in the city or the diocese, so that the mass of those either born free or liberated through enfranchisement, may not be corrupted again by any ferment of servitude, for even a small amount of ferment can corrupt a whole community, as a single wicked man could dishonour a multitude of virtuous men.[20]

The Prologue of Porta Procola is an impressive piece of medieval rhetoric. There is almost no mention of the political conflict that had accompanied the adoption of the award. The focus is on the ideological reasons that compelled the city of Bologna to take such a decision. The notary strikes an ambitious parallel between the Christian act of redemption and the measure taken by the Council of Bologna. The liberation in itself does not appear inspired by humanitarian

[20] My translation. An alternative English translation is available in J. CARPENTIER (ed.), *The Emergence of Human Rights in Europe: An Anthology*, Council of Europe Publishing, Strasbourg 2001, pp. 85–86 (M.R. Saulle and P. Tantucci contributed to the section on Italy). This is the original text: 'Paradisum voluptatis plantavit dominus Deus omnipotens a principio, in quo posuit hominem quem formavit et ipsius corpus ornavit veste candenti, sibi donans oerfectissima et perpetuam libertatem. Set ille miser sue dignitatis et divini muneris immemor, pomum vetitum supra preceptum dominicum degustavit, unde se ipsum et omnem suam posteritatem in hanc vallem misère traxit et humanum genus enormiter tosicavit aligans id miserabiliter nexibus diabolice servitutis et sic de incorrutibili factum est corruptibile, de immortali mortale, subiacens alteration et gravissime servituti. Videns vero Deus quod totus mundus perierat misertus est et humano generi et misit filium suum unigenitum natum de virgine matre cohoperante gratia Sancti Spiritus ut Gloria sue dignitatis diruptis vinculis servitutis quibus tenebamur captive nos restitueret pristine libertati, et idcirco valde utiliter agitur si homines ad initio natura liberos protulit et creavit et ius gentium servitutis iugo subposuit, restituantur manumissionis beneficio illi in qua nati fuerant libertatis. Cuius rei consideratione nobilis civitas Bononie que semper pro libertate pugnavit, preteritorum memorians et future providens in honorem nostri redemptoris domini Iesu Christi nummario pretio redemit omnes quos in civitate Bononie ac episcopate reperit servili condicione adstrictos et liberos esse decrevit inquisitione habita deligenti, statuens ne quis adstrictus aliqua servitude in civitate vel espiscopatu Bononie deinceps audeat commemorari, ne massa tam naturalis lbertatis quam redempta pretio, ulterius corrumpi possit fermento aliquot servitutis cum modicum fermentum totam massam corrumpat et consortium unius mali bonos plurimos dehonestet'. The critical edition of the *Liber*'s text is in ANTONELLI, *supra* note 16. For an Italian translation of the Prologues and a stylistic comment: M. GIANSANTE, 'I prologhi del *Liber Paradisus*. Fonti e problemi', in A. ANTONELLI and M. GIANSANTI (eds.), *Il* Liber Paradisus *e le liberazioni collettive nel XIII secolo. Cento anni di studi (1906–2006)*, Marsilio, Venezia 2007, pp. 201–228.

reasons, nor is it a recognition of the individual rights of the villeins (although the meticulous inscription of thousands of names of oppressed men, women and children — all those Aldrevandus, Bona, Taudescha, Ambroxius, Scarlatta, Caçadrago — in an official memorial book is in itself a sort of solemn recalling of the inherent *dignitas et divinum munus* of their being members of humankind). The serfs' liberation is a measure that first of all enhances the glory of the city and of its leaders — namely the *Capitano del Popolo*, Bonaccorso,[21] whose name is recurrent in the three prologues, which do not also recall Da Marengo, then the *Podestà*. In other words, the *Liber* celebrates the governing institutions of the *popolo*. Bologna *popolo*'s boldness and determination won against the resistance of the lords and gained for the city a new class of 'citizens': the almost 6,000 serfs who were separated from their masters. This is an accomplishment that must be celebrated, and the Prologues to the memorial books, especially those of Porta Procola and Porta Stiera, were accordingly written in a style similar to that of the *Liber Augustalis*, drafted by the chief chancellor of Frederick II Pier delle Vigne in 1231. The arguments that the Prologues introduce to provide a rationale to the massive manumission are taken from the Bible (Genesis, Paul's letters) as well as from the *Corpus iuris*. Indeed Bologna sets for its 'citizens' a 'natural law' status of freedom, by breaking and stigmatising the *ius gentium* institutions of serfdom and slavery, and restoring an unlikely but fascinating state of 'natural paradise'.[22] It is difficult not to see in such a programme, besides the obvious economic and political considerations that have been largely mentioned above, a genuine echo of a religious afflatus (perhaps the same that most probably presided over the liberation of serfs in Assisi by *popolo* and *magnati*, on a much smaller scale, with the 1203 and 1210 *concordiae*, presumably inspired by Saint Francis).

It would be anachronistic to find any fundamental rights (in the modern sense) inspiration in a policy which is a form of participation in the act of redemption performed by Christ. The programme is nevertheless very relevant in a fundamental rights context. In the Middle Ages, and indeed up to modern jusnaturalism, the principle of equality did not apply to individuals. The

21 Bonaccorso, *Capitano del popolo* in 1256, the following year was appointed *Podestà*. It is plausible that this unusual sequence of positions in his career at the service of the city was consequence of the delicacy of the programme of reform he had championed, epitomised in the *Liber Paradisus*. It might be of interest to notice that in 2008 the then mayor of Bologna, Sergio Cofferati, inaugurated a new headquarters of the Municipality named 'Palazzo Bonaccorso', facing a new square named 'Piazza Liber Paradisus'. The memory of the Heaven Book and of its main proponent is due to last for a long-time to come.

22 The Prologue of Porta Procola seems reminiscent of the famous excerpt from Ulpian's *Institutiones* about manumission and slavery as established by the law of the nations, not by the law of nature: '[…] utpote cum iure naturali omnes liberi nascerentur nec esset nota manumissio, cum servitus esset incognita: sed posteaquam iure gentium servitus invasit, secutum est beneficium manumissionis. Et cum uno naturali nomine homines appellaremur, iure gentium tria genera esse coeperunt: liberi et his contrarium servi et tertium genus liberti, id est hi qui desierant esse servi.' (*Digestum*, I.1.4). Cf. GIANSANTE, *supra* note 20.

reference was rather to the Ciceronian concept of *equabilitas*, that is the virtue to rule the *res publica* counterbalancing the various agencies that share the common space, as the Roman republic did with its mixed constitution (partly monarchic, partly oligarchic, and partly democratic).[23] 'Rights' were not an entitlement of the individual, but were rather associated with the social group or estate to which any individual belonged, and the 'liberty' of the individual corresponded to the 'liberties', 'immunities', and 'privileges' his[24] group was entitled to.

If we compare the arbitral award enshrined in the *Liber Paradisus* with the mass liberations of serfs in the thirteenth century by other Italian Communes — and indeed also by the kings of France, as well as in Cataluña and in many other parts of Europe — it is worth underlining two main characteristics of the Bologna initiative. First, the bold ideological investment that Bologna made on the occasion of the 1256–1257 liberation, as can be induced from the Prologues, and the fame that has accompanied that event up till the modern day. Second, whereas in all the other cases the so-called liberations were actually a mere cancellation — for the benefit of the disposing authority: a city, a king, etc. — of prior obligations contracted by freemen with other authorities (landlords, including church institutions) that removed them from the power (especially the fiscal jurisdiction) of the 'liberators', the award of 1256 in Bologna was a genuine emancipation of persons in non-free status.[25] This is perhaps evidence that, although political and economic reasons were also in this case of paramount importance, the decision to focus on the 'real' serfs and to use the 'classic' formalities of a *manumissio* '*nummario pretio*', according to the Roman law precepts, denotes the peculiar ideological message that Bonaccorso and his faction associated with this measure. This is why it can indeed be flagged as a *sui generis* and *sui temporis* fundamental rights declaration.

---

[23] *Equabilitas*, in Latin, only occurs in Cicero (notably in *De Oratore*, I.42.188). The term would be used by the Florentine humanist and historian Leonardo Bruni (Arezzo 1370 – Florence 1444), who would apply the notion to the governing system of Florence.

[24] Any gender concern was missing: one could apply to the Italian Middle Ages the remark that Papinian referred to Roman law: 'In multis iuris nostri articulis deterior est condicio feminarum quam masculorum' (*Digestum*, I.5.9).

[25] This point is particularly stressed by F. PANERO, 'Manumissioni collettive di servi in Francia e in Italia nel secolo XIII: riflessioni per una comparazione storica' in A. ANTONELLI and M. GIANSANTE (eds.), *Il* Liber Paradisus *e le liberazioni collettive nel XIII secolo. Cento anni di studi (1906–2006)*, Marsilio, Venezia 2007, pp. 351–368, at pp. 360–361. The case often compared to the Bologna liberation is that of Vercelli. This Commune stipulated in 1241 that no one but the Commune itself could impose any form of judicial dispute settlement, law enforcement measures (*districtio*), exaction of taxes, etc. It is worth noticing that at that time in Vercelli the *podestà* was a Guglielmo da Soresina, probably a relative of Bonaccorso, and that in 1228 a group of students (*universitas scholarium*) of the Padova *studium* established a similar institution in Vercelli. The *studium* of Padova had been created a few years earlier, in 1222, by a consistent group of students and teachers fleeing from Bologna. A thread maybe linked the cognate experiences of Bologna and Vercelli.

6. EPILOGUE

The *Liber Paradisus* — comprising the official list of those serfs who were to be liberated by their respective masters who in turn were entitled to receive the price of 10 or 8 lire per person — was not a statute and did not produce *per se* any juridical effect. One year after the arbitral award a normative instrument (a *statuto*) was enacted to execute the content of the arbitration and provide details of the procedures. The statute contained important and controversial novelties. First of all it specified that, while the masters were to receive the sums for the buy-back of their serfs, the latter were not entitled to receive their *peculium*, that is the property — if any — they had received from the masters during their service. This was entirely acquired by the Commune. Then, any freed individual was compelled (under threat of very harsh penalties) to enlist as a resident of the Bologna *contado* and immediately pay taxes thereto. These rules were undoubtedly evidence of the extreme financial stress that the Commune was experiencing. Another novel element was the repeal of some previous legal provisions that had allowed for the expansion of the number of serfs, including the norm that attributed servile status to the freeman who married an *ancilla*. Even more importantly, a clause was adopted providing that the *manentes* — that is the freemen who had stipulated with a landlord a contract whereby they and their descendants engaged to dwell in the land — were also 'liberated', and that in the future no more contracts of *manentia* were permitted. This meant that the only ongoing *manentes* were those who had inherited such a status (and the associated dwellings and immunities).

These provisions equated the legislation of the Commune of Bologna to that of the other cities that were adopting similar anti-aristocratic measures (Verbania, Verona, Treviso, Firenze, etc.). Between 1256 and 1257 in Bologna the *popolo* had gained full control of the city's institutions and started a vigorous policy to curb the resistance of the *magnati*. The passing of the *manentes* under the jurisdiction of the city was part of this strategy and aimed in particular to increase the tax income and to put under the municipality's control the land that the *manentes* — now free to move, but deprived of their main source of survival — had cultivated and inhabited.

The last decades of the thirteenth century were a period of tumult in Bologna. The town was torn by a furious conflict between the aristocratic families of the Geremei (supposedly Guelf) and the Lambertazzi (Ghibellines) and their respective factions. The aristocrats boycotted the initiatives of the municipality, to the extent of withdrawing without a fight on the occasion of a battle against Rimini and Faenza (1275). Asked why they had behaved in such a cowardly fashion, it is reported they replied: read the laws you have adopted, rotten *popolani*![26]

The Lambertazzi were expelled twice by the *popolani*, and in 1282 the Commune adopted radical legislation against the *magnati*, the so-called *ordinamenti sacrati*, exiling the turbulent aristocratic families from the town and, once again, prohibiting any form of voluntary subjugation of peasants and other members of the *popolo minuto* to the lords. Political and military instability however forced more and more families to seek protection of the landlords, so that the contracts of *manentia*, although prohibited and sanctioned with extraordinarily severe penalties, remained a constant practice and even increased, as insecurity and turmoil grew. The last explicit abolition was voted in 1304 by the *popolo*. In the meantime, however, the demographic and financial problems of the city had dramatically scaled down, along with the population, which dropped to around 40,000 inhabitants in the 1320s, and the prestige and political ambitions of the Commune. In 1350 the *Signore* of Bologna sold the town to the Visconti of Milan; in 1360 it started to be governed by a delegate of the Pope.

7. CONCLUDING REMARKS

The *Liber Paradisus* symbolises a moment in Italian history that can be singled out as the turning-point in which the city-states — including Bologna — were given a chance to build a more inclusive body politic. Dramatically, the Prologue to the *Liber* speaks of re-establishing for the human community a 'heaven of joy'. The path towards the realisation of such a heaven was provided for: it was based on a shared religion and a practice of government inspired by a respect for all members of society, whereby society members were considered as collective entities — families, corporations, guilds, orders, *universitates scholarium* — rather than individuals. Even the slaves and the serfs could have their place in such a picture.

The fresco of the *Buon Governo*, painted by Ambrogio Lorenzetti in 1338–1339 in Siena, both as an allegory and a realistic depiction of its effects, is a 'declaration and programme of action for human rights and good governance' put down in images, which is both illustrative of its time and remains eloquent to this day. The *Liber Paradisus*, set forth by visionary lawyers and political leaders for the glory of Bologna and for the benefit of the whole community, complements Lorenzetti's fresco. The vision has faded and the *Buon Governo* has been replaced by a lesser version (the *Cattivo* (bad) *Governo,* also painted by Lorenzetti on the opposite wall), but the endeavour to realise fundamental rights has been kept in motion.

---

[26] The anecdote is reported in ANTONELLI, *supra* note 16, p. xxxvii.

5. HUNGARY: THE HISTORIC CONSTITUTION AS THE PLACE OF MEMORY

Ivett CSÁSZÁR
Balázs MAJTÉNYI

'Very deep is the well of the past. Should we not call it bottomless?'
(Thomas Mann: Joseph and his brothers)

1. INTRODUCTION

Like Magna Carta in England, the Golden Bull in Hungary can be regarded as, if not necessarily the first, certainly a milestone document in the history of human rights. Parallels have often been drawn between the two documents: they have both been regarded as the result of efforts of the privileged to check the powers of kings in the feudal times of the thirteenth century, though it has also been pointed out that the differences between English and Hungarian social conditions make the comparison problematic.[1]

Rather than examining the text of the Golden Bull itself, which would be a heroic undertaking as there is no original sample, only later copies, we will look at how the document is read and interpreted. Readings of history are not only and perhaps not primarily about the past: what the discourse dominated by those in power in various periods brings into focus or silences about a certain historical period and its relics tells us as much about the past as about the interpreter of the past. The Golden Bull as part of Hungary's historic constitution has often been drawn on and has been the battlefield of the fight of identity politics, providing ground for egalitarian as well as anti-egalitarian aspirations.

2. THEORETICAL ASSUMPTIONS

Unified national history is a construction, an after-the-fact creation that is an important part of the national identity of states. At times of political transition it is reconstructed according to prevailing values. National history presents events

1 F. ECKHART, *Magyar alkotmány- és jogtörténet*, Budapest 1941.

from the vantage point of the privileged and creates an illusion of unity where in fact, taking into consideration the diversity of experiences of people of different ethnicity, religion, class and gender, none exists. Feminist criticism has been in the vanguard in pointing out that historical periods hailed as progressive and positive for men often had different implications for women's lives. The French Revolution, claims feminist criticism, emancipated non-aristocratic men, allowing for their inclusion in public life, but it excluded women of the popular classes and women of the aristocracy from power.[2]

Challenging dominant discourse that fosters national unity, and thereby conceals social differences, as well as realising the fact that 'history is a weapon',[3] Foucauldian 'counter histories' have appeared as critiques of traditional history-writing discourses.[4] Their fundamental goal has been to uncover the memories of oppressed and excluded groups and to criticise state power. Embracing such a critical standpoint, which is also in line with the universal values of human rights and equality, provides an opportunity for moral reflection and for building a human rights supportive political culture. Furthermore, counter-histories can supplement and run parallel with the history of human rights, which cannot be other than a 'retrospective teleology'.[5]

The cult that surrounds historical relics plays a huge part in fostering a sense of national unity and the illusion of collective identity. In turning to objects that symbolise unity and are accorded utmost respect, nationalism is tinged with fetishism. McClintock points out that '[d]espite the commitment of European nationalism (following Hegel) to the idea of the nation-state as the embodiment of rational Progress, nationalism has been experienced and transmitted primarily through fetishism — precisely the cultural form that the Enlightenment denigrated as the antithesis of "Reason".'[6] Among everyday fetish objects like flags, uniforms or anthems[7] the Holy Crown and the Golden Bull — conceived

[2] J.B. LANDES, *Women and the Public Sphere in the Age of the French Revolution*, Cornell, New York 1988, p. 147.

[3] See the online reader focusing on American counter history: <http://www.historyisaweapon.org/indextrue.html> accessed 20.03.2015 and H. ZINN, *A People's History of the United States: 1492 – Present*, HarperCollins, New York 1980.

[4] Foucault called critical history writing that stood in opposition to dominant historical writing 'counter history'. Counter history is an insurgent discourse aimed at the dominant discourse. It aims to integrate the points of view of groups that are pushed to social periphery or excluded into the writing of history, these include studies that give voice to the views of postcolonial, ethnic or social gender groups. M. FOUCAULT, *Society Must Be Defended: Lectures at the Collége de France, 1975–1976,* Picador, New York 2003.

[5] J-P. LEHNERS, 'Pleading for a New History of Human Rights' in A. MIHR and M. GIBNEY (eds.), *The SAGE Handbook of Human Rights*, SAGE, London 2014, p. 34.

[6] A. MCCLINTOCK, 'Family Feuds: Gender, Nationalism and the Family' (1993) 44 *Feminist Review* 71.

[7] The Szekler 'anthem' has increasing popularity in Hungary: since the anthem itself is an expression of nostalgia for the chopped off Hungarian territories, especially the territory of Transylvania, which includes the Szeklerland, it functions as a distinguishing mark and cohesive

together as part of the 'historic constitution' — are unique relics in Hungary that foster national unity and as such have become tools of a nationalist agenda. Having found their way into the new constitution of the country, accepted by an authoritarian government, these relics have been transformed into symbols with an anti-egalitarian reading — symbols of a thousand-year-old statehood and fetishes of national genius. As such they are subject to utmost reverence instead of judicious criticism, which in the case of medieval documents that left the masses of people unprotected from the power of the privileged is highly controversial.

3. THE BODY OF THE NATION FROM THE VIEWPOINT OF EQUALITY — A HISTORICAL PERSPECTIVE

The concept of the equality of rights draws a clear borderline between feudal societies and constitutional democracies. Let us look into this issue with respect to the concept of the nation since belonging or not belonging to the body of the nation has significant effects on rights and freedoms. In spite of the fact that Latin was the official language of the country until 1844, in the Middle Ages the majority of people living in the territory of Hungary most likely spoke Hungarian. This, however, did not mean that they were all considered Hungarians in the sense of the time. [8] To be Hungarian primarily meant to fill a *social* position. In the Middle Ages Hungarians were the subjects of the king, and social differences distinguished the 'Magyars' from the equally Magyar-speaking Szeklers. To be Magyar meant to have a certain social position, membership in an exceptional feudal class, the noble nation. It was principally the male members of this class that were granted rights. This concept of the Hungarian nation is clearly not identical to the modern egalitarian concept of the nation.[9]

With the appearance of nationalism in the nineteenth century and the introduction of the equality of civil rights in 1848, in theory all could belong to the nation regardless of social position, and the residents of the country — no matter what they thought — became members of the political nation through a public law construction.[10] This undoubtedly contributed to making society more

force of the community of Hungarian nationalists who would like to see a revision of the Trianon Treaty.

8 B. Majtényi and G. Majtényi, *Mi a cigány, mi a magyar, és van-e történelmü(n)k? Reflexió Lajtai Mátyás recenziójára.* No. 2. Budapesti Könyvszemle (BUKSZ) 2013, pp. 199–201.

9 B. Majtényi, *A nemzetállam új ruhája: Multikulturalizmus Magyarországon,* Gondolat, Budapest 2007.

10 Majtényi and Majtényi, *supra* note 8.

egalitarian, though women remained excluded from most realms of power.[11] Article 2 of Act V of 1848, for example, gave the right to vote to all regardless of religious affiliation, however, this general extension of the right to vote did not reach women; universal and equal suffrage was granted only in 1945.

The anti-egalitarian, pre-modern concept of the nation which included its members based on their social status did not entirely disappear and it remained the basis of prejudice against and exclusion of various minorities, e.g. Jews and Gypsies, and remains so to this day.[12] István Bíbó, a definitive figure in twentieth century Hungarian political thought, pointed out that the failure of the assimilation of Hungarian Jews was mainly due to the fact that 'Hungarian society, from the very beginning, assimilated or offered the opportunity to assimilate on dishonourable, disrespectful terms',[13] given that the adoption of the Hungarian language or the self-identification as a Hungarian did not result in the majority acknowledging one as a Hungarian.[14] Bíbó's observations can be extended to the Roma community as well: the Hungarian majority has blocked the masses of self-defined Hungarian, socially marginalised, Hungarian-speaking Roma from the opportunity to integrate. Assimilation is not only linguistic melting, but a phenomenon that necessitates the social acceptance of a group, and as such it cannot be realised through marginalisation and exclusion.[15] In the absence of social acknowledgment, those Roma who are successful in the labour world are challenged systematically when trying to assimilate in Hungary. Feischmidt, for example, highlights the example of micro-villages in South-Western Hungary where the economic success of Roma does not guarantee social acknowledgment, because the 'majority' is increasingly thinking in racial terms.[16] The result is that even if social differences decline, racist and mobility-obstructing thought constitute a new obstacle to integration.[17] The prejudiced

[11] E. GELLNER, 'The Coming of Nationalism and its Interpretation: The Myths of Nation and Class' in G. BALAKRISHNANA (ed.), *Mapping the Nation,* Verson, London and New York 1996, pp. 98–132.

[12] B. MAJTÉNYI and G. MAJTÉNYI, *Cigánykérdés Magyarországon 1945-től 2010-ig. (The Roma Issue in Hungary 1945–2010),* Libri, Budapest 2012, p. 26.

[13] I. BÍBÓ, *Válogatott tanulmányok,* Magvető, Budapest 1990 p. 746.

[14] Writing in 1944 he emphasised the collective responsibility of Hungarian society for the annihilation of the Jews, and encouraged that social memory treat the Holocaust as a crime committed against members of the Hungarian nation, i.e. against itself. BIBÓ, *supra* note 13.

[15] R. BRUBAKER, 'The Return of Assimilation? Changing Perspectives on Immigration and Its Sequels in France, Germany, and the United States' (2001) *Ethnic and Racial Studies* 531–548.

[16] M. FEISCHMIDT, 'Kényszerek és illeszkedések. Gazdasági és szimbolikus stratégiák aprófalvakban élő romák életében' (2012) *Szociológiai Szemle* 54–84.

[17] M. FEISCHMIDT, 'A mindennapi nacionalizmus és a másság cigányként való megjelölése' in M. FEISCHMIDT et al., *Nemzet a mindennapokban: Az újnacionalizmus populáris kultúrája,* L'Harmattan, Budapest 2014, pp. 401–447, 446 and Z. VIDRA and J. FOX, 'Mainstreaming of Racist Anti-Roma Discourses in the Media in Hungary' (2014) *Journal of Immigrant & Refugee Studies* 437–455.

environment obstructs social mobility, further weakening the egalitarian character of society.[18]

The continuing existence and recreation of historical social categories can be a barrier to equality. History is not only a part but a means of the fights of identity politics; historiography has always shaped the discourse of political identities. What is written in history books, academic or popular, or the textbooks written for students, has a crucial impact on the extent to which a society can accept the principle of constitutionality. Presenting history with an eye on aspects of equality will foster constitutional values, while foregrounding anti-egalitarian traditions will likely weaken those values.

The Hungarian history of fundamental rights (e.g. *habeas corpus*), unlike the Anglo-Saxon development of constitutional law, does not point towards the continuous expansion of rights, since Hungarian legal history has been frequently halted by rights-restricting dictatorial periods. It is of course true that, as Hörcher suggests, constitutional heritage cannot be discarded as if it did not exist just because the dictatorships introduced rights-restricting measures.[19] However, it has to be taken into account that political transitions were as a rule accompanied by the rewriting of history, and that heritage itself can be presented in various ways. Hungarian literature on the constitution as well as Hungarian historiography often discards the possibility of different interpretations and presents the historic constitution as if it were 'the result of organic development, what is more, it is itself the organic development.'[20] An interpretation of history that does not take into account the fact that historiography is part of the discourse of political identities and does not strive to present the past from the view of constitutional values undermines democratic political culture. Interpreting history as the place of memory[21] will make us understand readings that trace human rights or the rule of law back to medieval documents; these readings are primarily about now, too. In what follows we are examining the present-day mainstream interpretation of Hungarian history that disregards the demands of equality. The historic constitution, the Holy Crown and the Golden Bull, are read and interpreted by the social groups and political parties at present in power predominantly in a way that deepens inequalities and supports the privileged position of dominant social groups.

---

18 GELLNER, *supra* 11, pp. 98–132.

19 F. HÖRCHER, 'Communal Values in the New Hungarian Fundamental Law' in E. BOS and K. PÓCZA (eds.), *Verfassunggebung in konsolidierten Demokratien: Neubeginn oder Verfall eines Systems?* Nomos Verlag, Baden-Baden 2014, p. 357.

20 Á. RIXER, 'A történeti alkotmány lehetséges jelentéstartalmai' (2011) *Jogelméleti Szemle* <http://jesz.ajk.elte.hu/rixer47.html> accessed 20.03.2015.

21 P. NORA, *Entre Mémoire et Histoire. La problématique des lieux, in Les lieux de mémoire. I. La République*, Gallimard, Paris 1984, pp. xvii–xlii.

4. THE HISTORIC CONSTITUTION, THE HOLY CROWN AND THE GOLDEN BULL

Earlier legal history and constitutional law literature had a tendency to present the thousand-year-old or so assumed historic constitution as a crucial element of national identity, alleging that the spiritual roots of the historic constitution are to be found in the soul of the people and the depth of national genius.[22] The historic constitution as such is considered to be a sum of the various laws and customs of various periods that ensured freedoms and provided for constitutional guarantees of the institutional functioning of the Kingdom of Hungary. It is not a charter and is nowhere recorded, its content has changed from time to time, but the doctrine of the Holy Crown and the Golden Bull itself are key elements of it.[23]

The fundamental thesis of the historic constitution is that the origin of all public power is the Holy Crown, which was said to be the crown of King Stephen I (Saint Stephen, 1000–1038) and the inhabitants of the country are required to be loyal to and obey the Crown.[24] According to the theory Hungary's first Christian king, Stephen I, received the Crown from Pope Sylvester. The riddle whether King Stephen was given the crown by the pope or the emperor is a political issue and is linked with the sovereignty of the state. [25] The theories challenging the claim that it was given by the pope characteristically became more pronounced during state socialism.

The doctrine attributes state power to the Holy Crown,[26] and the nation (initially the nobility) and the king are together embodied in the Crown thus personified. At the same time the Crown, as the symbol of the unified kingdom, also meant the country's territorial integrity, that is, the cohesion of the Lands of the Crown of Saint Stephen.[27] The doctrine was elaborated in 1517 in a volume entitled *Tripartitum* by István Werbőczy, law scholar, who collected the laws and customs of the country in his work.[28] Thanks to the heritage of the 1848 revolution, in the light of the equality of civil rights the effects of the crown were extended to the entirety of the political nation, and were not narrowed to the

---

22 M. TOMCSÁNYI, *Magyarország Közjoga*, Királyi magyar Egyetemi Nyomda, Budapest 1932, p. 33.

23 See to this e.g. Z. SZENTE, *A historizáló alkotmányozás problémái — a történeti alkotmány és a Szent Korona az új Alaptörvényben* (2011) *Közjogi Szemle* or Z. SZENTE, 'The doctrine of the Holy Crown in the Hungarian Historical Constitution' (2013) *Journal on European History of Law*.

24 F. ECKHART, *A Szentkorona-eszme története*, Attraktor, Máriabesenyő–Gödöllő 2003, pp. 64 and 75.

25 See to this L. PETER, 'A nemzeti múlt legendái és tilalomfái' in L. PETER, *Elbától keletre*, Osiris, Budapest 1998, p. 95.

26 TOMCSÁNYI, *supra* note 22.

27 *Ibid.*, p. 253.

28 Werbőczy István Hármaskönyve, Franklin-Társulat, Budapest 1897.

exceptional orders any more.[29] Thus, legal historians sometimes link the sovereignty of the people to the doctrine.

After World War I, due to the Treaty of Trianon Hungary lost two-thirds of its territory and three-fifths of its population.[30] The country lost a population of 10.6 million of which the number of ethnic Hungarians was 3.5 million (today the latter number is less than 2.2 million). From this point on the Holy Crown has been held up as a unifying symbol for lost territories. Especially between the two World Wars the demand for territorial revision was an integral part of the theory of the Holy Crown.[31]

Like other similar theories, the doctrine describing statehood of a thousand years is partly founded on myths. Considering the fact that the Crown bears the picture of an emperor who ruled well after the reign of King Stephen, the byzantine emperor Michael VII Doukas (1071–1078), the Crown in its present form can never have been on his head. Theories that allege that pictures were replaced are not approved by historians. The earliest authentic description of the Holy Crown is from the sixteenth century.[32] According to Zoltán Péter '[i]t is doubtful whether there have ever been bestowed upon regalia, or indeed any object, in a European country the cult and such an enduring political role that have been accorded to the Crown of St Stephen.'[33] By way of comparison the author mentions that the Scottish Stone of Scone (Stone of Destiny) did not become a repository of rights.[34]

The Golden Bull, considered to be the most important founding document of the historic constitution, was issued on 24 April 1222 by King Andrew II (1205–1235). It was probably named after the stamp (bulla) made of gold that served to authenticate the document itself. The Golden Bull, however, came into prominence later on. In 1231 some of its provisions were repealed; nevertheless, in 1351 Louis I (the Great) (1342–1382) confirmed the document. The already mentioned *Tripartitum* of 1517 traces back the four freedoms of the noble orders — *habeas corpus*, subjection to the jurisdiction of the royal court, exemption from taxes and the right of resistance — to the Golden Bull. Historians often link the rule of law to the Golden Bull that restricted the powers of the king. No

29 TOMCSÁNYI, *supra* note 22, p. 252.

30 Treaty of Peace between the Allied and Associated Powers and Hungary and Protocol and Declaration, signed at Trianon 04.06.1920.

31 K. EGRESI, 'A köztársasági eszme és a szentkorona-tan a két világháború közötti magyar politikai gondolkodásban' in I. FEITL (ed), *A köztársaság a modernkori történelem fényében: tanulmányok*, Napvilág, Budapest 2007, pp. 240–272, 266.

32 G. PALFFY, 'A Szent Korona és a koronaláda balesete 1638-ban' in J. JANKOVICS, '*Nem sűlyed az emberiség!'...*, MTA Irodalomtudományi Intézet, Budapest 2007, pp. 1431–1444.

33 L. PETER, 'The Holy Crown of Hungary, Visible and Invisible' (2003) *The Slavonic and East European Review (SEER)* 422.

34 *Ibid.*

original sample of the document has survived; its earliest copy was made in 1318. Therefore, no one can be sure what the original document exactly contained.[35] Not even the golden bull (the stamp) survived; this is reproduced based on the stamp of other documents issued by Andrew II. Cieger claims that the Golden Bull subsequently raised the reputation and invited a positive evaluation of King Andrew II, who was otherwise considered a weak emperor.[36] Ironically, later periods came to associate the king with the Golden Bull, which was in fact enforced by the noble orders who demanded the reinforcement of their privileges and the restriction of royal power.

Though embedded in feudal times and born particularly close in time, as well as triggered by the intention of the privileged to restrict the powers of their king, it would be problematic to make too much of the parallel between Magna Carta and the Golden Bull, especially in the light of the very different paths of legal development that the two countries have taken.[37] The development of *habeas corpus* granted for the noble man in the Golden Bull is very different from its counterpart guaranteed by Magna Carta. For instance, during state socialism in Hungary the provision that made it possible to prosecute any member of the party only with the permission of the party was also considered *habeas corpus*.[38] That is, the guarantee against unlawful detention was transformed and distorted into a means of the state party to grant immunity for its members.

The traditions included in the Golden Bull might point in various directions and the question is what gets emphasised and reinforced as a result of a political decision: examples of rights extension or, quite to the contrary, examples of rights restriction. While extending the rights of the privileged, the Golden Bull restricted the rights of Jewish and Muslim people to hold office. What is more, following the 'achievements' of the Lateran Synod of 1215, in 1232 Andrew II called upon Jewish people to wear a distinguishing symbol and banned mixed marriages between Jews and Christians. If such practices are invoked and implicitly approved by the extreme right political parties at present to support their exclusionary politics, and if those in power, i.e. those who dominate political discourse, approve this endorsement with their silence, the Golden Bull will be reduced to a list of the rights of the privileged rather than extended into a milestone document of human rights.

Similarly, examining the document from the viewpoint of women's rights can lead to diverging conclusions. On the one hand, though the official Hungarian

---

35 Á. Timon, *Magyar Alkotmány- és jogtörténet*, Hornánszky, Budapest 1917, p. 295.

36 A. Cieger, 'A pecsét sok oldala. Az Aranybulla mint emlékezeti hely' in Z. Bódy, S. Horváth and T. Valuch (eds.), *Megtalálható-e a múlt? Tanulmányok Gyáni Gábor 60. Születésnapjára*, Argumentum, Budapest 2010, p. 406.

37 *Ibid.*, pp. 407–408.

38 See to this L. Péter, 'Montesquieu paradoxonja a szabadságról és a magyar alkotmány, 1790–1990' in L. Peter, *Elbától keletre*, Osiris, Budapest 1998, pp. 342–354.

version of the text uses the term 'ember', meaning 'human being', without making a distinction between the genders, it is likely that 'ember' referred to man and excluded woman since this term was mostly used in Hungarian dialects to refer to the male human being in spite of its seeming grammatical neutrality. On the other hand, the document protected some — very few — women's rights to property. It stipulated that the death of the husband shall have no effect on the dower of the wife, and that if a nobleman dies without any son, the daughter shall inherit a quarter of his wealth. Therefore, the document can be invoked as a point of reference both for the extension of human rights and the restriction of equality depending on political will.[39]

5. REVITALISATION OF THE HISTORIC CONSTITUTION AFTER THE FALL OF THE KINGDOM

After World War II the Crown was taken to the US.[40] The thousand-year-old historic constitution was replaced by a constitution that introduced a republic as the form of government (Act I of 1946) and this was followed by the state socialist constitution of the People's Republic (Act XX of 1949) when the Communists came to power. With Act I of 1946 the country became a parliamentary republic: article 19 stated that with the entering into force of the Act, the provisions and acts of the abolished kingdom, including the historic constitution, are no longer effective. Interestingly enough, the idea of the thousand-year-old constitution as the historic past that determines national identity did not come to an end during state socialism either. After its modification in 1972 (Act I of 1972), the state socialist constitution, parenthesising internationalism, referred to the historic past in the first sentence of the preamble: 'Hungary has been maintained and vitalised by the work and struggle of its people for a thousand years.' The US gave back the Crown to Hungary in 1978, when it was placed in the National Museum.

The constitution adopted at the political transition (Constitution of 1989)[41] did not found national identity on the historic constitution, and in building up the parliamentary system it relied on the parliamentary traditions of 1848, as well as on the parliamentary and republican public law traditions of Act I of 1946. At the millennium of the establishment of the state by Saint Stephen in 2000 the Crown was taken to the building of the Parliament and the Crown Act was

---

39 Cieger, *supra* note 36, pp. 410–411.

40 I. Bertényi, *A magyar Szent Korona*, Kossuth, Budapest 1996, p. 182.

41 The democratic constitution of the republic (Constitution of 1989), which was formally adopted in 1949 but was revised in light of the principle of the rule of law, democracy and fundamental rights after the political transition in 1989.

adopted.[42] (Act I of 2000 'To Commemorate the Establishment of the State by St Stephen and the Holy Crown').[43] The Act pointed out that the Crown shall be the embodying relic of the continuity and independence of the Hungarian state. What was believed to be the stamp of the Golden Bull suddenly became a public law symbol without any foundation in new legislation. A copy of the stamp has been worn by judges of the Constitutional Court on their chest since 1994 and in 2005 the new president of the Court, Mihály Bihari, was inducted in front of a medieval copy of the Golden Bull in the palace of the archbishop in Esztergom.[44]

With the change of government in 2010 a shift in public law took place and the achievements of the historic constitution[45] and the Holy Crown found their way into the Preamble of the new constitution, called Fundamental Law of 2011, as traditions determining national identity.[46] Although the republic remains the form of government, the Hungarian Holy Crown, appearing as the embodiment of national unity, retrieves some of its constitutional function.[47] The reference to 'the achievements of our historical constitution',[48] unlike the Anglo-Saxon development of constitutional law, does not point towards the continuous expansion of rights, since Hungarian legal history has been hampered by rights-restricting dictatorial periods. Using these terms is problematic because in Hungary neither the dictatorial periods, nor past national traumas like the Trianon Treaty have been adequately reflected on.[49]

Bringing back the tradition of the historic constitution and the Holy Crown has been hailed by some and denounced by others. Some critics consider the

---

42 See in detail I. HALÁSZ and G. SCHWEITZER, *Szimbolika és közjog: Az állami és nemzeti jelképek helye a magyar alkotmányos rendszerben*, Kalligram, Pozsony 2010 and I. HALÁSZ and G. SCHWEITZER, 'National and state symbols in the Hungarian legal system' (2010) *International Journal of Public Administration* 60–67.

43 Act I of 2000 to Commemorate the Establishment of the State by St Stephen and the Holy Crown.

44 CIEGER, *supra* note 36, p. 403.

45 G. SCHWEITZER, 'Fundamental Law – Cardinal Law – Historical Constitution: the Case of Hungary since 2011' (2013) 4 *Journal on European History of Law* 124–128.

46 The Hungarian Parliament passed Hungary's new constitution (entitled the Fundamental Law) on 18.04.2010, which entered into force 01.01.2012 and superseded the previous constitution (Constitution of 1989).

47 See the critical analysis of this process. S. RADNÓTI, *Az üvegalmárium*, Noran Libro, Budapest 2011.

48 See to this Z. SZENTE, 'A historizáló alkotmányozás problémái – a történeti alkotmány és a Szent Korona az új Alaptörvényben' (2011) *Közjogi Szemle* and Z. SZENTE, 'The doctrine of the Holy Crown in the Hungarian Historical Constitution' (2013) *Journal on European History of Law*.

49 P. GYÖRGY, *Állatkert Kolozsváron -- Képzelt Erdély*, Magvető, Budapest 2013 and M. FEISCHMIDT, 'Populáris emlékezetpolitikák az új nacionalizmus: a Trianon-kultusz társadalmi alapjai' in M. FEISCHMIDT et al., *Nemzet a mindennapokban. Az újnacionalizmus populáris kultúrája,* L'Harmattan, Budapest 2014, M. FEISCHMIDT, 'A fölény revíziója. A populáris emlékezetpolitikák Trianon-képe' in C. FEDINEC, Z. ILYÉS, A. SIMON and B. VIZI (eds.), *A közép-európaiság dicsérete és kritikája*, Kalligram, Pozsony 2013, pp. 151–182.

reference simply meaningless, others consider it as an attack on constitutionality, yet others regard it as incompatible with the traditions of the republic and the heritage of 1989. The role of the Holy Crown is indeed rather unclear in the Preamble, called National Avowal, of the Fundamental Law. At one point the Preamble stipulates that '[w]e honour the Holy Crown, which embodies the constitutional continuity of Hungary's statehood and the unity of the nation', but the provision of the former Constitution that defined the status of President of the Republic was left intact and incorporated into the Fundamental Law (THE STATE, article 9), saying that the President '[...] shall embody the nation's unity'. Thus, according to the Fundamental Law both the Hungarian Holy Crown and the President of the Republic embody the nation's unity. Can one conclude from the seemingly two contradictory provisions that the President is the Holy Crown? More in earnest, it is questionable whether the Holy Crown can symbolise the Republic at all.

6. CONCLUDING REMARKS

All in all, in addition to a close reading of the 793-year old Golden Bull or the 800-year old Magna Carta, for the purposes of a fundamental rights-focused approach it should also be relevant to look at how we interpret and conceive these documents that have shaped the national identity of states. Cieger points out that the Golden Bull is invoked both by the human rights activist and the radical nationalist who marches in paramilitary squads.[50] The discourse on history is a means of the struggles of identity politics and shapes political identity. We look upon the past with the values of the present and a document born in the Middle Ages can have a number of different interpretations.

While it can be positively evaluated as an important development in restricting the powers of feudal kings and thus a guarantor of certain rights of certain social groups, and in such capacity a forerunner of modern human rights documents, the uncritical endorsement of the values enshrined in the Golden Bull calls for cautiousness. After all it was only the privileged and not the masses of people who were the beneficiaries of the rights guaranteed therein and social groups of various categories, whether ethnic, religious or gender, were left unprotected or even disadvantaged. Elevating such historical relics to be the embodiment of national unity can also support an anti-egalitarian project as it posits relics from times when the masses of people were left powerless to be honoured and revered. The consideration of and emphasis on the aspects of constitutionality and equality strengthen democratic political culture, while an anti-egalitarian reading weakens it. Historians and politicians who shape national identity are responsible for which option they choose.

---

[50] CIEGER, *supra* note 36, p. 412.

6. BELGIUM: FROM COLLECTIVE PRIVILEGES TO INDIVIDUAL RIGHTS

Wim DECOCK
Koen LEMMENS

1. INTRODUCTION

Belgian constitutional law is usually associated with complex forms of federalism. If it is discussed in international legal scholarship, the focus is almost exclusively on the way the once Unitarian state has been gradually redesigned into a federal state with even some confederal features. Little attention is paid to the way fundamental rights are protected in the Belgian legal order. On the one hand, this is unsurprising given that Belgian constitutional law did not play a leading role in this field in the twentieth century. On the other hand, the omission is regrettable, as the Belgian constitutional rights catalogue has a long-standing pedigree.

In this chapter we will recall that the Belgian Constitution of 1831 was a leading document at the time of its adoption. The constitutional fathers, who themselves experienced the inconveniences of 'enlightened despotism', stressed the importance of solid protection of fundamental rights, especially in relation to executive power. What they feared most was arbitrary interference by public authorities in the exercise of fundamental freedoms. This idea corresponded very well with the then very popular idea of the minimal state.

This nineteenth century discomfort with, if not distrust of, public authorities was also fuelled by the romantic idea of a 'rebellious past'. In their relationship to central authorities, mostly of foreign origin, the local forces of power (e.g. the cities) had enjoyed a certain degree of autonomy since late medieval times. To the extent that they were represented by the Estates, citizens were given, albeit in a very hesitant way, the enjoyment of some 'fundamental' rights, guaranteed by medieval Charters. These texts can be seen as the local 'pendants' of the *Magna Carta.*

2. THE CONSTITUTIONAL TRADITION IN THE ANCIENT REGIME

2.1. PLURALISM AND DIVERSITY

The history of constitutionalism in Belgium before the revolutions of 1789 and 1830 is essentially pluralistic in nature. There are at least three reasons for that. One obvious factor is a phenomenon that can be observed across Europe in the *ancien régime*, namely the prevalence of collective privileges related to social class or personal status over the notion of individual rights applying indiscriminately to any single human being by virtue only of his birth in a democratic state.[1] The rights, or rather privileges, defended in the ancient constitutional texts pertain to the estates, that is representatives of collective groups such as towns, the nobility and the clergy.

It would be no exaggeration to say that deference to diversity rather than equal treatment was the starting-point for pre-revolutionary legal thought and practice.[2] A natural consequence of the pluralistic nature of constitutional law was that even the *summa divisio* of modern law between public and private law did not make much sense in the *ancien régime*. As François Laurent (1810–1887), the most prominent legal scholar in Belgium in the second half of the nineteenth century famously noted, if one had wished to codify private law in Belgian territories before the revolutions, one would have had to draft separate codes for each separate class of citizens.[3]

There is another reason why constitutional law in ancient Belgium should be thought of as diverse. During the late Middle Ages (eleventh to fourteenth centuries) Belgian territory as we know it today was still divided into at least four major realms of power, subject either to the count of Flanders, the count of Hainaut, the duke of Brabant, or the prince-bishop of Liège.[4] Alongside these bigger territories there were smaller ones such as the County of Loon, the Duchy

---

1 H. MOHNHAUPT, 'Der Entwicklungsgang von den wohlerworbenen, konzessionierten Rechten und Privilegien zu den dem Menschen zugehörigen Grundrechten' (2004) 31 *Europäische Grundrechte-Zeitschrift* 604–611.

2 For a brief yet crystal-clear analysis of constitutional culture in Europe before the French Revolution, see M. STOLLEIS, 'Vormodernes und postmodernes Recht' (2008) 37 *Quaderni fiorentini per la storia del pensiero giuridico moderno* 553–551 (547).

3 F. LAURENT, *Principes de droit civil français*, Bruylant, Brussels 1869, pp. 9–10: 'Il n'y avait pas plus d'unité dans les hommes que dans le territoire. La nation était divisée par ordres, et chaque ordre formait comme un peuple divers ayant ses privilèges et son droit particulier. Si l'on avait fait un code civil sous l'ancien régime, il aurait fallu, à bien des égards, un code distinct pour la noblesse (…).'

4 For an overview, including references to further literature, see L.J.R. MILIS, 'De periode van de landsheerlijkheden (elfde-dertiende eeuw)' in J.C.H. BLOM and E. LAMBERTS (eds.), *Geschiedenis van de Nederlanden*, HB, Baarn 2008, pp. 19–45, and F. STEVENS and A. TIXHON, *L'histoire de la Belgique pour les nuls*, First-Gründ, Paris 2010, pp. 57–78.

of Bouillon and the Principality of Stavelot-Malmédy. Under Burgundian (1384–1482) and then Habsburg (1482–1795) rule, top-down efforts were made to submit the different regions to uniform rule, but territorial particularities persisted.

Even when the first real bottom-up initiative for unification emerged, through the temporary 'Confederation of Belgian States' (1790) which came into existence during the revolt against Austrian rule, it did not include the Prince-Bishopric of Liège. It was not until 1792 that a so-called 'Manifest of United People from Belgium and Liège' was drafted, envisioning for the first time the unification of territories formerly belonging not only to Flanders and Brabant, but also to Liège. Ultimately, resentment of the French (1795–1815) and the Dutch (1815–1830) reign over Belgian territories probably did more to unite the formerly divided counties, duchies and principalities than anything which had come before.

The third element of diversity concerns the written or oral character of constitutional traditions in late medieval and early modern Belgium. Although in a limited number of places constitutional principles were solemnly written down on paper, in most regions they were transmitted orally. Famous examples of written constitutional texts are the 'Paix de Fexhe' (1316) for the Prince-Bishopric of Liège and the 'Blijde Inkomst' for the Duchy of Brabant (1356). However, from the absence of written constitutional texts in other regions one should not infer that they did not recognise a pact which sought to protect the rights of citizens against their rulers.

The basic procedural instrument used to seal the political contract was the so-called 'joyous entries', which saw the prince swear an oath at the beginning of his reign that he would respect the privileges of his subjects.[5] For example, the first mentioning of the count of Hainaut performing this oath during a 'joyous entry' reaches back to 1272, decades before the 'Paix de Fexhe' and the 'Blijde Inkomst' were drafted.[6] The same is true for Flanders, whose count is said to have observed this ceremony for the first time in 1297.

---

5 F. Zanatta, 'Pour une relecture du serment public entre le prince et les communautés d'habitants: l'exemple des joyeuses entrées des Archiducs' (2008) 377 *Revue du Nord* 729–745.

6 J-M. Cauchies, 'La constitution, le serment et le prince dans le Hainaut ancien' in *Liber Amicorum John Gilissen, Code et constitution: mélanges historiques*, Kluwer, Antwerpen 1983, pp. 51–60.

2.2. MAJOR LATE MEDIEVAL CONSTITUTIONS: 'PAIX DE FEXHE' (1316) AND 'BLIJDE INKOMST' (1356)

2.2.1. The misleading relevance of written documents

Two late medieval texts have later been interpreted as precursors of the modern Belgian constitution in preference to all other charters and oath-taking ceremonies from the *ancien régime*: the 'Blijde Inkomst' from the Duchy of Brabant, on the one hand, and the 'Paix de Fexhe' concluded between the Estates and the Prince-Bishop of Liège, on the other. From a historical-critical point of view, it is worthwhile stressing that this does not mean that in the other territories, which did not have written charters, no constitutional culture existed. The case of Flanders is revealing in this regard, and merits attention before we discuss the 'Paix de Fexhe' and the 'Blijde Inkomst'.

The unwritten basis of constitutional guarantees for the Flemish Estates against the Count of Flanders turned out to be much more effective in practice than the written documents in Brabant and Liège.[7] Although subjects in Flanders had already been invoking constitutional rights against central power two centuries before the 'Paix de Fexhe' and the 'Blijde Inkomst' were drafted,[8] and while charters had been concluded between cities and the count of Flanders on an individual basis during the eleventh and twelveth centuries,[9] a collective, written Flemish constitutional text did not emerge. As Blockmans and Van Uytven have pointed out, the lack of a constitution did not however prevent the Flemish estates from exercising 'de facto all authority granted by the English, Brabant and Liège documents, even earlier than the Brabant or Liège estates'.[10] In the absence of strong central power, prosperous cities such as Bruges, Ghent and Ypres simply did not need a written charter to protect their privileges.[11]

In terms of *Nachleben*, though, written documents had a considerable advantage in that they could be transmitted, remembered and interpreted extensively throughout the centuries (*scripta manent, verba volant*).

---

7 R. Van Uytven and W. Blockmans, 'Constitutions and their Application in the Netherlands during the Middle Ages' (1969) 47 *Belgisch Tijdschrift voor Filologie en Geschiedenis* 400–424 (413).

8 D. Heirbaut, 'Galbert of Bruges on the Flemish 1127–1128 Crisis — An Early Experiment in Constitutionalism, Parliamentarism and Popular Sovereignty Inspired by Feudal Law' in J.O. Sunde (ed.), *Constitutionalism Before 1789. Constitutional Arrangements From the High Middle Ages to the French Revolution*, Pax, Oslo 2014, pp. 49–59.

9 R. van Caenegem, 'Coutumes et législation en Flandre aux XIe et XIIe siècles' in *Libertés urbaines et rurales du XIe au XIVe siècle*, Pro civitate, Brussels 1968, pp. 245–279.

10 Van Uytven and Blockmans, *supra* note 7, p. 400.

11 *Ibid.*, p. 414.

2.2.2. The 'Paix de Fexhe': a temporary truce in Liège

The historical circumstances that led to the first famous text in Belgian constitutional history are typical of a more general phenomenon[12] and can be summarised as follows.[13] After his installment as the new prince-bishop of Liège in 1312, Adolphe de La Marck pursued a policy of centralisation of power which soon met with fierce resistance from the so-called 'Métiers', professional corporations, particularly in towns such as Awans. With bad weather leading to the rapid spread of disease and famine in 1315, the parties were forced to suspend hostilities.

To negotiate a truce, three representatives of the prince-bishop, namely two canons of the Cathedral of Saint-Lambert and a nobleman, met in Faixhe-le-haut-Clocher on 17 June 1316 with three representatives of the subjects, represented by a nobleman and two aldermen from the cities of Liège and Huy, respectively. One day later, the 'Paix de Fexhe' (Peace of Fexhe) was promulgated. Theoretically, it contained guarantees for the participation of the different interest groups ('le sens du pays'), especially the cities, in the political and legislative process. It also stipulated that every subject within the prince-bishopric should have the privilege to be judged by a court befitting his social status.

In practice, however, the prince-bishop ignored the 'Paix de Fexhe' and thwarted representation through bodies such as the Council of Twenty-Two, which united four ecclesiastical canons, four noblemen, and 14 representatives from cities in the Prince-Bishopric of Liège.

2.2.3. The 'Blijde Inkomst': an inauguration charter soon revoked

When Joan of Brabant and Wenceslas of Luxembourg were received ('ontfanghen') as the new dukes of Brabant on 3 January 1356, the cities required them to take an oath.[14] Joan and Wenceslas had to swear that they would not violate the privileges previously granted to the cities and the noblemen, for instance through the charter of Kortenberg (1312) and the so-called Walloon and Flemish charters (1314). These privileges mostly concerned fiscal advantages, judicial guarantees and the installation of a council that could control the treasury.

---

12 R. VAN CAENEGEM, *An Historical Introduction to Western Constitutional Law*, Cambridge University Press, Cambridge 1995, p. 81.

13 C. MASSON, 'La Paix de Fexhe de sa rédaction à la fin de la Principauté de Liège' (2006) 47 *Bulletin de la Commission royale des Anciennes Lois et Ordonnances de Belgique* 175–266. This article includes an edition of the text of the 'Paix de Fexhe' (pp. 262–266).

14 R. VAN BRAGT, *De Blijde Inkomst van de hertogen van Brabant Johanna en Wenceslas: een inleidende studie en tekstuitgave*, (Standen en Landen, 13), Nauwelaerts, Louvain 1956.

On the occasion of the reception of Joan and Wenceslas as the new dukes of Brabant, the cities submitted one great inauguration charter to them which collected the entirety of the previous charters. It is this text which has become known as the 'Blijde Inkomst', even though that term actually goes back to a later period: 'blijde incomste' was only used from the fifteenth century onwards, the Latin translation 'laetus introitus' and the French 'joyeuse entrée' emerging only in the sixteenth and seventeenth centuries.[15]

In the course of the nineteenth century the written constitutional text of the 'Blijde Inkomst' of 1356 was hailed as 'the most famous charter of our history'.[16] Since the second half of the twentieth century, though, historians such as Bryce Dale Lyon, Raymond van Uytven and Wim Blockmans have put the significance of the charter into perspective.[17] In fact, the Brabant constitution was dead letter only a few months after its promulgation.[18]

2.3. MEDIEVAL CONSTITUTIONAL THOUGHT AND THE REVOLUTIONS OF 1581 AND 1789

Because they had been written down, the 'Paix de Fexhe' and the 'Brabantse Blijde Inkomst' could serve throughout the ages as authoritative reference points for citizens who were in need of defending their liberties, privileges and rights against arbitrary rulers. In fact, their resurrection in subsequent times vested these texts with the authority they lacked at the time of their promulgation. For example, the Blijde Inkomst of 1356 served as the basis for a new Inauguration Charter applicable in the entire Burgundian Netherlands to which the Estates had Mary of Bourgondy swear allegiance in 1477.[19]

More importantly, during the revolt against the Spanish King Philip II, the Estates based their claim for independence, that is their right to literally 'leave' the Spanish king (Plakkaet van Verlatinge, 1581) on his violation of the privileges as contained in constitutional texts such as the 'Blijde Inkomst'.[20] Two centuries later, during the revolt of the Austrian Netherlands against Joseph II in

---

15 VAN BRAGT, *supra* note 14, p. 8.

16 See the panegyrical notes on the 'Joyeuse Entrée' in C. FAIDER, *Étude sur les constitutions nationales (Pays-Bas autrichiens et pays de Liège)*, Brussels 1842, and E. POULLET, *Histoire de la Joyeuse-Entrée de Brabant. Mémoire sur l'ancienne constitution brabançonne*, Brussels 1863.

17 B.D. LYON, 'Fact and Fiction in English and Belgian Constitutional law' (1956) 10 *Medievalia et humanistica* 82–101.

18 VAN UYTVEN and BLOCKMANS, *supra* note 7, p. 407.

19 W. BLOCKMANS E.A., *1477. Het algemene en de gewestelijke privilegien van Maria van Bourgondië voor de Nederlanden*, (Standen en Landen, 80), UGA, Kortrijk-Heule 1985.

20 P.A.M. GEURTS, *Het beroep op de Blijde Inkomste in de pamfletten uit de Tachtigjarige Oorlog*, (Standen en Landen, 16), Nauwelaerts, Louvain 1958, pp. 1–15; M.E.H.N. MOUT, *Plakkaat van Verlatinge. Vertaald, ingeleid en van aantekeningen voorzien*, Historische Uitgeverij, Groningen 2006. For an extended analysis of this constitutional text, see the contribution by our Dutch colleague Louis Berkvens in this volume.

1789, the Estates justified their cause on the grounds that the Habsburg emperor had violated the rights stipulated in the 'Blijde Inkomst'.[21] By the same token, during the revolt in the Prince-Bishopric of Liège in 1789, the Estates legitimised their disloyalty to the prince-bishop César-Constantin de Hoensbroeck with recourse to the privileges in the 'Paix de Fexhe'.[22]

2.4. A PRE-TASTE OF THE DREAM OF INDIVIDUAL RIGHTS OF MAN (FRANCHIMONT 1789)

First references to individual rights of man do not appear in the Belgian tradition until the revolutionary period at the end of the eighteenth century. Inspired by events in France, on 16 September 1789 the congress of Polleur adopted a 'Declaration of the Rights of Man and of the Citizen' to be applied in the small Marquessate of Franchimont, in the eastern part of the Prince-Bishopric of Liège.[23] Like its French counterpart, the so-called 'Déclaration des droits de l'homme et du citoyen pour le Franchimont' emphasised that all human begins were born free and equal.[24] It also consecrated the idea that the conservation of the inalienable, natural rights of man was the goal of any political community. Yet the significance of this document should not be overstated. As the Franchimont territory was conquered by the Austrians in January 1791, the dream of rights of man was soon shattered.

3. THE BELGIAN CONSTITUTION

3.1. THE HISTORICAL BACKGROUND

The Belgian Revolution (1830) was the result of an uprising of the intellectual middle class in Brussels. Many of its members were dissatisfied with the institutional functioning of the United Kingdom of the Netherlands (1815–1830),

---

21 G. VAN DIEVOET, *L'empereur Joseph II et la Joyeuse Entrée de Brabant. Les dernières années de la Constitution brabançonne*, (Standen en Landen, 16), Nauwelaerts, Louvain 1958, pp. 87–140; G. VAN DEN BOSSCHE, *Enlightened Innovation and the Ancient Constitution. The intellectual justifications of Revolution in Brabant (1787–1790)*, Paleis der Academiën, Brussels 2001.

22 MASSON, *supra* note 13, pp. 245–258; A. BORGNET, *Histoire de la révolution liégoise de 1789 (1785 à 1795) d'après des documents inédits*, De Their et Lovinfosse, Liège 1895.

23 A. DOMS, 'La déclaration des droits de l'homme et du citoyen au Congrès de Polleur: essai d'interprétation historique' (2005) 73 *Bulletin de la Société verviétoise d'archéologie et d'histoire* 35–96.

24 The text of the Declaration is included in F. STEVENS, P. POIRIER and P.A.J. VAN DEN BERG, *Constitutional Documents of Belgium, Luxemburg and the Netherlands 1789–1848*, Saur, Munich 2008, pp. 127–128.

a state created at the Vienna Congress (1815) encompassing the actual Netherlands, Belgium and Luxemburg.[25]

In theory, the United Kingdom of the Netherlands had many strengths which would have allowed it to become a leading nation in Europe. The North, at present the Netherlands, had colonies (Gold Coast, Surinam, Indonesia), and a longstanding tradition of trade. The South, today Belgium, rapidly became a leading industrialised country, due to the development of the Walloon coal and steel industry.[26] Yet, notwithstanding these assets, the state did not turn out to be a success story. Although many complex reasons may explain the failure of this state, it is generally believed that the authoritarian way in which its King, William I, reigned as an enlightened despot over the Kingdom was the main cause of discontent in the South.[27]

This discontent stemmed from three sources. Firstly, there was a feeling in the South that the state was dominated by the North. Southerners complained about the unequal repartition of taxes. They also contested the dominant position of Northerners in higher positions in public administration and the army. Secondly, problems were caused by the language policy of William I, who promoted the use of the Dutch language (and not of French) in the Southern provinces, where Dutch — albeit the Flemish version[28] — was the language spoken by the common people in what is now called 'Flanders'. At least in the Flemish part of the Southern provinces Dutch was to become the only official language. This policy irritated the francophone elite that was used to employing French, not only in Wallonia and Brussels, but also in the provinces known today as 'Flanders'. Thirdly, William's religious policy was a source of discontent: in the South, where Roman-Catholicism was the dominant religion, the idea that Protestantism and Roman-Catholicism would be treated on a par, led to frictions. On top of that, William I promoted the creation of public schools thus undermining the quasi-monopoly of the Catholic Church in educational affairs.[29]

The opposition against William I is known as the *Union Sacrée*, or in Dutch *Het Monsterverbond* (the Monster Alliance). Roman Catholics and Liberal Secularists joined forces to oppose the regime, managing to overcome the huge

---

[25] E. WITTE, J. CRAEYBECKX and A. MEYNEN, *Political History of Belgium. From 1830 onwards*, ASP, Brussels 2009, pp. 21 ff. On what happened during the revolutionary days: E. WITTE, *De Constructie van België: 1828–1847*, LannooCampus, Leuven 2006, pp. 53–63.

[26] Luxemburg formed a personal Union with the United Kingdom of the Netherlands.

[27] E. LEFEBVRE, *The Belgian Constitution of 1831: The Citizen Burgher*, (Zerp-Diskussionspapier 4/97), Bremen University, Zentrum für Europäische Rechtspolitik, 1997, p. 3; E.H. KOSSMANN, *The Low Countries (1780–1940)*, Clarendon Press, Oxford 1978, p. 115; A. ALEN and B. TILLEMAN, 'General Introduction' in A. ALEN (ed.), *Treatise on Belgian Constitutional Law*, Kluwer, Deventer 1992, p. 3.

[28] R. WILLEMYNS, *Het verhaal van het Vlaams. De geschiedenis van het Nederlands in de Zuidelijke Nederlanden*, Standaard Uitgeverij/Het Spectrum, Antwerpen/Utrecht 2003.

[29] ALEN and TILLEMAN, *supra* note 27, pp. 1–2; LEFEBVRE, *supra* note 27, p. 8.

ideological differences that divided them. Apart from French influences,[30] the Belgian Constitution (1831) is thus the direct result of both the reaction against the constitutional design of the United Kingdom of the Netherlands and an unusual coalition of ideologically opposed partners. The protection of fundamental rights and freedoms held a prominent place in the newly adopted Constitution.

Indeed, as intellectuals, the Belgian framers had experienced great difficulties in expressing themselves freely under the reign of William I.[31] Therefore, they strongly believed in the need to grant citizens strong 'intellectual' liberties. This meant that freedom of religion, of speech, of press[32], of assembly and association were amongst the core freedoms in the Constitution. Regarding the protection of these freedoms, the fathers of the Constitution adhered to fundamental principles.

Firstly, the drafters of the Constitution were convinced that governments should not intervene *a priori* in the exercise of fundamental freedoms,[33] although they clearly did not advocate unlimited freedoms. The abuse of fundamental freedoms could only be sanctioned afterwards, not by means of preventive measures; gone were the days of censorship. Secondly, according to the drafters, limitations on fundamental freedoms were only possible by formal laws, *viz.* acts of Parliament. Thus, they wanted to avoid the possibility that the Executive power would intervene to restrict fundamental freedoms.

When it comes to the content of the fundamental freedoms, it is hardly suprising that the focus was, back in 1831, on classic civil and political rights. As a result, the Constitution in its Title II ('The Belgians and their rights') initially focussed on the right of equality before the law, the right to individual liberty, the right to access to justice, the principle of legality in criminal affairs, the inviolability of the home, the protection of property, the right to freedom of belief and expression, the right to education, the right to assembly, freedom of association,

---

30 D. HEIRBAUT and J.F. GERKENS, 'In the shadow of France. Legal acculturation and legal transplants in the Southern Netherlands/Belgium' in J.A. SÁNCHEZ CORDERO (ed.), *Legal culture and legal transplants*, International Academy of Comparative Law, Universidad Autónoma de México 2012, pp. 167–193. Compare B. DELBECKE, 'Modern constitutionalism and legal transfer: the political offence in the French Charte Constitutionnelle (1830) and the Belgian Constitution' in T. DUVE (ed.), *Entanglements in legal history: conceptual approaches*, Max Planck Institute for European Legal History Open Access Publication, Frankfurt am Main 2014, pp. 427–460.

31 B. DELBECKE, 'Verdedigers van het eigen vrije woord. Advocaten en de ijver voor de persvrijheid in de Belgische grondwet (1830–31)' (2009) 11 *Pro Memorie* 142–158.

32 B. DELBECKE, *De lange schaduw van de grondwetgever. Perswetgeving en persmisdruiven in België (1831–1914)*, Academia Press, Gent 2012.

33 Freedom of assembly in public places being the only exception (article 26 Belgian Constitution).

the right to address petitions to public authorities, secrecy of correspondence and the right to free use of languages.[34]

It is striking that the right to life was not included in the list. It is said that the drafters believed this right was so obvious, that it did not need to be included in a constitutional catalogue of fundamental rights.[35] In 2005, an article was inserted however in the Constitution to confirm that death penalty has been abolished (article 14bis).

Be that as it may, the Belgian Constitution of 1831 was considered a hallmark of classic liberalism and the protection of fundamental freedoms. As such, it exerted considerable influence as a model for other constitutions across the world.[36] Moreover, it is not a surprise that Brussels became a safe haven for foreign intellectuals in the nineteenth century. Karl Marx, Victor Hugo, Rimbaud, Baudelaire and Multatuli all benefitted from the high protection of freedom of the press in Belgium.

3.2. THE EVOLUTION

The protection of fundamental rights has profoundly changed over the last 185 years. We can discern four major trends: the internationalization of constitutional rights, the recognition of an horizontal effect, the emergence of new rights and the development of a Constitutional Court. We will discuss each in brief.[37]

3.2.1. The internationalization of constitutional rights

It goes without saying that the developments in the field of human rights law since World War II have profoundly affected the Belgian legal order. Belgium has ratified most of the UN human rights treaties, is a Member State of the EU and has ratified the European Convention on Human Rights (ECHR) and the European Social Charter, as well as the Revised Social Charter. The role of the

34 V. Dujardin, 'Les droits constitutionnels originaires' in M. Verdussen and N. Bonbled (eds.), *Les droits constitutionnels en Belgique*, vol. I, Bruylant, Brussels 2011, pp. 48–71.

35 A. Alen and J. Clement, 'Fundamental Rights and Liberties' in A. Alen (ed.), *Treatise on Belgian Constitutional Law*, Kluwer, Deventer 1992, p. 193.

36 J. Gilissen, 'Die belgische Verfassung von 1831. Ihr Ursprung und ihr Einfluss' in W. Conze, *Beiträge zur deutschen und belgischen Verfassungsgeschichte im 19. Jahrhundert*, Klett, Stuttgart 1967, pp. 38–69.

37 For a more comprehensive overview, see P. Popelier and K. Lemmens, *The Constitution of Belgium. A contextual analysis*, Hart, Oxford 2015 (forthcoming), chapter 7. This part equally draws on G. Schaiko, P. Lemmens and K. Lemmens, 'Belgium' in J. Gerards and J. Fleuren (eds.), *Implementation of the European Convention on Human Rights and of the Judgments of the ECtHR in National Case-Law*, Intersentia, Cambridge 2014, pp. 95–143.

ECHR can hardly be underestimated. It is the major human rights treaty in Belgian legal practice.[38]

From a procedural and institutional point of view, it is important to stress that most of the ECHR's provisions, as well as many of the provisions of the additional protocols, have direct effect in the Belgian legal order. They can be directly invoked and applied before domestic judges.[39] Furthermore, the ECHR has priority over national legislation and even over the Constitution. The Supreme Court (*Cour de cassation*) has explicitly confirmed this in its case law.[40] Moreover, the Constitutional Court has a long-standing tradition of reading constitutional provisions and analogous international provisions as a whole.[41]

Hence, we discern two major consequences. First, the interpretation of constitutionally protected fundamental rights is highly conditioned by the international texts, primarily the ECHR. The importance of the proportionality test is perhaps the best illustration. As said before, the Belgian framers insisted on a formal legal basis of restrictions on fundamental freedoms. This idea echoes the concept of the inviolability of the law and is based on an unlimited faith in Parliament. Nowadays, however, the proportionality test, rooted in the ECHR, is unquestionably the key element in fundamental rights adjudication.

Secondly, the impact of international human rights law has proved to be an effective solution to the problem of the historical nature of the constitutional catalogue of fundamental rights. As we will explain under section 3.2.3., the list of constitutional rights has become outdated over time. The international human rights treaties offered a useful way to overcome this problem and to fill in some lacunae.

3.2.2. The recognition of a horizontal effect

Traditionally, it is said that the generalised horizontal effect of human rights is a fairly recent phenomenon, inspired by German legal thinking and case law. Yet it must be stressed that some provisions of the Belgian Constitutional Catalogue already envisaged the possibility that fundamental rights be applied between

---

38 On the position of the ECHR in Belgian Law, see SCHAIKO, LEMMENS and LEMMENS, *supra* note 37, pp. 113 ff.

39 *Ibid.*, p. 113.

40 Priority of international law over domestic law is based on the leading *Fromagerie Le Ski* case (Cass., 27 May 1971, *Pas.* 1971, I, p. 886). Priority over the Constitution has been confirmed in more recent judgments (Cass., 9 November 2004, Pas. 2004, n° 539).

41 See, e.g., Const. Court, judgment 16/2005, 19 January 2005, B.2.3.; Const. Court, judgment 61/2008, 10 April 2008, B.3.3.

private parties. This is, for instance, the case with the protection of the confidentiality of correspondence.[42]

The case law of the Belgian highest courts shows that fundamental rights are increasingly applied in horizontal relations. This is particularly so with regard to the protection of privacy. Recent cases and discussions concern conflicts between freedom of information and protection of privacy or reputation. In Belgian law, the law of torts is the mechanism *par excellence* to solve these conflicts. Judges frequently refer in those cases to the Strasbourg case law and they apply the criteria set forth by the Strasbourg Court.

However, there are also situations in which the horizontal effect of human rights is less straightforward. Thus, since the 1980s, Article 3 of the European Convention on Human Rights prohibiting inhuman and degrading treatment has been used in private litigation on gas and electricity supply.[43] This example, too, illustrates the previous point: international legal provisions can be used whenever there are no national provisions available.

It remains true, however, that to this day, there is no general theory in Belgian law on the horizontal effect of human rights law.[44] This explains, in part, why the application of anti-discrimination law has provesd to be very complicated.

3.2.3. The emergence of new rights

Clearly, since 1831, times and society have changed. The original catalogue of Belgian constitutional rights, with its focus on political and civil rights, has become outdated. Although Belgium developed a comprehensive welfare system after World War II, we had to wait until 1994 for constitutional protection of social, cultural and economic rights (article 23). The new provision protects the right to live in dignity. It then specifies, without being exhaustive, that this right includes: the right to employment, to social security and health care, the right to social, medical and legal aid, the right to decent accommodation, the right to the protection of a healthy environment and the right to cultural and social fulfilment. In 2014, when the Federal State transferred its competences pertaining to child allowances to the sub-state entities (viz. the 'Communities') further to the Sixth Reform of the State, the right to child allowances was inserted into the list. Thus, the sub-state entities will not be able to cancel child allowances, as they are constitutionally enshrined.

---

42 P. Lemmens and N. Van Leuven, 'Les destinataires des droits constitutionnels' in M. Verdussen and N. Bonbled (eds.), *Les droits constitutionnels en Belgique*, vol. 1, Bruylant, Brussels 2011, pp. 131 ff.

43 Schaiko, Lemmens and Lemmens, *supra* note 37, p. 134.

44 Schaiko, Lemmens and Lemmens, *supra* note 37, pp 131–135.

Since 1994, new rights have been included in the constitutional list of rights. We can mention, by way of example, an explicit recognition of equality between men and women (article 10 and article 11bis) or the rights of the child (article 22bis).

Yet, what matters most in the field of fundamental rights is the way the right to autonomy has become a leading principle in bio-ethical affairs. From a comparative perspective, Belgium adopted a statute decriminalising abortion quite late (1990), but from that moment onwards, a rapid evolution has taken place. In less than 15 years, under the impetus of the so called Purple Green (1999–2003) and Purple (2003–2007) coalition governments — cabinets comprising liberals and social-democrats and, during the first term, environmentalists — very liberal laws have been passed on euthanasia (2002), including for minors (2014), on same sex marriages in 2003 and on medically assisted procreation.

3.2.4. The creation of the Constitutional Court

Belgian Law has for decades been under the sway of the idea of the 'inviolability' of the law, which meant in practice that there was no constitutional review of legislation. Based on a strict interpretation of the 'separation of powers' it was argued that judges should not be allowed to interfere with the will of democratically elected Parliaments.

This idea has been abandoned in two stages. Firstly, the Court of Cassation delivered its famous *Fromagerie Le Ski* judgment in 1971,[45] affirming that self-executing provisions of an international treaty prevail over Belgian statutes. As a consequence, the Belgian judge was allowed to review statutes against self-executing international treaties, but not against the Constitution.

The second breakthrough took place in the aftermath of the Second Reform of the State (1980), when the Court of Arbitration (1983) was established.[46] Initially, the Court's role was to ensure that the Federal State and the sub-state entities respected their competences and did not overstep the boundaries. Only institutional parties could therefore file an application to the Court. With the Constitutional Reform of 1988, the Court was empowered to review federal and sub-state legislation against the equality provision (articles 10 and 11 of the Constitution) and the right to freedom of education (article 24 of the Constitution). Individual applicants were given standing. The Court then developed a very innovative case law based on a dynamic interpretation of the equality clause.

---

45 See *supra* note 40.

46 For its history, see: < http://www.const-court.be/> (presentation/the place of the Court) accessed 02.06.2015.

Indeed, the Court has turned into a true 'fundamental rights' Court. In 2003, this evolution was formally confirmed by Special Law: the Court could from then onwards review against all the rights included in Title II of the Belgian Constitution ('The Belgians and their rights') as well as against the rights of aliens (article 191 of the Constitution) and some specific provisions on tax law. In practice, these modifications did not bring about any significant change.

In 2007, the Court's name was officially changed to 'Constitutional Court'. This new name better covers the Court's function, but we should not forget that the Court is still not a full constitutional Court, since it cannot review legislation against all constitutional provisions.

4. CONCLUDING REMARKS

The scope of constitutional law in the ancient Belgian territories was not the protection of individual human rights. In this sense, the first part of this article adds weight to Samuel Moyn's thesis that the history of human rights is a relatively recent one.[47] Fundamental rights in the modern sense cannot be traced back to late medieval constitutional texts in the former Belgian territories.

Instead of granting rights to individual human beings the constitutional texts and ceremonies of the *ancien régime* were geared towards the protection of the interests of collective bodies or estates (the cities, the nobility, the clergy).[48] Whether expressed in writing or not, in pre-modern times constitutional principles were primarily concerned with the protection of these collective subjects against strong central power, not with individual fundamental rights in the modern sense of the phrase.[49]

Through such glorious texts as the Peace of Fexhe (1316) and the Joyous Entry of Brabant (1356), or simply through solemn oaths taken by the ruler at the beginning of his reign, the privileges of the Estates were confirmed. The Estates were granted a right to file petitions with the central authorities to express their grievances or even to revolt against a ruler if he infringed those privileges. Under the combined influence of a romantic tendency to glorify the past and the need to construct a national Belgian identity, the historical importance of texts such as the 'Paix de Fexhe' and the 'Blijde Inkomst' has been largely exaggerated since the niniteenth century.

---

47 J-P. LEHNERS, 'Pleading for a New History of Human Rights' in A. MIHR and M. GIBNEY (eds.), *The SAGE Handbook of Human Rights,* SAGE Publications, London 2014, p. 31.

48 A.M. BOS, *De voorgeschiedenis van de grondrechten. Van Magna Charta tot Déclaration des droits de l'homme et du citoyen*, Kluwer, Deventer 1976, p. v.

49 H.A. LLOYD, 'Constitutionalism' in J.H. BURNS and M. GOLDIE (eds.), *The Cambridge History of Political Thought 1450–1700*, Cambridge University Press, Cambridge 1991, pp. 254–297.

Nonetheless, the historical perception of ancient privileges and their confirmation in constitutional texts played a vital role in justifying revolutions against foreign rulers in subsequent times, regardless of whether a Belgian constitutional tradition truly exists.[50] Certainly in trying to justify the struggle for Belgian independence and the promulgation of the liberal constitution of 1831, contemporary historians and lawyers were happy to stress the continuity between the new constitution of the Belgian Kingdom and the old spirit of independence read into the medieval charters.[51]

The 1831 Constitution, in line with the 'new ideas' of the French Revolution, adopts a very individualistic perspective. Constitutional rights are conferred to individual citizens, and there are no longer class distinctions. The protection of collective privileges has been replaced by the guarantee of individual freedoms. The constitutional catalogue of fundamental rights echoes the universalist idea that everyone is equal before the law.

However, during the last decades we have witnessed a new trend to 'readjust' this credo. Thus, specific rights for children or women have been included in the constitution — are they not part of 'everyone'? Of course, this trend is not a specifically Belgian phenomenon. On the UN level we have seen a proliferation of category specific treaties, protecting human rights of women, children, persons with disabilities, migrant workers and so on.

Ironic as it may seem, the 'new approach' to human rights may have more in common with the pre-constitutional texts of the *ancien régime* than with the Belgian Constitution of 1831. In a strange way, post-modern constitutional culture seems to revert back to its pre-modern predecessors.[52] Will ancient traditions be our future solutions?

[50] On the problematic nature of the 'Belgian legal tradition' in general, see D. HEIRBAUT, 'The Belgian legal tradition: does it exist?' in H. BOCKEN and W. DE BONDT (eds.), *Introduction to Belgian Law*, Kluwer, Antwerpen 2000, pp. 1–22, as well as D. HEIRBAUT and M.E. STORME, 'The Belgian legal tradition: from a long quest for legal independence to a longing for independence' (2006) 14 *European Review of Private Law* 645–683.

[51] A. DE DIJN, 'In overeenstemming met onze zeden en gewoonten: de intellectuele context van de eerste Belgische constitutie (1815–1830)' (2002) 117 *Bijdragen en Mededelingen betreffende de Geschiedenis der Nederlanden* 25–45.

[52] Compare the reflections by STOLLEIS, *supra* note 2, on the rise and demise of the modern state over the last five centuries.

7. AUSTRIA: MANORIAL REGULATION OF MINING AND USE OF FORESTS AS POTENTIAL ANTECEDENTS IN FUNDAMENTAL RIGHTS

Marija WAKOUNIG

1. INTRODUCTION

Research on fundamental rights[1] is a relatively young scientific field, with the last three decades seeing a particular boom in research on the early history of these rights.[2] Notable here are the efforts towards an interdisciplinary approach, for instance to situate legal terms in a historical context and to explain them in this context (of origin)[3] — long before one can speak of 'inherent' and 'inalienable' rights, in a modern sense, to which every individual is entitled.[4] The

1 In relation to the *termini technici* see L. HUNT, *Inventing Human Rights: A History*, W. W. Norton & Company, New York/London 2007, pp. 22–26; M. KOENIG, *Menschenrechte*, Campus Verlag GmbH, Frankfurt am Main et al. 2005, p. 9; R. ALEXY, 'Grundrechte' in H.J. SANDKÜHLER (ed.), *Enzyklopädie Philosophie*, vol. 1: A–N, Meiner, Hamburg 1999, <http://www.unesco-phil.uni-bremen.de/Texte%20zur%20Vorlesung/Grundrechte-EPh.pdf> accessed 30.04.2015. Most recently T. SIMON, 'Die juristische Begründung der Grund- und Menschenrechte: Ein Ergebnis des Naturrechts? oder Kann man im Kontext der mittelalterlichen Rechtsgarantien von "Grundrechten" sprechen?' in B. SCHINKELE, R. KUPPE, S. SCHIMA, E.M. SYNEK, J. WALLNER and W. WIESHAIDER (eds.), *Recht – Religion – Kultur. Festschrift für Richard Potz zum 70. Geburtstag*, Facultas, Wien 2014, pp. 851–866, here pp. 853–857. (Many thanks to Mr Manfred Nowak for the reference of literature!).

2 See, e.g., the following two anthologies: G. BIRTSCH (ed.), *Grund- und Freiheitsrechte im Wandel von Gesellschaft und Geschichte: Beiträge zur Geschichte der Grund- und Freiheitsrechte vom Ausgang des Mittelalters bis zur Revolution von 1848*, Veröffentlichungen zur Geschichte der Grund- und Freiheitsrechte 1, Vandenhoeck & Ruprecht, Göttingen 1981; G. BIRTSCH (ed.), *Grund- und Freiheitsrechte von der ständischen zur spätbürgerlichen Gesellschaft*, Veröffentlichungen zur Geschichte der Grund- und Freiheitsrechte 2, Vandenhoeck & Ruprecht, Göttingen 1987. Interesting here as a comparison: M. GRANDNER, W. SCHMALE and M. WEINZIERL (eds.), *Grund- und Menschenrechte. Historische Perspektiven: Aktuelle Problematiken*, Querschnitte 8, Oldenbourg Wissenschaftsverlag, Wien/München 2002.

3 See S. MOYN, 'Die neue Historiographie der Menschenrechte' (2012) 38 *Geschichte und Gesellschaft* 545–572, 545.

4 See the explanation by SIMON, *supra* note 1, pp. 853–854.

origin of the 'rights of the individual' thus dates, depending on the study field, from ancient Greece to the early modern period.[5]

For the purposes of the preceding explanation, the question of when fundamental rights were guaranteed or applied for the first time in Austria must be considered complex and equivocal for several reasons. When trying to trace their early history, the chronological and geographical scope of Austria that one focuses on must be clarified, and, as a consequence, also the corresponding sources regarding the content/aspect of fundamental rights that could be consulted. In this context, the reasons and causes for the granting of rights as well as the beneficiaries of these rights, have to be considered.[6] These rights were not only formulated as privileges (exceptional laws, prerogatives), but also as private documents regulating legal matters addressing only a small, select group. Hegemonial territorial law codes or 'handfasts', which included issues which we now understand as fundamental rights (for example, the King's peace) were directed towards all subjects of the respective sovereign but they had the character of a commitment or a duty. Thus, in the late Middle Ages and the early modern period, the Austrian ancestral lands were still far from guaranteeing indivisible, fundamental rights for the benefit of the general public. Felix Ermarcora, for example, in an article on the development of human rights and fundamental freedoms, has pointed out that, when discussing the Middle Ages and early modern period, it is linguistically (more) correct to speak of the 'idea of human rights'.[7]

2. GENERAL FEATURES OF THE DEVELOPMENT OF FUNDAMENTAL RIGHTS

Until the appearance of humanism north of the Alps during the fifteenth century, and the resulting reception of Roman law one can consider there to have been a *human duties canon* rather than a *human rights canon*. At the threshold to the modern age, the new intellectual movement had a considerable influence on the gradual development of individual rights, especially as it shifted the common

[5] See the thoughts by O. HUFTON, 'Einleitung' in O. HUFTON (ed.), *Menschenrechte in der Geschichte: The Oxford Amnesty Lectures 1994*, Fischer Taschenbuch, Frankfurt am Main 1998, pp. 9–26, at p. 11. Elaborating on this topic: W. SCHMALE, 'Grund- und Menschenrechte in vormodernen und modernen Gesellschaften Europas' in M. GRANDNER, W. SCHMALE and M. WEINZIERL (eds.), *Grund- und Menschenrechte. Historische Perspektiven: Aktuelle Problematiken*, Querschnitte 8, Oldenbourg Wissenschaftsverlag, Wien/München 2002, pp. 29–100, at pp. 31–34, pp. 36–62.

[6] See MOYN, *supra* note 3, p. 475.

[7] F. ERMACORA, *Menschenrechte in der sich wandelnden Welt, Band 1: Historische Entwicklung der Menschenrechte und Grundfreiheiten,* Veröffentlichungen der Kommission für das Studium der Menschenrechte 1, VÖAW, Wien 1974, in particular heading of chapter 1. See also the Tyrolean Territorial Law Code (1406), explicitly mentioned by Ermacora, pp. 73–74. (Many thanks to Mr Manfred Nowak for the reference of literature!).

worldview from theocentric to humanistic.[8] (Renaissance) humanism encountered — in simplified terms — a transitioning society. The subjects increasingly tried, as a consequence of economic and social upheaval as well as technical innovation, to flee from their manorial lords and to gain their livelihood by engaging in other forms of employment. In the Austrian ancestral lands, for example, many people found work in the booming mines and in the ironwork industry. During Reformation and Counterreformation, however, these traces of individual fundamental rights of people were restricted and partly eliminated, thus interrupting their development until the Enlightenment in the eighteenth century. The ruler was able to implement disciplinary measures exploiting the religious contentions of the sixteenth and seventeenth centuries, particularly because the provisions of the Religious Peace of Augsburg 1555 and the Peace of Westphalia 1648 (*ius reformandi* and *ius emigrandi*[9]) passed pertinent instruments into his hands. Specifically, the authorities were aware of who was catholic or converted permanently to Catholicism or who, through failure to comply with mandatory conversion, was forced to emigrate to adjacent protestant territory, as long as he/she could pay the necessary ransom to be released from serfdom. Exempt from this were the clergy and the imperial estates (*cuius regio, eius religio*). The *ius reformandi* can thus be considered a Janus-faced law, because it granted both freedom of religion (to the imperial estates) as

---

8 See F. BAAB, *Was ist Humanismus*, Verlag Friedrich Pustet, Regensburg 2013, pp. 34–36; further P.G. SCHMIDT, 'Mittelalterlicher Humanismus' in *Humanismus in Europa*, Stiftung 'Humanismus heute' des Landes Baden-Württemberg, Heidelberg 1998, pp. 75–88. Recently published on Roman law: J.M. RAINER, *Das Römische Recht in Europa: Von Justinian bis zum BGB*, Manzsche Verlags- und Universitätsbuchhandlung, Wien 2012. Compare also the explanations by K-H. OHLIG, 'Christentum – Individuum – Kirche' in R. DÜLMEN (ed.), *Entdeckung des Ich: Die Geschichte der Individualisierung vom Mittelalter bis zur Gegenwart*, Böhlau, Köln/Weimar/Wien 2001, pp. 11–40, at pp. 32–33.

9 See the text of § 24 of the Peace of Westfalia (right of emigration upon change of religion): 'Wo aber unsere, auch der churfürsten, fürsten und stände unterthanen der alten religion oder Augspurgischen Confession anhängig, von solcher ihrer religion wegen aus unsern, auch der churfürsten, fürsten und ständen des h. reichs landen, fürstenthumen, städten oder flecken mit ihren weib und kindern an andere orte ziehen und sich nieder thun wolten, denen soll solcher ab- und zuzug, auch verkauffung ihrer haab und güter gegen zimlichen, billigen abtrag der leibeigenschafft und nachsteuer, wie es jedes orts von alters anhero üblichen, herbracht und gehalten worden ist, unverhindert männiglichs zugelassen und bewilligt, auch an ihren ehren und pflichten allerding unentgolten seyn. Doch soll den oberkeiten an ihren gerechtigkeiten und herkommen der leibeigenen halben, dieselbigen ledig zu zehlen oder nicht, hiedurch nichts abgebrochen oder benommen seyn.' <http://www.lwl.org/westfaelische-geschichte/portal/Internet/finde/langDatensatz.php?urlID=739&url_tabelle=tab_quelle> accessed 30.04.2015. See also B. RUTHMANN and S. EHRENPREIS, 'Ius reformandi – Ius emigrandi. Reichsrecht, Konfession und Ehre in Religionsstreitigkeiten des späten 16. Jahrhunderts' in M. WEINZIERL (ed.), *Individualisierung, Rationalisierung, Säkularisierung: Neue Wege der Religionsgeschichte*, Beiträge zur Geschichte der Neuzeit 22, Verlag für Geschichte und Politik, R. Oldenbourg Verlag, Wien/München 1997, pp. 67–95; G. SCHMIDT, *Der Dreißigjährige Krieg*, Verlag Beck, München 2003, p. 17.

well as prohibition of religion (to subjects).[10] The *ius emigrandi* can also be seen as two-faced: on one side as a precursor of freedom of religion and conscience, and on the other as a constraint, because this freedom to choose was dependent on emigration and ransom.[11]

How difficult it is to speak of universal fundamental rights before the eighteenth century is proven by dress codes and dress regulations, which made religious (Star of David), social and economic status immediately recognisable and visible, regulated the traffic in goods (silk), defined luxury goods etc.[12]

The maintenance of serfdom until 1781 and the only superficial attempts to contain the persecution of witches stand in stark contrast to any potential fundamental rights. An indication of an altered and advanced understanding of individual rights and human dignity is, though, apparent in the fate of the *Constitutio Criminalis Theresiana* (Nemesis Theresiana).[13] This code was perceived as outdated, despite having tried, for the first time, to unify the penal (procedural) law in the Austrian ancestral land and the Kingdom of Bohemia (but not in Hungary). The Empress Maria Theresa introduced the controversial criminal code but her son Joseph II overruled it with the Josephinian Criminal Code in 1787.[14]

3. POTENTIAL EXAMPLES OF INDIVIDUAL RIGHTS (FOURTEENTH – SIXTEENTH CENTURIES)

3.1. CHANGING SOCIAL CONDITIONS LEADING TO NEW RULES

How can fundamental rights be defined in medieval times and in the early modern period? What can be interpreted as a fundamental right? As mentioned above, there are currently different approaches to and interpretations of the early days of European individual rights and their concepts,[15] and one should beware arbitrariness. Vested rights, so-called *iura quaesita*, which some corporations

---

10 For details see B.C. SCHNEIDER, *Ius Reformandi: Die Entwicklung eines Staatskirchenrechts von seinen Anfängen bis zum Ende des Alten Reiches*, Jus Ecclesiasticum 68, Mohr Siebeck, Tübingen 2001.

11 See also J. ZIEKOW, *Über Freizügigkeit und Aufenthalt: Paradigmatische Überlegungen zum grundrechtlichen Freiheitsschutz in historischer und verfassungsrechtlicher Perspektive*, Ius Publicum 21, Mohr Siebeck, Tübingen 1997, p. 85.

12 <http://www.habsburger.net/de/kapitel/dienstag-und-samstag-ist-markttag-handwerk-maerkte-und-lebensmittelversorgung-im>; <http://www.habsburger.net/de/kapitel/die-idee-der-toleranz>. See also <https://www.uni-muenster.de/FNZ-Online/sozialeOrdnung/stadtgesellschaft/quellen/kleider.htm > accessed 01.05.2015.

13 <https://archive.org/details/ConstitutioCriminalisTheresiana-1768> accessed 30.04.2015.

14 <http://alex.onb.ac.at/cgi-content/alex?apm=0&aid=jgs&datum=10040003&zoom=2&seite=00000007&ues=on&x=5&y=6> accessed 29.04.2015.

15 MOYN, *supra* note 3, pp. 545–572.

had acquired, were 'the exact opposite of "inherent rights"; they rather were rights *acquired* through customary law, privileges or legal contracts'.[16]

Knowing that this complex research topic cannot be dealt with exhaustively in one chapter and that modern parameters can in any event not be used as a standard *ex post*, this contribution will focus on two examples of acquired rights (*iura quaesita*) with far-reaching consequences. These examples are based on an interpretation of entitlement to the forest, which with its resources (building material, energy, workplace, property) secured survival, as a fundamental right. From 1300, employment opportunities in the non-agrarian sector increased in the area of the Eastern Alps, leading to social differentiation, regulations and gradually to the limit of existing resources. In the mining sector, for example, a differentiation evolved between owners of manually operated bellows and farmers: although the former were still bound to the working process, there was a difference with respect to ownership. At the end of the fourteenth century, the introduction of water-operated bellows and hammer mills, as well as an increase in production, engendered the local separation of mines from blast furnaces and generated employers and employees. The blast furnaces were heated with wood and coal, which, in the sixteenth century, increased the value of the forest enormously. Conflicts between the manorial lords occurred, as forest cover had been decimated due to the land clearing by colonists, yet there were an increasing number of mines and ironworks. These conflicts were particularly significant in the Duchy of Carniola. Several regulations by the territorial lord were dedicated to this situation, with the manorial mining regulation of Aßling (Jesenice) 1381 and the manorial forest regulation of Gottschee (Kočevska) 1406 serving as models until 1771, when Carniola obtained its own forest regulation. The issuer of both regulations was Count Friedrich of Ortenburg (approx. 1360–1418) who had vast land and forestry possessions at his disposal, predominantly in the duchies of Carinthia and Carniola, owned several provincial courts and served temporarily as imperial vicariate over the patriarchy of Aquileia for the Holy Roman Empire.[17]

---

16 SIMON, *supra* note 1, p. 857 (italics in original).

17 On Ortenburg see: M. WAKOUNIG *Die Besitzungen der Grafen von Ortenburg in Krain (1202–1377)*, phil. Dipl. Arb., Wien 1982, pp. 79–80; M. WAKOUNIG, *Dalmatien und Friaul: Die Auseinandersetzungen zwischen Sigismund von Luxemburg und der Republik Venedig um die Vorherrschaft im adriatischen Raum*, Dissertationen der Universität Wien 212, Wien 1990, pp. 32–46.

3.2. THE MINING REGULATION OF ASSLING (JESENICE)

As early as 1381, Ortenburg was forced to issue a mining regulation in his manorial territories in Aßling. Although this legislative landmark did not explicitly mention wood, with which the blast furnaces were heated — probably because it did not yet pose a problem — Ortenburg 'regulated the question of ownership, the status of persons and the organisation of enterprises, as well as the questions of jurisdiction: the owners of the blast furnaces and hammer mills were designated as mining foremen [Bergmeister], who were free to do as they pleased with their own property. If they were also in possession of oxgangs, they were also granted burgage tenure. [...] The mining foremen were free, their social status was autonomous and they were allowed to vote annually for a judge, who had to be confirmed by Ortenburg'.[18] If a mining foreman constructed a furnace or a hammer mill at his own expense, he enjoyed the rights described above as long as he resided in Aßling. 'He who, however, acquired the craft entirely or partly through purchase and subsequently sold it, lost the rights of a mining foreman',[19] which seems to indicate that company shares were also available. Regarding the employees, who were made up of sons of farmers, poorer city dwellers or others, the mining regulation was subordinating. They had no 'right to vote for the appointment of the judge, although they were assigned to him [...] but they were subject to the disciplinary powers of the mining foreman'.[20] The catalyst for the mining regulation which eventually eliminated several legal uncertainties was riots, triggered by the workers.[21]

This mining regulation was considered a prototype for subsequent ones, which had to be enacted due to disputes over forest resources. However, the decrees and mining regulations by Maximilian I (1515), Ferdinand I (1530 and 1553), and Karl II (1575, valid in Gorizia) *de facto* disempowered the manorial lords, because the supervision of the woodlands was assigned to the profit-thirsty mining foremen, without concern for the forests themselves. After many protests

---

18 M. WAKOUNIG, 'Von Přemysl Otakar II. bis zu Maximilian I. von Habsburg' in A. SUPPAN (ed.), *Zwischen Adria und Karawanken*, Deutsche Geschichte im Osten Europas 7, Siedler Verlag, Berlin 1998, pp. 54–110, at pp. 90–91.

19 *Ibid.*

20 *Ibid.*

21 The mine regulation of Aßling (Jesenice 1381) is contained, among others, in A. MÜLLNER, *Geschichte des Eisens in Krain, Görz und Istrien: Von der Urzeit bis zum Anfang des XIX. Jahrhunderts*, Verlag von Halm & Goldmann, Wien 1909, pp. 374–377. See also: S. VILFAN, *Pravna zgodovina Slovencev: Od naselitve do zloma stare Jugoslavije*, Ljubljana Izd. Slovenska Matic, Ljubljana 1961, pp. 190–191; S. VILFAN, *Rechtsgeschichte der Slowenen bis zum Jahre 1941*, Grazer rechts- und staatswissenschaftliche Studien 21, Leykam, Graz 1968, pp. 129–130. Recently published: D. MIHELIČ, 'Usoda gozdov na Slovenskem do 16. stoletja' (2008) 4/4 *Ekonomska i ekohistorija* 27–51, 34.

from the estates, the utilisation of the woodland was regulated by decree in favour of the manorial lords.[22]

3.3. THE FOREST REGULATION OF GOTTSCHEE (KOČEVSKO) 1406

As is apparent from the preceding discussion, the boom of mining and the ironwork industry in the Eastern Alps occurred due to the abundance of forests and wood. Wood was, however, also a resource which was important for survival in this area. It had multiple uses as building material for residential houses, stables and barns, as a tangible and renewable heat and energy source, and also as material for different timber products, which could be sold by the subjects either at markets or as peddlers. Prudent and responsible exploitation of this resource was therefore required. The tension between the two types of use meant that wood mutated into a permanent source of discord, between manorial lords and the local rulers' authorities, between the manorial lords and their subjects and, most seriously, among the subjects themselves. The latter was what triggered Friedrich Ortenburg to issue the forest regulation of Gottschee 1406, which was valid throughout Carniola until 1771.

After many armed conflicts and murders relating to forest disagreements, he laid down in the introduction to the regulation that the forest was his property and that therefore he decided over its usage. Subjects who for nine years and one day had used (unspecified) parts of the forest would be allowed to continue doing so and were granted the right to sell, to lease or to deliver the wood. Forest rights were inheritable both by males and females; for daughters they could be passed on as a dowry, as long as they married inside the Ortenburg dominion of Gottschee. Constraints concerned those who moved away from a barren region or who did not offer to sell a bird of prey to the sovereign within three years. Linked to the free use of the woodlands was also the duty to declare hawk nests and to deliver five dormice to the sovereign. Theft, encroachment or acquisition of forest and hunting rights (of birds of prey and dormice) under false pretences was punished severely.[23] By the sixteenth century, despite the forest regulation, and probably due to the mining industry, there was a shortage of lumber, which caused the landlord (at that point Count Auersperg) to intervene.[24]

---

22 WAKOUNIG, *supra* note 18, p. 90.

23 All the quotes and further reprimands at WAKOUNIG, *supra* note 18, pp. 77–78. See also MIHELIČ, *supra* note 21, p. 36.

24 WAKOUNIG, *supra* note 18, p. 78.

4. CONCLUDING REMARKS

It would — lest there are new findings leading to new insights — not be legitimate to insist on constructing an early history of fundamental rights, in the modern sense, in the Austrian ancestral lands before the eighteenth century. It would be interesting to compare, as a further step and within the framework of an interdisciplinary research project, different legislative landmarks, to juxtapose them with emerging issues and through this, to expose traces or early stages of fundamental rights thought. In such a context it would be interesting to investigate the actors and institutions who promoted such thought, and to identify the arguments of those who sought to oppose it.

Comparing the two legislative landmarks discussed in this chapter, it becomes evident that (by coincidence) the same manorial lord was forced by disputes and, particularly, killings, to enact two pioneering regulations. While the first case (Mining Regulation) revolves ostensibly around the question of ownership, which without wood — that on the face of the regulation played no role — would not have been as contentious, the Forest Regulation is instead a qualitative question of survival. The manorial lord had in both cases tried to establish order through customary law, or to generate customary law through order, to, on the one hand, curb labour unrest and at the same time clarify pending ownership questions and, on the other hand, to make wood available. The manorial lord achieved a temporary resolution of the claim to wood, less so to work (in the sense of *iura quaesita*), and had provided territorial legislation of a provisional nature lasting until the eighteenth century. This occurred, however, not because of a humane or an equality impetus, but rather to reduce unrest, which wasted energy and time. It is possible that the solution lies, and not only in this case, in semantics. In future, one will have to look more closely at the word *order* when dealing with the question of fundamental rights, to find out which legal-qualitative differences existed between regulations adopted by sovereigns and those by manorial lords.

8. SPAIN: THE FIRST CRY FOR JUSTICE IN THE AMERICAS — FROM ANTONIO DE MONTESINOS TO THE LAWS OF BURGOS (1512)

Felipe GÓMEZ ISA

1. INTRODUCTION

Although it is always a risky intellectual exercise to judge past events and legal developments by contemporary categories and paradigms,[1] it can be argued that one of the first attempts in Spain to protect human dignity took place in the context of the encounter with the *New World*. The Spanish Conquest of the Americas after 1492 and the debate about the treatment to be given to the Indians paved the way for a very passionate and challenging discussion as to both the nature of indigenous people and the duties of the *conquistadores* towards them.[2] Against this background, Antonio de Montesinos, a Dominican friar sent to the Americas to accompany the conquerors and to guarantee that Catholic principles would lead the colonial enterprise, preached a revolutionary sermon in 1511 that shocked the conscience of both the conquistadores and the Spanish Crown. He openly denounced the unjust ill-treatment that the Indians were suffering. This sermon had a profound impact in imperial Spain, and moved the King to convene an official discussion of theologians and jurists that led to the adoption of the *Laws of Burgos* on 27 December 1512, whose main goal was to protect and humanise the Indians and to regulate the rights and duties of the conquistadores. The aim of this chapter is to analyse the religious and philosophical climate in which these Laws were adopted, and to explore to what extent they can be considered an early proclamation of fundamental rights.

---

1 For a relevant reflection on the need to adopt an historical approach to human rights see J-P. LEHNERS, 'Pleading for a New History of Human Rights' in A. MIHR and M. GIBNEY (eds.), *The SAGE Handbook of Human Rights*, SAGE, London 2014, pp. 22–23. A critical perspective of the role played by the historiography of human rights can be found in B. CLAVERO, *Derecho Global. Por una historia verosímil de los derechos humanos*, Trotta, Madrid 2014.

2 P. LEUPRECHT, *Reason, Justice and Dignity. A Journey to Some Unexplored Sources of Human Rights*, Martinus Nijhoff Publishers, Leiden-Boston 2012, pp. 75–101.

2. THE SERMON BY ANTONIO DE MONTESINOS

On the Sunday before Christmas in 1511 Dominican Father Antonio de Montesinos delivered a highly provocative sermon in the Holy Mass in *Isla Española* (today's Dominican Republic and Haiti), the first colonial town erected in the New World after the Spanish Conquest. The content of the sermon had been agreed by the whole group of Dominicans, the Order of Preachers, and its principal aim was to publicly protest against the treatment the Indians were receiving. As Lewis Hanke has underlined, this sermon can be seen as 'the first cry on behalf of human liberty in the New World'.[3] The strong words used by Montesinos are highly illustrative of the suffering of the Indians caused by the colonists:

> In order to make your sins against the Indians known to you I have come up on this pulpit, I who am a voice of Christ crying in the wilderness of this island …; this is going to be one of the strangest voice that ever you heard, the harshest and hardest and most awful and most dangerous that ever you expected to hear … This voice says that you are in mortal sin, that you live and die in it, for the cruelty and tyranny you use in dealing with these innocent people. Tell me, by what right or justice do you keep these Indians in such a cruel and horrible servitude? On what authority have you waged a detestable war against these people, who dwelt quietly and peacefully on their own land? … Why do you keep them so oppressed and weary, not giving them enough to eat nor taking care of them in their illness? For with the excessive work you demand of them they fall ill and die, or rather you kill them with your desire to extract and acquire gold every day. And what care do you take that they should be instructed in religion? … Are these not men? Have they not rational souls? Are you not bound to love them as you love yourselves?[4]

The main focus of the harsh criticism by Montesinos was the so-called *encomienda* system. The encomienda was the institution that articulated the master-servant relationship between the colonists and the Indians in the very first phase of the colonisation process,[5] and served both the religious interests of the

---

3 L. HANKE, *The Spanish Struggle for Justice in the Conquest of America*, University of Pennsylvania Press, Philadelphia 1949, p. 17. A critical approach to the position defended by Hanke in R.A. WILLIAMS, *The American Indian in Western Legal Thought: The Discourses of Conquest*, Oxford University Press, New York 1990.

4 One of the most accurate accounts of the sermon by Antonio de Montesinos can be found in Bartolomé de Las Casas' book *History of the Indies*, 1561, III, pp. 4–5.

5 One of the deepest analyses of the Encomienda is to be found in S. ZAVALA, *La Encomienda Indiana*, Junta para la Ampliación de Estudios, Madrid 1935. See also R. HIMMERICH Y

Crown and the economic purposes of the conquistadores.[6] By virtue of it, the King distributed land and entrusted Indians (*repartimiento*[7]) to the settlers (*encomenderos*) for compulsory labour. In return, 'the encomenderos were obliged to provide religious instruction for the Indians and to protect them'.[8] The Spanish conceived the encomienda as a form of serfdom that did not give actual ownership of the Indian workers to the encomenderos, but 'in practice it differed little from slavery'.[9]

The sermon by Montesinos on the last Sunday of Advent created much unrest among the Spanish colonists, since it openly questioned the encomienda system and advocated more humane treatment for the Indians. The encomenderos protested angrily before both the Dominican Order and the Spanish Crown, fiercely trying to defend their privileges. King Ferdinand the Catholic was so astonished by the testimony of Montesinos that he set up the *Junta de Burgos*, a consultative body of theologians, jurists and officials, including Montesinos himself, to reflect on the proper treatment to be given to the native Indians and to draft new legal principles accordingly. After more than 20 meetings of this group in the city of Burgos, the *Royal Ordinances for the Good Governance and Treatment of the Indians* were promulgated by the Spanish King on 27 December 1512. The 35 ordinances enshrined in the so-called Laws of Burgos can be considered as the first systematic code to regulate the conduct of Spanish colonists in the Americas, particularly in their relations with indigenous people.[10]

3. THE LAWS OF BURGOS

While one cannot properly argue, as some scholars do through overly anachronistic projections, that the Laws of Burgos were 'the first Declaration of human rights in Spain',[11] there are nonetheless sound reasons to assert that they

---

VALENCIA, *The encomenderos of New Spain, 1521–1555*, University of Texas Press, Austin 1991.

6 R. SÁNCHEZ DOMINGO, 'Las Leyes de Burgos de 1512 y la Doctrina Jurídica de la Conquista' (2012) 28 *Revista Jurídica de Castilla y León* 25.

7 M. SEGURA ORTEGA, 'El Derecho de Indias' in G. PECES-BARBA and E. FERNÁNDEZ (dirs.), *Historia de los Derechos Fundamentales. Tránsito a la Modernidad, Siglos XVI y XVII*, Dykinson, Madrid 1998, p. 719.

8 HANKE, *supra* note 3, p. 19.

9 J. ANAYA, *Indigenous Peoples in International Law*, Oxford University Press, Oxford 2004, p. 35, note 3. Along the same lines see T.J. YEAGER, 'Encomienda or Slavery? The Spanish Crown's Choice of Labor Organization in Sixteenth-Century Spanish America' (1995) 55 *The Journal of Economic History* 842–859.

10 R.A. WILLIAMS, 'The Medieval and Renaissance Origins of the Status of American Indians in Western Legal Thought' (1983) 57 *Southern California Law Review* 11–48.

11 SÁNCHEZ DOMINGO, *supra* note 6, p. 1.

constituted a 'significant advance'[12] in the long journey for the defence of justice and dignity, and strongly influenced the subsequent evolution of Spanish Law. The primary aims of the Laws of Burgos were 'the salvation of the souls'[13] of the Indians and 'the conservation of their lives',[14] imposing very detailed obligations to the encomenderos. For the first time in history, and probably the last time,[15] an Empire such as Spain transparently questioned the colonisation process itself[16] and seriously reflected about the treatment that local populations should receive.[17]

The Laws of Burgos did not abolish the encomienda system[18] but instead they limited it to a great extent through strict regulations on food and accommodation

---

12 F. MACÍAS, 'The Laws of Burgos: 500 Years of Human Rights', *The Library of Congress* <http://blogs.loc.gov/law/2012/12/the-laws-of-burgos-500-years-of-human-rights/> accessed 11.03.2015.

13 Laws of Burgos, Preamble.

14 *Ibid.*

15 J.L. DE LEÓN AZCÁRATE, 'La Biblia y la dignidad de los indios del Nuevo Mundo. O cuando la teología ilumina la política de una época' in C. BERNABÉ and C. GIL (eds.), *Reimaginando los orígenes del cristianismo. Relevancia social y eclesial de los estudios sobre Orígenes del cristianismo*, Verbo Divino, Estella 2008, p. 452.

16 Some of the participants at the Junta de Burgos denied the Papal donation to the Spanish Crown as a legitimate title to legally acquire lands in the Americas. Pope Alexander VI granted land title to Spain by virtue of his Bull *Inter Caetera*, adopted on 3 May 1493. Incredibly, this Papal Bull has not been officially revoked so far. There is a very challenging project led by some academics and some indigenous leaders from the US and Canada to organise a march to Rome in 2016 to ask Pope Francis I to revoke it and to 'Shout out the Lie that a man can be considered as less than human purely because he does not worship at the same altar as other men from other land', *The Long March to Rome* < http://longmarchtorome.com/> accessed 11.03.2015.

17 Some years later, in 1550, Spanish Emperor Charles V convened the so-called *Controversia de Valladolid*, to continue discussing both about the legitimacy of the Conquest and about the brutality of the methods used by the conquistadores. Bartolomé de las Casas was the driving force behind this unique exercise of imperial self-criticism. This official debate in the then capital of Spain, Valladolid, has been described as an 'astounding trial' by K-M. SIMONSEN, 'The Politics of Universalism. Strategic Uses of Human Rights Discourses in Early Modernity' (2013) 5 *Journal of Aesthetics & Culture* 5 <http://www.aestheticsandculture.net/index.php/jac/article/view/23157> accessed 11.03.2015. For a very interesting analysis of the contemporary ideological implications in Western political thought of the Controversia de Valladolid see D. VELASCO, 'Autoconciencia del Norte e historia de la "razón cínica". De la Conferencia de Valladolid (1550) a la Conferencia de Río (1992)' (1992) 7 *Inguruak* 141–155. Others see the Controversia de Valladolid as the starting-point for the evolution of human rights, J. DUMONT, *El amanecer de los derechos del hombre: la Controversia de Valladolid*, Encuentro, Madrid 1997.

18 The encomienda was formally abolished by Charles V with the adoption of the *Laws and ordinances newly made by His Majesty for the government of the Indies and good treatment and preservation of the Indians* (Barcelona, 20 November 1542), also known as the *New Laws*, but, due to the protests and threats of rebellion by colonists in the Americas, it continued as the main institutional pillar of Spanish colonization. For a detailed account of the fight between those that considered that the encomienda was the principal enemy of the Indians, mainly Bartolomé de Las Casas, and those that defended it see HANKE, *supra* note 3, pp. 83–101.

for Indians, on the labour regime to be applied, on access to health,[19] on the prohibition of ill-treatment,[20] on the protection of some native customs,[21] and on religious instruction. First of all, the Indians should be given sufficient means for their *subsistence*,[22] 'the most important consideration for the good treatment and increase of the Indians'.[23] In this respect, Ordinance XV commanded 'that all persons who have Indians shall be obliged to maintain those who are on their estates and there to keep continually a sufficiency of bread and yams and peppers, and, at least on Sundays and feast days, to give them dishes of cooked meat'. Given the harsher conditions undergone by the Indians working in the mines, 'they shall be given bread and peppers and a pound of meat a day, and on feast days fish or sardines or other things for their subsistence'.[24] The Indians should also be 'well situated and housed'[25] and be given 'to each of them a hammock in which to sleep continually'[26] so that they need not sleep on the ground.

In terms of *labour conditions*, the Laws of Burgos also detailed the specific obligations that the encomenderos had to respect *vis-à-vis* the Indians working for them. Those Indians extracting gold at the mines will work 'for five months in the year and, at the end of these five months, the said Indians shall rest forty days'.[27] During these 40 days of rest, the persons having those Indians in encomienda 'shall be obliged ... to indoctrinate them in the things of our Faith'.[28] These Laws also prescribed some obligations to protect pregnant women. According to Ordinance XVIII, 'no pregnant woman, after the fourth month, shall be sent to the mines, or made to plant hillocks, but shall be kept on the estates and utilised in household tasks'. Along the same lines, a very generous maternity leave period was established, since 'after she bears her child she shall nurse it until it is three years old, and in all this time she shall not be

19 The Preamble of the Laws of Burgos stated that 'if some Indian should fall sick he will be quickly succored and treated, and thus the lives of many, with the help of Our Lord, will be saved who now die because no one knows they are sick'.

20 As stated in Ordinance XXIV, 'no person or persons shall dare to beat any Indians with sticks, or whip him, or call him dog, or address him by any name other than his proper name alone; and if an Indian should deserve to be punished for something he has done, the said person having him in charge shall bring him to the visitor for punishment'.

21 Ordinance XIV commanded that the Indians shall not be prevented from performing their customary dances (*areytos*) 'on Sundays and feast days, and also on work days, if they do not on that account neglect their usual work stint'.

22 Ordinance I of the Laws of Burgos refers explicitly to 'half a fanega of maize, ... a dozen hens and a cock to raise and enjoy the fruit thereof, the chickens as well as the eggs ... It is given them in exchange for what they are leaving behind, *to enjoy as their own property*' (emphasis added).

23 Laws of Burgos, Ordinance XV.

24 *Ibid.*

25 Laws of Burgos, Ordinance I.

26 Laws of Burgos, Ordinance XIX.

27 Laws of Burgos, Ordinance XIII.

28 *Ibid.*

sent to the mines, or made to plant hillocks, or used in anything else that will harm the infant'.[29]

A very progressive amendment to the Laws of Burgos related to child labour was introduced on 28 July 1513. The said modification ordered that 'Indian children under fourteen years of age shall not be compelled to work at adults' tasks until they have attained the said age or more; but they shall be compelled to work at, and serve in, tasks proper to children, such as weeding the fields and the like, on their parents' estates'.[30] In the area of labour conditions, these Laws clearly 'seem to be ahead of their time',[31] anticipating some protective measures that were to be adopted centuries later.

Finally, approximately one third of the provisions of the Laws of Burgos were devoted to the *religious instruction* of the indigenous people 'with great love and gentleness'[32]. First of all, every encomendero is obliged 'to erect a structure to be used for a church',[33] and each morning, before they go to work, 'the Indians shall be obliged to go to the said church and pray as they do in the evening'.[34] Those who have more than 50 Indians in encomienda 'shall be obliged to have a boy taught to read and write, and the things of our Faith, so that he may later teach the said Indians, because the Indians will more readily accept what he says than what the Spaniards and settlers tell them'.[35] The encomenderos were also obliged 'to have all infants baptised within a week of their birth',[36] and to assure that all Indians 'be given the sacraments'.[37]

But the truth is that the Spanish Crown 'used the Catholic faith as the principal justification of its conquest'.[38] This is well illustrated by the introduction of the *requerimiento* by the Junta de Burgos in 1513. The requerimiento was a statement to be announced to the Indians before military hostilities could be legally launched. It basically *required* Indians to acknowledge 'the Church as the Ruler and Superior of the whole world' and the Papal donation to the Spanish Crown of all territories they discover.[39] Additionally, the native Indians should

29 Laws of Burgos, Ordinance XVIII.

30 *Amendments to the Laws of Burgos*, given in the City of Valladolid, 28 July 1513, Amendment II.

31 MACÍAS, *supra* note 12, p. 2.

32 Laws of Burgos, Ordinance IV.

33 Laws of Burgos, Ordinance III.

34 *Ibid.*

35 Laws of Burgos, Ordinance IX.

36 Laws of Burgos, Ordinance XII.

37 Laws of Burgos, Preamble.

38 J. GILBERT, *Indigenous Peoples' Land Rights under International Law. From Victims to Actors*, Transnational Publishers, Ardsley 2006, p. 7.

39 See *supra* note 16.

allow the Catholic faith to be taught to them.[40] If they resisted, the requerimiento threatened the Indians with the eloquent words that follow:

> if you do not this or if you maliciously delay in doing it, I certify to you that with the help of God we shall make war against you ..., we shall take you and your wives and your children and shall make slaves of them ...; and we shall take away your goods and shall do to you all the damage that we can ...; and we protest that the deaths and losses which shall accrue from this are your fault ....[41]

Obviously, the Indians did not fully understand the real meaning of the formula used in the requerimiento.[42] Therefore, it turned into a legal formalism to justify the Conquest and the war against those who resisted,[43] in other words an act of profound hypocrisy. Some years later, Bartolomé de Las Casas strongly criticised these forms of evangelisation, since the Catholic faith can only be preached by peaceful means and through persuasion.[44] But what Las Casas never questioned was the colonisation process itself as a legitimate way to Christianise the Indians.[45]

A very relevant feature of the Laws of Burgos was the establishment of an institutional mechanism to supervise their implementation and punish violations. Each community in the Americas should have two *visitors* to monitor the way in which the encomenderos were fulfilling their obligations. As proclaimed by Ordinance XXIX of the Laws of Burgos, the visitors were:

> in charge of inspecting the whole community, together with its mines and estates, its shepherds and swineherds, and they shall ascertain how the Indians are being taught in the things of our Faith, and how their persons are being treated, and how they are being maintained, and how they or the persons who have them in

40 A detailed analysis of the requerimiento can be found in L. HANKE, 'The Requerimiento and its Interpreters' (1938) *Revista de Historia de América* 25–34.

41 An English translation of this document can be found in HANKE, *supra* note 3, p. 33.

42 As pointed out by Amber Ferris, 'the observance of the proper application of The Requirement varied depending on the expedition. Some conquistadors read this in a "grotesquely absurd" way while others took pains to make sure the natives understood what they were hearing'. A. FERRIS, 'Bartolome de las Casas Revisited', Seminar Paper Presented to the Department of History, Western Oregon University, in partial fulfillment of the requirements for the degree of Bachelor of Science in History, 2009, p. 17, <https://www.wou.edu/las/socsci/history/senior_seminar_papers/2009/Amber% 20Ferris%20HST%20499.pdf> accessed 12.03.2015.

43 SEGURA ORTEGA, *supra* note 7, p. 719.

44 B. DE LAS CASAS, *De unico vocationis modo omnium gentium ad veram religionem* (*On the Only Way of Attracting All Peoples to the True Religion*), 1540.

45 R. MESA, 'Bartolomé de las Casas, Maestro contemporáneo' in A. MANGAS (ed.), *La Escuela de Salamanca y el Derecho Internacional en América. Del pasado al futuro*, Asociación Española de Profesores de Derecho Internacional y Relaciones Internacionales, Salamanca 1993, p. 79.

> charge are obeying and fulfilling these our ordinances ...; we command them to have a particular care in all this, and we charge their consciences with it.

The visitors were selected 'from among the oldest inhabitants of the communities',[46] and were obliged to 'keep a book in which to enter every person who has Indians in encomienda, and the Indians that each one has ... so that those who are born may be entered, and those who die removed, and the visitors have continually a complete record of the increase or decrease of the said Indians'.[47] The visitors were obliged 'twice a year to inspect all the places where there are Indians of their charge'.[48] Finally, the Laws of Burgos also set up a far-reaching system of accountability for the activities performed by the visitors themselves. According to Ordinance XXXIV, the Admiral, judges and officers of the Indies should 'inquire once every two years into the way in which the said visitors are fulfilling their duties'.

The Laws of Burgos constituted a great innovation, since they were the first systematic body of law aimed at regulating the conduct of the conquistadores in the Americas. Given their relevance, the Spanish King ordered the Laws to be published, something that was limited to legal documents of major importance. Thus, 50 copies of the Laws of Burgos were issued to be sent to America.[49] In this connection, the Laws themselves ordered the visitors 'to have and keep in their possession a copy of these our ordinances ..., by which they may better know what they must do, observe and obey'.[50]

In essence, the Laws of Burgos were the result of a delicate balance between the expansionist interests of the Spanish Empire, the extension of the Catholic faith sponsored by the Pope, and the economic goals of the colonists. This combination of somewhat conflicting interests helps explain the limited impact the Laws had in the development of the Conquest. In practice, the ordinances were manifestly violated and could not prevent the systematic ill-treatment of the indigenous peoples in the Americas.[51] As a consequence of this dramatic lack of implementation, a Mexican scholar has recently argued that the Laws of Burgos have to be interpreted as a 'sophisticated justification of domination'[52] rather than as a defence of the dignity of the Indians in the context of the colonisation of the Americas. In my view, although both the Spanish Crown and a high

---

[46] Laws of Burgos, Ordinance XXX.
[47] Laws of Burgos, Ordinance XXIII.
[48] Laws of Burgos, Ordinance XXXI.
[49] Sánchez Domingo, *supra* note 7, pp. 17–18.
[50] Laws of Burgos, Ordinance XXXIII.
[51] Segura Ortega, *supra* note 7, p. 723.
[52] M.J. Bailón Corres, *Derechos Humanos de los pueblos indígenas: el debate colonial y las Leyes de Indias de 1681*, Comisión Nacional de los Derechos Humanos, México D. F. 2014, p. 39.

number of ecclesiastics had good intentions, the reality of the Conquest was fully driven by the imperial expansion of Spain and by the economic interests of the conquistadores.

4. LAS CASAS AS 'PROTECTOR OF THE INDIANS'

Bartolomé de Las Casas (1484–1566) is a very controversial character still today, and there is a high 'plurality'[53] of interpretations of Las Casas' intellectual legacy. His admirers defend the paradigmatic voice of Las Casas as 'the first clear announcement of the modern language of human rights',[54] while his detractors see him as a prominent example of what they refer to as 'ecclesiastical imperialism',[55] and as a promoter of the so-called *black legend*[56] against Spanish colonisation of the Americas associated with some forms of Hispanophobia.

Bartolomé de Las Casas first arrived in 1502 as a colonist in the Americas,[57] where he was essentially seeking adventure and riches. Like many other settlers, he fought the natives and was given a group of Indians in encomienda to forcibly work for him. He was present in the church when Dominican Antonio de Montesinos gave his famous Christmas sermon in December 1511, and, as he himself accounted, was strongly touched and moved by it. In fact, Las Casas was ordained as a Catholic priest only a year later, in 1512. But it was not until 1514 that he *converted*, and publicly committed to devote his entire life to fight the ill-treatment the Indians were receiving from the Spaniards. He travelled to Spain with Antonio de Montesinos to inform both the Spanish Crown and the Catholic Church about the atrocities being perpetrated in the Americas and about the lack of implementation of the Laws of Burgos. As a response to his dramatic testimony he was appointed 'Protector of the Indians' by Cardinal Cisneros in

---

53 B. CLAVERO, *Genocidio y Justicia. La Destrucción de las Indias, ayer y hoy*, Marcial Pons, Madrid 2002, p. 69.

54 P.G. CAROZZA, 'From Conquest to Constitutions: Retrieving a Latin American Tradition of the Idea of Human Rights' (2003) *Human Rights Quarterly* 291. In the same vein see M. BATAILLON, *El Padre Las Casas y la defensa de los Indios*, Ariel, Barcelona 1974; L. HANKE, *All mankind is one. A Study of the Disputation between Bartolomé de Las Casas and Juan Ginés de Sepúlveda in 1550 on the religious and intellectual capacity of the American Indians*, Northern Illinois University Press, Illinois 1974; M. BEUCHOT, *Los Fundamentos de los Derechos Humanos en Bartolomé de Las Casas*, Anthropos, Barcelona 1994; P.S. VICKERY, *Bartolome de Las Casas: Great Prophet of the Americas*, Paulist Press, New York 2006.

55 D. CASTRO, *Another Face of Empire: Bartolomé de Las Casas, Indigenous Rights and Ecclesiastical Imperialism*, Duke University Press, Durham 2007.

56 R. MENÉNDEZ PIDAL, *El Padre Las Casas: su doble personalidad*, Espasa-Calpe, Madrid 1963; J. LAWRANCE, *Spanish Conquest, Protestant Prejudice: Las Casas and the Black Legend*, Cultural and Communications Press, Nottingham 2009.

57 An account of the life and work of Las Casas can be found in J. FRIEDE and B. KEEN (eds.), *Bartolome de Las Casas in History: Toward an Understanding of the Man and his Work*, Northern Illinois University Press, Illinois 1971.

1516.[58] Once back in America, he became an ardent defender of the Indians,[59] and defined the encomienda system as the principal enemy for the very survival of native populations.[60] This particular dimension of the vital trajectory of Las Casas is of utmost importance in understanding both the theoretical and practical scope of his reflections. As it has been rightly underlined by Paolo Carozza:

> what distinguishes Las Casas from his contemporaries is his combination of speculation and experience, his engagement in practice with the struggle for justice ... In this way he also foreshadowed the typical dynamic of how human rights thinking developed in the 20th century.[61]

In this sense, Bartolomé de Las Casas could easily be considered as one of the very first examples of an *engaged intellectual* in history.[62]

Las Casas and the Spanish School of International Law[63] based their arguments in the Aristotelian-Thomist idea of the natural sociability and rationality of

---

58 E. GARCÍA GARCÍA, 'Bartolomé de las Casas y los derechos humanos' in M. MACEIRAS and L. MÉNDEZ (coords.), *Los derechos humanos en su origen. La República Dominicana y Antón de Montesinos*, Editorial San Esteban, Salamanca 2011, pp. 2–4.

59 A clear-cut example of Las Casas as a figure ahead of his time is that he defended the *obligation of restitution* and *reparation* to the Indians given the injustices suffered by them. This issue of restitution and reparation of the historical injustices to indigenous peoples is still under discussion at national and international level almost five centuries later. For a detailed analysis of this claim see F. GÓMEZ ISA, 'Repairing Historical Injustices: Indigenous Peoples in Post-Conflict Scenarios' in G. ORÉ AGUILAR and F. GÓMEZ ISA (eds.), *Rethinking Transitions. Equality and Social Justice in Societies Emerging from Conflict*, Intersentia, Cambridge-Antwerp 2011, pp. 265–300.

60 The most open criticism to the encomienda can be found in his work *De Regia Potestate*, 1571.

61 CAROZZA, *supra* note 54, p. 291.

62 According to one of the most relevant experts on Scholastic legal philosophy in sixteenth-century Spain, Las Casas is a leading example of those intellectuals trying to adequately combine 'theory and praxis'. A-E. PÉREZ LUÑO, *La polémica sobre el Nuevo Mundo. Los clásicos españoles de la Filosofía del Derecho*, Trotta, Madrid 1992, p. 163.

63 The so-called *Spanish School of International Law* was composed by a number of theologians and jurists (Francisco de Vitoria, Domingo de Soto) that taught at the University of Salamanca, and that can be considered as the precursors of modern International Law. See in this respect J.B. SCOTT, *The Spanish origin of International Law: Francisco de Vitoria and his law of nations*, Clarendon Press, London 1934; R. HERNÁNDEZ, 'The Internationalization of Francisco de Vitoria and Domingo de Soto' (1991) 15 *Fordham International Law Journal*, Issue 4, 1031–1059. On the other hand, one has to recognise that traditional International Law, embedded with an inherent Eurocentrism, has played a major role in the history of conquest, usurpation of indigenous peoples' sovereignty, and dispossession of their lands, territories and natural resources. See in this sense, among many others, P. KEAL, *European Conquest and the Rights of Indigenous Peoples: The Moral Backwardness of International Society*, Cambridge University Press, New York 2003; A. ANGHIE, *Imperialism, Sovereignty and the Making of International Law*, Cambridge University Press, Cambridge 2004; E. KEENE, *Beyond the Anarchical Society: Grotius, Colonialism and Order in World Politics*, Cambridge University Press, Cambridge 2002; M. KOSKENNIEMI, *The Gentle Civilizer of Nations: The Rise and Fall of International Law 1870-1960*, Cambridge University Press, Cambridge 2002.

human beings,[64] but went well beyond this in defending the essential humanity and freedom of the Indians. One key pillar of Las Casas' thinking was the principle of the *universality of humankind*.[65] As affirmed by the Dominican friar:

> all the races of the world are men, and of all men and of each individual there is but one definition, and this is that they are rational. All have understanding and will and free choice, as all are made in the image and likeness of God ... Thus the entire human race is one.[66]

Given that all men, including native Americans, 'are made in the image and likeness of God', they are *equal* and *free*[67] according to sacred principles of Natural Law.[68] By this process, Las Casas progressively departed from the Thomist tradition of voluntarist Natural Law and advocated a rationalist approach to the said principles of Natural Law.[69] This evolutionary reading of Natural Law allowed Las Casas to introduce the very idea of *subjective natural rights* that could not be found in his predecessors' writings.[70] In the view of Tierny, the greatest achievement by Las Casas on a theoretical level 'was to graft, quite consciously, a juridical doctrine of natural rights onto Aquinas' teaching on natural law'.[71] While recognising the added value of the theories of Natural Law and subjective natural rights developed by Bartolomé de Las Casas and his colleagues at the University of Salamanca, one has to accept that 'the human rights of his time were different from human rights in the twenty-first century'.[72] On the other hand, they contributed significantly by anticipating some of the ideas that opened the door to the modern conception of human rights after the liberal revolutions of the eighteenth century. In the view of Pérez Luño, the Spanish School promoted a 'rationalist and humanist natural law of a democratic character that gave birth to the genesis of modern human rights and the rule of

64 On the influence of Aristotle on Las Casas see G.L. HUXLEY, *Aristotle, Las Casas and the American Indians*, Royal Irish Academy, Dublin 1980.

65 J.A. CARRILLO SALCEDO, 'Aportación de Francisco de Vitoria a los fundamentos filosóficos de los derechos humanos' in MANGAS, *supra* note 45, p. 51.

66 B. DE LAS CASAS, *Apologética historia summaria de las gentes destas Indias* (*Apologetic Summary History of the People of these Indies*), 1552.

67 This is one of the main differences between Las Casas and Aristotle, since the Greek philosopher defended slavery as in conformity with Natural Law. Natural slavery was the principal issue under discussion in the *Controversia de Valladolid* in 1550 between Bartolomé de Las Casas and Ginés de Sepúlveda. See *supra* note 17.

68 C. DEL ARENAL, 'La visión de la sociedad mundial en la Escuela de Salamanca' in MANGAS, *supra* note 45, p. 33.

69 PÉREZ LUÑO, *supra* note 62, p. 156.

70 GARCÍA GARCÍA, *supra* note 58, p. 12.

71 B. TIERNEY, *The Idea of Natural Rights: Studies on Natural Rights, Natural Law, and Church Law, 1150–1625*, Eerdmans Publishing Co., Cambridge 1997, p. 276.

72 FERRIS, *supra* note 42, p. 29. See also in this sense J. HÖFFNER, *La ética colonial española del Siglo de Oro*, Ediciones Cultura Hispánica, Madrid 1957, p. 303.

law'.[73] They can be considered as the precursors of a theological and philosophical foundation for contemporary human rights.[74]

5. CONCLUDING REMARKS

As evidenced by the always contradictory evolution of human rights throughout history, prophetic voices such as those of Antonio de Montesinos and Bartolomé de Las Casas are necessary to make oppression and domination visible, and to advance ideas calling for justice and human dignity. Unfortunately, as rightly pointed out by Simonsen, the Indians (as many other sub-altern and marginalised groups in history) did not speak for themselves, they were only 'represented';[75] thus they were viewed as *objects* of protection rather than as *subjects* of rights.[76]

The Laws of Burgos (1512) were a significant attempt to humanise and protect the indigenous inhabitants of the Americas. They had an openly paternalistic nature, and expressed the said protection in terms of obligations of the conquistadores rather than in terms of *rights* of the Indians. Although not formulated as proper rights, some of their provisions protected access to health for the Indians, some introduced labour safeguards or established generous maternity leave for pregnant women working in encomiendas. While one cannot affirm that any gender perspective whatsoever was present in the Laws of Burgos, it can be maintained that women (and children) were considered as objects of specific protection.

At the same time, the Laws of Burgos articulated a sophisticated system of supervision and control of the way in which the encomenderos were applying the constellation of obligations established in the Laws of Burgos, the *visitors*.

But the Laws of Burgos were not adopted in a vacuum. On the contrary, they are the result of a number of competing interests, namely the colonial objectives of both the Spanish Crown and the conquistadores, and the religious aims of the Catholic Church. This is the main explanation of their systematic lack of implementation in the framework of the colonial enterprise. The distance between rhetoric and practice was immense.

The intellectual climate in which these Laws were adopted was characterised by a transition from medieval Scholasticism to a progressive incorporation of

---

73 PÉREZ LUÑO, *supra* note 62, p. 181.

74 CARRILLO SALCEDO, *supra* note 65, p. 54.

75 SIMONSEN, *supra* note 17, p. 9.

76 F. GÓMEZ ISA, 'Pueblos Indígenas: de objeto de protección a sujetos de derechos' in M.C. BARRANCO and C. CHURRUCA (eds.), *Vulnerabilidad y protección de los derechos humanos*, Tirant lo Blanch, Valencia 2014, pp. 167–186.

rational principles into the prevailing theories of Natural Law. The ecclesiastic humanism advocated by the Spanish School of International Law paved the way for the emerging protection of the human dignity of all human beings, including the Indians, and can be considered as one of the first manifestations of the recognition of fundamental (natural) rights in Spanish legal history.

9. LITHUANIA: FROM EQUALITY TO INEQUALITY AND TO EQUALITY AGAIN

Vygantė MILAŠIŪTĖ

1. INTRODUCTION

The Constitution of the Republic of Lithuania of 1992,[1] which is currently in force, explicitly mentions in the preamble its link with the sixteenth century Statutes of Lithuania and the Constitutions of the Republic of Lithuania from the period between World War I and World War II. Lithuanian legal scholars also note the importance of the 1791 Constitution of the Polish-Lithuanian State for the history of the constitutional law of Lithuania.[2] Presently researchers into the history of Lithuanian constitutional law hold that the earliest written sources of Lithuanian constitutional law are ducal privileges from the end of the fourteenth century.[3] Among these privileges, the privilege issued in Vilnius by the Grand Duke Jogaila to Catholic nobility on 20 February 1387 stands out as the earliest constitutional document on fundamental rights.

The privilege of 1387 is important in that it marked Lithuania's transition from the ancient law based on equality, to the Medieval law based on inequality of estates. The resulting hierarchy of society, which resulted in the nobility becoming the segment of society whose rights and liberties were widely protected, was fully developed in the sixteenth century as reflected in the three versions of the Statutes of Lithuania. The next change of revolutionary importance for the law of Lithuania in general and the protection of fundamental rights in particular took place only in 1918 when Lithuanian law entered the modernity marked by respect for the principle of equality.[4] This chapter

---

1. Lietuvos Respublikos Konstitucija. *Valstybės žinios*, 1992, nr. 33–1014. Constitution of the Republic of Lithuania (25.10.1992), translation into English is available electronically at <http://www3.lrs.lt/home/Konstitucija/Constitution.htm> accessed 10.06.2005.
2. A. BUMBLAUSKAS, 'Gegužės 3-iosios Konstitucija ir Lietuva (Pranešimo tezės)' (2006) 1 *Konstitucinė jurisprudencija. Lietuvos Respublikos Konstitucinio Teismo biuletenis* 318.
3. J. MACHOVENKO and L. GRIŠKEVIČ, 'Bendravalstybinės LDK privilegijos kaip Lietuvos konstituciniai aktai' (2014) 93 *Teisė. Vilniaus universitetas* 46.
4. For a description of these two milestones in the development of Lithuanian law see *ibid.*, p. 51.

examines the privilege of 1387, the Statutes of Lithuania, and the Interim Constitution of 1918 in turn.

2. THE 1387 LAND PRIVILEGE TO THE NOBLES

2.1. HISTORICAL CONTEXT AND GENERAL OVERVIEW

Lithuanians in 1387 and Western Lithuanians, or Samogitians, in 1417 were the last in Europe to accept the Roman Catholic faith. A pagan Lithuanian state which was formed in the middle of the thirteenth century suffered from aggression by the Teutonic Order which sought to gain control of the country and then convert the population without granting the new Christians any political or social rights. A potential acceptance of baptism from the Teutonic Order by Jogaila, the Grand Duke of Lithuania, could mean the loss of Samogitia to the Order. Acceptance of the Orthodox version of Christianity via the marriage of Jogaila to a daughter of the Duke of Moscow which was planned for 1383 would have meant vassalage for Lithuania, as the Duke of Moscow demanded that Jogaila should call himself the 'junior brother' of the father-in-law. Therefore baptism and a union with Poland was Lithuania's best choice. In 1386 Jogaila was crowned King of Poland for which he promised to baptise Lithuania, and unite Lithuania and Poland under the Polish crown, while leaving Lithuania with its own rule. Lithuania accepted baptism from Poland and joined Western civilisation. This political union of Poland and Lithuania lasted 400 years.[5]

After being baptised and then crowned at Krakow, Jogaila returned to Lithuania, convened the country's nobles to Vilnius, the capital city, and demanded that they consent to be baptised as proof of their allegiance to him. To help create conditions more conducive to the spread of Catholicism, Jogaila promulgated a number of decrees called privileges. Notably, by his second privilege issued on 20 February 1387 Jogaila expanded the rights of those nobles who had accepted Catholicism.[6] Other important privileges issued by Jogaila in connection with the Christianisation of Lithuania were addressed to the bishop and residents of Vilnius. Thus, Jogaila's privileges initiated the formation of the estate system in Lithuania.[7]

---

5 M. JUČAS, *Krikščionybės kelias į Lietuvą*, Baltos lankos, Vilnius 2000. The summary in English is available electronically at <http://viduramziu.istorija.net/socium/krikscionybe-en.htm> accessed 10.06.2015.

6 Katalikų bažnyčia Lietuvoje, 'History of the Catholic Church in Lithuania. The Baptism of Lithuania (1387–1417)', <http://www.lcn.lt/en/bl/istorija/1/blistorija2.html> accessed 10.06.2015.

7 MACHOVENKO and GRIŠKEVIČ, *supra* note 3, 54. See also A. EIDINTAS et al., *Lietuvos istorija*, Vilniaus universiteto leidykla, Vilnius 2013, pp. 42–43, available in other language versions electronically at <http://www.eu2013.lt/en/History-of-Lithuania-Book> accessed 10.06.2015.

The privileges of the fourteenth century were the first written legal acts in Lithuania. They marked the transition to written law and added certainty to legal relations. Generally privileges confer special rights on one group of people and impose obligations on another group. Two major types of privileges can be discerned in the law of the Grand Duchy of Lithuania: land privileges which applied to the whole territory of the Duchy and provincial privileges which applied to parts of it.[8] Despite having a defined territorial scope, the privileges were nevertheless applied based on the principle of personal application. The addressees of the 1387 privilege to the nobles were those noblemen of the Grand Duchy of Lithuania who had adopted Catholicism. At the time of the adoption of privileges the principle of personal application of the law still prevailed in ethnic Lithuania, the political centre of the Grand Duchy of Lithuania, even though in other parts of the Grand Duchy of Lithuania the law was mainly applied on a territorial basis. Both principles were possible in the Grand Duchy of Lithuania. Written privileges belong to the Western tradition of law.[9] The Lithuanian privileges differ from the Western royal privileges in that in the West those privileges would first be granted to concrete persons and only afterwards expanded to cover the whole social group to which those persons belonged whereas in Lithuania they were from the very outset addressed to the whole social group in question.[10]

Under the 1387 privilege nobles who had adopted Catholicism were granted specific privileges and their legal position was equalised with that of the Polish nobility. The tendency to equalise the position of the nobility in both sectors of dual states can be observed in other dual states of that period, notably Hungary-Croatia.[11] However, even after the adoption of privileges the Lithuanian nobles were not equal with the Polish nobility by position and rights, as the Grand Duke had far more power in Lithuania than the King did in Poland, e.g. the nobles of the Grand Duchy of Lithuania could not elect estate courts, and the privileges did not address this issue. On the whole, the social development of Lithuania followed the Polish pattern, with a delay of about 150–200 years.[12]

The validity of privileges was not limited temporally. Issuance of new privileges did not affect the validity of previous privileges. Thus, the principle *lex posterior derogat legi priori* did not apply. Even though it was not legally necessary, all

---

8 MACHOVENKO and GRIŠKEVIČ, *supra* note 3, p. 55.

9 J. MACHOVENKO, 'Lietuvių ir slavų teisės vaidmuo kuriant Lietuvos Didžiosios Kunigaikštystės teisės sistemą' (2005) 55 *Teisė. Vilniaus universitetas* 70, 76.

10 A. ŠENAVIČIUS, 'Lietuvos teisinės kultūros ištakos' in G. ŠAPOKA (ed.), *Teisės raida: retrospektyva ir perspektyva. Liber Amicorum Mindaugui Maksimaičiui*, Mykolo Romerio universitetas, Vilnius 2013, p. 94.

11 J.W. SEDLAR, *East Central Europe in the Middle Ages, 1000–1500*, University of Washington Press, Seattle 2011, p. 71, available electronically at ProQuest ebrary, accessed 07.03.2015.

12 E. GUDAVIČIUS, 'The Grand Duchy of Lithuania' in *Lietuvos Statutas. The Statute of Lithuania. Statuta Lituaniae*, Teisingumo ministerija, Vilnius 2004, p. 54.

privileges issued by Grand Dukes were confirmed in later privileges, at the request of the rights holders.[13] They were codified in the Statutes adopted in the sixteenth century[14] but stayed valid, were confirmed *inter alia* by the 1791 Constitution of the Polish-Lithuanian state and remained a source of law as long as the statehood of the Grand Duchy of Lithuania existed.[15]

Of the three privileges issued by Jogaila in 1387, the privilege to the Catholic nobility is the only one which could be issued exclusively by the Grand Duke of Lithuania as privileges to a local bishop and to residents of a particular town could be issued by other landholders too.[16] This privilege therefore amounts to a constitutional act.

2.2. FUNDAMENTAL RIGHTS CONTENTS

Of importance for the issue of fundamental rights are those provisions of the 1387 privilege which deal with: 1) property rights of the nobles and exemption of duties to the Grand Duke; 2) the gender aspect, i.e. marriage rights of women and property status of widows; 3) the judicial system.

2.2.1. Property rights and exemption of duties

The privilege stipulated that Catholic noblemen and their heirs were guaranteed the right to dispose of their patrimonial land.[17] The Grand Duke thus renounced his right to interfere with the management of patrimonial property of nobles.[18] Such rights had already been granted to the nobility in Poland[19] and were generally among the rights contained in various charters of rights and liberties adopted in various European countries in the thirteenth and fourteenth century.[20]

---

[13] J. MACHOVENKO, 'Europos ius commune Lietuvos Didžiosios Kunigaikštystės teisinėje sistemoje' in G. ŠVEDAS (ed.), *Europos Sąjungos teisės įtaka Lietuvos teisinei sistemai*, Vilniaus universitetas, Vilnius 2014, pp. 97–98.

[14] J. MACHOVENKO, 'Nacionalinės teisės tradicijos ir paveldo vaidmuo reguliuojant piliečio ir valstybės santykius 1791 m. gegužės 3 d. Konstitucijoje' (2012) 3 *Parlamento studijos* <http://www.parlamentostudijos.lt/Nr13/13_teise_1.htm> accessed 10.06.2015.

[15] MACHOVENKO and GRIŠKEVIČ, *supra* note 3, p. 63.

[16] *Ibid.*, p. 56.

[17] The text of the privilege is quoted from its Lithuanian translation published in R. GELUMBAUSKIENĖ and G. ŠAPOKA, *Lietuvos teisės istorijos chrestomatija*, Justitia, Vilnius 2012, p. 33. Its original in Latin can be found in *Zbiór praw litewskich od roku 1389 do roku 1529 tudzież rozprawy sejmowe o tychże prawach od roku 1544 do roku 1563*, Drukarnia na Garbarach, Poznań 1841, pp. 1–2, available electronically at <https://archive.org/stream/zbirprawlitewsk00sogoog#page/n16/mode/2up> accessed 10.06.2015.

[18] S. VANSEVIČIUS, 'Lietuvos didžiojo kunigaikščio ir ponų tarybos valdžia XV–XVI a.' in V. ANDRIULIS (ed.), *Teisės bruožai Lietuvoje XV–XIX a*, Mintis, Vilnius 1980, p. 29.

[19] As the text of the privilege indicates. See also A. ŠAPOKA, *Lietuva ir Lenkija Jogailos laikais*, Šviesos sp., Kaunas 1935, pp. 34–35.

[20] 'Rights that were to become commonplace in charters of the thirteenth and fourteenth centuries included obliging the organs of the crown to adjudicate per legem, to conserve omnibus

A distinctive non-Western feature of this privilege was that it acknowledged existence of allodial property and did not envisage possession of fiefs by vassals, which was the prevailing form of feudal land tenure in Western and Central Europe in the fourteenth and fifteenth century.[21] Property as envisaged in the privilege of 1387 was allodial property as it was not related to military service or other public duties: nobles performed military service for the benefit of the duke because he was a ruler and the nobles were his subjects, but not in exchange for land.[22]

In addition, the privilege provided that Catholic noblemen were exempted from an obligation to perform any task for the benefit of the Grand Duke with the exception of the obligation to participate in the building or reconstruction of castles, and in military action. As far as an obligation to participate in the military action of persecuting the enemy who is fleeing the country is concerned, the privilege indicated that it was the task of every man who was able to carry a weapon and thus was not limited to nobles.

The privilege is important in that it recognised the nobility as a social group[23] and started defining its rights. The Grand Duke, in adopting this privilege, weakened his own economic and political power.[24] Granting privileges to certain groups led from ancient legal equality to medieval inequality of estates.[25] It should be observed that at the time of the issuance of the 1387 privilege the difference between nobles and other warriors was not very clear: even though military service was the main feature of nobility, alongside the noblemen military service was at those times also performed by persons who were dependent on the nobles, i.e. town residents and peasants. While the privilege of 1387 still recognised that in certain military actions every man who was able to carry a weapon, and not only the nobles, was to participate, there were no such reflections of ancient military democracy in land privileges issued later.[26] The privilege of 1387 thus provided a basis for further strengthening of the estate of the nobility which led to the creation of the 'republic of the nobles' whose

---

iustitium, to not arbitrarily violate the personal integrity of subjects, to not impede the liberty to stay and choose one's residence once certain dispositions had been observed, to not impede certain forms of association, and to guarantee certain aspects of patrimonial right'. See R. BUONAMANO, *Rights and Subjectivity: A Pre-History of Human Rights*, Cambridge Scholars Publishing, Newcastle upon Tyne 2008, available electronically at ProQuest ebrary, accessed 07.03.2015.

21 MACHOVENKO, *supra* note 9, p. 76.

22 J. MACHOVENKO, 'Lietuvos Didžiosios Kunigaikštystės bajorų žemės nuosavybė kaip viešosios teisės institutas' (2011) 78 *Teisė. Vilniaus universitetas* 28, 34.

23 MACHOVENKO and GRIŠKEVIČ, *supra* note 3, p. 55.

24 VANSEVIČIUS, *supra* note 18, p. 29.

25 MACHOVENKO, *supra* note 13, pp. 94–95.

26 J. MACHOVENKO, 'Lietuvos Didžiosios Kunigaikštystės visuomenės luominės struktūros susidarymo teisiniai pagrindai' (2001) 39 *Teisė. Vilniaus universitetas* 53, 59.

constitutional description was provided in the Statutes of Lithuania in the sixteenth century.

2.2.2. Gender aspect

Under the privilege Catholic noblemen were also entitled to freely give their daughters, granddaughters, other female relatives and widows into marriage, in keeping, however, with the Catholic rites. A widow of a Catholic nobleman was entitled to remain in the property of her late husband and use it as long as she did not remarry. Here, rudiments of the property status of widows were provided, which would be elaborated in further privileges and systematised in the Statutes of Lithuania.[27] The right of giving dependent females in marriage without the ruler having any role to play in this was proclaimed,[28] thus paving the way for the understanding of the freedom to choose one's spouse without external interference.

2.2.3. Judicial system

The privilege also introduced in the Grand Duchy of Lithuania the same court system as in Poland. Namely, in a territorial unit there had to be one judge who was to examine complaints and impose punishments (applying customs and laws) and one lawyer who was to execute those decisions. Commentators note that it was impossible at that time to ensure proper reception of the Polish law courts system because the Grand Duchy of Lithuania lacked a developed system of administrative divisions as well as a consolidated estate of the nobles. There were three levels of noblemen in Lithuania differing in their legal status (dukes, lords and nobles) and, moreover, the confessional division between the Catholics and Orthodox noblemen was also an obstacle.[29] The attempt to introduce such a system, however, can be seen as the first attempt in Lithuanian constitutional law to establish elements of fair trial in the modern understanding of this term: cases had to be decided by a designated institution applying existing law and the decisions taken had also to be enforced by a designated institution. It is noteworthy that the 1387 privilege did not limit the judicial powers of the Grand Duke who was the highest judicial authority with regard to his subjects. It was the land privilege of 1447 which gave nobles the right to administer justice with regard to their dependent persons.[30] As we shall see, the idea of an independent institution specifically devised for the task of administering justice was

---

27 J. KUNSMANAITĖ, 'Widows, property, and law in Lithuania' in M. KORPIOLA (ed.), *Regional Variations in Matrimonial Law and Custom in Europe, 1150–1600*, Brill, Leiden 2011, p. 102.

28 R. JUOZAPAITIENĖ, 'Tėvų valia kaip santuokos sudarymo sąlyga' (2011) IX *Res humanitariae. Klaipėdos universitetas* 10, 16.

29 A. JURKEVIČIUS, 'LDK teismų santvarkos apraiškos rašytiniuose teisės dokumentuose 1387–1529 m.' (2014) 1(41) *Jaunųjų mokslininkų darbai. Šiaulių universitetas* 66.

30 S. VANSEVIČIUS, 'Teismas ir jo procesas pagal 1529 metų Lietuvos Statutą' in V. ANDRIULIS (ed.), *Teisės bruožai Lietuvoje XV–XIX a.*, Mintis, Vilnius 1980, p. 60.

significantly strengthened in the sixteenth century with the adoption of the Statutes of Lithuania.

2.3. SIGNIFICANCE AND FURTHER DEVELOPMENTS

Having issued the first privileges the Grand Duke of Lithuania became a constitutional figure who had certain powers and at the same time acknowledged himself as being subject to law. Every new privilege issued by the Grand Duke constitutionally limited his powers to an even greater extent.[31]

For the protection of fundamental rights specifically, the 1387 privilege was important in that being a noble of Catholic faith was a prerequisite for having rights. At the same time it is noteworthy that, whilst being a male was necessary for full enjoyment of rights, women's rights were mentioned in the 1387 privilege for the first time in written Lithuanian law.

The year 1387 is seen by legal historians to mark the transition from the ancient to the medieval legal system in Lithuania as well as the adoption of European *ius commune* and the integration of Lithuanian law into the Western tradition.[32] From a comparative perspective, one of the most successful explanations of Lithuania's belated acquisition of the features of late medieval European civilization is a 'theory of delay'.[33] This theory notes distinctive local circumstances and, while acknowledging the belated start of European civilization in Lithuania, at the same time posits that certain phenomena developed in Lithuania in an accelerated way which led, for example, to the level of development of legislation and codification in Lithuania in the sixteenth century being in quite an advanced state compared to neighbouring countries.[34]

3. THE STATUTES OF LITHUANIA OF 1529, 1566 AND 1588

3.1. HISTORICAL CONTEXT AND GENERAL OVERVIEW

In the personal union between Poland and Lithuania created in 1385, Poland put forward suzerainty claims and Polish politicians sought to introduce in both countries the rules introduced by Žygimantas (Sigismund) the Old, the

---

31 MACHOVENKO, *supra* note 13, p. 97.

32 MACHOVENKO and GRIŠKEVIČ, *supra* note 3, p. 51.

33 R. PETRAUSKAS, 'Vėlyvųjų viduramžių Europa ir Lietuvos Didžiosios Kunigaikštystės visuomenės ir kultūros raida XIV–XVI amžiuje' (2009) 23 *Lietuvos istorijos studijos. Vilniaus universitetas* 69, 70.

34 *Ibid.*, p. 82.

Sigismundina Code. The Lithuanian nobles underlined the necessity of having national law and the codified Statute of Lithuania was adopted in 1529.[35]

Constitutional norms adopted as land privileges were codified and enacted as a single legal Act, the Statute of Lithuania, in 1529.[36] Two subsequent versions of it were adopted in 1566 and 1588. The three versions are commonly known as the First, Second, and Third Statute of Lithuania. Originally enacted in Ruthenian which was the language of the administration of the Grand Duchy of Lithuania, the Statutes, a codification of laws which were in contemporary use,[37] were soon translated into Latin and Polish.[38] The Statute was the law of the nobles, and the rights of their subjects were taken into account inasmuch as they were related to the duties of these subjects to the Grand Duke: if they were exempted from these duties (for the benefit of the nobles), it was indicated in the Statute.

The Statutes were still privileges, as they conferred special rights on some persons and imposed special obligations on others.[39] Like modern constitutions, however, the Statutes set out the system of government and the functions of state institutions. The First Statute consolidated the rule of the Council of the Lords, the Second Statute established the parliamentarian system and the democracy of the nobility whereas the Third Statute for the first time in Europe separated legislative, executive and judicial powers.[40]

The First Statute did not regulate relations between the state and the Church, it did not provide for a notion of an insult to religion or the Church but generally it expressed Christian ideology. The Second Statute proclaimed freedom of religion and the Third Statute established equality of all Christian denominations.[41] Overall, the Statutes were rather secular and religion seemed to be gradually losing its role as a determinant of the scope of rights.

---

35 E. Gudavičius, 'A short survey of the First Statute of Lithuania' in *Lietuvos Statutas. The Statute of Lithuania. Statuta Lituaniae,* Teisingumo ministerija, Vilnius 2004, pp. 36–37.

36 J. Machovenko, 'Nacionalinės teisės tradicijos ir paveldo vaidmuo reguliuojant piliečio ir valstybės santykius 1791 m. gegužės 3 d. Konstitucijoje' (2012) 3 *Parlamento studijos,* <http://www.parlamentostudijos.lt/Nr13/13_teise_1.htm> accessed 10.06.2015.

37 Gudavičius, *supra* note 35, p. 21.

38 V.A. Vaičaitis, 'XVI amžiaus Lietuvos Statutai ir Europos teisės tradicijos' in G. Švedas (ed.), *Europos Sąjungos teisės įtaka Lietuvos teisinei sistemai,* Vilniaus universitetas, Vilnius 2014, pp. 116–118. For a description of the amount of influence these three versions of the Statute had on the life in Lithuania see A. Plateris, 'Codification of the Law in the Grand Duchy of Lithuania' (1965) 11(2-Summer) *Lituanus. Lithuanian Quarterly Journal of Arts and Sciences,* available electronically at <http://www.lituanus.org/1965/65_2_03_Plateris.html> accessed 10.06.2015.

39 Machovenko and Griškevič, *supra* note 3, p. 55.

40 I. Valikonytė, 'Lietuvos Statutas — Lietuvos Didžiosios Kunigaikštystės bajorų konstitucija' (2012) 4(28) *Konstitucinė jurisprudencija. Lietuvos Respublikos Konstitucinio Teismo biuletenis* 276, 278.

41 *Ibid.*

3.2. FUNDAMENTAL RIGHTS CONTENTS

Using the analysis of the 1387 privilege as a starting-point, it can be observed that the Statutes contained, *inter alia,* provisions dealing with the following matters pertaining to fundamental rights: 1) property rights and *status libertatis* of the nobles; 2) the gender aspect, i.e. marriage rights of women, property status of widows, enhanced protection of women; 3) the judicial system.

3.2.1. Property rights and status libertatis

Created 'by the nobles for the nobles', the Statute ensured their rights and liberties. All three versions of the Statute contained a separate chapter devoted to the subject of the liberties of the nobles.[42] At the very outset of this chapter the sovereign pledged to the state and the Council of Lords 'to belittle nothing', i.e. to observe existing rights and privileges of the nobles.[43]

The First Statute of Lithuania linked land property with military service by the nobles. The right to dispose of patrimonial land was limited: nobles could now freely dispose of only one third of such land. The remaining two thirds could be mortgaged to protect the interests of the family or for the purposes of military service. Allodial land property was thus transformed and became close to a fief although not in the full meaning of that term as it was still possible to dispose of one third or mortgage the two thirds of land without the authorisation of the sovereign; the only requirement was to register these transactions. Notably, under the First Statute inequality among the nobles was obvious: the nobles in possession of patrimonial land (the lords) had wider political rights including the right to exercise judicial functions on their land — a power not held by the owners of other types of land.

The Second Statute of Lithuania improved the situation of the nobles who earned their land for services, by eliminating the differences between patrimonial land, land provided for services, and purchased land and removing restrictions on the disposal thereof but preserving the link between land property and the military or other type of service to the sovereign. Exclusive ownership of land inhabited by peasants, along with the right to elect the Grand Duke and exercise jurisdiction with regard to their dependent persons, became the basis of the economic and political power of the nobles. Peasants and town dwellers could no longer purchase the nobles' land and aspire to nobles' rights. With the adoption of the Second Statute of Lithuania a hierarchical society of estates was fully formed.[44]

---

42 VALIKONYTĖ, *supra* note 40.

43 The First Statute of Lithuania, chapter 3, article 1. Translation of the First Statute of Lithuania into English is quoted from *Lietuvos Statutas. The Statute of Lithuania. Statuta Lituaniae*, Teisingumo ministerija, Vilnius 2004.

44 MACHOVENKO, *supra* note 22, pp. 35–39.

The nobility became quite homogenous as the rights of lords and the rights of other nobles were formally equalised although the difference in actual opportunities remained.[45]

Under the influence of the so-called 'Christian law', which referred to Roman law or *ius commune europaeum*, the Third Statute provided nobles with the *status libertatis* which comprised the right to the presumption of innocence, personal inviolability, the treatment of a person as a full subject of law, and equality of arms in court proceedings.[46] The *status libertatis* granted to the nobles also included the right to leave the country (except to go to enemy lands), to dispose of their property, and to be legally represented, primarily in court proceedings. In addition, the *status libertatis* also imposed on the nobles the duty to defend the state.[47]

3.2.2. Gender aspect

Under the First Statute of Lithuania, the duty to defend the state was incumbent not only on male but also on female nobles (widows were specifically mentioned in the text of article 1 of chapter 2). This meant that women were also understood as holders of certain rights. One full chapter of the Statute was devoted to inheritance by women and the giving of girls in marriage. Women's property rights were narrower than men's. The husband was the head of the family; however, a dower defended the property interests of the wife. Girls could get married only with the consent of their guardians; however, they had the right to appeal against those who abused these powers. In this aspect the situation of a woman in Lithuania did not in essence differ from that in countries of Western Europe.[48] The Third Statute of Lithuania more explicitly provided for the free will of a female to choose whom to marry, i.e. a right not to be given in marriage against her will.[49] There is some controversy in historiography regarding the relative importance of the free will of a woman and the requirement of consent of the family as conditions for marriage.[50]

The size of the dower under the Statute could not exceed one third of the amount of the husband's immovable property although there had been no such limit previously. This limitation was, however, related to the general rule applicable to nobles under the First Statute allowing free disposal of one third of the estate.

---

45 VALIKONYTĖ, *supra* note 40, p. 279.

46 V.A. VAIČAITIS, 'Lietuvos Statutai kaip Lietuvos konstitucionalizmo šaltinis' (2013) 89 *Teisė. Vilniaus universitetas* 55, 60–61.

47 VAIČAITIS, *supra* note 38, p. 127.

48 GUDAVIČIUS, *supra* note 35, p. 32.

49 The Third Statute of Lithuania, chapter 3, article 39. The text of the Third Statute of Lithuania is quoted from its Lithuanian translation published in R. GELUMBAUSKIENĖ and G. ŠAPOKA, *Lietuvos teisės istorijos chrestomatija*, Justitia, Vilnius 2012, p. 151.

50 See discussion in JUOZAPAITIENĖ, *supra* note 28, pp. 16–18.

The specificity of Lithuania compared to its neighbour Poland was that in Lithuania contractual provisions played a more important role for widows in the event of remarriage: if a widow with no dower (i.e., to whom default legal provisions applied) decided to remarry, the absence of contractual provisions was to her disadvantage as she would not get any of her husband's property.[51]

The Statutes provided for enhanced protection of women and foresaw compensation for injury or killing of a woman which was double in size compared to that foreseen in the case of injury or killing of a man of the same estate.[52]

3.2.3. Judicial system

Under the First Statute, the Grand Duke was the supreme judge and he was competent to decide certain categories of cases as the first (and only) instance court. The general rule was that cases were to be decided at a local court but decisions could be appealed against either to the Grand Duke or, should he be away in Poland, to the Council of the Lords.[53] The Third Statute clearly showed the intention to transfer judicial powers from the executive and legislative branches to the specially devised judicial power with the Supreme Tribunal at its top.[54]

As mentioned earlier, the Statutes provided for certain fair trial elements. These included the presumption of innocence, the public nature of the court, equality of arms, the right to defence, the right to be legally represented, and so on. The Statutes also expressed the principles of independence, impartiality and impeccable reputation of the court although not yet in the fully modern sense.[55]

Under the influence of the 'Christian law' the Statutes also envisaged renunciation of relics of pagan law such as cruel punishments, torture, slavery, or collective responsibility[56] although some of these practices remained.[57] For example, the First Statute stipulated that a thief apprehended with evidence might be tortured three times in one day to extract admission of his guilt, upon which he had to pay damages. And if this man, knowing sorcery, at the time of torture did not feel the torture, and it was as though he was sleeping, then he had to pay damages to the plaintiff to the extent to which the plaintiff swore.[58]

---

51 KUNSMANAITĖ, *supra* note 27, p. 113.
52 VALIKONYTĖ, *supra* note 40, pp. 278–279.
53 VANSEVIČIUS, *supra* note 30, pp. 61–62.
54 VAIČAITIS, *supra* note 38, p. 129.
55 *Ibid.*, pp. 128–129.
56 *Ibid.*, pp. 120–121.
57 VAIČAITIS, *supra* note 46, 60. See also VANSEVIČIUS, *supra* note 30, p. 69.
58 See the First Statute of Lithuania, chapter 13, article 14.

3.3. SIGNIFICANCE AND FURTHER DEVELOPMENTS

As mentioned previously, the Statutes of Lithuania showed an approach to law and codification which was comparable to the codes of laws of other European states. The Statutes were perceived as an achievement not only by historians but also by the contemporary addressees, i.e. the nobility of Lithuania who found them a useful instrument for the protection of their rights and liberties.

The cult of rights and liberties became the basis of the ideology of the noble society of the Grand Duchy of Lithuania. It was understood that the state protected the liberties of the nobles and it did so by means of the Statute which was seen to be 'the greatest safeguard of universal freedom'. The Statute remained a symbol of political identity and the statehood of the Grand Duchy of Lithuania long after it disappeared from the map of Europe following the partitions of the Polish-Lithuanian state in the eighteenth century. Participants in the 1830 uprising against the Russian Czar seem to have relied on the understanding that a Lithuanian is 'he who believes in freedom and abides by the Statute'. For comparison, the Constitution of the Polish-Lithuanian state of 1791, even though it too provided for the rights of the nobility,[59] does not seem to have left such a deep imprint on the minds of its contemporaries in Lithuania.[60]

The privilege of the nobles to undertake military service, and on that basis to have the least restricted property rights, ensured their full capacity to have rights and duties, much wider than was the case for others.[61] Being a noble was a prerequisite for enjoying rights but the requirement to be of a particular faith was relaxed as the equality of all Christian denominations was recognised. Women still had narrower rights than men but the protection of women's rights was strengthened compared to the 1387 privilege.

Furthermore, certain seeds of equality of rights for everyone, and not only the nobles, can be seen in the Statutes. Notably, the preamble of the First Statute of Lithuania mentioned the desire to grant Christian rights to all subjects regardless of their class or origin. Article 9 of chapter 1 provided for equal requirements for trial: 'We desire to establish that all our subjects, poor and rich alike, whatever their condition or position, be tried equally and identically by these written laws.' Article 12 of chapter 11 of the Third Statute stipulated that rape of a woman or a girl, whether noble or not, was to be punished identically, by death,

---

59 E. Jarašiūnas, 'Apie pirmąsias konstitucijas ir jų reikšmę' (2010) 2(120) *Jurisprudencija. Mykolo Romerio universitetas* 23, 44.

60 Valikonytė, *supra* note 40, p. 283.

61 Gudavičius, *supra* note 35, p. 31.

unless the victim wished to marry the perpetrator. These provisions were very democratic for the hierarchical estate society of those times.[62]

4. THE INTERIM CONSTITUTION OF 1918

4.1. HISTORICAL CONTEXT AND GENERAL OVERVIEW

On 16 February 1918 The Act of Independence of Lithuania was adopted by the Lithuanian Council formed at the time of the German occupation during World War I. The Act provided for the restoration of an independent Lithuania, governed democratically, and established that it was up to the Constituent Seimas (Parliament) democratically elected by all the residents of Lithuania to finally determine the foundation of the Lithuanian State.[63] Germany was strictly opposed to the Lithuanian pursuit of independence. The military defeat of Germany brought about a radical change in the political situation and the Lithuanian Council was allowed to adopt a constitution and form its own government. On 2 November 1918 it adopted the interim constitution named the Fundamental Principles of the Interim Constitution in which the Council *inter alia* committed itself to convene the Constituent Seimas as soon as possible.[64] The adoption of this Act is seen as the start of modern law in Lithuania as the law was based on equality of citizens.[65] More specifically, it is also the legal Act which established women's electoral rights in Lithuania.

4.2. FUNDAMENTAL RIGHTS CONTENTS

The Interim Constitution, a very laconic document, contained a chapter on fundamental rights of citizens.[66] The first provision of this chapter, article 22, proclaimed equality before the law irrespective of sex, ethnicity, religion or estate and specified that there should be no privileges based on estate. This chapter also contained a provision (article 24) to the effect that pre-war legal Acts remained valid only insofar as they did not contradict the Interim Constitution. This provision was included into the chapter on rights because legal Acts of Russia which had been valid in the main part of Lithuania's

---

62 T. BIRMONTIENĖ, 'Moterų teisių raida Lietuvoje: konstitucinis pripažinimas, politinio lygiateisiškumo siekis' (2006) 12(90) *Jurisprudencija. Mykolo Romerio universitetas* 34, 35.

63 See Lietuvos nepriklausomybės aktas (Act of Independence of Lithuania, 16.02.1918) published in M. MAKSIMAITIS, *Lietuvos valstybės konstitucijų istorija*, Justitia, Vilnius 2005, p. 321. The relevant extract translated into English is available electronically at <http://www3.lrs.lt/pls/inter/w5_show?p_r=5691&p_k=2> accessed 10.06.2015.

64 M. MAKSIMAITIS, *Lietuvos valstybės konstitucijų istorija*, Justitia, Vilnius 2005, pp. 382–383.

65 MACHOVENKO and GRIŠKEVIČ, *supra* note 3, p. 51.

66 Lietuvos Valstybės Laikinosios Konstitucijos pamatiniai dėsniai (Fundamental Principles of the Interim Constitution of the State of Lithuania, 02.11.1918) published in M. MAKSIMAITIS, *Lietuvos valstybės konstitucijų istorija*, Justitia, Vilnius 2005, pp. 323–325.

territory before World War I were based on the privileges of estates and not on equality of all citizens.[67] Inviolability of the person, home and property as well as freedom of the press, self-expression, peaceful assembly and association were guaranteed in article 23 on condition that their objectives and measures were not in contradiction with the laws of the State. The possibility of derogation in times of emergency was foreseen in article 25.

The Interim Government had to adopt the Law on the Election to the Constituent Seimas based on the principles of general, equal and direct elections and secret ballot (chapter VI, articles 26–27). The Law on the Election to the Constituent Seimas adopted on 20 November 1919 spelt out these constitutional principles in greater detail and, notably, mentioned women as holders of both active and passive electoral rights. Women actually participated in the elections and seven of them were elected to the Constituent Seimas. Thus, the 1918 Interim Constitution granted legal protection of the electoral rights of women and put into effect the 1905 documents of the Grand Seimas of Vilnius — a meeting of 2000 representatives of Lithuanians, including women, in which the idea of the statehood of Lithuania had been promoted and the principles of the future state, including those of equal elections and other aspects of gender equality, had been declared.[68]

The Interim Constitution was silent on issues such as the right to property, matters of religion, the court system, procedural rights, etc. as these were left to be decided by the Constituent Seimas.

4.3. SIGNIFICANCE AND FURTHER DEVELOPMENTS

Under the interim Constitution which proclaimed equality, the only prerequisite for enjoying rights was that of citizenship. Notably, women's full rights, including electoral rights, were recognised. Adoption of this legal act was one step in the constitutional development of the Republic of Lithuania which gave legal expression to the provisions of the Act of Independence of 16 February 1918 and paved the way for the adoption of a democratic Constitution of 1922 which also guaranteed rights to citizens but not to all human beings as such.[69] Afterwards, Lithuanian constitutional law experienced ups and downs in terms of the protection of fundamental rights until 1940. It then suffered a period when its development was made impossible as the statehood of the Republic of Lithuania

67 MAKSIMAITIS, *supra* note 64, pp. 67–68. Interestingly, reception of Russian laws meant that the link with the Statutes of Lithuania was preserved as norms of Russian empire, especially those pertaining to civil, matrimonial, and family law, had been heavily influenced by the Statute of Lithuania. See M. MAKSIMAITIS, 'Istorinės LDK teisės aidas moderniojoje Lietuvos teisėje' (2012) 19(3) *Jurisprudencija. Mykolo Romerio universitetas* 843, 854–855.

68 BIRMONTIENĖ, *supra* note 62, p. 36.

69 MAKSIMAITIS, *supra* note 64, p. 128.

was denied by the occupying powers. The independence of the Republic of Lithuania was re-established only in 1990. These developments, however, pertain to the still recent history of Lithuania and are therefore outside the scope of this chapter.

5. CONCLUDING REMARKS

The beneficiaries of the 1387 privilege were limited to nobility and, within that, only to Catholics. Women's rights were ensured but to a lesser extent than men's and property rights were regulated. Political rights as rights to participate in the governing of the country were not mentioned. The judicial system was seen as an expression of the sovereign power but nonetheless preconditions for fair trials rights were created.

The Statutes were addressed to the nobles and different versions of the Statutes reflected a tendency towards more equality between the different types of nobles. There were also seeds of equality for all, although in very limited areas. Religion was gradually losing its role as a determinant of the scope of rights. Women's rights were regulated in more detail but the notion of a woman as less than a full holder of rights persisted. Political rights as rights to participate in the governing of the country were becoming more important although property was a precondition for enjoying these rights. The judicial system showed tendencies towards nobles aspiring to expand their jurisdictional powers and to limit those of the sovereign. Meanwhile, fair trial rights were being developed.

The 1918 Interim Constitution proclaimed equality, abolished privileges of estates and declared fundamental rights for all. Religion was not a factor in determining the scope of rights and women were granted equality with men. Political rights as rights to participate in the governing of the country were specifically listed, no longer with property as a precondition. Property rights seemed to be losing some of their importance compared to political rights whilst the judicial system and, consequently, fair trial rights were considered to be of such importance that they could only be determined by the parliament.

Generally, analysis of the above stages in the development of Lithuanian constitutional law shows how written law, starting with the protection of certain rights of a small elite group and via the development of a system for the protection of more numerous rights of a broader category of beneficiaries, became a tool for the protection of fundamental rights of every citizen. Although written law first moved away from ancient equality, it then developed towards modern equality. The currently prevailing concept of fundamental rights for everyone within the jurisdiction of the state was, however, still absent.

10. POLAND: FROM THE GOLDEN LIBERTY OF THE NOBLES TO FUNDAMENTAL RIGHTS

Agata HAUSER
Zdzisław KĘDZIA

1. INTRODUCTION

This chapter presents the development of fundamental rights in Poland. Before discussing specific fundamental rights documents it is necessary to explain that the history of Poland until World War I is customarily divided into four periods, depending on the organisation of the state: the patrimonial state (the tenth to fourteenth century), the estate monarchy (13201454), the republic of nobles (1454–1795) and the partition of Poland (1795–1918).[1]

It is also important to clarify that until the First Republic, Polish society was divided into several social estates (nobility, clergy, townsmen and peasants). In case of each of the estates, both the legal status and applicable laws were different.

2. ESTATE MONARCHY

The first fundamental rights documents applicable to all nobles and in the territory of the whole country were adopted in the fourteenth century. However, some relevant sectorial rulings were already in force before then. For example, economic or legal immunities were granted to individual landowners (lords and the church).[2] The clergy gained significant tax privileges as early as thirteenth century. In 1264, a Kalisz Statute issued in the region of Great Poland granted the Jews legal protection and regulated the main juridical and economic issues

---

1 For details see E. BORKOWSKA-BAGIEŃSKA, 'Historical development of public law in Poland' in W. DAJCZAK, A.J. SZWARC and P. WILIŃSKI, *Handbook of Polish Law*, ParkPrawo, Warszawa–Bielsko-Biała 2011, pp. 25–31.

2 J. BARDACH, B. LEŚNODORSKI and M. PIETRZAK, *Historia ustroju i prawa Polskiego*, LexisNexis, Warszawa 2003, p. 33.

concerning them. It also included some provisions relating to religious freedoms.[3] For example, Jews could not be forced to give back collaterals on the days of their religious holidays. The Statute also forbade accusing Jews of using Christian blood. This provision was especially important because, at the time, many people believed that Jews slaughtered Christian children in order to use their blood for ritual purposes.[4] Kings of the unified Poland later confirmed and updated this privilege, in order to apply it to the whole territory of the country.[5]

The period of estate monarchy was characterised by the growing importance of the nobles. The kings, wanting to secure their support in wars or in issues such as succession, acceded to the demands of this powerful and wealthy estate. The privileges applicable to the nobility in this period concerned four main categories: fiscal obligations and other monetary responsibilities towards the state; military obligations; the right to property and its protection and specific rights related to court procedure.

The first two privileges applicable to the whole country were issued in 1355 in Buda and in 1374 in Koszyce. These acts related to two issues: economic privileges of the nobles and guarantees related to military service by them.

According to the Buda privilege, the king could no longer impose taxes in an arbitrary and excessive fashion. In exchange, the nobility agreed that Louis the Hungarian would succeed Casimir III on the Polish throne. Subsequently, the Koszyce privilege excluded the possibility of imposing new taxes on the nobility without their consent. After 1381 this privilege was also applicable to the clergy.

The introduction of these economic privileges for the nobles had major political implications. In particular, the so-called 'tax freedom of the nobility', introduced by the Koszyce privilege, had a significant influence on the growth of the power of that estate: future kings often had to concede to the will of the nobles on certain political issues in order to gain their support for an introduction of a new tax.[6]

A second group of rights concerned guarantees related to military service by the nobles. It should be explained that in the fourteenth century Poland did not have a standing army. In each instance, the king had to call a *pospolite ruszenie* (*levée en masse*, military mobilisation). According to the Koszyce privilege, the nobles

---

3 This act was inspired by the privilege of 1236 issued by Emperor Frederick II. H. HAUMANN, *A History of East European Jews*, CEUPress, Budapest 2002, p. 4.

4 HAUMANN, *supra* note 3, p. 9.

5 A. BOSIACKI, H. WAJS, M. WĄSOWICZ, R. WITKOWSKI and M. ZNOJEK, *60 Years oft he Universal Declaration of Human Rights: Anniversary Collection, Volume I: The Monuments of Human Rights*, The Office of the Commissioner for Civil Rights Protection, Warszawa 2008, pp. 45–46.

6 BARDACH, LEŚNODORSKI and PIETRZAK, *supra* note 2, p. 91.

were obliged to 'furnish unpaid military service for operations within the frontiers of the Crown'.[7] However, at the same time, the nobility sought assurances related to campaigns conducted abroad. The Buda and Koszyce privileges guaranteed that the king would, firstly, compensate for all damages suffered by the nobility during military expeditions abroad and, secondly, buy out nobles captured or injured during military expeditions abroad. All the privileges related to foreign campaigns were supposed to ensure that Louis the Hungarian, and any future foreign kings, would not lead the troops away from Polish lands, leaving them unprotected.[8]

The Buda and Koszyce privileges also included a general confirmation of all rights previously acquired by the other estates: the clergy, townsmen and peasants. All the succeeding acts dealt only with the rights of the nobility and, more rarely, the clergy.[9] What is more, in general, the new privileges of the nobility and of the clergy restricted rights and freedoms of other estates, in particular, the peasants.

The next important privilege, issued in Czerwińsk in 1422, concerned the right to property of the nobility. The king was prohibited from confiscating nobles' land without a court order. The courts' rulings were to be based on written law in cases regarding members of the nobility. In this way another guarantee against arbitrary decisions and misuse of trials by the king against his political opponents was also put in place.[10]

Privileges of Jedlnia (1430) and Cracow (1433) introduced the rule of '*neminem captivabimus nisi iure victum*', which meant that the nobles could not be imprisoned or punished without a court judgment. This rule, despite its different name, was in fact very similar to the *habeas corpus* principle.

The privilege of Nieszawa (1454) confirmed earlier privileges, in particular that only the courts might order confiscation of property and arrest. According to this Act, the king could not issue new laws or call a *pospolite ruszenie* (military mobilisation) without the consent of the local parliaments, which were composed of nobles.

It should be noted that this act caused significant disadvantage to the other estates, in particular the townsmen and peasants.[11] In the case of townspeople,

---

7 N. DAVIES, *God's Playground. A History of Poland. Volume 1: The Origins to 1975*, Oxford University Press, Oxford 2005, p. 90.
8 D. MAKIŁŁA, *Historia prawa w Polsce*, PWN, Warszawa 2008, p. 71.
9 *Ibid.*, p. 68.
10 *Ibid.*, p. 72.
11 BARDACH, LEŚNODORSKI and PIETRZAK, *supra* note 2, p. 92.

the privilege limited their access to a separate court system.[12] The privilege also restricted the freedom of movement of peasants.[13]

3. REPUBLIC OF NOBLES — THE FIRST REPUBLIC

The Nieszawa privilege marks the beginning of the shift of power from the king towards the nobility of the country, often at the cost of other estates. The unique position of the nobility was further strengthened with the 1505 *Nihil novi nisi commune consensu* (nothing new without the common consent) Act, according to which the king could not issue any law without the consent of the parliament. However, some nobles interpreted 'common consent' as a basis for the principle of unanimity in the parliament. For a long time, this understanding of the 1505 act did not pose any major problems, but from 1652 it led to the acceptance of the *liberum veto* principle, according to which a single deputy could block the adoption of law by the parliament (more about this principle below).[14]

The process of strengthening the powers of the nobles brought further limitations on the rights and freedoms of other estates (excluding the clergy). According to the Piotrków privilege of 1496, townsmen could not own or be given land. However, this privilege was even harsher for peasants. It virtually bound them to the land owned by the nobles: only one peasant a year could leave a village and only one son of each family could change profession and move to a city, provided he was not an only child.[15]

The legal status of peasants further deteriorated in subsequent years. From the beginning of the sixteenth century a peasant who wanted to leave his village had to obtain the permission of his landowner. Similarly, a peasant's daughter needed permission to marry someone from outside her master's lands.[16]

The restrictive rules were applicable not only to the personal affairs of peasants, but also to their socio-economic situation. In particular, the extent of *pańszczyzna* (serfdom) was gradually increased. It should be explained that under feudal laws, peasants had to provide unpaid services to the owner of the land they were cultivating, which meant in the case of Poland, mainly to the nobility and clergy. Two acts adopted in 1520 (Bydgoszcz and Toruń constitutions) provided that peasants were bound to work for the landowner at least one day a week. However, in practice, they worked for three to five days a week.[17]

---

12 *Ibid.*, p. 97.
13 T. MACIEJEWSKI, *Historia ustroju i prawa sądowego Polski*, C.H.Beck, Warszawa 2011, p. 26.
14 BARDACH, LEŚNODORSKI and PIETRZAK, *supra* note 2, p. 223.
15 MAKIŁŁA, *supra* note 8, p. 103.
16 *Ibid.*
17 MACIEJEWSKI, *supra* note 13, p. 47.

From 1519, only the patrimonial courts could adjudicate in cases between peasants and private landowners as the king declined the right of the former to have access to royal courts.[18] This was further confirmed in 1573. However, as J. W. Sedlar notes, 'in practice the lords often referred the more serious cases to these [i.e. royal] courts anyway, in order to let the odium of a heavy punishment fall on the government rather than on themselves'.[19]

Taking into account the legal status of the peasants, the extent of their economic exploitation and the principle of bondage to the land, it is possible to compare their situation to slavery.

Poland was an electoral monarchy from 1370 but parliament customarily elected the eldest son of the previous monarch, always a member of the Jagiellonian dynasty.[20] After the death of the last Jagiellonian in 1572, the king was elected by the noblemen in free elections. Each newly elected king had to sign the *henrican articles* upon his coronation. This document, named after the first king elected in this procedure, Henri de Valois in 1573, listed all fundamental rights of Poland that the king had to accept. It guaranteed all the privileges of the nobility and their political rights. It also included a modern *ius resistendi*, according to which the nobles could disobey the king if he did not comply with the laws and privileges provided for in the *henrican articles*.

Apart from public rights, the *henrican articles* also confirmed the principle of religious tolerance. This principle first appeared in a general legal Act in 1573, when the Warsaw Confederation declared a religious peace between people of different faiths.[21] This Act included non-Catholic religions, however, religious freedom applied only to the nobles.[22] The practical impact of this declaration was limited by the catholic counter-reformation movement which was, though, comparatively moderate in Poland due to the tradition of religious tolerance. Yet, in 1668 a legal Act was adopted, which provided that conversion from Catholicism to other Christian faiths was punishable with exile and confiscation of property.[23] The situation of non-believers was even worse, historic accounts mention instances of burning atheist nobles at the stake.[24]

---

18 A. JEZIERSKI and C. LESZCZYŃSKA, *Historia gospodarcza Polski,* KeyText, Kraków 2003, p. 40.

19 J.W. SEDLER, *East Central Europe in the Middle Ages, 1000–1500,* University of Washington Press, Seattle 2011, p. 320.

20 D. STONE, *The Polish-Lithuanian State, 1386–1795,* University of Washington Press, Seattle 2001, p. 116.

21 BARDACH, LEŚNODORSKI and PIETRZAK, *supra* note 2, p. 209.

22 *Ibid.*, p. 210.

23 MACIEJEWSKI, *supra* note 13, pp. 50–51.

24 For details of the case against Kazimierz Łyszczyński see: M. TETER, *Sinners on trial,* Harvard University Press, Cambridge 2011, pp. 84–87.

The legal status of the nobility in the period of the First Republic included certain political rights and freedoms rather typical for that period of history. They included: *ius resistendi*, *vox libera* (freedom of speech), *ius vetandi* (right to vote), *aequitas* (equality), freedom of association and *liberum veto*.[25]

An especially interesting trait of the Polish nobility was the legal equality within that estate. The Law on Foreign Titles from 1638 clearly proclaimed that all people of the knights' (nobles) estate were equal and it prohibited the use of aristocratic titles.[26] Additionally, the abolition of old honours and titles, as well as creation of new ones, was forbidden by law.[27]

This legal equality is particularly remarkable if one takes into account the extent of nobles' estate in Poland. According to the historians, in the sixteenth century around 10 per cent of the whole population were members of the nobility.[28]

4. THE GREAT DIET AND THE CONSTITUTION OF 3 MAY 1791

The recognition of the aforementioned principle of *liberum veto* had serious constitutional consequences. According to the doctrine, the opposition of any individual noble, being a member of the Sejm (the Diet), to a resolution of parliament not only prevented its adoption, but also led to the dissolution of the Sejm which could be convened again in two years for a regular session. Moreover, all laws passed during the given session were declared null and void.[29]

Liberum veto was primarily conceived as the guarantee of liberty. It might also be interpreted as a tool to encourage members of the parliament to work for consensus; an idea which nowadays is understood as a guiding principle of good governance. However, the practical meaning of this, as of any other, principle may only be precisely assessed while measuring its actual impact. Many commentators say that it influenced the fate of the country in a dramatic way and its consequences lasted for generations. In practice, this instrument did not enable primarily honest, courageous, and determined individuals to oppose attacks against freedom and counter a misguided or corrupted majority, but in the event helped corrupted nobles to prevent the adoption of laws that were incompatible with their or their patrons' particular interests. The neighbouring

---

25 Makiłła, *supra* note 8, pp. 79–83.

26 Bardach, Leśnodorski and pietrzak, *supra* note 2, p. 193.

27 J. Lukowski, *Diorderly Liberty: The Political Culture of the Polish-Lithuanian Commonwealth in the Eighteenth Century*, A&C Black/Bloomsbury Publishing, London, Delhi, New York, Sidney 2010, p. 4.

28 Maciejewski, *supra* note 13, p. 44.

29 J.T. Lukavski, *Liberty's Folly: The Polish-Lithuanian Commonwealth in the Eighteen Century*, Routledge, Abingdon, Oxon 2013, p. 91.

powers quickly recognised this opportunity to expand their spheres of influence. *Liberum veto* was used in the seventeenth and eighteenth centuries 73 times. As a result, parliamentary work continued to be paralysed for decades, which badly affected the treasury and army. *Liberum veto*, supposedly the vehicle for freedom in the country, undermined its ability to survive. Jean-Jacques Rousseau wrote about this principle as it was applied in Poland: 'The liberum veto is not in itself a pernicious right, but when it oversteps its limits it immediately becomes the most dangerous of abuses. Once it was the guarantor of public freedom; now it is only an instrument of oppression.'[30]

In the second half of the eighteenth century some members of the nobility finally began to realise that their 'golden liberty' posed a threat to the future of the whole state. They endeavoured to introduce reforms, but met strong opposition from other members of their estate. In 1768 the parliament adopted the so-called 'cardinal laws'. In this Act, the conservative nobles, supported by Poland's neighbouring states, were able to affirm the existing state organisation and privileges in order to stop the proposed reforms. The Act confirmed, *inter alia*, the free election of the king, the privileges granted to the nobles and the *liberum veto* principle. In 1772, the three neighbouring powers, Prussia, Russia and Austria, carried out the first partial partition of the weak and largely defenceless state. This was the final warning to enlightened circles in society. As a consequence, progressive forces launched a process of constitutional reforms, including the abolishment of *liberum veto*. On 6 October 1788, the Great Diet (Sejm Walny) was convened and allowed to work on the majority principle. After nearly three years of debates, on 3 May 1791, it passed the first constitution in the history of the country, the so-called 'May Constitution', which was the first written Constitution in Europe drafted and adopted in a democratic way.

This step gave rise to strongly divided reactions. Enlightened circles both in Poland and abroad welcomed the May Constitution with a great deal of enthusiasm. One of its great admirers, Edmund Burke, wrote about the constitutional reforms in Poland in language which today might sound somewhat exaggerated:

> But in what manner was this chaos brought into order? The means were as striking to the imagination, as satisfactory to the reason, and soothing to the moral sentiments. So far as it has gone, it is probably the most pure and defecated public good which ever has been conferred on mankind. We have seen anarchy and servitude at once removed; a throne strengthened for the protection of

[30] J.-J. ROUSSEAU, *Considerations on the Government of Poland and on its Proposed Reformation. April 1772 (completed but not published), ch. IV – Specific Causes of Anarchy; retrieved from the Constitution Society* <http://www.constitution.org/jjr/poland.htm> accessed 31.03.2015.

> people without trenching on their liberties.[31] [...] All, from the king to the day-labourer, were improved in their condition. [...] To add to this happy wonder (this unheard of conjunction of wisdom and fortune) not one drop of blood was spilled; no treachery, no outrage, no system of slander more cruel than the sword; no studied insults on religion, morals or manners; no spoil; no confiscation; no citizen beggared; none imprisoned; none exiled; the whole was effected with a policy, a discretion, an unanimity and secrecy, such as have ever been before known on any occasion; but such a wonderful conduct was reserved for this glorious conspiracy in favour of the true and genuine rights and interests of men.[32]

This lengthy quotation is an indicator of the profoundness of the change designed by the May Constitution. The principle of limited Government opened up a new and modern perspective of the relationship between the state power and the people. However, people were not understood as a community of equal individuals. Their position was determined by the legal status of the relevant social estate. The Constitution recognised in article I 'the sacred Roman Catholic faith' as the dominant religion and forbade apostasy but it also guaranteed 'freedom to all rites and religions in the Polish lands'. Rights-holders were primarily members of the nobility. The Constitution reiterated their previous privileges by saying: 'we most solemnly assure to the noble estate all liberties, freedoms, and prerogatives of precedence in private and public life, and more particularly we confirm, assure and recognise as inviolable the rights, statutes and privileges justly and lawfully granted to that estate' by previous kings. It continued 'we desire to preserve and do preserve sacred and intact the rights to personal security, to personal liberty, and to property, landed and movable, even as they have been the tide of all from time immemorial;'. The Constitution also declared the guarantee of personal security and of all property belonging to anyone by virtue of law.

Separately, the May Constitution referred to the distinguished status of citizens of cities which was regulated by the Law on Royal Cities (not belonging to nobles), promulgated slightly prior, on 19 April 1791, and referred to by the Constitution as one of its parts. While reaffirming their recognition as free people, this Law extended several rights to the citizens of independent royal cities, including *inter alia*, the privilege *neminem captivabimus nisi iure victum* (before benefiting only nobles); the right to property; access to city offices, the

[31] *An Appeal from the New to the old Whigs: in consequence of some late discussions in Parliament, relative to the Reflections on the French revolution*, (by E. Burke), III edition, London, 3 September 1791, p. 127.

[32] *An Appeal from the New to the old Whigs*, *supra* note 31, p. 128.

officers' corps of the army and careers in legal chancelleries, and participation in and access to the administration of justice.

Finally, the May Constitution undertook to improve the situation of peasants who continued to be subordinated to their landlords and largely deprived of any rights of their own. In this spirit, referring to justice, humanity, Christian duty, and the self-interest of the state, the Constitution recognised the peasants as the most numerous populace in the nation and hence, the greatest strength of the country, as well as the most copious source of the country's wealth. In the same provision, the Constitution extended the protection of the law and of the national government to this part of the population. This found expression in the principle that liberties, assignments and agreements of peasants agreed by the landowner constituted a mutual obligation protected by law and the government. The Constitution also guaranteed freedom of settlement, movement and economic activity to all persons newly arriving in the country, as well as those returning to the country after having been removed from its territory.

The question arises whether the May Constitution was comparable with other documents of the epoch regarding rights and freedoms. Enacted three months before the 1791 French Constitution but two years later than the French Declaration on the Rights of Man and the Citizen and 15 years after the Virginia Bill of Rights, the May Constitution still reflected a compromise between the *ancient régime* and the ideas of the modern constitutionalism. It did not proclaim a Bill of Rights proper. Nevertheless, its text proves the influence of fundamental rights ideas, sometimes hidden behind the social structure, sometimes captured in specific contexts. R. Ludwikowski rightly stressed that unlike the French and American Bills, the language of the May Constitution was focused on rights of the main social groups rather than on individual rights. '[...] the Polish Constitution did not recognize these rights as "inherent in the human nature". Rather, it referred to "ancestors as first founder of liberties" and particularly to the kings who — on the basis of social agreement with the estates — granted "laws, statutes and privileges".'[33]

5. TIME OF DESPAIR

Regrettably, all efforts to heal the governance of the country, although so roundly praised by contemporary and later commentators and being still today a source of pride to the nation, came too late to revert the course of history. The powerful neighbours, afraid of the prospects of Poland's recovery, completed the

---

33 R.R. Ludwikowski, 'Constitutions and Human Rights' in D.P. Forsythe (ed.), *Encyclopedia of Human Rights*, Oxford University Press, Oxford 2009, p. 407.

partition process of the country which thus ceased to exist as an independent state in the years between 1795 and 1918.

During this period, foreign emperors governed the divided country. The legal entitlements of the Polish population, if any, originated in the will of their rulers. Nevertheless, the nation did not abandon its struggle for independence which on some occasions was also exploited by foreign actors. In 1807 Napoleon, supported in his campaigns by military units composed of Poles, proclaimed the establishment of a Duchy of Warsaw with a constitution that abolished slavery and reaffirmed the equality of citizens but did not contain any bill of rights. After Napoleon's fall, at the Vienna Congress in 1815, the Duchy of Warsaw (with some territorial amendments) was given to the Russian Empire which created a dependent Kingdom of Poland with the Russian Czar as the Polish King. On 15 November 1815 the Czar issued a Constitution for the Kingdom. Its chapter 'General Guarantees' comprised 24 articles related to what we would call today a charter of rights. They proclaimed *inter alia* freedom of religion, extending, however, special protection to the Roman Catholic faith and guaranteeing equal rights of all Christian worshippers. Freedom of the press was declared, subject to limitations established by law with a view to restraining its abuses. Protection of the law was guaranteed without regard to social status. The already mentioned principle *neminem captivabimus* (habeas corpus) covered the entire population. The Constitution established some modern principles of the penal procedure, such as the obligation to inform immediately and in writing the person deprived of liberty of the cause of arrest and the obligation to bring an arrested person within three days, at the latest, before a competent tribunal to have his case examined. Nobody should be punished except in conformity with law and by a decision of the competent magistrate. Expulsion from the country was essentially forbidden. Property was recognised as sacred and inviolable. Expropriation was only admissible for public good and against appropriate compensation. Public affairs were to be conducted in Polish, and public offices were to be filled only by Poles. Foreigners legitimately present in Poland were to be treated according to the national standard.[34] However, these rights largely existed only on paper. In the framework of reprisals after the failed November 1830 uprising of the Polish population, the Constitution was replaced by a statute and the kingdom eventually became a province of the Russian Empire.

6. THE SECOND REPUBLIC — REGAINED SOVEREIGNTY AND DEMOCRACY

The continuing efforts of the nation to restore its nationhood and freedom, including three armed uprisings and tireless diplomatic work, brought results

[34] Art. 11–34 of the 1815 Constitution.

first when the neighbouring powers had been defeated or weakened by the consequences of World War I. The immediately decisive factor was the Fourteen Points Peace Plan by the American President Woodrow Wilson, announced during the end phase of World War I, on 8 January 1918. The Plan specifically called for the restoration of Poland as an independent country, which occurred on 11 November 1918.

Shortly after its rebirth, on 21 March 1921, Poland adopted its new Constitution (called the March Constitution) which was a modern document, establishing a democratic republic on the Westminster model. The Constitution embraced Chapter V entitled 'General Duties and Rights of Citizens'. The title might be somewhat misleading by mentioning duties at the forefront; in fact, Chapter V set out a typical list of civil and political, as well as some economic, social and cultural rights. The exposition of duties had its historical reasons. Poland was facing huge challenges related to social and legal reunification, as well as to defence of its territorial integrity. In other words, the intention of the Constitution's drafters was clear: without questioning liberal values, to emphasise the importance of joint efforts in building an independent and democratic state.

The constitutional bill of rights remained, as far as its content was concerned, very much in line with the comprehensive catalogues of rights of the time. Even from the present perspective, it looks quite modern with perhaps one exception. Namely, the Constitution still spoke primarily of citizens as rights-holders. The fundamental rights standard started to dominate in constitutions of the world some decades later. Only in some cases did the March Constitution go beyond this limitation. Moreover, rather typically for the dominant perception of the rights of aliens at that time, it made their rights dependent on the principle of reciprocity. Nevertheless, article 95 § 1 stated that 'The Republic of Poland guarantees on its territory, to all, without distinction of origin, nationality, language, race, or religion, full protection of life, liberty, and property'.[35] Consequently, guarantees of personal liberty, in particular in the context of criminal proceedings, were applicable to all. The principle of equality before the law was, however, addressed only to citizens.

The Constitution did not specify any groups of rights. Applying current language to their categorisation, under civil and political rights the Constitution spoke *inter alia* about freedom of movement and settlement; the inviolability of the home and confidentiality of correspondence; freedom of conscience and religion; freedom of expression and of the press (prohibition of censorship); freedom of association and unions; and the protection of national, religious, and linguistic minorities. Under economic and social and cultural rights the Constitution

[35] Compare also article 97 of the March Constitution on limitations of liberty.

provided for property rights; the right to choose one's profession or occupation; the protection of labour relations; the right to social security; the right to education; the right to found schools and educational institutions; academic freedom; and the protection of children. The Constitution established the right to have access to court; the right to compensation for damages inflicted by the State or territorial self-government; and the right to petition as procedural and institutional guarantees. On the other hand, citizens had the duty to observe the law; submit to any public burdens, services, and duties; provide military service; demonstrate fidelity to the country; and to bring up children as righteous citizens. The latter duties were evidently rooted in the recent history of the country.

The March Constitution was finally replaced by the Constitution of 23 April 1935 which completed the process of giving the state an authoritarian profile which had started with the coup d'état in May 1926. This basic law, ensuring the supremacy of the executive not only over other state agencies but also over citizens did not contain a bill of rights. Although there were some references to freedom of conscience, expression and association, these were contrasted with the principle that they could not infringe the common good. Moreover, the rights of the citizen to influence public affairs were to be measured by the individual's contribution to the common good.

7. THE IMPACT OF YALTA AND STRUGGLE FOR DEMOCRACY

The Yalta Agreement reached by the Allied Powers in 1945 located Poland after World War II in the Soviet sphere of influence, and this fact pre-defined, by and large, Polish constitutional development until 1989. There was obviously no room for a liberal bill of rights. Although the Constitution of the Polish Peoples' Republic adopted on 22 July 1952 included Chapter 8 'The Fundamental Rights and Duties of Citizens', the meaning of the provisions laid down therein was declaratory only. According to the courts' interpretation, the constitutional provisions were not applicable directly but required implementing legislation. Moreover, the Constitution itself drew political limits on the enjoyment of individual rights.

Nevertheless, after the liberalization of the regime in 1956 following Stalin's death, some mutually supportive factors ongoingly undermined the imposed political order and the monopoly of political power in Poland. In particular, the powerful and independent Catholic Church challenged the authorities with a different concept of social and political relations, as well as with a competing set of values, and discreetly offered shelter to dissident activists. On another front, the private property nature of farm land potentially provided a source of living independent from the state. These factors, together with vigorous cultural circles, and repetitive protests by workers, intellectuals and students created the space for calls for reforms, increased freedom and democracy. The wave of strikes in Polish shipyards in the summer of 1980 finally brought a breakthrough. The demands of striking workers supported by intellectuals were captured in the so called '21 postulates' adopted in Gdansk Shipyard in August 1980. It is to be pointed out that while many of the demands were related to socio-economic deficits, the first four focused, in fact, on fundamental rights, namely: the admission of free trade unions independent from the communist authorities and from enterprises, in accordance with International Labour Organisation Convention No. 87; a guarantee of the right to strike and of the security of strikers; compliance with the constitutional guarantee of freedom of speech, the press and publications, including freedom of independent publishers and the accessibility of the mass media to representatives of all faiths; as well as the release of all political prisoners and the cessation of repression against persons because of their personal beliefs.[36]

The imposition of martial law in the country on 13 December 1981 temporarily suppressed the democratic movement. However, the seeds of freedom and democracy were already planted and helped the society to continue its struggle during the eighties. The authorities on their part were trying to combine repression with some appeasement measures in the form of scattered reforms. In 1980, an Administrative Court was established, competent to consider complaints against administrative decisions affecting individuals. In 1986, the Constitutional Tribunal[37] was put in place, empowered to examine the constitutionality of laws. Finally, one year later the Commissioner for Human Rights (ombudsman) was created and gained great authority in a very short time, somewhat against the expectation that it would be only a fig leaf, set-up by the authorities to demonstrate their good will. The figure of 50 thousands complaints sent to the Commissioner during the first year of her tenure illustrates how much this office was needed.

8. DEMOCRATIC TRANSITION — THE THIRD REPUBLIC

In the light of the described developments, it was not surprising that the Round Table negotiations between the opposition acting under the umbrella of Solidarity and the authorities in 1989, which opened the road to political and economic transformation, focused *inter alia* on fundamental rights and the rule of law. It was notable that the first legislative changes in the follow-up to the Round Table embraced guarantees of freedom of association seen as the guarantee of political pluralism; abolishment of censorship, freedom of movement; and the reform of electoral law. All this happened as soon as April 1989. On 17 October 1992, a constitutional reform of state organs was put in place. The adoption of a new Bill of Rights was postponed until the adoption of a

---

36 A. HAUSER, J. JARACZEWSKI, J. JABŁOŃSKA and Z. KĘDZIA, 'An Introduction to Polish Constitutional law' in W. DAJCZAK, A.J. SZWARC and P. WILIŃSKI (eds.), *Handbook of Polish Law*, ParkPrawo, Warszawa–Bielsko-Biała 2011, p. 113.

37 According to the Polish legal tradition, courts of particular significance are called 'tribunals'.

new Constitution which happened, after a long consultative process, on 2 April 1997. Fundamental rights and freedoms take a prominent place in the present Polish Constitution, in comparison with the previous constitutional Acts of Poland. The Bill of Rights is enshrined in Chapter 2 of the Constitution, although some relevant provisions are also located in its other parts, in particular the first one laying down the principles of the State. Similarly to the Universal Declaration of Human Rights and many contemporary constitutions, human dignity is the underlying concept. By recognising the inherent nature of human dignity as the source of rights and freedoms, the Constitution links the origin of these rights with a supra-state set of values.

In addition to the protection of human dignity, the constitutional catalogue of rights is based on the principles of freedom, equality and non-discrimination. It embraces all categories of rights: civil and political, economic, social and cultural.

9. CONCLUDING REMARKS

This brief snapshot of the history of fundamental rights and freedoms in Poland may be finished with a couple of final remarks from the point of view of natural law and international law.

Firstly, in the Polish Kingdom, the guarantees of rights and freedoms were seen as a commitment of the crown towards different estates of society, primarily nobles. The issuing of privileges by Kings usually followed agreements reached in this respect with the representatives of the parliament before elections. Under these conditions, there was little space for arguments based on the law of nature. It is striking that the idea of rights and freedoms as originating in natural law has been explicitly articulated only in the present Constitution of 1997. The historical developments outlined above would seem to explain this phenomenon.

Secondly, after 1945, international human rights standards played an increasingly important role in the struggle for freedom and democracy in Poland, as well as in Polish academic publications. Reference to international commitments of the State was often a convenient and in some cases an effective tool for confronting the authorities. At the same time, personalism as a socio-philosophical school found support among intellectuals, including those within the Catholic Church, which gave an impetus to place human rights as an obligation of the state also from a moral perspective. In existential terms, the two sets of arguments not only coincided but also supported each other. Finally, in the present Constitution they together provide the foundation for the Bill of Rights. This common function does not, of course, prevent tensions between interpretations based primarily on one or another argument, in particular with regard to rights and freedoms in morally highly sensitive areas.

PART II

11. FRANCE: FOUNDATIONAL IMPORTANCE OF THE DECLARATION OF 1789

Florence BENOIT ROHMER

1. INTRODUCTION

Much has already been said about the Declaration of the Rights of Man and of the Citizen adopted in 1789, a fundamental text in the field of human rights in France. The Declaration has often been considered as a model, in Europe and also in the rest of the world.[1]

The Declaration was adopted during the emergency of the French Revolution of 1789, at the cost of several compromises. It took just a week to draft the document, between 20 and 26 August 1789. It was originally used only as the preamble to the first French constitution, the Constitution of 1791, but it outlived this constitution, and is now part of French positive law. Indeed, the French Constitutional Council stated in a decision of 16 July 1971 that the Declaration of the Rights of Man has constitutional value and therefore must be respected by the French legislature. This means that it has an impact on all French legislation and that any text that violates the Declaration, whether it comes from the administration or the legislature, will be censored by judges.

2. MULTIPLE SOURCES OF PHILOSOPHICAL INSPIRATION

2.1. BACKGROUND

The origin of the Declaration is unclear and has given rise to much debate. The Chinese even believe that the revolutionaries of the time were inspired by the writings of Confucius, thanks to translations made by Jesuits in China, and that Confucius thus influenced the Declaration of the Rights of Man.

In fact, there were many philosophical influences that impacted on the Declaration of the Rights of Man and the Citizen, and they arose from various

---

1 <http://www.conseil-constitutionnel.fr/conseil-constitutionnel/root/bank_mm/anglais/cst2.pdf>

schools of modern political philosophy.[2] Modern natural law played a leading role in the drafting of the Declaration and Judeo-Christianity also had an influence on the humanist thought of the time.

2.2. MODERN NATURAL LAW

The theories of natural law based on the social contract and developed in particular by Hobbes and Locke in the UK and Rousseau in France were a determining source of inspiration for the Declaration of the Rights of Man. The very term 'Declaration' means that all the text does is declare and therefore record the rights inherent to human nature, and pre-existing in nature. However in the French Declaration natural law no longer has divine origin, which it does in the American Declaration.

Indeed, for the Americans of the period, it was God who bestowed mankind with rights that are considered natural, and natural law is 'naturally' in accordance with the will of God. The American Declaration of Independence reflects this divine influence: 'We hold these truths to be self-evident, that all men are created equal, that they are endowed by their Creator with certain unalienable Rights, that among these are Life, Liberty and the pursuit of Happiness. That to secure these rights, Governments are instituted among Men.'

Conversely, for the French revolutionaries, religion was discarded and the cult of Reason prevailed under the influence of the Enlightenment thinkers, who promoted the idea of natural religion. God was therefore no longer the source of natural law, and it fell to mankind to discover the rights, based on nature, which were revealed through the gift of reasoning that mankind possesses. Modern naturalist theories are highly influenced by Enlightenment philosophy and emphasise the importance that must be given to reason and to the individual. God is not the creator of rights; the individual alone is capable of reason, and is therefore the only one able to discover natural law.

These recognised natural rights of man were enshrined in the 1789 Declaration. The document does not claim to create new rights, but simply to state the existence of some of these rights, to 'display' them. These rights are supposed to exist regardless of their recognition by the legislature, as indicated in the text of the Preamble of the Declaration: 'resolved to set forth in a solemn declaration the sacred and inalienable rights of man. Therefore, the National Assembly recognises [not 'grants' –FBR] and declares the following rights ...'.

---

[2] S. RIALS (éd), *La déclaration des droits de l'homme et du citoyen*, Hachette, Paris, 1988; C-A. COLLIARD, *La déclaration des droits de l'homme et du citoyen de 1789*, La documentation française, Paris, 1990; G. CONAC, M. DEBENE and G. TEBOUL (éd), *La Déclaration des droits de l'homme et du citoyen de 1789; histoire, analyse et commentaires*, Economica, Paris 1993.

2.3. JUDEO-CHRISTIANITY

Judeo-Christianity also had a strong influence on the humanist thought of the time, and was another source of inspiration for the Declaration. It is based on the principle of the equal dignity of human beings, equality being the corollary of human dignity. Most articles of the Declaration insist on equality between men precisely because the purpose of the French Revolution was to remove the privileges — the 'private laws' that guaranteed a number of advantages to the French aristocracy and that the people sought to abolish. In most of its articles the Declaration emphasises equality between men. The law must be the same for all, either when it protects, or when it punishes (art. 6), and '[e]ach citizen has the right to ascertain, by himself or through his representatives, the need for a public tax, to consent to it freely, to know the uses to which it is put, and of determining the proportion, basis, collection, and duration' (art. 14).

Judeo-Christianity also creates favourable conditions for the recognition of individual rights enforceable against the state by asserting the principle of separation of temporal and spiritual power. The Caesar, or the emperor, should not interfere in the domain of spiritual power, that is to say the power of God. Judeo Christianity therefore emphasises the idea that the state should not be omnipotent, but that its scope should be restricted solely to temporal affairs. Men can therefore invoke rights enforceable against the state and thus limit its power.

3. THE CONTROVERSIAL IMPACT OF THE AMERICAN DECLARATION OF INDEPENDENCE

The impact of the American Declaration of Independence cannot be denied, even if it was not the only source of inspiration for the French revolutionaries. However, they themselves not only refuted any American influence, but sought to show themselves as being even bolder than the Americans. The French revolutionary Rabaut Saint Etienne thus stated that '[i]f the Assembly decides on a declaration, it should not slavishly follow and restrict itself to the example of the United States'.[3] Since then, French doctrine has consistently highlighted the differences between the French and American Declarations.[4]

---

3 Rabaut Saint-Etienne, Boissy d'Anglas, Discours et opinions de Rabaut-Saint-Etienne suivis de ses deux derniers écrits, H. Servier, 1827, p. 50.

4 We all know about the controversy between Jellinek and Boutmy (beginning of the twentieth century), Jellinek arguing that the Virginia Declaration of the Rights of People had inspired the Declaration of 1789 and Boutmy insisting on the influence of the French philosophical theories of the eighteenth century on the drafting of the Declaration (G. JELLINEK, *La Déclaration des droits de l'homme et du citoyen: contribution à l'étude du droit constitutionnel moderne,* traduit de l'allemand par Georges Fardis, A. Fontemoing, Paris 1902 Access on Gallica. E. BOUTMY, *Etudes politiques,* A. Colin, Paris 1907, Access on Gallica.

The American Declaration of Independence in any event reinforced the idea among the French revolutionaries of drawing up a Declaration of the Rights of Man and of the Citizen. In the registers of grievances of the time, citizens demanded that a Declaration be drawn up. They complained of taxes, censorship, discrimination and arbitrary arrest. It was the significance and number of these grievances that led the French revolutionaries to draft a declaration.

In addition, the first American declarations, in particular the Declaration of Virginia, were known to the French revolutionaries, as they had been translated into French. They undoubtedly served as a reference point for the French Constituent Assembly. Thomas Jefferson, future president of the United States was at that time the US Ambassador in Paris. He was consulted by Lafayette before the latter submitted to the Constituent Assembly a draft declaration, which was in the event not accepted by the Convention responsible for drafting the Declaration.

The American Declaration is however more pragmatic than the Declaration of the Rights of Man. In the United States, the American Declaration responded to the political will of the 13 British colonies that broke free from the yoke of the mother country following the war of independence. The Declaration of Independence is therefore presented as an internationally oriented text. In France, the revolutionaries sought to make the Declaration a text of universal scope, aimed both at remoulding French society and generally defining the founding principles of a new political society in line with the aspirations of the people.[5]

4. THE CONTENTS OF THE DECLARATION OF THE RIGHTS OF MAN AND OF THE CITIZEN

Like the English Bill of Rights, the French Declaration was based on liberalism. The purpose of both texts is to protect freedoms. Therefore both provide effective limits to political power, the former by codifying the rights and freedom that had been bequeathed to the English by their ancestors to be transmitted for posterity, the latter by stating loud and clear the new ideals of the French revolutionaries. The French revolutionaries were profoundly anti-statist; in their view, freedoms were guaranteed only if the state did not intervene. Jellinek points out the 'negative status' of these freedoms, characterised by the abstention of the State in areas of freedom granted to individuals.[6] The State

5 F. BENOÎT-ROHMER, 'Des divergences de conception des droits de l'homme en Europe et en Amérique du Nord' in Y. JEANCLOS (dir.), *La sécurité de l'Europe et les relations transatlantiques au seuil du XXIe siècle*, Bruylant, coll. études stratégiques internationales, Bruxelles 2003; R. LETTERON, 'L'universalité des droits de l'homme: apparences et réalités — L'idéologie des des droits de l'homme en France et aux Etats Unis' (2001) *Annuaire français des relations inernationales*, vol. II, pp. 146–164.

6 JELLINEK, *supra* note 4.

must undertake not to hamper the exercise of freedoms (if the freedoms enjoyed a positive status, the government should commit to intervening in order to guarantee them).

This explains the limited role of the law when considered as the expression of general will. The law can only intervene in borderline cases, and mainly to enforce the rights of others. Anything that is not forbidden by law may not be prevented.

In addition, the sole purpose of society envisaged by the revolutionaries was to preserve the rights and freedoms of individuals. Society is at the service of mankind, to preserve the rights granted it, including freedom, security of ownership and resistance to oppression as reflected in article 2 of the Declaration: 'The goal of any political association is the conservation of the natural and imprescriptible rights of man. These rights are liberty, property, safety and resistance against oppression.'

The Declaration of 1789 does not describe all natural rights, it selects those natural rights that the revolutionaries believed deserved to be guaranteed by society. The Declaration was in fact drawn up in response to the abuses of the Ancien Régime, to denounce king's abuses of his subjects' rights. Furthermore, each of the freedoms enshrined in the Declaration is the result of an abuse of the Ancien Régime. For example, the prohibition of arbitrary arrest and the right to security are proclaimed in the Declaration of Human Rights to fight against the practice of *lettres de cachet* that allowed the king to imprison whomever he wished with no special procedure. Freedom of opinion, freedom of expression and freedom of religion are also recognised, to fight against censorship and to protect Protestant victims from religious persecution. The double enshrinement of property rights responds to the desire to release property, in particular land ownership, from feudal charges and the restrictions on use that affected certain lands. However, it also reflects the influence of the bourgeoisie of the era on the revolution, anxious to protect their property. This is incidentally the only right that is considered 'sacred and inviolable' by article 17 of the Declaration.

The Declaration of the Rights of Man also recognises political freedoms, namely the right to participate in the formation of the law, the equal eligibility of all to all public titles, public posts and places, as well as the equal distribution of taxes.

Finally, the concept of freedom is considered inseparable from the concept of equality, since the revolutionaries' objective was to abolish privileges. This is a *de jure*, not *de facto*, equality, as stated in article 1 of the Declaration: 'Men are born and remain free and equal in rights'. Individuals should have the same rights, but may find themselves in different situations.

We find that the revolutionaries did not seek to grant the right to happiness; unlike the American Declaration of Independence, this does not appear in the Declaration of the Rights of Man. This is indeed a denial, not a simple omission.

The revolutionaries expressly rejected drafts that mentioned such a right. This was the case with the draft Declaration of the Rights of Man presented to the Constituent Assembly by Lafayette that mentioned, among the inalienable and enduring rights, the pursuit of well-being and resistance to oppression, as well as with Mounier's draft, which clearly stated that 'the purpose of any government should be universal happiness'.

5. CRITICISM OF THE DECLARATION OF THE RIGHTS OF MAN AND OF THE CITIZEN

5.1. CRITICISM OF THE REVOLUTIONARIES

The Declaration, from the day after its publication, has been the subject of philosophical criticism, hostile to classical liberalism. The anti-revolutionary current was reflected in the writings of Burke, British author of the eighteenth century and fervent monarchist, keen to protect the interests of the British Crown and monarchies in general. His aim was to prevent the spread of revolutionary ideas in England and to ensure that the possibility for individuals to invoke human rights did not undermine the monarchy, which was synonymous with tyranny in the eyes of the revolutionaries.

In his book written in 1790 entitled 'Reflections on the Revolution in France',[7] Burke demonstrated total hostility to French liberal thinking as it was expressed in the 1789 Declaration. In his view, the revolution of 1789 should be considered as a punishment sent by God to discipline the French for their support of the American colonies in their struggle against British rule.

Burke first contested the overly abstract and highly ideological nature of the rights proclaimed in the French Declaration, and their futility given that they are devoid of practical consequences. He also predicted that the many freedoms granted by the Declaration of the Rights of Man would constitute 'an infinite source of disorder'. In his view it was necessary to state the purposes of those freedoms and provide procedural safeguards alongside them. The 'Parisian philosophers' should have made clear how to reconcile these freedoms with public security, the maintenance of order and the recognised freedoms of others. He also disputed the break that the French Revolution made with the past because, in his mind, societies should take root in the institutions inherited from the past, especially those that ensure the exercise of tangible freedoms.

---

[7] The work's full title is *Reflections on the Revolution in France, And on the Proceedings in Certain Societies in London Relative to that Event. In a Letter Intended to Have Been Sent to a Gentleman in Paris, 1790.*

5.2. THE FEMINISTS OF THE REVOLUTIONARY ERA

The 'Feminists' of the revolutionary era also courageously challenged the sexist character of the 1789 Declaration. Olympe de Gouges was quite bold in drafting, in 1791, a Declaration of the Rights of Woman and the Female Citizen, modelled on the 1789 Declaration.[8] She dedicated it to Queen Marie Antoinette and dared to write: 'Woman is born free and remains equal to men in terms of rights'.[9] In it she calls for civil and political equality between both sexes and demands that women be given back the natural rights that had been taken away from them due to the 'perpetual tyranny that man subjects her to'; 'these boundaries must be reformed by the laws of nature and reason' (article 4).

It was not just a counter-project aiming to replace the word 'man' with the word 'woman'. For de Gouges, it was obvious that the nation was formed by both sexes together (art. 3). In most of the articles of her Declaration, Olympe de Gouges replaced 'man' with 'woman and man', so as to make clear the harmony between the two sexes. Article 7 states more firmly that there are no special rights for women: 'No woman is exempt; she shall be accused, arrested, and detained in the cases determined by the Law'. The most famous section of the Declaration is the one in which she demands the right to expression for women: 'Women have the right to mount the scaffold, they must also have the right to step up to the speaker's rostrum'.

It is hardly surprising that the draft Declaration was rejected by the Convention. This project had been completely ignored politically until recently. Olympe de Gouges was in fact guillotined in November 1793 for defending equality between women and men, and proposing in one of her brochures that the people, by referendum, should choose the form of the political system that best suited France. Thus her attempt to demand equal civil and political rights between the sexes ended in failure and fell into oblivion for two centuries. Now no longer neglected, Olympe de Gouges' Declaration is a stirring plea in favour of feminist demands.[10]

---

8 <https://chnm.gmu.edu/revolution/d/293/>

9 Article 1 is the equivalent of article 1 of the Declaration of the Rights of Man and of the Citizen: 'Men are born and remain free and equal in rights'.

10 J-L. DEBRÉ and V. BOCHENEK, *Ces femmes qui ont réveillé la France*, Arthème Fayard, Paris 2013; S. MOUSSET, *Olympe de Gouges et les droits de la femme*, Le Félin, Paris 2003; A. ROSA, *Citoyennes. Les femmes et la Révolution française*, Messidor, Paris 1988; J.B. LANDES, *Women and the Public Sphere in the Age of the French Revolution*, Cornell University Press, Ithaka 1988; S.E. MELZER and L.W. RABINE, *Rebel Daughters and the French Revolution*, University of California Humanities Research Institute Series, Oxford University Press, Oxford 1992.

5.3. MARXIST CRITICISMS

Marxists have criticised the profound liberalism of the Declaration, as well as its bourgeois nature.[11] Marx believed that the Declaration separated the human rights granted to a person relating to private life — such as religious freedom, the right to property — from the rights of the citizen, granted because of membership of a political community, for example the right to vote. This dissociation between human rights and citizens' rights is not acceptable in the Marxists' view, because it ends up isolating and opposing individuals against one another in society. For Marx, human rights are simply 'selfish rights', the rights 'of man separated from man and the community', which allow individuals to oppose to each other and make man an isolated being. Other persons appear as the main obstacle to the achievement of freedoms. Society seeks only to guarantee each member the preservation of his own person, to serve the individualistic interests of individuals. In this context, society appears as a framework that will limit the exercise of these fundamental rights. This selfish notion, according to Marxists, is characteristic of the bourgeois state which results in a rupture of the social bond, and a rupture between man and society.

The second criticism levelled by Marx lies in the 'formal' nature of the freedoms recognised by the 1789 Declaration. Marx believes that these freedoms are abstract formulas, thus empty of all substance. They are illusory and are not surrounded by sufficient conditions and guarantees to ensure that the majority of men can authentically benefit from them. The inequality of social and economic conditions means that some of the rights can benefit only the property-owning class. For example the right to property is a hypocritical right that is granted to the proletarian, even though ownership of property is refused to him due to his lack of financial resources. For Marx, it is not enough to confer rights on individuals, it is necessary to put people in a position to actually exercise those rights.

[11] K. MARX, 'On the Jewish Question' in *K. Marx/F. Engels, Collected Works*, vol.3, London 1975, pp. 146–174.

6. ADDITIONS TO THE DECLARATION OF THE RIGHTS OF MAN AND OF THE CITIZEN

6.1. THE ECONOMIC AND SOCIAL RIGHTS GUARANTEED BY THE PREAMBLE TO THE CONSTITUTION OF 1946

The Declaration of the Rights of Man was complemented by the Preamble to the 1946 Constitution that founded the fourth French Republic. The Preamble added what were thought of as necessary economic and social rights to the list of civil and political rights of the Declaration of Rights of Man and of the Citizen. France had just come out of a bloody war, in which fundamental rights were violated en masse. It was necessary to prevent another war breaking out in Europe.[12]

Thus, the preamble to the 1946 constitution referred to the rights and freedoms recognised by the Declaration of Rights of 1789 and the fundamental principles recognised by the laws of the Republic before setting out a series of political economic and social principles that were 'particularly necessary in our time'. These principles focused mainly on workers' rights and social rights, but they also concerned international law. Equality between men and women in all areas was finally enshrined, as well as the duty to work and the right to obtain employment, the right to trade union action, the right to strike, the right to participation and the collective determination of working conditions as well as the management of businesses, nationalisation of national public services and *de facto* monopolies. It was also stated that the nation guaranteed the right to health protection, material security, rest and leisure, especially for the child, the mother and old workers, the right to obtain a decent means of living from the community, and equal access of the child and adult to education, vocational training and culture. The right to asylum in the territory of the Republic for any person persecuted because of their actions in favour of freedom was also enshrined. It should also be noted that the French Republic complies with international law and establishes the principle of the consent of France to the limitations of sovereignty necessary for organisation and the defence of peace.[13]

Under the fifth French Republic, the Constitutional Council in 1971 conferred a constitutional value upon the preamble of the 1946 Constitution and the Declaration of the Rights of Man,[14] which today obliges both the legislature and the executive power to respect these two texts, or else face sanctions. Thus for

---

[12] Y. POIRMEUR, 'La réception du préambule de la constitution de 1946 par la doctrine. La construction de la juridicité du préambule par ses premiers commentateurs' in G. KOUBI (dir.), *Le préambule de la constitution de 1946. Antinomies juridiques et contradictions politiques*, PUF, Paris 1996.

[13] G. KOUBI (dir.), *Le préambule de la constitution de 1946. Antinomies juridiques et contradictions politiques*, PUF, Paris 1996.

[14] Decision 71–44 DC of 16 July 1971 of the French Constitutional Council.

example, a law that violates the Preamble to the Constitution of 1946 or the Declaration of the Rights of Man may be declared non-compliant with the Constitution and so be repealed on the basis of constitutional priority.[15]

It is also worth noting that the French Constitutional Council subsequently expanded the list of fundamental rights in France, based on the phrase 'fundamental principles recognised by the laws of the Republic' mentioned in the Preamble to the 1946 Constitution. While these principles were not specifically stated by the drafters of the 1946 Constitution, the Constitutional Council used the phrase as a basis to define in its case law a number of constitutional principles drawn from the great liberal laws adopted by Parliament under the third French Republic. These include among others freedom of association, freedom of education and freedom of conscience.

6.2. THE CHARTER FOR THE ENVIRONMENT

Following a revision of the French Constitution of 1958, and at the request of President Chirac, the Charter for the Environment was incorporated into the French Constitution in 2005. Indeed, since the adoption of Constitutional Law No. 2005–205 of 1 March 2005 on the Charter for the Environment, the first paragraph of the Preamble to the Constitution now reads: 'The French people solemnly proclaim their attachment to the Rights of Man and the principles of national sovereignty as defined by the Declaration of 1789, confirmed and complemented by the Preamble to the Constitution of 1946, and to the rights and duties as defined in the Charter for the Environment of 2004.'

It therefore adds to the civil and political rights of the Declaration (first-generation rights) and the economic and social rights of the Preamble of 1946 (second-generation rights), rights borrowed from the third generation of rights that were already enshrined in French legislation or international texts. The Charter of Fundamental Rights is original in that it guarantees not only rights but also obligations relating to the protection of the environment.[16]

The Charter enshrines a new individual right, that of the right of each person to live in a balanced environment that respects their health (article 1). It recognises the duty of each person, private or public, to participate in the conservation of the environment. This concept of duty has been criticised by some writers who consider that the citizen should only benefit from individual rights, and that a citizen's sole duty should be to respect the rights of others.

---

15 *Les grandes décisions du Conseil constitutionnel* de Patrick Gaïa, Richard Ghevontian, Ferdinand mélin-Soucramanien, Eric Oliva, André Roux, Dalloz-Sirey, Collection Grands arrêts.

16 <http://www.conseil-constitutionnel.fr/conseil-constitutionnel/english/constitution/charter-for-the-environment.103658.html>.

The Charter enshrines three principles: the polluter-pays principle of environmental responsibility, which means that the polluter must repair the damage caused to the environment; the principle of prevention of environmental damage and the precautionary principle. Regarding the latter principle, the utmost care was taken when drafting to avoid abuses of interpretation that could hamper technological progress. The wording of article 5 of the Charter differs from the traditional phrasing of this principle as found in the Rio Summit Declaration. Article 5 of the Charter states that '[w]hen the occurrence of any damage, albeit unpredictable in the current state of scientific knowledge, may seriously and irreversibly harm the environment, public authorities shall, with due respect for the principle of precaution and the areas within their jurisdiction, ensure the implementation of procedures for risk assessment and the adoption of temporary measures commensurate with the risk involved in order to preclude the occurrence of such damage.'

Referring to the law on genetically modified organisms of 2008, the Constitutional Council ruled in its decision No. 2008–564 DC of 19 June 2008, that the provisions of article 5 'like all the rights and duties defined in the Charter of the Environment, have constitutional value' and 'that they are binding on public authorities and administrative authorities in their respective areas of responsibility'. Since that decision, the Council has on several occasions had to respond to complaints stemming from lack of knowledge of the Charter, in terms of ex ante and ex post checks, and clarifying that all provisions of the Charter have constitutional value.

7. CONCLUDING REMARKS

The Declaration of the Rights of Man adopted in 1789 is the French founding text for the protection of fundamental rights. Its significance is not just ideological and symbolic; it is a catalogue of the founding rights of French republican values which combine liberal ideals with democratic principles.

This explains why the Constitution of the French fifth Republic (the current constitution) does not include a list of fundamental rights as other constitutions do but simply refers in its Preamble to the Declaration of 1789 and to the texts which complement it. The Preamble states that '[t]he French people solemnly proclaim their attachment to the Rights of Man and the principles of national sovereignty as defined by the Declaration of 1789, confirmed and complemented by the Preamble to the Constitution of 1946, and to the rights and duties as defined in the Charter for the Environment of 2004'.

The French Constitutional Council played a decisive role in recognising in 1971 the binding nature of the Preamble of the fifth Republic Constitution. Since then, the principles set forth in the Declaration, complemented by economic and social rights in 1946 and in 2004 by rights related to environmental protection, have constitutional value and serve as the reference standard for constitutional review of fundamental rights. Many laws and regulations have been annulled because they did not comply with those principles as interpreted by the Constitutional Council or by the domestic courts.

The French Declaration is a reference text not only in France but also in the rest of the world. It has been drafted with universal scope and addresses fundamental rights in general and not just the rights of French citizens. It has influenced many declarations in Europe and has had a major impact on the development of liberty and democracy in Europe and worldwide.

12. SWEDEN: FREE PRESS AS A FIRST FUNDAMENTAL RIGHT

Anna-Sara LIND

1. INTRODUCTION

In 2016, the 250th anniversary of the Freedom of the Press Act (FPA) will be celebrated in Sweden.[1] This Act is one of the four constitutional laws that together form the Swedish constitution.[2] Although not unchanged, having evolved with developments in society, several of the main principles in the original Freedom of the Press Act have survived to the present day. In this chapter, I intend to identify these core principles and show how important the Act has been for the development of modern Sweden both as a fundament of the society and also as a tool to enable individuals and the media to contribute to public debate.

Even though it is fundamental to Swedes' understanding of society and a strong constitutional symbol, the Freedom of the Press Act is today facing new challenges as the constitutional landscape changes nationally and internationally. New forms of fundamental rights as granted through the European Convention for the Protection of Human Rights and Fundamental Freedoms as well as the direct applicability of binding (constitutional) European Union law put the Freedom of the Press Act to new tests. These new phenomena are also discussed, or at least touched upon, in this chapter.

---

1 The father of the original Freedom of the Press Act was Anders Chydenius, from Karleby, in the part of Sweden that later on became Finland. He was a student at both the Royal Academy in Åbo (Turku) and Uppsala University and studied, amongst other things, economics and science.

2 As is expressed in the Swedish Instrument of Government (hereafter IoG) Chapter 1, Article 3: The Instrument of Government, the Freedom of the Press Act, the Fundamental Law on Freedom of Expression and the Act of Succession are the four fundamental acts in Sweden. See also J. NERGELIUS, *Svensk statsrätt*, 3rd ed., Studentlitteratur, Lund 2014, pp. 133–134.

2. THE FREEDOM OF THE PRESS ACT — THEN AND NOW

The history of written constitutions in Sweden can be traced back to the oaths of the medieval kings.[3] As early as the fourteenth century, the oath of the King was an expression of his willingness to serve the people, to treat people alike and to respect the law. For hundreds of years, this promise to the people served as a firm bond between the King and his people. As time passed and Sweden became one country with one King, the King's power started to become a matter of family ties as the Crown was inherited from father to son. Nevertheless, the oath continued to play a role as the custom was that every new King swore an oath to the people.[4] Accordingly, the bond between the King and his people continued to be a true political reality for centuries.

This tradition was, however, promptly put aside when King Karl XII inherited the crown at only 15 years of age in 1697. At the time, Sweden was a huge country, with a territory embracing great parts of Northern Europe and the Baltic Sea. The young King chose to put the oath aside; he crowned himself (literally!) and said that his powers came directly from God. The bond to the people was redefined or even broken, even more so as the King almost never stayed on Swedish soil being much occupied in going to war in foreign countries.[5] After King Karl XII had passed away, an era of political vagueness and uncertainty emerged in Sweden. During this period many of the most important legal reforms in Swedish history took place. An initial form of parliamentarianism was born and the period is often called the 'Freedom Era' or the 'Age of Liberty' even though no freedoms or rights were given to the citizens. The name indicates the liberty in the political system, leading up to a system with two political parties in a proto-parliamentary system and, at the same time, the increasing numbers of rights that were given to political and societal groups in Sweden: the

---

3 This oath is linked to the Charter of Alsnö proclaimed by King Magnus Ladulås at the house Alsnö, in, probably, 1280. Some researchers have stated that this Charter was the first document expressing 'worldly nobility' ('ett världsligt frälse') in Sweden. More recently it has been concluded that the Charter is the codification of an already existing system and not something new. See O. BRING, *De mänskliga rättigheternas väg*, Atlantis, Stockholm 2011. See also J. HIRSCHFELDT, 'Den återerövrade tryckfriheten' in M. BRUNDIN and M. ISBERG (eds.), *Maktbalans och kontrollmakt: 1809 års händelser, idéer och författningsverk i ett tvåhundraårigt perspektiv*, Sveriges riksdag, Stockholm 2009, pp. 373–414. H-G. AXBERGER, 'Justitieombudsmannen, tryckfriheten och maktdelningen' in M. BRUNDIN and M. ISBERG (eds.), *Maktbalans och kontrollmakt: 1809 års händelser, idéer och författningsverk i ett tvåhundraårigt perspektiv*, Sveriges riksdag, Stockholm 2009, pp. 415–450.

4 Needless to say, Sweden as a nation was a reality as Gustave I of the house Wasa managed to control the territory. The first king of Sweden marked, heavily, a distance against the Catholic Church as he decided that Sweden should become a protestant country adhering to the Lutheran beliefs. This meant that the Swedish State Church was born, closely linked to and loyal with the King/State ever since even though the Church was separated from the State in 2000. See P. PETTERSSON, 'State and Religion in Sweden: Ambiguity Between Disestablishment and Religious Control' (2011) 24 *Nordic Journal of Religion and Society* 119–135, 121.

5 AXBERGER, *supra* note 3.

nobility, the clergy, the bourgeoisie and the land-owning farmers (peasants).[6] The General Code of 1734 (to some extent still in force) was enacted as was the Freedom of the Press Act, in 1766, including the very important principle of access to public documents.

The Freedom Era was, however, efficiently closed down by the King Gustave III. He managed to rescind the Freedom of the Press Act for some years, but it remained in the minds of his political opponents and as soon as they had the opportunity the important Freedom of the Press Act was back, in force, in 1792. Since then, it has been a living document that is referred to, applied and seen as the core of the Swedish constitution.

3. COMMUNICATING RIGHTS FOR INDIVIDUALS OR A MERE STEERING DOCUMENT?

3.1. A MULTI-CONSTITUTIONAL PROTECTION OF THE FREEDOM OF EXPRESSION

The literal meaning of the Freedom of the Press Act in Swedish is 'Printing freedom ordinance',[7] and it might not necessarily be easy to assume that the main function of this constitutional act is to grant individuals fundamental rights. Fundamental rights have, however, never played a major role in Swedish constitutional history. The liberal enlightenment that in other countries paved the way for Bills of Rights and Declarations, did not reach the Swedish constitution. Against this background, freedom of the press and the right to access public documents nonetheless remained from the eighteenth century up until the 1970s the only constitutionally protected rights. Since the present Instrument of Government (IoG) was created at a very late stage and a specific chapter on fundamental rights was only introduced a couple of years later, in 1978, it must be understood that considerable parts of present constitutional law have been created through 'the back door'. By this I mean that the Instrument of Government was written in order to match already existing laws that imposed limitations on rights. In the previous Instrument of Government, from 1809, freedom of the press with direct reference to the Freedom of the Press Act was stated in article 16 IoG.

The prohibition of censorship was established in the Freedom of the Press Act from the outset. This principle has from early on changed and in some ways steered society. Many people in Sweden could already read in the eighteenth century, unlike in some other countries, and they were also, notably, allowed to

---

6 On the political liberties, see M. Roberts, *The Age of Liberty: Sweden 1719–1772*, Cambridge University Press, Cambridge 1986.

7 Tryckfrihetsförordningen (1949:105).

read. To this should be added that the judiciary was, with some reluctance, for many years one of the instruments that the King used to steer the country. This gradually started to change. The Freedom of the Press Act was and still is an expression and symbol of freedom. But it has always been an important way to steer society and at the same time an important tool to *control* how the exercise of public power is carried out. Today, the fundamental right to access public documents is guaranteed in Chapter 2 FPA. In this chapter it is also stated that the only possible way to limit this right and make an exception to the Freedom of the Press Act is when explicitly provided for in the Transparency and Secrecy Act.[8]

The constitutional protection of the freedom of expression is today granted through three fundamental acts: the Instrument of Government, the Freedom of the Press Act and the Fundamental Law on Freedom of Expression. Freedom of expression gives everyone the right to express him or herself in different ways. The IoG is generally applicable to forms of expression which do not fall within the scope of the Freedom of the Press Act or the Fundamental Law on Freedom of Expression. The Freedom of the Press Act is applicable to 'all written material produced using a printer press' (Chapter 1, article 5) or when such material is duplicated according to the criteria put forth in the Act. Not surprisingly, an urgent need for a new version of the Act arising from the use of other forms of media led to the enactment of the Fundamental Law on Freedom of Expression in 1991.[9] This Act mirrors the Freedom of the Press Act but is applicable to radio and TV programmes and to internet based programmes when certain conditions are met.[10]

The protection granted through the Freedom of the Press Act and the Fundamental Law on Freedom of Expression is much stronger than the general protection granted in the Instrument of Government (Chapter 2 article 1). It follows from the IoG that freedom of expression can be limited by law in accordance with the rules in Chapter 2 articles 20–24. These limitation clauses are not applicable when a matter falls within the scope of the Freedom of the Press Act or the Fundamental Law on Freedom of Expression since these two specific fundamental acts prevail over the Instrument of Government (Chapter 2 article 1 paras. 2 and 3 IoG; Chapter 1 article 3 FPA). The only way to make an exception from these two fundamental freedom of expression Acts is in accordance with the rules in the Freedom of the Press Act. This means that these two acts are *exclusive* in character.

---

8 Offentlighets- och sekretesslag (2009:400).

9 Yttrandefrihetsgrundlagen (1991:1469).

10 In this chapter, I will focus on the Freedom of the Press Act (FPA) as the Fundamental Law on Freedom of Expression (FLFE) mirrors the FPA. The FLFE contains almost the same rules as the FPA and refers to the FPA regularly.

As has been shown above, the Freedom of the Press Act and the Fundamental Law on Freedom of Expression are unique as fundamental laws if we compare the Swedish Constitution to the constitutions of other countries. This is so because they only regulate matters relating to freedom of the press and freedom of expression, and also because the rules they contain are very unusual from a comparative perspective as they contain materially very detailed rules of criminal and procedural law. These constitutional rules are to be applied directly to concrete and actual cases as if they were rules of lower hierarchical value, i.e. laws or ordinances.

The Freedom of the Press Act aims at strengthening free and public debate in society. In order for this to happen, it is applicable to 'all written material produced using a printing press' (Chapter 1, article 5) or when such material is duplicated according to the criteria put forth in the Act and when it has been published (article 6). It is important to know if and when the person in charge of the message clearly chooses to take responsibility for its expression and therefore merits the stronger constitutional protection the Freedom of the Press Act entails. But exceptions to this stronger protection are also provided in Chapter 1 articles 9 and 10. The Act is accordingly, for example, not applicable to expressions that are commercial advertising[11] or to child pornography.[12] These expressions are instead governed by ordinary laws. This does not, however, mean that these expressions lack constitutional protection. They do fall, of course, within the scope of the Instrument of Government, Chapter 2 article 1.

3.2. THE CORE PRINCIPLES OF THE FREEDOM OF THE PRESS ACT

To the fundamental features of the Freedom of the Press Act, such as exclusivity and superiority, should also be added the core principles supplementing the complex structure of free press protection.

The *prohibition of censorship* dates back to the original Act of the eighteenth century. It is today expressed in Chapter 1 article 2 FPA and is fundamental for the protection of freedom of expression. The idea behind this prohibition is that the expression should always be printed and made public before action against it

11 The tensions between free speech (as in freedom of expression), commercial speech and gender impact have been discussed by Eva Maria Svensson in several articles. E-M. SVENSSON and M. SVENSSON EDSTRÖM, 'Freedom of Expression vs. Gender Equality: Conflicting Values when Regulating Gender Stereotypes in Advertising' (2014) 127 *Tidsskrift for Rettsvitenskap* 479–511; E-M. SVENSSON, 'Nordic Regulation of Gender Discriminatory Advertisements' in M. EDSTRÖM and R. MØLSTER (eds.), *Making Change: Nordic Examples of Working Towards Gender Equality in the Media*, Nordicom, Göteborg 2014, pp. 99–105; E-M. SVENSSON, 'Traditionskonform tolkning: Om tolkning av förhållandet mellan könsdiskriminerande reklam och grundlagsskyddade yttranden' in J. FEJØ, U. NERGAARD, C.D. TVARNØ and G. SKOVGAARD ØLYKKE (eds.), *Festskrift Liber Amicarum et Amicorum in Honour of Ruth Nielsen*, DJØF, København 2013, pp. 323–342.

12 See Government Bill, prop. 1997/98:43 pp. 67–69 and 151.

can be taken. It is absolute and includes all measures in the public sphere that could prevent or hinder an expression being made public. This also means that it is not allowed to forbid a particular form of technology, a radio device for example, in order to hinder the reception of certain information. Together with the idea that *no one should be hindered to have or use printing devices*, as was established in the Freedom of the Press Act of 1812, there is a solid base for a truly free freedom of expression.[13] This right is, naturally, easier for a company or corporation to exercise, even though it is not limited to legal persons.

The prohibition of censorship is also enforced through a strong *right to be anonymous* when using *the right to communicate information* and messages to the press (Chapter 3). The right to communicate the information is, of course, as strong if one wants to do so openly. Crucially, in no case should one fear being prosecuted or being liable. In order for this to work, the public sector has no right to investigate who could have sent the message or given the information. This is an important part of public administrative law; no one working in the public sphere has the right to investigate outside the rules of the Freedom of the Press Act. Also, no one can use the fact that a person has or might have exercised their constitutionally provided rights against him or her. An employer at a national agency is accordingly forbidden to threaten employees about the passing of information to the press, and even the slightest suggestion of questioning would be considered to be a threat. This prohibition of 'punishment' is still an important part of public administrative law.[14]

The Freedom of the Press Act also contains *special procedural rules* that apply if a case falls within the scope of the Act (Chapter 9). These rules differ considerably from the normal proceedings in Swedish courts. First of all, the Chancellor of Justice is the only person who can decide that a case should be investigated and the only person who has the right to prosecute as stated in the rules in the FPA. Secondly, if the Chancellor of Justice decides to prosecute, a jury is involved in the proceedings (Chapter 12).

We also find *special rules of criminal law* enumerated in the Freedom of the Press Act. These rules are very detailed and state all the offences that are considered to be breaches of the Freedom of the Press Act. According to these rules, the responsibility for committing a crime cannot be shared between several persons nor can one person pass on responsibility to anyone else. Liability is to be decided according to a special 'chain of command' which provides that only

---

13 See Chapter 4 FPA. H-G. AXBERGER, *Yttrandefrihetsgrundlagarna*, Norstedts Juridik, Stockholm 2012, pp. 80–81.

14 See, for example, the decisions taken by the Parliamentary Ombudsmen (JO). In the last year book, the Parliamentary Ombudsmen indicate that 374 complaints could be related to freedom of expression. See also T. BULL, 'Offentligt anställdas yttrandefrihet och repressalieförbudets räckvidd' in J. EKROTH and K. SWANSTRÖM (eds.), *JO: lagarnas väktare*, Riksdagens ombudsmän – JO i samarbete med Riksbankens jubileumsfond, Stockholm 2009, pp. 51–70.

one person can be responsible (Chapter 8). The one who is responsible according to the rules is presumed to have knowledge about the content of the printed material. According to the principle of 'double criminalization', the offence set out in the Freedom of the Press Act should also be part of the ordinary criminal code. The idea behind this is that it should be more complicated to enact new limitations to freedom of expression than to remove hindrances to it. As the Swedish constitution requires constitutional rules to be approved by two parliaments, the procedure of creating new limitations is indeed quite complicated.

When applying the criminal and procedural rules, the judge, jury or Chancellor of Justice need to respect the so-called 'instruction' stated in Chapter 1 article 3:

> Any person entrusted with passing judgment on abuses of the freedom of the press or otherwise overseeing compliance with this Act should bear constantly in mind in this connection that the freedom of the press is fundamental to a free society, direct his or her attention always more to illegality of subject matter and thought than to illegality of expression, to the aim rather than the manner of presentation, and, in case of doubt, acquit rather than convict.[15]

To conclude, the system as a whole aims at protecting the system that strives to secure public debate. The idea behind all this is, accordingly, not primarily to guarantee individuals' rights but rather to secure a system for maintaining a certain (high) level of freedom of expression.[16] Indeed this system, with all its special proceedings and material rules regulated in detail, is constructed so as to hinder the individual in gaining justice in an efficient way. A free debate exposed to as few hindrances as possible is still the supreme goal of the constitutional construction.

3.3. DEMOCRACY OR A 'MERE STEERING DOCUMENT'? THE FREEDOM OF THE PRESS ACT IN PRACTICE — A NATIONAL PERSPECTIVE

The 'people' is described as the sovereign in the Instrument of Government and the will of the people is the common theme of the Constitution. In Chapter 1 Section 1 IoG it is also written that '[a]ll public power proceeds from the people' and that Swedish democracy is based upon the free formation of opinion. The

15 H-G. Axberger, 'JK och yttrandefriheten' in U. Göranson (ed.), *Justitiekanslern 300 år*, Iustus förlag, Uppsala 2013, pp. 125–152. See also T. Bull, 'Justitiekanslern och granskningssamhället' in U. Göranson (ed.), *Justitiekanslern 300 år*, Iustus förlag, Uppsala 2013, pp. 153–160.

16 T. Bull, 'EU-medlemskapet och våra grundlagar' (2011) *Svensk juristtidning* 375–381.

expression 'free formation of opinion' is a core component and includes the Freedom of the Press Act, the Fundamental Law on Freedom of Expression and the freedom of expression rights stated in the Instrument of Government.

The person who contributes to public communication is crucial to the systematic functioning of the Freedom of the Press Act as its aim first and foremost is to guarantee free opinion and debate and an open society. The special protection guaranteed through the Freedom of the Press Act and the Fundamental Law on Freedom of Expression is constructed around established forms of media. Publishers (of journals and books), journalists and media corporations have in fact a stronger constitutional protection than individual persons whose messages do not reach the established media. This means that the protection for individuals not falling within the scope of the FPA (for example consumers) is weaker (only containing the dimension of the Instrument of Government) which in turn means that they are more easily subjected to sanctions for prohibited communications. This unequal system does not match the protection that individuals are guaranteed in the European Convention on Human Rights or under European Union law.

The Governmental Committee on the Freedom of Expression acknowledged the above-mentioned issue of media corporations in the autumn of 2010.[17] In its report the Committee suggested three new alternative models for a new fundamental Freedom of Expression Act, instead of the two present ones. One of these models aimed at strengthening and underpinning the importance of media corporations and explicitly recognised their importance for freedom of expression.[18] This was also stressed in the Committee's final report; however no major changes to the two present fundamental acts were suggested.[19]

4. ENCOUNTERING INTERNATIONAL LAW: THE FREEDOM OF THE PRESS ACT IN A PLURALISTIC LEGAL ENVIRONMENT

Sweden became a member of the European Union in 1995 and ever since, the Freedom of the Press Act has created strong constitutional tensions between EU law on the one hand and Swedish law, on the other hand. These tensions can be traced in the explicit wording of the Instrument of Government where it is expressed that the Riksdag (Parliament) in cooperating with the EU may transfer decision-making authority which does not affect the basic principles by which

---

17 Statens offentliga utredningar (Sweden's Official Investigations), hereafter SOU, SOU 2010:68 Ny yttrandefrihetsgrundlag? Yttrandefrihetskommittén presenterar tre modeller.

18 SOU 2012:55 En översyn av tryck- och yttrandefriheten.

19 H-G. AXBERGER, 'Constitutional Responsibility for the Free Flow of Information and Ideas in the Internet Age' in A-S. LIND, J. RECIHEL and I. ÖSTERDAHL (eds.), *Information and Law in Transition: Freedom of Speech, the Internet, Privacy and Democracy in the 21st Century*, Liber förlag, Stockholm 2015.

Sweden is governed (Chapter 10, article 6). Sweden is a dualistic country, which means that public international law needs to be implemented into the Swedish legal system in order to become directly applicable.[20] Since Sweden is dualistic, it is understandable that it was a major constitutional experience to discover that in practice EU law prevails over national (even constitutional) law and realise the impact of this direct effect.

As the Instrument of Government is worded, it follows that the constitutional position of the Riksdag, the right to access public documents and the fundamental principles of the Freedom of the Press Act form the basic principles by which Sweden is governed. This was also clearly stated during the negotiations that preceded Swedish membership. Sweden made a clear and explicit Declaration on Open Government that was attached to the Treaty of Accession in which Sweden welcomed greater openness and transparency in the European Union. Sweden also declared that public access to official records as well as the constitutional protection afforded to those who give information to the media are fundamental principles which form part of Sweden's constitutional, political and cultural heritage.[21] The Committee on the Constitution of the Swedish Parliament also made a statement on the importance of openness to the Swedish system of government. The Committee underlined that public access to official documents as well as the freedom to give information to the media form an integral part of the basic principles of Sweden's constitutional system, together with other provisions stated in the Freedom of the Press Act and the Fundamental Law on Freedom of Expression. The Committee underlined that law-making powers which would substantially modify these constitutional principles could not be transferred to the EU.[22]

An evaluation of how the rules on delegation of powers expressed in Chapter 10 IoG have been applied is a task given to the Committee on the Constitution of the Riksdag. The evaluation has been continuously carried out when Sweden has been asked to ratify new treaties in the EU. Up until the present day, the conclusion has been that the Instrument of Government has been respected.[23] But the delegation must also respect the protection of fundamental rights as expressed by the Swedish Constitution and the European Convention on Human Rights. Until now, this has been seen as an issue solely for the legislator and the

[20] I. Cameron and T. Bull, 'Legislative review from human rights compatibility: A view from Sweden' in M. Hunt, H. Hooper and P. Yowell (eds.), *Parliaments and human rights: Redressing the democratic deficit*, Hart, Oxford 2014, pp. 279–295.

[21] See I. Österdahl, 'Transparency versus Secrecy in an International Context: a Swedish Dilemma' in A-S. Lind, J. Recihel and I. Österdahl (eds.), *Information and Law in Transition: Freedom of Speech, the Internet, Privacy and Democracy in the 21st Century*, Liber förlag, Stockholm 2015.

[22] Government Bill, prop. 1994/95:112 pp. 17–18.

[23] See Government Bill, prop. 2007/08:168 s 67 and the Opinion of the Legislative Council of 28 June 2005.

general opinion has been that courts should not rule in this matter. However, in the last revision of the Instrument of Government it was stated in the *travaux préparatoires* that this should change.[24] A new possibility to consider these deeply fundamental matters in court was discovered and this has underlined the importance of the protection of the Freedom of the Press Act and the European Convention on Human Rights.

Open government, transparency and the right of access to documents was important to Sweden when joining the EU.[25] And when Sweden was to become a member of the EU amendments to the Swedish Secrecy Act were suggested in order to strengthen transparency and openness even more in the encounter with the new international legal environment that the EU was considered to be.[26]

In the *travaux préparatoires* relating to the negotiations it was stated that Sweden focused on the question of what effect EU membership would have on the right of access to documents set out in Chapter 2 FPA. Also the far-reaching right to give information to the media had been one of the questions attracting the highest degree of attention in the general debate. This has not decreased; the debate is still vigorous today if it is suggested that these two fundamentals should be limited. As we shall see, however, the present debate has revealed new matters to discuss.

5. CONCLUDING REMARKS

The Freedom of the Press Act does not appear to be waning in importance. When approaching the 250th anniversary of the Act, it is clear that the fascination for trying to find new ways to make the constitution functional in modern society continues. Even though parliamentary committees during the last decades have been reluctant to make any major changes, the practical problems surrounding our Freedom of the Press Act are increasing in number. These challenges are due to technical development, the globalization of national law and the fact that the Freedom of the Press Act is a fundamental act enumerating a lot of very detailed rules.

There is, as we have seen in this chapter, a certain reluctance to change this fundamental act in a more thorough way than just taking care of details. The last major review ended up in a no-change situation where the parliamentary

[24] SOU 2008:125, p. 500.

[25] See the *travaux préparatoires*: SOU 1993:14, Departementsserien (Departmental report series) Ds 1993:36; Government Bill, prop. 1993/94:114. See also Government Bill, prop. 1994/95:112 p. 17.

[26] These constitutional tensions are thoroughly analysed by Inger Österdahl in her research programme on free speech, right to information and access to public documents. See ÖSTERDAHL, *supra* note 21.

committee refused to suggest any changes to the parliament even though their initial task had been to try finding new and modern approaches to the growing threat of EU law.[27] Yet another committee has now been appointed, the Committee on the fundamental media act.[28]

The problems that this new committee will investigate are linked to the deep constitutional tradition of the Freedom of the Press Act but seem at the same time to be rather superficial. There are several examples. Emerging new technologies taken together with the fundamental principles of the Act create new practical situations. The rules on how to decide periods of limitation for liability according to the Freedom of the Press Act and the Fundamental Law on Freedom of Expression cause problems for a new editor-in-charge who automatically becomes liable for the work of his or her predecessor when an article is published on an internet page of a newspaper. The rules on periods of limitation are much more generous when the newspaper is printed as the period of six months starts to be counted from the moment the article was published. But for the internet version of the newspaper, time starts to run when the article is removed. This is a strange outcome of new technologies connecting to an old way of regulating and considering freedom of expression and the press. It also means that the fundamental idea of one person being solely responsible and liable does not always function as it was intended.

Another very important question is how the fundamental right to access public documents should interact with new technologies and the demands that are formulated in European law. In 2014, an internet service called Lexbase was launched. The responsible editor had achieved a certificate of no legal impediment to publication and was accordingly within the scope of the Freedom of the Press Act protection. As the Freedom of the Press Act is superior to ordinary law, this led to a situation where the Personal Data Act could be put aside. Lexbase's business idea was to gather judgments from courts in Sweden. Judgments and court rulings are public documents in Sweden. The selling philosophy behind Lexbase was to indicate on a map on an internet site where the persons convicted were living and when clicking on the map one could order the judgments that could be linked to the place or the persons living at a certain place. It is questionable whether such an internet service is an expression of editorial activity that the protection put forth in the Freedom of the Press Act is intended to protect.

The Committee needs to strive for new solutions in the detailed text of the Freedom of the Press Act, but also for new ways to reconcile the balance between freedom of expression and protection of the personal integrity of

---

[27] See SOU 2012:55.

[28] Dir. 2014:97. Mediegrundlagskommittén was appointed in 2014. The Committee should present their conclusions in September 2016.

individuals.[29] The discussion regarding the linkage between automatic fundamental protection and the traditional media is bound to continue as the internet and social media are today the site of a vast amount of public debate and accordingly could be a bigger part of the special constitutional rules on freedom of expression. Maybe the era of special status for established media companies is approaching an end in Sweden as the Freedom of the Press Act is moving beyond a quarter of a millennium.

[29] Interestingly enough, the Committee has not been given the task of proposing a new crime on integrity that could be added to the lists in the FPA and the FLFE.

13. THE NETHERLANDS: THE BATAVIAN STAATSREGELING AS THE FIRST FUNDAMENTAL RIGHTS DOCUMENT

Louis BERKVENS

1. INTRODUCTION

This article gives a short overview of the evolution of fundamental rights from medieval 'liberties', through the developments in the Dutch Republic in the early modern period, until the first modern constitution, i.e. the Batavian Constitution of 1 May 1798.

In the Netherlands the first fundamental rights documents were issued by dukes and counts in the territories, which nowadays form part of the kingdoms of Belgium and the Netherlands, in the form of privileges for the individual towns in their realms. The late thirteenth and early fourteenth centuries heralded the beginning of a fundamental rights movement on the aggregate level of counties and duchies, at first in Flanders and Brabant, where nobility and cities combined their efforts to maintain their rights against arbitrary rule by their lords.

These first fundamental rights documents on the local and provincial level are very similar to the Magna Carta of 1215 in England, as the example of the Charter of Kortenberg shows. The main goal of the Charter of Kortenberg (1312) is the protection of the privileges and liberties of the nobility and towns of the Duchy of Brabant. Against the background of infractions against 'the law of the land', Duke John II of Brabant solemnly promised to maintain the country 'by law and judgement' ('*te wette ende te vonnisse*') (article 2), thus guaranteeing the people of Brabant judgment according to their laws and liberties. A permanent commission of four knights and ten representatives of the towns of Leuven, Brussels, Antwerp, 's-Hertogenbosch, Tienen and Zoutleeuw, the so-called 'Council of Kortenberg', was created to oversee the execution of the Charter (article 4). In the event of non-compliance with the orders of the Council, the courts of law were allowed to stop administering law and the nobility and towns were given the right to deny service to the duke, until he amended his ways (article 7, article 10).[1]

According to Coopmans there is a strong connection between the medieval principle of '*te wette en te vonnisse*' and the prevention of arbitrary behaviour by the government. The subjection of government to the rule of law and rules of due process forms the nucleus of modern fundamental rights. These principles protect subjects from arbitrary arrest by the government and arbitrary sentencing.[2] From these principles followed the exclusive competency of the urban aldermen courts over the 'burghers' of their towns, protection against unlawful arrest in criminal cases, protection against torture and ordeals and the obligation of judges to strictly apply material criminal law.[3]

Although the formulation of the principle of 'te wette en te vonnisse' is not gender specific, it stands to reason that is applied to men and woman equally.

The legality principle and the temporary disobedience clause or *ius resistendi* of the Charter of Kortenberg became the basic elements of the 'Joyeuse Entree' of the medieval dukes of Brabant and the lords of the Burgundian and Habsburg Netherlands afterwards, until the Dutch Revolution of the sixteenth century.[4] The Joyeuse Entree was a constitutional document in which the fundamental principles governing the exercise of political authority were laid down, as negotiated between the successive dukes and the Estates of Brabant since 1356, before their inauguration. *Inter alia* the Joyeuse Entree stipulated the principles of indivisibility and inalienability of the land, the rule of law, the principle of due process and the disobedience clause.[5] In the fifteenth century new articles were added, granting the Estates of Brabant freedom of expression and immunity from '*wangunste*' or 'disfavour' by the Duke in relation to their expressed opinions.[6]

---

1 J.M. LOOVENS, *Practycke stiel ende maniere van procederen in Haere Majesteyts Souvereynen Raede van Brabant*, Philippus Josephus Lemmens, Brussel 1745, vol. I, pp. 26–31.

2 J.P.A. COOPMANS, 'Te wet en te vonnis. Enkele beschouwingen over de rechtsgebondenheid in de middeleeuwse strafrechtsbedeling' in H. VAN DEN BRINK e.a. (eds.) *Samenwinninge. Tien opstellen over rechtsgeschiedenis geschreven ter gelegenheid van het tienjarig bestaan van het interuniversitair instituut Nederlands Centrum voor Rechtshistorische Documentatie*, W.E.J. Tjeenk Willink, Zwolle 1977, pp. 163–177.

3 *Ibid.*, pp. 172–173.

4 And in the Southern Netherlands until its abolition by Joseph II in 1789. R.C. VAN CAENEGEM, *An Historical Introduction to Western Constitutional Law*, Cambridge University Press 1995, p. 81.

5 E.g., Joyeuse Entree of Duke Wenceslaus and Duchess Joanna of Brabant 1356 (LOOVENS, *supra* note 1, p. 47); recognition of the Charter of Kortenberg by duke Wenceslaus 1372 (LOOVENS, *supra* note 1, p. 71); Joyeuse Entree of duke Anthonie 1406 (LOOVENS, *supra* note 1, p. 83).

6 Joyeuse Entree of Duke Philip I 1427, article 43 'liberteyt van opinien' (LOOVENS, *supra* note 1, p. 93); Joyeuse Entree of Duke Philip of Burgundy 1430, article 56 'sonder enige indignatie oft wangunste' (LOOVENS, *supra* note 1, p. 101).

In the sixteenth century the Joyeuse Entree of the German Emperor Charles V as Duke of Brabant (1514) consisted of 66 articles and 17 additional articles, dedicated to protection against arbitrary government, safeguarding the rule of law, the principle of due process, freedom of expression in the meetings of the Estates of Brabant and immunity from disfavour for opinions expressed in those meetings. It still also contained the same disobedience clause as the Charter of Kortenberg of 1312.[7]

Under the government of Charles V the Low Countries were subjected to a process of political unification, being successfully welded into a single, increasingly integrated state.[8] In the period 1516–1543 he acquired the territories of Utrecht, Overijssel, Drenthe, Frisia and Guelders in the northern part of the Low Countries, which were integrated into the Habsburg Netherlands. At the same time as creating a modern centralised administrative organisation, Charles V encountered immense difficulties caused by the rise of Protestantism in the Netherlands, against which he gradually mobilised a formidable system of repression, creating the Dutch Inquisition under the inquisitor-general Frans van der Hulst in 1522 and executing many Protestants in 1526–1527. By targeting the intellectual elite, especially clergy, booksellers, schoolmasters and officials and making it impossible for such men to adhere openly to the Reformation without sacrificing their posts, possessions and lives, Charles V created an atmosphere of repression, which under his son Philip II (1556–1598) culminated in the Dutch Revolt (1568–1648).[9] In this revolt the tradition of the protection of privileges and liberties of the Estates, and the protection of religious liberty as a new element, came to play an important role.

2. THE UNION OF UTRECHT AS FUNDAMENTAL LAW OF THE DUTCH REPUBLIC (1579–1795)

During the Dutch Revolution the Northern Netherlands formed the Union of Utrecht, an association against their lord Philip II of Spain. The two main goals of this Union were military resistance against Philip II and protection of the liberties and rights of the separate members of the Union.[10] According to the

---

7 A. ANSELMO, *Codex Belgicus seu ius edictale a principibus belgarum sanctitum*, Petrus Bellerus, Antwerp 1662 (Reprint 114, Algemeen Rijksarchief en Rijksarchief in de provinciën, Brussels 1998), vol. II, pp. 84–99.

8 J.I. ISRAEL, *The Dutch Republic. Its Rise, Greatness, and Fall 1477–1806*, Oxford University Press, Oxford 1995, p. 129.

9 *Ibid.*, pp. 82–83.

10 A.T. VAN DEURSEN, 'Tussen eenheid en zelfstandigheid. De toepassing van de Unie als fundamentele wet' in S. GROENVELD and H.L.P. LEEUWENBERG (eds.), *De Unie van Utrecht. Wording en werking van een verbond en een verbondsacte*, Martinus Nijhoff, Den Haag 1979, pp. 136–154.

Dutch historian Van Deursen the Union of Utrecht was the expression of the unity of the sovereign provinces of the Northern Netherlands. The main obligation that followed from the Union was the collective duty to maintain the privileges and liberties of the separate provinces as signatories of the Union. The signatories of the Union of Utrecht solemnly promised 'to maintain' 'the particular privileges, liberties, exemptions, rights, statutes and commendable customs', of 'each and every province, town, member and inhabitant in particular' (article I). Because of religious repression, they added the provision, in article XIII, 'that everybody is free in in his religious beliefs, and that nobody can be investigated or prosecuted because of his religion'. This article formed the basis of Dutch religious tolerance in the seventeenth and eighteenth centuries. Although it granted freedom of conscience, it did not mean freedom of religion in the modern sense, because Reformed Protestantism became the official religion of the Dutch Republic: Roman Catholics, Jews and religious dissenters were only 'tolerated'.[11]

At first the Northern Provinces stayed within the limits of the medieval *ius resistendi* in order to protect their rights and liberties, but in the so called '*Plakkaat van Verlatinghe / Placard of Abandonment*', issued by the Estates-General of the seven provinces in 1581, they went a step further, by declaring Philip II a tyrant and deposing him as their overlord, thus setting the example for the American Declaration of Independence of 1776.[12] This far reaching declaration was later on defended by the '*stadhouder*' or lieutenant governor William of Orange in his famous Apology of 1580, in which he formulated six fundamental restrictions to sovereign power, derived from the Joyeuse Entree of Brabant — still regarded as the principal province of the Netherlands — as an example of Dutch constitutional rights and liberties. These restrictions concerned the safeguarding of personal liberty by the legality principle; the cooperation between the sovereign and the Estates-General or provincial estates in creating laws; no taxation without consent of the Estates; no standing armed forces in peacetime; no monetary changes without the consent of the Estates, and the binding of the sovereign and his officers to the principles of due process.[13]

Although the Dutch Revolution was motivated by the protection of constitutional rights and liberties, in practice there was much debate about 'True Freedom' in

---

11 O.J. DE JONG, 'Unie en religie', in S. GROENVELD and H.L.P. LEEUWENBERG (eds.), *De Unie van Utrecht. Wording en werking van een verbond en een verbondsacte*, Martinus Nijhoff, Den Haag 1979, pp. 155–183.

12 M.E.H.N. MOUT, *Plakkaat van Verlatinge 1581*, Staatsuitgeverij, Den Haag 1979; for the similarities between both documents, see: J.P.A. COOPMANS, 'Het Plakkaat van Verlatinge (1581) en de Declaration of Independence (1776)' in (1983) 98 *Bijdragen en Mededelingen betreffende de Geschiedenis der Nederlanden* 540–567; J.P.A. COOPMANS, *Verzet en opstand als factoren in de vorming van het constitutiebegrip*, Kluwer, Deventer 1990.

13 COOPMANS (1983), *supra* note 12, 549; for the text of the Apology see: *Apologie van Willem van Oranje. Hertaling en evaluatie na vierhonderd jaar. 1580-1980*, Lannoo, Tielt 1980.

the Dutch Republic during the seventeenth and eighteenth centuries. Although the Dutch printing press theoretically was restricted by oft-repeated ordinances of the Estates-General, or the Estates of the separate provinces, there was actually near complete freedom of the press.[14] Thanks to a wealth of printed material, the Dutch were laying the foundation of a public sphere that contributed in the late eighteenth century to the emergence of the Radical Enlightenment. The passion for political debate illustrates one of the striking features of Dutch politics since the early seventeenth century, in a period of constant reinvention of the newly formed state as it arose to become a leading Republic in Europe.[15]

The political debate on 'True Freedom' in the Dutch Republic was dominated by the question of the stadholderate and its role in the Union. Since its separation from Spain the political structure of the Netherlands was comprised of the Estates of the Provinces as bearers of sovereignty, and the Estates-General and *stadhouders* from the House of Orange governing the external relations and the common defence of the Republic. At the beginning of the seventeenth century a political debate arose about political supremacy in the Republic: to whom belonged supremacy, to the sovereign provinces or to the Union? In this debate the wealthy (republican) 'regents' of the Dutch province of Holland, represented by Johan van Oldenbarneveldt and Hugo de Groot in 1617, and by Johan and Cornelis de Wit in 1672, defended the thesis that the provinces were the bearers of political supremacy and the defenders of 'True Liberty'; the Estates-General and the *stadhouder* defended the opposite (Orangistic) position. During the seventeenth and eighteenth centuries both views were alternately dominant until in 1747 William IV of Orange, who had already acquired the stadholderate of Friesland (1711), Groningen (1718), Drenthe and Gelderland (1722), was also appointed as hereditary *stadhouder* of Holland, Zeeland, Utrecht and Overijssel and Captain-general of the Union, thereby assuming nearly monarchical power in the Dutch Republic. During his administration the republican regents, were removed from office in favour of Orangists.[16]

Under his successor William V the political debate on 'True Liberty' took new form, because of the disastrous Anglo-Dutch war of 1780–1784, resulting in 'a

---

14 H.A. ENNO VAN GELDER, *Getemperde vrijheid. Een verhandeling over de verhouding van kerk en Staat in de Republiek der Verenigde Nederlanden en de vrijheid van meningsuiting in zake godsdienst, drukpers en onderwijs gedurende de 17e eeuw*, Wolters-Noordhoff, Groningen 1972, pp. 150–190.

15 C. SECRETAN, '"True Freedom" and the Dutch Tradition of Republicanism' in (2010) 2 *Republics of letters: A Journal for the Study of Knowledge, Politics, and the Arts*, no. 1, 82–92, p. 82 <http://rofl.stanford.edu/node/81>.

16 E.H. KOSSMANN, 'The Crisis of the Dutch State 1780–1813: Nationalism, Federalism, Unitarism' in G.A.M. BEEKELAAR et al. (eds.), *Vaderlands Verleden in Veelvoud*, Martinus Nijhoff, The Hague 1975, pp. 435–452, p. 441.

Patriot call to Arms'.[17] Republican regents and the middle classes collaborated in order to restore the former greatness of the Dutch Republic. From about 1782 to 1787 democratic 'Patriotism' was able to establish itself as a major force in parts of the Republic. Their programme was expounded in a pamphlet by Johan Derk van der Capellen, under the title *Grondwettige Herstelling van Nederlands Staatswezen / The True Principles of the Dutch State Restored* (1784). According to this pamphlet Orangism equated despotism. In the patriotic view, the best possible state is a confederative one, combining the strength of a great state with the governability and good order of a small state, thanks to its division into small republics. Both elements are equally important: small states form the best guarantee against despotism, favouring civil order and liberty. Confederated, these small states collectively possess the strength of a large state whilst retaining the decency of government found in smaller states.[18] In order to regain national strength a democratic reform of the Dutch Republic was deemed necessary: as many people as possible should be transformed into fully respected citizens taking part in political life. After the collapse of this democratic movement, under foreign pressure, in 1787, many 'patriots' went into exile in the Southern Netherlands and in France, returning to the Dutch Republic in the wake of the French armies invading the Low Countries in the winter of 1794, as leaders of the Batavian Revolution of 1795.

3. THE 'HOLLAND' DECLARATION OF THE RIGHTS OF MAN AND OF THE CITIZEN OF 31 JANUARY 1795 AND THE BATAVIAN CONSTITUTION OF 1 MAY 1798

Although the Netherlands is traditionally regarded as a country where civil liberties play an important role, it was only after the Batavian Revolution of 1795 that the first modern catalogue of fundamental rights was published, at first on the provincial level, by the 'Provisional Representatives of the People of Holland', followed later on by the 'Provisional Representatives' of the other Dutch provinces and the Estates-General of the Dutch Republic on 4 March 1795.[19]

The Holland Declaration of 1795 was inspired by the Bills of Rights of Virginia (12 June 1776), Pennsylvania (28 September 1776), and Massachusetts (2 March 1780) together with the French Declarations of the Rights of Man and of the Citizen of 1789 and 1793, but it predates the French Declaration of the Rights and Duties of Man and of the Citizen of August 1795. Another important source

---

[17] I. Leonard Leeb, *The Ideological Origins of the Batavian Revolution. History and Politics in the Dutch Republic 1747–1800*, Martinus Nijhoff, The Hague 1973.

[18] Kossmann, *supra* note 16, p. 444.

[19] F.H. van der Burg and H. Boels, *Tweehonderd jaar Rechten van de mens in Nederland*, F.M. van Asbeck Centrum voor Mensenrechtenstudies, Leiden 1994.

of the Holland Declaration of Rights can be found in a pamphlet by the French politician Honoré Gabriel Riqueti, Count de Mirabeau (9 March 1749 – 2 April 1791), written in 1788, at the request of Dutch political refugees in Brussels, after the repression of the patriot revolt in 1787. His *Avis aux Bataves sur le Stathoudérat* also included a *Déclaration des droits du tout peuple qui veut la liberté*.[20] In this document we can already find some of the radical notions that returned in the French Jacobin constitution of 1792, such as the idea that the government is established for the happiness of the People, hence giving the People the inalienable right to reform, correct or change the form of government whenever their happiness so requires (article 3); and the right of the People to assemble in order to deliberate about the common good and to address their representatives in the legislative body in order to seek redress for their sufferings (article 6). Here we also find the idea that the legislative, executive and judicial branches of government should be completely separated in order that laws, not men, should govern (article 10). To prevent arbitrary rule, Mirabeau also denied the executive and judiciary the right to suspend laws or stop their execution, leaving this prerogative in the hands of the legislative body exclusively (article 11). In his opinion no people can have a free government unless there is a 'firm and constant adherence to the rules of justice, moderation, temperance, economy, virtue, and a frequent "recours" to fundamental rights' (article 12): freedom of the press must therefore be maintained 'inviolablement' (article 26).

According to the Declaration of the Provisional Representatives of Holland, all people are born with equal rights, of which they cannot be deprived (article 1). Those natural rights consist of equality, liberty, security, property and resistance to oppression (article 2). Liberty is defined as the power of each man to do all he can that does not disturb the rights of others (article 3). Therefore all people are allowed to disclose their thoughts and feelings, by making use of the freedom of the press (article 4). From the principle of liberty also follows freedom of religion (article 5). Security is defined as the guarantee not to be disturbed in the exercise of one's rights or the peaceful possession of one's legally acquired properties (article 6).

All people should have a vote in the legislative body of society, whether personally or by elective representation (article 7). Since the main goal of civil society exists in the assurance of the peaceful enjoyment of the natural rights of men, the enjoyment of these rights can only be restricted when necessary for the common good, by resolution of the People or their representatives (articles 8–10). Therefore nobody can be deprived of his property for the common good without resolution of the People or their representatives and without proper compensation (article 11).

---

[20] VAN DER BURG and BOELS, *supra* note 19, pp. 13–14.

The law is the free and solemn expression of the general will; it is the same for all, in punishment as well as in reward (article 12). In consequence thereof nobody can be legally prosecuted, arrested or imprisoned without an antecedent criminal law (article 13). No detainee may be treated more harshly than necessary to keep him under arrest (article 14).

The next articles contain some provisions in regard to those in public office. They stipulate that because of the equality of men, everyone is eligible for public office on the basis of his virtues and competences alone (article 15). Public functionaries always are accountable for their actions (article 16); the right of every 'Burger' to address those in public power cannot be lawfully restricted under any circumstances (article 17). The People is the bearer of sovereignty, therefore the People always are entitled to change, improve or to elect a new form of government (article 19).

The Declaration of the Provisional Representatives of the People of Holland formed the beginning of a complex discussion about the most desirable form of government for the former Dutch and now Batavian Republic: was it preferable to have a unitary republic like France, or should the republic continue to be a federation of sovereign provinces like the ancient Dutch Republic?

On 30 December 1795 the Estates-General decided to organise elections for a National Assembly, which held its first meeting on 1 March 1796. During the first meeting the president of the National Assembly, Pieter Paulus, stated in his opening address that the Assembly was congregated 'to lay the immovable foundations of the People's national happiness and prosperity, by giving them internal and external peace and finally a constitution, founded on the eternal and inalienable Rights of Man and of the Citizen'.[21]

From the beginning there was no consensus about the concept of a constitution. The views of the 'Moderates', who advocated a restricted form of elective democracy, and of the 'Federalists', who wanted to preserve provincial sovereignty, clashed with the views of the more radical 'Unitarians', who wanted to create a strong unitary Batavian Republic with a more democratically elected government. Thus the first and second drafts of the Batavian Constitution were rejected.[22] In January 1798, after a bloodless coup d'état — the so-called 'Velvet Revolution' — the Federalists were excluded from the National Assembly and a

---

21 The acts of the first constitutional commission are published by L. DE GOU, *Het plan van constitutie van 1796*, Martinus Nijhoff, The Hague 1975; L. DE GOU, *Het plan van constitutie 1796*, p IX; *Aanspraak van Mr. Pieter Paulus, Eerste praesident der Nationale Vergadering, gedaen bij de opening van dezelve vergadering op den 1. Maart 1796, het tweede jaar der Bataafsche Vrijheid.* Landsdrukkerij, The Hague 1796.

22 For the acts of the second constitutional commission see: L. DE GOU, *Het ontwerp van constitutie van 1797*, Martinus Nijhoff, The Hague 1983–1985 (vol. I–III).

Unitarian constitution, the *Staatsregeling voor het Bataafsche Volk*, was, under French pressure, finally adopted.[23]

The *Staatsregeling* of 1 May 1798 can be considered as the first modern Dutch constitution. It consists of the following elements: *Algemeene Beginselen* / General Principles (articles 1–8); *Burgerlijke en Staatkundige Grondregels* / Civil and Governmental Fundamental Rules (articles 9–72); the *Acte van Staatsregeling* / Constitutional Act (303 articles) and five procedural regulations, two of which related to the election procedure in the voting districts (39 resp. 38 articles). The other regulations specifically concern the election of members of the executive branch of government (18 articles), the budget and the national treasury (17 articles), and the revision of the constitution (32 articles).

In the *Algemeene Beginselen* the Batavian People pay tribute not only to the *Déclaration des droit du tout peuple qui veut la liberté* of count De Mirabeau (1788) but also to the political philosophy of Rousseau and his ideas of the social contract, the *volonté générale*, the sovereignty of the people and the equality of all people before the law, stipulating that nothing that is in accordance with the inalienable rights of the people can be prohibited by law.[24]

In the *Burgerlijke en Staatkundige Grondregels* we find a wide range of fundamental rights, such as the right to vote and to elect the members of the *Vertegenwoordigende Macht /Representing Power* as the supreme authority of the Batavian Republic (articles 11–12), freedom of the press (article 16), freedom of religion (article 19), freedom of assembly (article 18) and the right of petition (article 17), which are essential for the concept of democratic states in which the People have real influence on government. Article 28 stipulates the codification of civil law, penal law and procedural law within two years after the implementation of the *Staatsregeling*. Article 29 protects people against arbitrary arrest and detention and guarantees them legal process and judgment. Article 30 prohibits harsh treatment of prisoners and declares illegal the arbitrary delay of the execution of condemned prisoners (in the case of the death penalty) or in the implementation of their sentences. Article 34 guarantees people access to justice in conformity with the *Staatsregeling* or the law. Article 36 declares the abolition of legal torture in the Batavian Republic. Article 39 guarantees the inviolability

---

23 The acts of the third constitutional commission were also published by L. de Gou: L. DE GOU, *Staatsregeling 1798*, Martinus Nijhoff, The Hague 1988–1990 (vol. I–II); about the complex relations between France and the Batavian Republic, see R. KUBBEN, *Regenerations and Hegemony. Franco-Batavian Relations in the Revolutionary Era, 1795–1803*, Brill Publishers, Leiden 2011 (Legal history Library, vol. 3; Studies in the History of International Law, vol. I).

24 On the influence of political theory on the *Staatsregeling* see: W. WITTEVEEN, 'Politieke theorie en de Bataafse Staatsregeling' in E.J.M.F.C. BROERS and R.M.H. KUBBEN (eds.), *Ad Fontes. Liber Amicorum prof. Beatrix van Erp-Jacobs*, Wolf Legal Publishers, Oisterwijk 2014, pp. 281–293.

of private homes. Article 40 prohibits the expropriation of private property for the common good, unless with adequate compensation.[25]

In the sphere of social fundamental rights, the *Burgerlijke en Staatkundige Grondregels* also formulate some duties for society, namely to provide labour to the industrious and assistance to the disabled (article 47), and to care for the education of abandoned children (article 49). Society also offers security and protection to all foreigners who wish to share the benefits of freedom peacefully (article 50).

From the gender perspective it must be remarked that neither under the Holland Declaration of 1795 nor under the Batavian Constitution of 1798 was the right to vote extended to women; they had to wait until 1921 before suffrage was granted to them in the Netherlands.

The practical significance of the *Staatsregeling* has been very limited: it was succeeded in 1801 and in 1805 by new and less democratic constitutions for the Batavian Republic; and in 1806 by the constitution for the (Napoleonic) Kingdom of Holland, which in 1810 became part of the French Empire under Napoleon. After the Napoleonic wars, the Netherlands became independent again in 1813 and in 1814 the 'sovereign prince' William of Orange (who in 1815 became King William I) granted his people a rather autocratic constitution, which in 1815, after the creation of the 'United Kingdom of the Netherlands' by the Congress of Vienna, combining the Netherlands, Belgium and Luxemburg in a single state, was replaced by a new constitution. This in turn, after the independence of Belgium in 1840, was replaced by an adapted version, which in 1848 was further replaced by a more liberal one.[26]

4. CONCLUDING REMARKS

In Dutch historiography the constitution of 1848 is often considered to be the beginning of modern Dutch parliamentary democracy. In the 1998 commemoration of 150 years of the constitution, the 200th anniversary of the *Staatsregeling* of 1798 was neglected completely. According to the Dutch legal historian Moorman van Kappen this was due to an oversight of the commemorative commission, who wanted to make use of the 150th anniversary of the 1848 constitution for initiating a discussion about the fundamental

[25] T. Veen, 'Het volk, de leden van de maatschappij en de ingezetenen van de republiek. Opmerkingen over het democratisch gehalte van de Bataafse Staatsregeling' in O. Moorman van Kappen et al. (eds.), *De Staatsregeling voor het Bataafsche Volk van 1798*, Gerard Noodt Instituut, Nijmegen 2001, pp. 9–34.

[26] For text editions of these constitutions see: Van Hasselt, *Verzameling van Nederlandse Staatsregelingen en Grondwetten*, N. Samson Alphen aan de Rijn, several editions.

principles of modern public law. In his view the Batavian *Staatsregeling* is still an important historical document, which reflects the original views of the part of Dutch society that before 1795 was excluded from political participation. The *Staatsregeling* can be considered as testimony of the original Dutch version of the European and North-American enlightened political philosophy of safeguarding the fundamental rights of the people against oppression by the state, and as such still merits attention today.[27]

The Netherlands has a rich fundamental rights tradition originating from the 'liberties' granted through medieval ducal charters. Subject to elaboration since the late sixteenth century in the Dutch Republic, which saw the further development of the idea of 'true liberty', the concepts were translated into a more enlightened version during the Batavian Republic, creating the basis of modern fundamental rights in the modern Kingdom of the Netherlands.

[27] O. MOORMAN VAN KAPPEN, 'De betekenis van de Staatsregeling-1798 toen en nu' in O. MOORMAN VAN KAPPEN et al. (eds.), *De Staatsregeling voor het Bataafsche Volk van 1798*, Gerard Noodt Instituut, Nijmegen 2001, pp. 1–8; J.T. VAN DEN BERG and J.J. VIS, *De eerste honderdvijftig jaar parlementaire geschiedenis van Nederland 1796–1946*, Bert Bakker, Amsterdam 2013, pp. 76–77.

14. PORTUGAL: 'TROPICAL VERSAILLES' IN THE BEGINNING OF THE NINETEENTH CENTURY

Teresa PIZARRO BELEZA
Helena PEREIRA DE MELO

1. INTRODUCTION

In November 1807 the French army, led by General Jean-Andoche Junot, occupied Lisbon and invaded Portugal. In order to avoid the consequences of the French invasion, the Royal Court of Portugal left for the Portuguese colony of Brazil at almost the same time. Queen Mary of Portugal, the Prince Regent at the time, Dom João VI of Braganza, other members of the royal family, together with elements of the nobility, high clergy, Council of State and high courts, physicians, librarians, musicians, and even a riding master, fled to Rio de Janeiro, so that Napoleon would not be able to depose the House of Braganza from the throne. Many assets were also taken, namely the Royal Library, silver, jewels and a printing press. In March 1808, the court arrived in Rio de Janeiro.

With the partial evacuation of Lisbon and the lack of preparation of the Portuguese army, it was easy for Junot's army (of 25,000 soldiers) to occupy Lisbon. Initially he tried to rule Portugal without creating major conflicts, as he hoped, like Murat in Naples, to become the king of a new French satellite state. He attempted to gain the approval of the people by leaving almost untouched the judicial, fiscal and administrative structures and by giving privileges to the *afrancesados* (the pro-French Portuguese). He even tried to convince Napoleon to bestow a Constitution to Portugal as he had done in July 1807 to the Grand Duchy of Warsaw. In order to achieve this Junot convened, in May 1808, a traditional assembly which had not been functioning for more than a century, where the three main groups of Portuguese society (the nobility, the clergymen and the people) had seats. This *Junta dos Três Estados* begged Napoleon for a Constitution for the Portuguese Kingdom that would be a constitutional monarchy (whose king would be Junot), where the principle of equality before the law would be respected and the Napoleonic Civil Code applied.[1]

But Portugal remained unappeased and the population resisted the French occupation. Junot altered his position, declared the Braganza dynasty officially deposed in February 1808, and dissolved the regency council. He began to adopt harsh reforms and the intensity of reaction of the population grew steadily: uprisings against the French occupation occurred all over the territory and local associations were created in order to resist foreign control. These associations recognised the supremacy of one of their number: the *Oporto Junta Suprema*, led by Bishop Dom António José de Castro.

Meanwhile, the British were trying to help the Portuguese to expel the French. Britain had a long-standing alliance with Portugal and a secret agreement between the Portuguese and British states had been signed in October 1807. Under this agreement, the British supported the evacuation of the Court and undertook not to recognise as Portuguese king a person who did not belong to the House of Braganza.

The Oporto Junta efforts to resist the French occupation were successful after the British Army, commanded by Arthur Wellesley, the future Duke of Wellington, arrived in August 1808. Junot's troops were defeated by a joint Anglo-Portuguese force at the Battle of Vimieiro, and left Portugal. The reformation of the Portuguese army was entrusted to William Carr, later the Viscount Beresford. Two further invasions by the French, under the command of Generals Soult and Massena were defeated, mostly as result of Wellington's skillful tactics. At the end of the war with the French, however, the king did not return to Portugal. Absolute monarchy was restored but Dom João VI ruled the kingdom from Rio de Janeiro (called by some authors 'the tropical Versailles') and appointed several governors to represent him in Portugal. The influence of the English, namely of Beresford, in national politics was huge.

In 1815 Brazil was raised to the status of a Kingdom, and Rio de Janeiro was chosen as the unofficial seat of the United Kingdom of Portugal, Algarve and Brazil. Three years later the acclamation of Dom João was celebrated in Rio, consolidating his domain in the Brazilian territory within the Royal Union of States. Portuguese observers were increasingly afraid that the permanent seat of the monarchy would no longer be Lisbon. As Gabriel Paquette states:

> Dom João displayed little inclination to return to the Old World. The *Governadores* sent him strongly worded letters imploring him to do so, describing the "delicate" situation that demanded "great

[1] J. Bacelar Gouveia, *Manual de Direito Constitucional*, vol. I, 5th ed., Almedina, Coimbra 2013, pp. 378–380.

> attention" and "prompt remedies". Two urgent matters cropped up routinely in this correspondence: first, that revenues had declined drastically since 1808 and the ordinary expenses of even a skeletal administration went unmet, resulting in a mounting public debt; second, that the "prolonged absence" of the king generated widespread "disgust and mistrust", diminishing the "spirit of the nation".[2]

Many factors led to the 1820 Liberal Revolution: the court's refusal to return to Portugal, the consequences of the French and British occupations, the huge public debt, the agriculture and commercial crises partially due to high taxation, and the influence of French political ideas. The *afrancesados* were collaborationists during the French occupation and that made people distrust them. But when the British occupation took place, the pro-English began to be distrusted and the anti-clerical, masonic, liberal *afrancesados* were respected again. In 1818, a secret society was created in Oporto called the *Sinédrio*. It aimed at ending the British influence in Portugal, adopting a constitution that would declare a constitutional monarchy based on the regeneration of the traditional Portuguese institutions, and halting a situation where Portugal had the undignified status of a colony of a former colony. They wanted the King to return to Lisbon and to restore Portuguese traditional public institutions grounded on the rights, liberties and customs that had characterised the Portuguese legal system since its beginnings.

Conspiracies spread all over the country. They culminated in the Oporto August 1820 revolution led by *Sinédrio* that quickly spread through Portugal. A Provisional Government Committee, formed to rule the country, decided to elect a revolutionary parliament (with a single chamber) to write the first Portuguese Constitution.

2. ADOPTING THE FIRST PORTUGUESE CONSTITUTION

The Revolutionary Parliament (*Cortes Extraordinárias e Constituintes da Nação Portuguesa*) began its work in the last week of January 1821. The main model that the liberals wanted to follow was the Cadiz Constitution of 1812. In November 1820 it was even thought that it would be a good idea to put the Spanish Constitution into effect in Portuguese national territory. Bentham, who wrote several letters to members of the Portuguese Revolutionary Parliament, even urged them to adopt it: 'Adopt it as a mass: time admits not picking and choosing. (…) Take it for all in all, nothing as yet practicable can be so good for

---

2 G. PAQUETTE, *Imperial Portugal in the Age of Atlantic Revolutions The Luso-Brazilian World, c. 1770–1850*, Cambridge University Press, Cambridge 2014, p. 107. See also P. OTERO, 'O Brasil nas Cortes Constituintes Portuguesas de 1821–1822' (1988) July–December *O Direito* 399–453.

you. For them it is good; for you it will be still better: this you shall see. To find ready-made a work so suitable, is a blessing too great for expectation; an advantage beyond all price'.[3]

Wholesale adoption did not happen, but the election of the deputies for the Revolutionary Parliament followed the rules (founded on the principle of proportional representation, being the number of candidates elected per constituency proportional to the number of electors) laid down in this Spanish Constitution.

Influence by foreign constitutional models clearly occurred: as the Cadiz Constitution was inspired by the French revolutionary constitution of 1791, adopted after the end of the *Ancien Regime* and the Absolute Monarchy, and by the liberal French Constitution of 1795, the Portuguese Constitution of 1822 was also guided by these French Constitutions. Thus, the ideas of French Constitutionalism were one of the main inspirations of the Portuguese First Fundamental text, although they were mitigated by Bentham's utilitarianism.[4]

If we compare the text of the Portuguese Constitution with the text of the Spanish Constitution we reach the conclusion that they are very similar. Their structure is almost the same and the content overlaps significantly. Almeida Garrett (a politician and one of the most important Portuguese writers of the first half of the nineteenth century) considered that both constitutions were 'almost identical, distinguished only by terms of phrasing, words or emphasis', that both belonged to 'the meridional system of freedom'.[5] Nevertheless, some differences could be found between the constitutional texts: the Portuguese constitution has an autonomous title on 'Rights and Duties' and the Spanish Constitution has not; the Portuguese Constitution stated that the king was a 'constitutional monarch' whereas the Cadiz Constitution determined that the kingdom was a 'moderate monarchy'; according to the Portuguese Constitution the executive power was shared between the secretaries of state and the king, while according to the Spanish Constitution, this power resided only in the king; the Portuguese Constitution allowed direct suffrage, the Spanish universal indirect suffrage; freedom of the press was better guaranteed in the Cadiz Constitution,[6] and so on.

---

3 J. Bentham, *On the Liberty of Press, and Public Discussion and Other Legal and Political Writings for Spain and Portugal* (editors: Catherine Pease-Watkin and Philip Schofield), Oxford University Press, Oxford 2012, p. 101.

4 See J. Miranda, *Manual de Direito Constitucional*, vol. I, 2, 10th ed., Coimbra Editora, Coimbra 2014, pp. 29–30.

5 J. Baptista Da Silva Leitão De Almeida Garrett, 'Da Europa e da América e de Sua Mútua Influência na Causa da Civilização e da Liberdade' (1826) IV *O Popular, Jornal Político, Literário e Comercial* nº XIX (May) pp. 25–81.

6 See Miranda, *supra* note 4, pp. 30–31.

The method adopted by Parliament to write the constitutional text was peculiar and was never again adopted by Portuguese parliaments when drafting a Constitution. First, the Revolutionary Parliament wrote a provisional text called the 'Basis of the Constitution of the Portuguese Monarchy' that contained the main principles that would be developed in the Constitutional text. These 37 principles were considered 'the most adequate principles to ensure the individual rights of the Citizen and the organization and limits of the State political powers'.[7] It was approved by the assembly and enacted as a decree on 3 March 1821. The Prince Regent and the other religious, civil and military authorities had to swear it, and it was a 'provisional constitution' that was intended to serve during a transitional period, until the permanent constitution was adopted.

3. FUNDAMENTAL RIGHTS IN THE CONSTITUTION OF 1822

The new Constitution, signed on 23 September 1822, aimed at achieving a compromise between tradition and the new liberal and democratic trends. This is quite clear if we read its preamble: 'In the name of the Holy and Indivisible Trinity, the Constituent Assembly of the Portuguese Nation, entirely convinced that the public disgraces that have affected it and still do so, have had their origin in the contempt of the citizen's rights and in the disrespect of the main laws of Monarchy (...) adopt the following Political Constitution, in order to ensure the rights of each person and the common benefit of all Portuguese'. Under the Constitution, the official religion of the State is still Roman Apostolic Catholicism and the political regime is a monarchy: as is stated in article 31, a noble house of Portuguese origin, 'the Most Serene House of Braganza is the reigning house of Portugal'. The King, John VI, whose title is declared to be 'most faithful Majesty' must swear the new Constitution and to respect it. The origin of his political legitimacy is national sovereignty and no longer divine right. He is chosen in accordance with a predefined order of hereditary succession and he has no political or other responsibility.[8] The Kingdom of Portugal thus became a constitutional monarchy, the King being the head of State.

The Constitution recognised the creation of a United Kingdom, in which Brazil had been raised to the status of a kingdom, coequal with Portugal. It states that the Portuguese Nation is 'the union of all Portuguese from both hemispheres'. To the national territory belonged in Europe the kingdom of Portugal and the kingdom of Algarve, Madeira Island, Porto Santo Islands and Azores; in America the kingdom of Brazil; in Africa Guinea-Bissau, Angola, Cape Verde, S. Tomé and Principe and Mozambique; in Asia, Goa, Daman and Diu, Macao,

---

7 CORTES GERAIS EXTRAORDINÁRIAS E CONSTITUINTES DA NAÇÃO PORTUGUESA, *Bases da Constituição da Monarquia Portuguesa*, Tipografia de J. F. M. Campos, Lisboa 1821, p. 2.

8 Articles 25.º, 31.º, 121.º, 126.º and 127.º of the Constitution of 23 September 1822.

Timor. A complex system of representative government is established by the Constitution in order to rule this huge empire. Popular sovereignty resides in the body of the free and independent Nation and can only be exercised by its legally elected representatives. The constitution must be written by deputies that represent the general will of the nation; by a revolutionary assembly. The king does not have the power to sanction the constitutional text.[9]

According to the Constitution the Portuguese State was a representative monarchy where legislative, executive and judicial powers were separated and independent from each other. The constitutional separation of powers meant that the king and his secretaries of state had executive power; the unicameral parliament (called *Cortes*), elected every two years by direct and universal suffrage (with the exclusion of women and illiterate men), had legislative power and the judges held judicial power. The king could not participate in ordinary sessions of the Parliament and had the right to sanction laws adopted by the parliament, but not to veto them.[10]

Title I of the Constitution concerns the fundamental rights and duties of Portuguese Citizens. Its 19 articles were directly influenced by the French Declaration of the Rights of Man and of the Citizen, passed by France's National Constituent Assembly in August 1789.

The main values of the 1822 Portuguese Constitution can be found at article 1 and are the typical traditional liberal values: liberty, security and property. Liberty is understood as the citizens' faculty of 'not being obliged to do what law does not order them to do, nor to be forbidden to do what law does not prohibit'. It is to be exercised within strict respect of existing laws.[11]

Several expressions of liberty are protected by the constitutional text. Liberty of conscience and expression was qualified as 'one of the most precious human rights'; every Portuguese must be free to express his thoughts without prior censorship. Freedom of the press also could not be restrained in advance by any authority, and a special court was to be created by Parliament in order to protect it. This freedom could only be abridged in religious matters: in this case the Bishops could exercise censorship after the text had been published and the government had the duty to help them punish those considered guilty of infringing freedom of expression in the field of 'dogma and morals'.[12] This

9 Articles 20.º, 27.º and 112.º of the Constitution.

10 Articles 41.º, 91.º and 110.º of the Constitution. See C. Blanco De Morais, Curso *de Direito Constitucional Teoria da Constituição em Tempo de Crise do Estado Social*, T. 2, Vol. 2, Coimbra Editora, Coimbra 2014, p. 144.

11 Article 2.º of the Constitution.

12 Articles 7.º and 8.º of the Constitution. See M. Caetano, *Constituições Portuguesas*, 7th ed., Editorial Verbo, Lisboa / São Paulo 1994, p. 18.

Catholic censorship was intended to please the church which distrusted the members of the Constitutional Assembly, since many of them were Freemasons.

In addition, liberty of religion in the case of foreigners (but not Portuguese citizens) was protected by the Constitution. The official religion of the state was, as stated, Catholicism. Nevertheless, foreigners were free to manifest their religions and confessions in private.[13]

Freedom to teach is also guaranteed by the text, it being free to any citizen to open a school for public teaching. An education policy is foreseen in the Constitution: the State shall open schools all over the national territory where boys and girls (both sexes) will learn to read, write and count and be instructed in religious and civil obligations. The concern with literacy led to another constitutional solution: in the future, the right to vote would not be recognised to men that 'being older than 25, do not know how to read and write, if they were less than 17 at the time of the adoption of the Constitution'.[14]

Security of the person is a fundamental right explicitly mentioned and protected by the Constitution, and it consists of the protection that the Government will ensure to all persons, so that they can exercise their rights.[15] In general, no one shall be sentenced under criminal law unless he was previously considered guilty and no criminal law will be enacted unless it is strictly necessary, according to the principle of *ultima ratio* in the field of criminal law. The fundamental principles of liberal criminal law *nulla poena sine lege*, of proportionality of penalties must also be respected by the future Portuguese Criminal Code (which was only adopted in 1852), according to the Constitution. Criminal liability is considered not to be transferable and torture, confiscation of property, whippings, hot iron branding, public humiliation and other forms of cruel or infamous penalties are abolished.[16]

The humanisation of prison law also occurred. The goal of humanising prison punishment underlay the new constitutional solutions: jails were to be 'safe, clean and with good air circulation' and their aim was to 'ensure safety and not to torment prisoners'. Inmates were to be separated according to 'their personal characteristics and the type of crime they have practiced'. Unconvicted prisoners were to be the subject of special treatment and when the prison was visited by a controlling authority no prisoner could be hidden from it.[17]

---

13 Article 25.º of the Constitution.

14 Articles 33.º, 237.º and 239.º of the Constitution.

15 Article 3.º of the Constitution.

16 Articles 4.º, 10.º and 11.º of the Constitution. See T. Pizarro Beleza and F. Lacerda Da Costa Pinto, 'Criminal Law' in C. Ferreira de Almeida, A. Cristas and N. Piçarra (eds.), *Portuguese Law: An Overview*, Faculdade de Direito da Universidade Nova de Lisboa e Almedina, Lisboa 2007, pp. 148–149.

17 Articles 208.º and 209.º of the Constitution.

As also stated in the French Declaration of the Rights of Man and of the Citizen, property was 'an inviolable and sacred right' of every Portuguese citizen. Expropriations in the public interest could only be undertaken on a legal basis and on the condition that the owner had been previously indemnified.[18]

Other first generation rights are also proclaimed in the Constitution: inviolability of the home and of correspondence, the right to vote and to be elected. Concerning the inviolability of domicile, unless there is a decision duly passed by a competent authority in cases explicitly defined by law, no domicile may be entered.[19]

Portuguese citizenship was given to all people who were sons of a Portuguese father and who had been born on the territory of the United Kingdom or on foreign territory if the Portuguese father was serving the Portuguese Nation; to all people who having a foreign father, were born and resided in the Portuguese territory, and declared once they had reached majority that they wanted to be Portuguese citizens; to children born out of wedlock to a Portuguese mother if they were born on national territory or afterwards decided to reside there; to abandoned newborns that were found on national territory; to freed slaves, and to naturalised foreigners.[20]

The right to vote was accorded to every male citizen who had attained the age of 25. Also eligible to vote were Portuguese citizens who were older than 20 and married, or military officers, or had a university degree, or were clergymen. The Constitution defined other groups that were not eligible to vote: *filius familiae* who lived with their parents unless they were civil servants; domestic servants; homeless people; monks and those that being older than 25 were illiterate.[21]

The same rules applied to recognition of the right to be elected as a member of Parliament. Those who did not have the right of suffrage could not be elected. Among those who had this active right to vote, some were excluded from passive suffrage: those who did not have enough property to provide for their personal needs; people who had gone bankrupt, until it was proven that they had acted in good faith; foreigners, even if naturalised Portuguese; people employed as Secretary of State or State Counselors or in the Royal House, and freed slaves born outside Portuguese territory. Special ineligibilities are also foreseen: the right to be voted for is not recognised to those who are not naturalised or do not reside, for at least five years, within the province where the election takes place; to bishops and priests within their parishes; to judges in the districts where they exercise their judicial function (this does not apply to judges of the Supreme

18 Article 6.° of the Constitution.
19 Articles 5.° and 18.° of the Constitution.
20 Article 21.° of the Constitution.
21 Article 33.° of the Constitution.

Court of Justice or of other courts that have jurisdiction over the whole kingdom) and to higher army personnel in elections in which their subordinates vote.[22]

The Constitution recognises the principle of equality, stating that all citizens are equal before the law. This recognition implies that every citizen has equal access to law and effective judicial protection in order to defend his rights protected by law, there being admitted no court privileges in either civil or criminal procedures, nor the creation of 'special commissions' (linked with seigneurial or ecclesiastical jurisdictions) to try any person.[23]

The recognition of the principle of equality also implies that every citizen has the right of access to public offices under equal conditions, without any distinction other than his 'talents and virtues'. Public offices are considered not to belong to anyone and their number shall, according to the constitutional text, be limited to the strictly necessary. Civil servants have the duty to respect the Constitution and the laws, to be faithful to the government and to perform their job well. The Constitution also recognises the right of all Portuguese citizens to be rewarded for 'important national services'.[24]

All citizens have the right to petition, to address complaints to the legislative and executive powers and to have their complaints examined, and to protest against infractions of the Constitution.[25]

It is interesting to note that the 1822 Constitution pays special attention to what came to be considered, more than 100 years later, economic and social rights: the Parliament and the Government are in charge of building civil and military hospitals, homes for newborn babies who have been abandoned by their parents, and other charity establishments. As the Constitution was drafted and approved for application also to Brazil, the Government had the additional duty to 'civilise' the Indians.[26] Ecological concerns can be found, as well, in the Constitution: town halls have the duty to plant trees on common lands.[27]

The Portuguese citizen also has fundamental duties, which are: the duty to be fair, to respect religion, to love and defend his homeland, and to obey the Constitution and the laws.

---

22 Articles 34.° and 35.° of the Constitution.
23 Article 9.° of the Constitution.
24 Articles 12.°, 13.° and 15.° of the Constitution.
25 Articles 16.° and 17.° of the Constitution.
26 See C. Nogueira da Silva, *Constitucionalismo e Império A Cidadania no Ultramar Português*, Almedina, Coimbra 2009, pp. 266–297.
27 Articles 223.° and 240.° of the Constitution.

4. CONCLUDING REMARKS

The king returned to Portugal in July 1821 and left his son, Dom Pedro, in Rio de Janeiro, with full regency powers. In 1822 Brazil declared its political independence and Dom Pedro de Alcântra e Braganza was crowned as its emperor.[28]

The Constitution was in force from September 1822 to June 1823: less than one year. It was never fully implemented and the ideas it contained were contested by a conservative, anti-masonian and catholic political discourse.

The country suffered serious economic problems and the political disputes between the liberal and conservative parties became extreme. In 1823 a new revolution occurred, under the command of the youngest son of Dom João VI, Dom Miguel. The King was obliged to dissolve Parliament and to revoke the Constitution, and a new Committee was appointed to draft a new absolutist Constitutional Charter. As Jorge Miranda wrote, the Constitution of 1822 would become 'the symbol of an ideal that was very far from being reached'.[29]

---

28 See F.J. Da Rocha Martins and M. Lopes De Oliveira, *A Primeira Constituição Portuguesa*, Edições Excelsior, Lisboa 1946, pp. 18–20.

29 See Miranda, *supra* note 4, p. 32.

15. LUXEMBOURG: FUNDAMENTAL RIGHTS IN A SMALL STATE

Charlotte WIRTH[1]

1. INTRODUCTION

In the context of constitutional history, Luxembourg is a valuable example of the development of a small state. Although Luxembourg only received a truly independent government in 1839, the creation of the current state is a result of the Congress of Vienna in 1815. In the centuries before 1815, the territory was a legal part of different empires and fell under different constitutional systems. The focus of this analysis will lie on the development of Luxembourg in the nineteenth century, yet we will see that movements in favour of fundamental rights can be identified earlier on a local level during the Middle Ages and throughout the state's development, as various influences interacted with an increasingly emancipated society. The development of Luxembourg from state to nation was triggered by the territory's reorganisation at the Congress of Vienna in 1815 and progressed through the achievement of sovereignty in the years from 1839 to 1868. The latter was the initial catalyst for the development of a national conscience and even a national identity that became increasingly manifest during the political instabilities of 1848 and the developments during the post-March era[2] from 1848 to 1870.[3]

1 The author would like to thank Jean-Paul Lehners for his substantial assistance with this publication as well as Norbert Franz, Michel Pauly and Renée Wagner for placing their articles at the author's disposal and providing valuable assistance and advice.

2 The terms 'pre-March' and 'post-March' used in this article are referring to the 1848 revolutionary wave, a series of liberal and democratic revolutionary movements against the conservative — in the case of France also liberal — European monarchies. In this analysis, 'pre-March' refers to the period from the Congress of Vienna 1815 until the years leading up to the 1848 Revolution, while 'post-March' refers to the period from the Revolution to the Constitution of 1868.

3 N. FRANZ 'Artikel Luxemburg' in W. DAUM (ed.), *Handbuch der europäischen Verfassungsgeschichte im 19. Jahrhundert. Institutionen und Rechtspraxis im gesellschaftlichen Wandel*, vol. 3: 1848–1870, Dietz Verlag, Bonn, in print, p. 1. Quotations from the submitted typoscript of the author.

This analysis will focus on the different constitutional systems that Luxembourg was subjected to during the nineteenth century, and special attention will be given to the national Luxembourgish constitutions. The aim is to identify movements in favour of fundamental rights — such as ideas of liberty, equality, solidarity, inclusion or justice — in the different documents of a constitutional nature. The partition of power will also be considered — especially the interplay between the ranges of influence of the monarch, the government and the representative bodies — as well as the possibilities for political participation of representative organs. The development of the administration in the years of the achievement of state sovereignty will also be briefly addressed, along with suffrage and the gender question.

2. HISTORICAL CONTEXT

The political history of the territory that we now call Luxembourg is a complex one, starting well before the actual territorial configuration in 1839.[4] While the Grand Duchy was created during the Congress of Vienna in 1815, the major part of its territory is constituted of the former county of Luxembourg that had become a Duchy in the fourteenth century and was the ancestral homeland of the Luxembourg dynasty that counted several emperors. Following the death of the last emperor, the Duchy became part of the Burgundian territories, stretching between France and the German Empire. As part of the Holy Roman Empire of the German Nation, Luxembourg was then ruled by the Habsburg dynasty during the sixteenth and seventeenth centuries. Following the Spanish war of succession, it fell under the Austrian Habsburg dynasty in the beginning of the eighteenth century, under which rule Luxembourg knew a rather long period of stability and economic expansion. However, in 1795, Luxembourg was conquered by the French Republic and became an integral part of France.[5] After the downfall of the Napoleonic Empire and the reorganisation of Europe during the Congress of Vienna in 1815, the situation of Luxembourg changed and the territory was re-formed as the Grand Duchy of Luxembourg and accorded to the King of the United Kingdom of the Netherlands, while its capital became a fortress of the German Confederation and was occupied by Prussian troops. King William I of the Netherlands integrated Luxembourg as a Province into the United Kingdom of the Netherlands. The distinct status of the Grand Duchy was a result of its allegiance to the German Confederation.

---

4 When speaking of 'Luxembourg' we speak of the area of the current state. For this chapter see M. PAULY, *Geschichte Luxemburgs*, C.H. Beck Verlag, Munich 2011 or M. PAULY, *Histoire du Luxembourg*, Éditions de l'ULB, Brussels 2013.

5 And insofar the various French Constitutions issued during the time granted rights of fundamental nature to the people, they also applied to the area of current Luxembourg.

However, the Dutch Kingdom collapsed in the Belgian Revolution of 1830 and the major part of the Grand Duchy became the Province of Luxembourg of the newly founded Kingdom of Belgium. Only its capital, with the fortress of the German Confederation, remained under Dutch rule. In 1839, following the conference of London, the western part of the Grand Duchy remained with Belgium, while the eastern part of the reduced Grand Duchy stayed under Oranian rule and continued to be part of the German Confederation. This agreement was of utmost importance for the sovereignty of Luxembourg. Only now was the Duchy ruled by a Luxembourgish government and acquired its first State Charter under King and Grand Duke William II in 1841. During the period until the Revolution of 1848, the foundations of the Luxembourgish state system were created and implemented and in just a few years, Luxembourgish legislation and state organisation were of the highest level, which marked the history of the state well beyond the nineteenth century.[6]

In 1848, Luxembourg was gripped by the wave of liberal and democratic revolutionary movements against the conservative — in the case of France also liberal — European monarchies. It was triggered by hunger crises, mass poverty and unemployment, and was also a result of an emancipatory process of the middle and lower classes. Some politicised groups claimed social and political fundamental rights, such as freedom of opinion and association, the right to free education, universal suffrage, minimum wages, measures for the provision of work and for the abolition of speculation with food and a strengthening of the representation of the people. The riots were stopped with help of Prussian troops and the tensions were resolved by the elaboration of the 1848 Constitution, modelled on the liberal Belgian Constitution of 1830, which strengthened the representation of the people and defined some fundamental rights of citizens. However, in 1856, William III reacted to the German Federal Assembly's opposition to the increasing possibilities of participation of the people and replaced the liberal Constitution of 1848 with a new constitution that re-strengthened the authority of the monarch. The collapse of the German Confederation due to the Prussian-Austrian war in 1866 led to the *Luxembourg Crisis* of 1867, following William III's intention to sell Luxembourg to France, which created tensions amongst the major European powers. The crisis was finally resolved by the Treaty of London of 1867, establishing the perpetual neutrality and demilitarisation of Luxembourg. In 1868 the parliament restored the liberal Constitution of 1848, maintaining just a few institutions of the authoritarian constitutional system of 1856.

These crises of the nineteenth century show that the new state had consolidated in the sense that strong nation-building tendencies can be identified. In principle,

---

6 N. FRANZ, 'Artikel Luxemburg' in W. DAUM (ed.), *Handbuch der europäischen Verfassungsgeschichte im 19. Jahrhundert. Institutionen und Rechtspraxis im gesellschaftlichen Wandel*, vol. 2: 1815–1847, Dietz Verlag, Bonn 2012, pp. 543–573, pp. 4–7.

the Constitution of 1868 has formed the basis of the political life of the Grand Duchy to the present day and is still the current constitution of the state, although it has been subject to a number of fundamental reforms.

3. CONSTITUTIONAL SYSTEMS

From 1815 to 1830, Luxembourg was subjected to the Netherlands *Grondwet*, according most powers, such as executive and military power, to the King. Only legislative power was shared with the Dutch Assembly of the Estates. This Assembly was formed of the nobility, the municipalities and the rural communities, yet its range of influence was very small and it had only restricted legislative and budgetary competences. State finances and the finances of the monarch were not separated and the Luxembourgish population was put under a high fiscal strain due to the national debt. Upon the Belgian Revolution, Luxembourg was subject to a parliamentary monarchy. The executive power lay with a government controlled by parliament, while the legislative power was shared between the latter and the King. The administrative authority of the representative body of the people increased and both the parliament and the assemblies now played an active part in the budgetary, legislative and administrative decisions. The first Luxembourgish State Charter of 1841 had some similarities and continuities with the Dutch *Grondwet*, such as assigning executive power to the monarch, who also had significant legislative authority. At the level of state administration, a national government and a central administration were put into place. A national, Luxembourgish Assembly of the Estates, nominated by the grand duke, represented civil society and was involved in state decisions of a legislative, administrative and budgetary nature. The state's and monarch's finances were separated, which limited the authority of the monarch over financial questions.

The Constitution of the 1848 Revolution, largely inspired by the liberal Belgian Constitution of 1831, increased the rights of representation of the people[7] in opposition to the monarch's authority, while a slightly lowered census now allowed parts of the upper middle class to participate in the election of the representative bodies. By contrast, the 1856 Constitution — imposed by the monarch without the consent of the representatives of the people — largely restricted their rights while it re-established the authority of the monarch,[8] who held all state authority and whose person became not only inviolable but also sacred. The legal authority of the Court of law was reduced in order to limit its

[7] Especially in budgetary matters.

[8] Yet, the state authority of the monarch was not absolute, as it was bound to the statute of the German Confederation and hence on the national constitution and laws; cf. FRANZ, *supra* note 3, p. 5.

authority within the state.[9] This was again revised in the liberal Constitution of 1868 that shared a tradition with the 1848 Constitution. Released under the State Minister Emmanuel Servais, after the dissolution of the German Confederation in 1866, it strengthened the authority of the representative bodies considerably while it weakened the position of the monarch.

We can conclude that the relations of power changed with the different constitutional systems but despite all tensions and retrograde steps, the range of influence of the representative organs gradually increased. Nonetheless, we must take into account that the latter was mainly formed by a certain segment of society, namely the wealthiest people. While they were able to defend their interests in major state decisions, we must bear in mind that those interests were not necessarily those of the common people. Only with the emancipation of the people and the lowering of the census, did parts of the middle class attain the chance to become involved in political activities in the second half of the nineteenth century.[10]

4. FUNDAMENTAL RIGHTS

4.1. EARLY TENDENCIES

While the focus of this analysis lies on the nineteenth century, it should be mentioned that tendencies in favour of fundamental rights can be seen earlier. If it is right, indeed, that there is no continuity between the urban charters of the Middle Ages conceding personal and collective rights to the bourgeoisie of western towns[11] and the movement for democracy in the nineteenth century, some fundamental concepts of civil and political rights can nonetheless be identified in these charters as well as for instance in the famous *Magna Charta Libertatum* (1215).

An example indicating such tendencies is the Charter of Freedom for the Luxembourg citizens, issued by Countess Ermesinde in 1244. The Charter was a reaction to the freedom and emancipation movements and town liberations of the thirteenth century. Indeed in the course of the thirteenth century, a number of towns[12] obtained a separate constitution. This measure was an integrative part of urban development and planning: in order to control their territories, the Counts needed towns as centres of administration, citizens fit for military service,

---

9 Cf. FRANZ, *supra* note 3, p. 13.

10 Cf. FRANZ, *supra* note 3, pp. 5–8.

11 Cf. M. PAULY and A. LEE (eds), *Libertés et citoyenneté urbaines du moyen âge à nos jours / Städtische Freiheiten und bürgerliche Partizipation vom Mittelalter bis heute / Urban liberties and citizenship from the Middle Ages up to now. Actes du Colloque 2009 de la Commission internationale pour l'Histoire des villes*, Publications of CLUDEM, 41, Trier/Luxembourg 2015.

12 Echternach, 1236; Thionville, 1239; Luxembourg 1244; Grevenmacher, 1252.

potential administrators and taxpayers. The privilege of freedom made the cities areas of separate peace that stood out in the settlement network. In the context of rural exodus, population growth and urban development, granting the privilege of freedom was a measure to gain new citizens, also insofar as those citizens were no longer the serfs of a landlord. As *citizens*, they became subject to taxation and military service, and they obtained 'pax et quies', freedom and security for themselves and their trade and commerce in return.

Similar to other charters, the so-called Charter of Freedom of 1244 granted important fundamental rights to citizens: it abolished the arbitrary rule of the Count and offered protection, military security, legal security and better trading conditions to the citizens. The equality of all citizens was established and they enjoyed personal freedom, free inheritance and free movement.[13] On the other hand they had to pay higher taxes and as free citizens they had to fulfil military duties, but here, social criteria were now taken into account. The privileges of freedom for the citizens further encouraged the emancipation of the people, who began to organise in communities, gained influence and autonomy, obtained the possibility to participate in the administrative municipal decisions and could defend their interests and petition for more rights. Yet, it is important to note that the urban council of jurymen who exercised these jurisdictional, executive and legislative rights was formed of people who came from a certain segment of society: not all inhabitants of a town were *citizens* in the legal sense.

All in all, we can conclude that there have been fundamental rights tendencies long before the nineteenth century. However, the Burgundian Conquest interrupted the remarkable development in this area during the thirteenth century for a short period.[14]

4.2. THE PRE-MARCH ERA

The Dutch Constitution of 1814[15] was already a considerable achievement in terms of fundamental rights, since — on the grounds of a united state territory without privileged provinces — it retained legal equality and religious liberty of the citizens. These fundamental rights were later embedded in the Dutch

---

13 Cf. K. ANDERMANN, 'Bürgerrecht. Die Speyrer Privilegien von 1111 und die Anfänge persönlicher Freiheitsrechte in deutschen Städten des hohen Mittelalters' (2012) *Historische Zeitschrift* 295, 593–624.

14 This subject has been analysed in depth by Michel Pauly: M. PAULY, 'Der Freiheitsbrief der Stadt Luxemburg: herrschaftlicher Machtanspruch oder bürgerliches Emanzipationsstreben?' in M. MARGUE (ed.), *Ermesinde et l'affranchissement de la ville de Luxembourg. Etudes sur la femme, le pouvoir et la ville au XIIIe siècle*, CLUDEM, Luxembourg 1994, t.7, pp. 235–253; M. PAULY, 'Bürgerfreiheiten im Interesse des Stadtherrn? Das Freiheitsprivileg von 1244 für die Stadt Luxemburg' in W. REICHERT, G. MINN and R. VOLTMER (eds.), *Quellen zur Geschichte des Rhein-Maas-Raumes. Ein Lehr- und Lernbuch*, Kilomedia, Trier 2006, pp. 33–57.

15 See the chapter on the Netherlands by Louis Berkvens in this volume.

Constitution of 1815 and they thereby also applied to the Grand Duchy of Luxembourg. Yet other fundamental rights, such as freedom of the press and the right to education were not endorsed. The Belgian Constitution of 1831 extended the rights of citizens. In addition to the rights already granted by the Dutch Constitution and the abolition of the estates, crucial fundamental rights were retained: the freedoms of education, of association, of press, of opinion and of petition as well as confidentiality of correspondence were now granted to the citizens.[16] The Luxembourgish Charter of 1841 guaranteed freedom of religion — and even the right to express any religious views and hence also agnostic or atheistic ideas. Equality before the law, without regard to religious affiliation, social status or origin, was also guaranteed and with the re-organisation of justice in 1840, jurisdiction was now assumed by Luxembourgish citizens.[17] Further, the right to individual liberty — which meant that no one could be persecuted or arrested outside the law — was granted, as well as the inviolability of the home and the protection of property. The Constitution also retained the right of Luxembourgish citizens to petition the Assembly of the Estates and guaranteed access of Luxembourgish citizens to public positions. Yet, the new constitutional systems did not necessarily grant more rights or increase the authority and possibility for participation of the citizens.

While the 1841 Charter guaranteed some important fundamental rights, the people were deprived of other essential fundamental rights granted under the Belgian Constitution: freedoms of the press, of assembly and of association were abolished. In 1847, censorship was tightened[18] and was now executed directly by the monarch and his commissaries.[19] Gender equality was obtained in none of the constitutional systems and only became an issue in the twentieth century.[20]

4.3. POST-MARCH ERA

In the 1848 Constitution, the fundamental rights of the people were significantly extended. It guaranteed personal freedom, the inviolability of the home, the protection of property and freedom of religion, yet the most important acquisition was freedom of the press and of opinion. Censorship was lifted and the right of assembly, association and petition were granted, as well as confidentiality of correspondence, albeit with restrictions. The death penalty for political crimes was abolished as was *civil death*, which was an increased penalty that led to the loss of fundamental rights, such as the right of property or of

---

16 See the chapter on Belgium by Wim Decock and Koen Lemmens in this volume.

17 Cf. FRANZ, *supra* note 6, pp. 543–573, pp. 17–18.

18 Law of 22 November 1847 by William II.

19 This tightening of the censorship was a clear answer to the fragile relationship between the Oranian monarchs and an expression of the insecurity of the monarchical rule, yet under this angle, it can also be interpreted a response to the emancipatory tendencies of the people. Cf. FRANZ, *supra* note 6, pp. 543–573, pp. 20–23.

20 Cf. FRANZ, *supra* note 6, pp. 543–573, pp. 13–14.

tutelary authority, the annulation of matrimonial and family relationships and the denial of the possibility to be heard as witness or to conclude legal transactions. Branding, the last corporal punishment still executed, was also abolished. Public primary education became a state responsibility.

The Constitution of 1856 did not touch these fundamental rights to a wide extent. However it restricted the right of association 'for the sake of public order'. Whilst freedom of press remained a civil right, state pressure on the press was critical. The right to petition was limited insofar as personal interests could not be subject of petitions. An exception was made for complaints against unlawful acts of the governmental or administrative authorities. The Constitution of 1868 reversed the 1856 restriction of the right of association and extended the confidentiality of correspondence to telegrams. Yet, state pressure on the press was maintained to a large extent.[21] Hence, the various fundamental rights that were introduced by the 1848 Constitution were widely maintained during the reactionary phase of the 1850s. However, the restrictions on the rights of association and petition were not negligible. The law of 10 June 1898 reinforced the criminal code (article 310) by punishing any attempt to restrict the liberty of labour by strike or any other threat. Freedom of the press was formally maintained, but it was considerably limited by other measures.[22]

After this overview of the civic rights granted or restricted under the different constitutions, a few will be looked at in detail.

4.4. EDUCATION, ECONOMY AND SOCIAL RIGHTS

Even if national sovereignty was marked by tensions between the Church and the State on the question of education, the Church played an important part in the promotion of education.[23] But freedom of education was one of the rare rights that were not transferred from the Belgian into the Luxembourgish Constitution of 1848. The national Luxembourgish Education Act of 1843 conferred the educational duties to the municipalities, who were obliged to set up primary schools, ensure a continuous education and guarantee the education of the poor and the needy.[24] Schooling became compulsory only in 1881. Until the twenty-first century education was a state prerogative and any private or religious initiative to create a school required governmental authorisation.

The post-March era was marked by continuous efforts at development of the educational system. With the 1848 Revolution, the efforts of the state were extended to the promotion of secondary and further education and even under the

---

21 Cf. FRANZ, *supra* note 3, p. 16.
22 Cf. FRANZ, *supra* note 3, pp. 9–10.
23 This thanks to the efforts of the sisters of the congregation *Unserer Lieben Frau*.
24 Cf. FRANZ, *supra* note 6, pp. 543–573, pp. 25–27.

restrictive 1856 Constitution, decisive efforts at the development of the educational system were made.[25] The economy and the social sector were still widely neglected parts of state activity during the pre-March era. A large part of the population suffered from economic crises and mass poverty. The situation of the state was characterised by considerable structural problems. Industry was underdeveloped, trade suffered from unfavourable customs frontiers and mass poverty prevailed. While these problems were only partially confronted under the Dutch and Belgian rules, they were addressed by the first national Luxembourgish administration: between 1840 and 1847, central laws and regulations on suffrage, government and justice organisation, traffic engineering, the public school system, the public health system and care of the poor were issued. The accession of the Grand Duchy to the *German Zollverein* opened up a considerable market to the Luxembourgish economy and generated an important customs revenue to the state.

In spite of these efforts, the population of the Grand Duchy was marked by mass poverty and unemployment. The textile industry and the steel industries were underdeveloped, as was agriculture — problems that led to the 1848 Revolution. In the following years, continuous investments in the development and promotion of the transport infrastructure, the economy, the public sector, religious communities, schools and social and healthcare were made. Even under the restrictive 1856 Constitution, William III continued the development of the infrastructure and in doing so, created the grounds for the economic upswing of the state. In the 1850s, the Luxembourgish railway network was created; an essential step towards the state's development.[26]

As for public welfare, social care, healthcare and care of the poor were institutionally strengthened after national sovereignty and became the object of state interest and promotion especially after the 1860s. However, many aspects remained neglected until well into the twentieth century and the Grand Duchy was far from being a *social state*. Help was only given to people whom the state actually recognised as needy. Furthermore, the measures for poor relief often went hand in hand with the combat of delinquency, and as a result, they did not necessarily arise out of solidarity but had a repressive character.[27]

---

25 Cf. FRANZ, *supra* note 6, pp. 543–573, pp. 18–19.

26 Cf. PAULY, *supra* note 4; for the history of railways: *150 Joer Eisebunn zu Lëtzebuerg 1859–2009*, Société Nationale des Chemins de Fer Luxembourgeois, Ministère du Développement durable et des Infrastructures, Luxembourg 2009.

27 Cf. FRANZ, *supra* note 3, pp. 20–23.

5. SUFFRAGE AND THE RIGHT TO VOTE

Suffrage and the right to vote were essential indicators of the right to political implication; therefore a brief account of their development will be given. Indeed, during the whole nineteenth century a certain census had to be paid in order to participate in both the direct and indirect elections of the representative bodies. The amount varied with the constitutional systems, yet it limited the suffrage to those who were able to afford the census.[28]

Even though the census was gradually lowered in the post-March Constitutions,[29] an overwhelming majority of men were excluded from an active participation in the political decision-making, while women did not have any right to vote at all.[30] This would only change with the constitutional reform after World War I, where universal, equal suffrage for women and men as well as the principle of the people's sovereignty were finally introduced.[31]

6. GENDER

While over the nineteenth century, feminist movements have arisen throughout Europe, Luxembourg has been largely exempt from this development. Women's voices were not heard and in this context, we can name the nineteenth century, the 'the silent century',[32] when referring to the Grand Duchy. While the mid-nineteenth century was characterised by an emancipation of the bourgeoisie, women did not participate in this movement and did not, or not appreciably, claim their rights — they remained silent. They were excluded from politics and even though the 1848 Constitution guaranteed legal equality and thus implied gender equality, it was counteracted by the 1804 patriarchal Civil Code that firmly entrenched the inferiority of women and especially married women.[33] Their legal situation was far inferior to that of men, which was also linked to the fact that the family image during the nineteenth century was that of a unit with the man as head and decision-maker.

---

[28] An exception was the passive election of the eight Luxembourg delegates for the government during the Belgian rule.

[29] With exception of the 1856 Constitution that dramatically limited the eligible voters; cf. FRANZ, *supra* note 3, pp. 8–9.

[30] Cf. FRANZ, *supra* note 3, pp. 10–13.

[31] R. WAGENER, *'... wie eine frühreife Frucht' Zur Geschichte des Frauenwahlrechts in Luxemburg*, Forum, Luxembourg 1994.

[32] R. WAGENER, 'Bye Bye Siegfried. Der lange Abschied der Luxemburger Frauen vom Patriarchat' in CENTRE D'INFORMATION ET DE DOCUMENTATION DES FEMMES 'THERS BODÉ' (LUXEMBOURG) (ed.), *Not The Girl You're Looking For – Melousina Rediscovered. Objekt + Subjekt der Frau in der Kultur Luxemburgs = Objet + Sujet – La femme dans la culture au Luxembourg*, CID Femmes, Luxembourg 2010, pp. 212–238.

[33] *Ibid.*, pp. 212–238, pp. 220–221.

Only female teachers were an exception; both men and women could become teachers and women could even become school principals. This did not only give them access to further education,[34] but made teachers pioneers in women's employment and opened up the possibility of articulation of emancipatory claims. However, the silence of women was maintained and their voices campaigning for political, social and legal equality were not heard until well into the twentieth century.[35]

7. CONCLUDING REMARKS

We have seen that due to political tensions and upheavals, Luxembourg was subjected to a series of different rules and constitutional systems that influenced the power relations between monarch, government and representative bodies and alternatively limited or increased the fundamental rights granted to the people as well as their possibilities for participation in the decision-making process. The pre-March era has shown that a change of constitutional system does not necessarily imply an increase of rights and liberties. Changing constitutional systems not only created new rights or liberties, but some rights or liberties also disappeared. The pre-March era was characterised by economic backwardness, domestic political change and an endangerment of the national sovereignty. In the post-March era the state-building process made considerable progress and the state administration professionalised. State responsibilities covered the typical responsibilities of the Western and Middle European states, from the instruments of power, through transport infrastructure and the education sector to healthcare and care of the poor.

All in all, during the period in focus, fundamental rights have gradually increased with the emancipation of the people. Especially after national sovereignty and the post-March crises, a national conscience developed, giving birth to a political movement that found followers from all social classes, who — despite all differences — identified with the state and enhanced the nation-building process. Yet, while emancipatory processes and claims began to form and take shape during the nineteenth century, it is the time after the turn of the century that can be considered the era of social and political awakening. Only then were there first attempts to form political parties, increased petitions for the expansion of fundamental rights and, finally, the raised voices of women.

---

[34] In 1857, one third of the female population could neither read nor write; cf. WAGENER, *supra* note 32, p. 220.

[35] And only in 2006, a constitutional modification of 2006 retained that 'All Citizens have equal rights and duties' and that the State 'shall ensure the active promotion of the elimination of obstacles that might exist to equality between men and women'. WAGENER, *supra* note 32, pp. 212–238, pp. 219–223 and p. 241.

16. GREECE: REFLECTIONS FROM THE HELLENIC LEGAL TRADITION

Stelios PERRAKIS
Maria Daniella MAROUDA

1. INTRODUCTION

The identification, description and analysis of documents of similar importance to Magna Carta, for a country like Greece, with a legal culture that transcends the actual creation of the Greek Modern State (1832), is certainly not an easy exercise. This is due to the fact that from the era of the Greek City-State (Polis) of antiquity to modern times and the post-1945 human rights period, important documents and references of the Hellenic legal tradition related, directly or indirectly, to the recognition of fundamental rights and democratic institutions and the rule of law in a legal order of principles and values. An interesting feature of the historic process from Greek City-State to contemporary Greece is that it culminated with the adoption of important texts of constitutional character and value, addressing the concerns of the citizen, the human person and his rights.

It is true that the legal assessment and political significance of such texts should take into account that they were formulated in different historic periods and within different societal and political contexts. They have autonomous characteristics, especially in the field of fundamental rights. From the philosophical streams and perspectives of Ancient Greece, to the codifications of legal provisions up to the period of the Enlightenment and beyond, including the War of Independence/Revolution of 1821, the emergence of Greece as a State and its transformation during the nineteenth century from Kingdom to Republic, the very notion of fundamental rights does not seem to have had an identical perception and recognition in the evolution of the society and space called Greece. Analysis reveals, however, important insights into such legal tradition, because it highlights the principles and values that underlie the organization of Greek societies where fundamental rights seem to be *prima facie* absent. And even if, in the Poleis/Cities in the golden period of Athenian democracy and beyond, these fundamental rights and the modern version of civil rights do not necessarily find an absolute match,[1] whether because of the institution of slavery (and its corollary 'eleutheroi') or because of the unequal position of women, the antithesis is interesting.[2] As long as we focus on the relationship between the state and the citizen, these ancient rights reflect the fundamental rights of equality before the law, freedom of expression, political rights to participate in public life and the direct participation of the citizen in the legislative and judicial bodies, giving expression to the the unique definition of democracy by Aristoteles, according to which democracy means that the majority is ruling and the minority is controlling.[3] All these concepts have inspired the nucleus of the fundamental rights of the Enlightenment and the French Revolution.

It is also true that in societies such as ancient Greece, one can identify precursor forms and separate functions, but not the codified expressions of fundamental rights as they appeared in the eighteenth century and beyond.[4] This is why, in these early documents, it is safer to depart from the use of terminology referring to individual rights (or human rights) and rather focus on the enshrined fundamental rights, which, however, as a notion or term, is not to be found in any ancient Greek texts. Certain documents refer, on the other hand, to specific civil rights (family, personal status or property rights, as is evident in the first European legal code, the Great Code of Gortyn (adopted in the fifth century BC), which we also decided to briefly analyse, as one of the fundamental texts reflecting the Greek legal tradition.

Individual approaches in the form of codified legal provisions or nineteenth century constitutional texts ranging from the Revolutionary Period of the War of Independence to the First Greek Constitution of 1844, or the Constitutional Acts of the Ionian Islands (1806, 1817), or of Crete (1822, 1899), regions that were not yet incorporated in the newly founded Greek state, give the perception of a solid and democratic state organisation and in particular of a legal order in which the individual or citizen enjoys basic rights. The works of Rigas Velestinlis and especially his masterpiece: *The New Political Constitution* (containing *Ta dikaia toy anthpopou*, eng.: human rights) precedes, dominates and inspires these constitutional Acts.

---

1 G. TENEKIDES, 'La Cité d'Athènes et les droits de l'homme' in G. TENEKIDES, *Les relations internationales dans la Grèce Antique*, Fondation A.G.Leventis, Athènes 1993, pp. 457-460.

2 See, on the status of women in Ancient Greece a contradiction with the power of women in the cities P. DIMAKIS, 'Indices du pouvoir des femmes dans l'Athènes classique', in H. JONES, (ed.) *Le Monde Antique et les droits de l'homme*, Centre de droit comparé et d'histoire du droit, Bruxelles 1998, pp. 147–154.

3 H. JONES (ed.), *Le monde antique et les droits de l'homme* (Actes de la 50e session de la Société Internationale Fernand de Visscher pour l'Histoire des Droits de l'Antiquité, Bruxelles, 16–19 septembre 1996), Centre de droit comparé et d'histoire du droit, Bruxelles 1998.

4 *Ibid.*

The pluralism of such important documents directed our decision to include in the current contribution, instead of a single 'fundamental text' compared to Magna Carta provisions, three important sets of documents that cover the historic dimension of important achievements before the formal emergence of fundamental rights in Greece. The first, although mostly concerning civil rights and the position of women in that society is the Gortyn Code (fifth century BC) and the second is the works of Rigas Velestinlis, while the third focuses on the revolutionary Constitutional Acts during and following the War of Independence up to the first formal Constitution of 1844, which was imposed on King Otto by the people of the newly founded state.

2. THE GREAT CODE OF GORTYN: A FIRST EUROPEAN SET OF LEGISLATION

The famous inscription of laws at Gortyn on the island of Crete,[5] dating back to the beginning of the fifth century BC, or the Great Code (although not a Code in the strict legal sense) contains an organisation of provisions that were unearthed 120 years ago. Expressions in the Code referring to 'as is written' in interconnected legal texts gives the impression of a unified set of laws that might have been the inspiration for one of the greatest legislative achievements of Ancient Greek Law, often referred to as the 'Queen of Inscriptions'. In 12 columns and 621 lines, the Code gives us a very important glimpse into the early Greek, Crete and Dorian customs, in addition to constituting the earliest law code and the first European one.[6] The Code shows a tremendous effort by Gortynians to organise their legislation logically and coherently, with provisions that are to be used in their daily lives. Two-thirds of the main body of the Code consists of regulations about the family and its property.

The Great Code is the largest document of ancient Greek Law in existence, containing 35 independent legislative acts, with provisions mostly of a civil and penal nature. We find articles on sexual assaults (II.2–10, 11–16, 16–20, and 20–45), estate settlement due to divorce or death of one of the spouses (II.45–III.37), two laws on protection of children (IV.17–23), and a section on inheritance and on the heiress (VII.15–VIII.30, VIII.30–IX.1 and IX.1–24). According to the logic of the provisions, a husband may choose to divorce his seduced wife, but then the wife is entitled to compensation if the husband is the cause of the divorce. The laws on the protection of children born after the divorce of their

---

5 The Code is located in the archaeological site of Gortyna, on the island of Crete. The Code is well preserved, open to the public and worth visiting.

6 J.K. Davies, 'Deconstructing Gortyn: When is a Code a Code?' in L. Foxhall and A.D.E. Lewis (eds.), *Greek Law in its Political Setting*, Clarendon Press, Oxford 1996, pp. 33–56; J.K. Davies, 'The Gortyn Laws' in M. Gagarin and D. Cohen (eds.), *The Cambridge Companion to Families in the Greek and Roman Worlds*, Cambridge University Press, Cambridge 2005, pp. 305–327.

parents have the logical consequence that they belong to the paternal *oikos* (home), and then the laws that follow deal with inheritance issues. Important provisions refer to Gortynian citizens who were taken captive when abroad, with the paying back of ransom as an obligation. Children of a mixed marriage between a free woman and a slave are dealt with under separate laws, as well as the liability of slave owners after the conclusion of the sale.

In this archaic legislation, the law consists of a general ban against a behaviour (e.g rape), followed by a *protasis* (definition of the act of the perpetrator) and an *apodosis* (punishment and/or size of the fine). The law on seduction, for example, separates the case of the seduction of a *doulos* (slave) from other cases. The laws on divorce between a free man and a free woman cover only the estate settlement (property). Moreover, in the laws on adoption, the provisions are extensive. The permission to adopt, the actual process of adoption (an act that is valid and public), the adopter's obligations and the fact that it applies to adopters of citizens' status are all dealt with.

One of the most important features of the Code refers to the position of women. Although in Greece women had unequal status, according to Gortyn women enjoyed a remarkable independence compared to Athenian practice. They could choose their spouse from among either free men or slaves, they could divorce, and instead of a dowry, daughters were entitled to a specific portion of the inheritance equal to half of that of a son. Even an heiress was able to choose her husband, and on divorce a woman could keep her own property and half of the cloth she had woven during the course of the marriage.[7] Moreover, women in Gortyn could own property in their own right and could manage and dispose of it without the need of a 'guardian' (*kyrios*), such as we find in Athens. They could appear in court on their own as plaintiffs or defendants. Divorced women were entitled to any property that they brought to the marriage, as well as half of the joint income, if derived from her property. The code also provides for a portion of the household property to belong to the woman on divorce. Women were also protected from sexual assault, seizure, rape, forcible intercourse with a slave, attempted seduction, adultery, and separation of spouses. Specific provisions refer to the children of divorced women, the remarkable — for the period — reference that unwed slave mothers should have the protection of the law, the distribution of property among children, the law on gifts to women and gifts to a daughter.[8] There were also other interesting features in the Code. For example,

---

7 See, Laws relating to women in Gortyn/Crete, ca. 450 B.C. (Excerpts from the Gortyn Law Code, *Inscr. Creticae* 4.72, cols. ii.3–27, ii. 45–iv.54, v. 1–9. vi.31–46, vi.56–vii.2, vii.15–viii.19, xi. 18–9. G).

8 The law allows a father, if he wishes, to give his daughter a gift when she is getting married worth up to the amount of her share of inheritance, after which she is not to receive anything more (4.48–5.1). Husbands and sons are explicitly allowed to give gifts (10.13–17, 12.1–5) to women, either at the time of the wedding, or later. If the husband dies, his wife may choose to remarry, and she is allowed to keep gifts or other property or what her husband gave her

regarding sexual offences, rape of a free person, male or female, was to be punished by a fine largely determined by the difference in social status between the victim and the accused. A free man convicted of raping a serf or a slave would receive the lowest fine; a slave convicted of raping a free man or female would warrant the highest fine. Adultery was punished similarly to rape under the Code, but also takes into consideration the location of the crime. The Code dictated higher fines for adultery committed within the household of the female's father, husband, or brother, as opposed to another location.

Another important section refers to an antithesis if compared to Athenian traditions; privileges enjoyed by slaves. These included the right to choose a spouse without the permission of the 'master', the right to own property which could not be confiscated by the owner and an implicit assumption that slaves have the capacity to obtain legal redress if the owner infringes these privileges. The aim was to clarify complex relationships, including the division of property of free citizens in complex scenarios, such as if they choose to marry *doulous* (serfs).

The existence of a Code, as early as in the fifth century BC, with such important regulation of the relationships in society, with special status for women and girls, as well as the protection of children and their interests, provides a clear image of a society willing to protect the vulnerable through a statutory regime. Therefore, even though scholars have argued that in that era there were no such concepts as fundamental or individual rights, these provisions reflect the concrete idea of a legal organisation in the society and between its members, with an implicit recognition of rights and privileges, an interesting gender perspective (military training for both men and women, right to choose a spouse, property rights, etc.) and a connection to the everyday organisation of life.

3. RIGAS VELESTINLIS: TA DIKAIA TOU ANTHROPOU (HUMAN RIGHTS)

Rigas Feraios from Velestino, Thessalia/Greece, also known as Rigas Velestinlis (1757–1798), is one of the most important figures of Modern Greece as well as of the Balkans. He was a major figure of the Greek Enlightenment and an active player in the Greek Resurgence in the late eighteenth century, and he was the first martyr of the Greek cause following his assassination by the Ottomans in Belgrade (1798). Rigas influenced his contemporary environment by spreading

according to three witnesses that should testify before a court, if disputes arise (3.17–37) (17.20). We can infer from the wording of the laws at Gortyn that women's rights in these respects had been granted recently or had been expanded, in order to further protect the property of women. See M. GAGARIN, Women's property at Gortyn, Dike, 15 2012, pp. 73–92, <http://riviste.unimi.it/index.php/Dike/article/view/3492>.

the principles of the French Revolution onto Greek territory.[9] Rigas Velestinlis was a complex personality, who tried numerous strategies in an attempt to organise a revolution in the area of the Balkans and to create an independent democratic state. The ideas of Rigas Velestinlis, influenced by the French Revolution and its Declaration of the Rights of Man and the Citizen, contributed to the rise of a culture of freedom, democracy and fundamental rights under Ottoman Rule in the Balkans in the eighteenth century.

Out of the entire revolutionary project of Rigas Velestinlis some elements are worthy of particular mention: *Thoureios,* a patriotic anthem;[10] *the Map of Greece (Harta),* a geographical Map of Greece with political significance[11] and most importantly the *New Political Constitution of the Inhabitants of Roumeli, Asia Minor, the Islands of the Aegean and the Principalities of Moldavia and Wallachia*, written in Vienna in 1797.

The New Political Constitution of Rigas is a masterpiece; a document describing the governance of his envisioned Greek Democracy (containing 124 articles). The first part of the document refers to the Declaration of Human Rights (*Dikaia tou Anthropou*). The second part refers to his vision of a Democratic State (Constitution). He includes, *inter alia*, a definition of the people, the status of the Greek citizen, the organisation of the administration, and finally the judicial system and the relationship of the Greek Republic with foreign nations. Notably, an Annex contains a vivid description of the new Greek flag, the uniform of the Greek soldier, as well as the helmet all Greek men and women should wear to be recognised as free democrats and equal brothers.[12]

It is interesting to note that the document as a whole reflects the vision of Rigas not only on individual human rights, but also on the rights of peoples or nations exercising self-determination within the organisation of a federal State in

---

9 For Rigas and his work see A. MANESSIS, 'L'activité et les projets politiques d'un patriote grec dans les Balkans vers la fin du XVIIIe siècle' (1962) 3 *Balkan Studies* 75–115; P. KITROMILIDES, *Greek enlightenment. Political and social ideas*, 2nd ed., Cultural Foundation of the National Bank of Greece, Athens 1999, p. 575; N. PANTAZOPOULOS, *Studies about Rhigas Velestinlis, published by the Scientific Society of Studies,* Pheres-Velestino-Rhigas, Athens 1994, p. 106.

10 This Revolutionary Song (Thoureios) Rigas stressed the essential values of the people namely freedom and human dignity which in the human life with universal and social content. The same text recognises the individual and the collective character of these rights.

11 J-Y. GUIOMAR and M-T. LORAIN, 'La carte de Grèce de Rigas et le nom de la Grèce', *Annales historiques de la Révolution française*, no. 319, 2000, pp. 101–125. The cartographic work of Rigas Velestinlis, is a masterpiece the twelve-sheet Charta (1797) reflecting the 'Space' in which he envisioned the Greek State, populated by Greeks, or where Greece attested a presence by mythology and history. La Charta is mainly described as an intellectual work rather than a real cartographic product. See C. BOUTOURA, 'On the map projection of Rigas Velestinlis Charta' (2008) 3 *e-Perimetron* No. 3 146–160.

12 For the full text of the document see H. KYRIAKOPOULOS, *The Constitutions of Greece*, Εθνικόν Τυπογραφείον, Athens 1960, pp. 3 et seq.

accordance with the rule of law. Indeed Rigas, at a time in which slavery and tyranny were still present, formulated the first memorandum of association of the Balkan area under the name New Political Administration, in which were included fundamental rights and the constitution. Thereby the revolutionary Greek Democracy and the other Balkan nations could have an effective and workable plan to democratically govern the new state, which was to replace Ottoman authoritarian rule. Rigas' new political government declares the equality of citizens before the law, private and national freedom, freedom of the press, the security of citizens, the right of ownership, the abandonment of slavery, and opposition to violence and inequity.

In Rigas' vision, fundamental rights refer to the rights of the person as a citizen.[13] As a consequence political freedoms guaranteed within fundamental rights are recognised on behalf of individuals or groups of persons. The right of resistance against tyrannical governance is furthermore recognised. Rigas' standards were the French Revolution and ancient Athenian Democracy and his ideas were later present in all Constitutions of revolutionary Greece.

In the part of the document on Human Rights, a commendable gender dimension is included, referring to the obligatory training not only of boys but also of girls (Human Rights, article 22), which reveals that Rigas was a proponent of equality between men and women. The introduction of protection of citizens against exploitative money-lending (Human Rights, article 35[14]) is equally important. Moreover, every citizen of the new state would be equal before the law, and they would enjoy religious freedom and respect of their language. The people who were to be a part of this democratic state would enjoy the benefits of a democratic administration which showed respect for their life and their

13 See for example: 'Article 1.- ...People.... enjoy their natural rights, something that no one on earth has the right to take away from them Article 2.- These Natural rights are: firstly all to be equal and not someone superior to the other. Secondly, to be free and no one slave to the other. Thirdly, to be secure in our life and no one to be *able to imagine that he can deprive it unfairly and forthly, no one to be able to claim the property we own because it belongs to us and to* our heirs. Article 5.- All fellow citizens can have access to public offices of equal value. Article 6.- Freedom is that force which man owns in order to act in a way that cannot clash with his neighbours rights. Article 7.- The right to reveal our opinion and thoughts through printing, as well as many other ways; the right of gathering peacefully; the freedom of all religions Article 9.- Law has the duty to protect the common freedom of the whole nation as well as that of every person, inhabitant of this country, against the depression and despotism of the governors. When they govern well the law must protect them, when wrongly, to expel them...'.

14 Article 35.- 'When the administration violates, brakes and despises the rights of the people and does not listen to their complaints, then the revolution of the people or part of the people and the punishment of the tyrants is most sacred of all their rights and the most indispensable of all their duties. In case the revolutionaries live in a place where the tyrants are more in number, the most courageous and freedom-loving patriots should hold the crossings of the streets and the mountains heights, until they become many in number and multiplied and only then they should start the attack against the tyrants'.

property.[15] Professor Nicolaos Pantazopoulos explicitly states that 'Rigas went beyond the declaration of the French Revolution, that gives rights to the individual and not to the societies meaning the minorities. In that way Rigas was to become the pioneer of the Universal Declaration of Human Rights, which recognizes human rights within the spirit of Rigas for small or great groups, such as Communities and Societies'.[16]

In the document a separate reference is made to the right and the duty of the people to proceed to a revolution when the administration violates their rights. It is referred to as a sacred right and the most necessary of their duties (article 35). This same reference is reflected in later Constitutional Texts and in the preamble of the Universal Declaration of Human Rights.

4. THE HERITAGE OF RIGAS: FROM THE FIRST REVOLUTIONARY CONSTITUTIONS DURING THE WAR OF INDEPENDENCE TO THE FIRST CONSTITUTION OF GREECE IN 1844

The very important influence of Rigas dates back to the period of the War of Independence of Greece against Ottoman Rule. This influence was felt even though his works remained at a declaratory level; they were a source of inspiration for the development that followed, the first constitutional provisions reflecting fundamental rights. It is of particular importance that during the whole period of the struggle for independence, the revolutionary Greeks, even without the formal existence of the state, proceeded innovatively and adopted constitutional texts with particular reference to fundamental rights.

In particular, the National Assembly meeting that took place in December 1821 proceeded to adopt legal documents containing provisions of a constitutional character on the Greek Polity (*Politeuma*).[17] All of these Acts, passed by the elected delegates of the Greek people who were struggling for freedom, incorporated references to fundamental rights, as envisaged by Rigas and the instruments of the French Revolution.

Indeed in the provisional Constitution of Greece, as adopted by the first National Assembly of Epidavros (December 1821), a series of provisions relate to general rights, such as the tolerance of the administration towards religions (paragraph

15 P. KITROMILIDES, *Greek enlightenment. Political and social ideas*, 2nd ed., Cultural Foundation of the National Bank of Greece, Athens 1999, p. 575.

16 N. PANTAZOPOULOS, *Studies about Rhigas Velestinlis*, Scientific Society of Studies Pheres-Velestino-Rhigas, Athens 1994, p. 106.

17 For the text of the revolutionary constitutions, see KYRIAKOPOULOS, *supra* note 12, pp. 31 et seq.

a), the equality of Greeks before the law without discrimination (paragraph c), the enjoyment of political rights without distinction (paragraph b), the assimilation of foreigners with the indigenous inhabitants before the law, the right to personal safety, property, and dignity (paragraph i), etc. All of these are included in Section B, under the title 'On the General Rights of the Inhabitants of Greece'.

The second National Assembly of Astros (20 March 1823) moved towards a revision of the Epidavros text. Whereas religious rights remained the same, with an explicit prevalence of the Greek Orthodox Church, Section B referred to Political Rights of Greeks. We find a specific reference on who is a Greek and what are his civil and political rights. The conditions for the naturalization of foreigners are striking (e.g. five years of residence). Most importantly, though, the Constitution prohibited slavery, incorporated freedom of expression, the right to file complaints and the right to access to justice. The Law of Epidavros was, thus, complemented with new provisions on the organisation and the functioning of the State.

The third Review National Assembly held in Troizina voted in 1827 for the Political Constitution of Greece. This document was adopted as a formal Constitution. Since then, Greek Constitutions have had a similar form in the separation of Chapters. The first chapter declares freedom of religion (with the predominance of the Greek Orthodox Religion), freedom of the press, the protection of personal freedom and the protection of property. In the second chapter organisational arrangements for the Greek territory are set out. Chapter 3 refers to the public law of Greece, including the people's sovereignty and fundamental rights. The naturalisation of foreigners is dealt with in Chapter D.

The arrival of Kapodistrias as the Governor of Greece, in 1828, inexorably led to the suspension of previous constitutional provisions and to the institution of a new governance framework.

The philosophy of the Constitution of Epidavros and subsequent texts were restored by the Fifth National Assembly held at Nafplion in 1832 following the assassination of Kapodistrias (in September 1831). The National Assembly adopted a constitution, which was recognised as the fundamental law of the nation, named the 'Political Constitution of Greece'. The National Assembly declared that the Constitution would be submitted to the Sovereign Prince of Greece (Otto) for his approval. In Chapter B certain fundamental rights are declared, on the public or common law of the Greeks, on religion, on the distinction between Greeks and citizens, and on citizenship and naturalisation, as well as on the common rights and duties of the Greeks (in Greek, the terminology used is that of *dikaia*, referring to just causes, fairness and the concept of rights — the same term as used by Rigas).

With the London Protocol of 1832 Prince Otto of Bavaria would become the King of Greece. The National Assembly held in Argos ratified the election of

Otto as King. However, on 25 January – 6 February 1833, following his arrival at Nafplion, the then capital of Greece, the Regency issued a declaration that Otto became King of Greece ελέω θεού (with gods benediction), thereby establishing an absolute monarchy and sidestepping the constitutional texts.

On 3 September 1843, the people of Greece forced the King to accept a change of regime. In November 1843, the First National Assembly adopted a Draft Constitution, which was sent to King Otto for acceptance and ratification. The Constitution referred to a contract between the monarch and the Nation re-establishing the Constitutional Monarchy. The Greek Kingdom passed the first Constitution, which provides for fundamental rights, following the existing *aquis*, and included the public law of Greeks (article 3–14). The content of these articles repeat the fundamental rights found in all previous revolutionary constitutions and particularly the one drafted in Troizina in 1827. Like all previous revolutionary constitutions, the Constitution of 1844 endorsed the principle of the separation of powers and guaranteed basic fundamental rights and freedoms. Still, from the constitutional point of view this Charter was a pact between the monarch and the people, recognising the monarch as the supreme organ of the State and the head of the Executive. He had the right of legislative initiative, and the competence to appoint the members of the Upper House and the judges. It was a largely liberal document by the standards of the day, providing for virtually universal male suffrage (although women were barred from voting until as late as 1952).

5. CONCLUDING REMARKS

In Greek history and legal tradition, Greeks, as human persons, were defined essentially as being free (*eleutheroi*) and as members of a city (citizens).[18] Moreover, freedom was considered to be the foundation of a democratic regime, guaranteeing rights and privileges. In this context, each citizen was a member of the legislative body (*Vouli*), or the Assembly (*Ekklisia tou Dimou*) and sat as a Judge, as an expression of the people's sovereignty. *Eunomia* (rule of law), virtue, principles and values for human dignity, and the status of the citizen constituted the common rules of Greeks (Thucydides).

These concepts were then and are today the essential core components of a democracy and the foundational prerequisites of true enjoyment of fundamental rights. Even if at that time, there was no explicit recognition of the term fundamental rights, the spirit and the practical expression of values for human persons and citizens is present, reflecting the legal tradition that survived and

[18] Aristoteles, *Politics*, 22, viii, 557b3.

found expression in the first constitutional acts of the newly founded Greek State of the nineteenth century. From this perspective, the Greek contribution to the rise of a law and culture of fundamental rights and democracy is important.

17. DENMARK: IN LOVE WITH TRADITION

Eva Maria LASSEN

1. INTRODUCTION

On leaving Copenhagen Central Station, the visitor to Denmark will see a 20-meter tall obelisk taking up a prominent position in the station square. This column has traditionally been named the 'Danes' symbol of liberty', 'a symbol of national cohesion', or 'a foundation stone of democracy'. Officially it is called the Liberty Column.

The foundation stone for the Liberty Column was laid by the Crown Prince in 1792, and was a gift from the citizens of Copenhagen to commemorate the abolishment of adscription of the peasants (i.e., feudalism) in 1788 and the agricultural reforms that followed.

The inscriptions of the column read that the King realised that 'freedom for his citizens laid down by just law' gives birth to 'love of the Fatherland, courage to protect it, a zest for knowledge, a desire for industrious work'. The King decreed that adscription should be abolished so that the peasant might be 'enlightened', 'hard-working and good', and 'an honest citizen'.

The perception that the abolition of adscription in 1788 was *the* stepping stone to democracy has transmitted to modern times. Thus it was in accordance with celebrated tradition that the Danish queen in 1988, on the occasion of the celebration of the 200th anniversary of the abolition of adscription, in a speech said that 'With the Act of 20 June 1788 the foundation was laid, not only for freeing the farmers but also for our society today'.[1]

Can we conclude, then, that the Act of 20 June 1788 abolishing adscription is the first Danish fundamental rights document? On closer inspection, this conclusion calls for qualification. First of all, there are earlier documents in Danish history which contain substantial and fundamental rights, albeit only relevant to a few

[1] Quoted from F. STENDAL PEDERSEN, *Den ulige frihed: Studier i myten om stavnsbåndsløsningens betydning*, Odense Universitetsforlag, Odense 1990, p. 37.

segments of society. This applies most notably to the Coronation Charter of 1282, issued by King Erik Klipping.[2] This charter, which in some ways is the Danish parallel to Magna Carta, was the result of severe clashes between King Erik Klipping and the noblemen of the country caused by the king's abuse of power.[3] Thus he had used his judicial power to execute disobedient and difficult subjects, typically noblemen, for lese-majesty, and to take over their property. The conflict ended with the king being forced to issue the Coronation Charter, in which his judicial power was curbed and property rights were ensured. Most importantly, the *habeas corpus* rule is included in the Charter.

The Coronation Charter of 1282 and subsequent coronation charters predominately benefitted the highest echelons of society. From 1660 to 1848 absolutist monarchs reigned with practically no restraint on royal power: the days of coronation charters were over.

The Coronation Charter of 1282 is sometimes named 'Denmark's first constitution'[4] and as such is an important document in Danish political history. Outside the circle of historians, however, it does not hold a central place in Danish self-perception and national identity. In this sense, the Coronation Charter is *not* Magna Carta to the Danes.

We have to look to the eighteenth century to find fundamental rights documents which benefitted larger segments of society in a fundamental way, and which have had 'staying power' in Danish national identity. In this sense it could be said that it is safe to focus mainly on the reforms of the eighteenth century when we are looking for fundamental rights documents.

But this view, too, has to be qualified. New ways of looking at society in history have resulted in novel perspectives on legal and social history, including the perspective of the less fortunate in society. Historians have in recent decades become increasingly interested in topics of paramount importance to modern fundamental rights, for instance the conditions of women and children, the situation of crofters in the countryside and of workers and the unemployed in the city. The many studies of legal, political and economic and social conditions of these groups are examples of the confluence of interest between human rights scholars and historians. This confluence of interest provides new insight for both human rights researchers and historians and opens up any given historical period to new interpretation. This has a bearing on how we look at the agricultural reforms and the abolition of adscription in Denmark in the eighteenth century.

---

2 C. FRIISBERG, *En nation dannes: Danmark og danskerne til 1920*, Vestjysk Kulturforlag, Varde 2006, pp. 54–58.
3 *Ibid.*
4 D. TAMM, *Retshistorie, Vol. I: Dansk retshistoire*, Jurist- og Økonomforbundets Forlag, Copenhagen 1990, p. 29.

New studies have, for instance, drawn attention to the fact that crofters benefitted far less from the agrarian reforms than the farmers, legally and in social practice, and as for women, they gained even less. From the point of view of non-discrimination and equal opportunity, the agrarian reforms of the eighteenth century do not score well.[5]

This does not mean that the agrarian reforms of the late eighteenth century, and the abolition of adscription in particular, are not important from a fundamental rights perspective. First, the abolition of adscription and the agrarian reforms explicitly had significance for large segments of society. Second, the agrarian reforms had an impact on and can be seen as a forerunner of the Constitution of 1849, which may be called the first proper fundamental rights document in Denmark, because it concerned the whole of society (albeit in a not fully democratic manner). When in 1848, after almost 200 years of absolutism, a 'free constitution' was to be created, the founding fathers were looking for a new constitutional paradigm. The free European constitutions profoundly inspired the first Danish constitution, which nevertheless did not systematically follow these European constitutions. The social and political context of the Danish constitution gave the constitution a particularly Danish expression, and this context was strongly influenced by the agrarian reforms of the eighteenth century. Third, the agrarian reforms and in particular the abolition of adscription are important because of the position they have held, and continue to hold, in national perceptions of Danish democracy.

In this chapter the focus will therefore be first on the abolition of adscription and on the agricultural reforms in the last part of the eighteenth century, followed by the creation of the first 'free' Danish constitution of 1849. Then we will see how the constitution, by means of amendments, gradually became a fundamental rights document proper in the twentieth century. Even today the Danish constitution is not a fully-fledged rights document referring to the entire range of human rights. It will be argued that the reason is partly to be found in the tradition of viewing Danish democratic history as an evolutionary history, which starting with the agrarian reforms and the abolition of adscription takes place slowly, peacefully — and largely outside the constitutional framework. This traditional view gives the development of constitutional rights a particular expression.

---

5 A. Faye Jacobsen, *Husbondret: Rettighedskulturer i Danmark, 1750–1920*, Museum Tusculanum Publishers, København 2008, pp. 111–191.

2. REFORMS WITHOUT REVOLUTION: REFORMS IN THE EIGHTEENTH AND EARLY NINETEENTH CENTURY

In the 1750s and 1760s some large landowners introduced reforms on their estates, for instance by remodelling the common land (separate strip holds were exchanged for compact holdings) and scattering of farms, and abolishing tenant farms and 'hoveri' — a term derived from the German language and referring to the obligation of tenants to work on the land of the estate owners as rent for their land plots.[6] These experiments were often financially advantageous for the large estate owners as well as for the tenant farmers turned owner occupiers.[7] They inspired other large estate owners and contributed to the creation of fertile ground for extensive agricultural reforms carried out under the auspices of the absolutist government.

In 1784 a Land Commission was established, and a reform period started, changing though not revolutionising agricultural conditions. The most famous of these reforms is the abolition of adscription by the Act of 20 June 1788, putting an end to a practice stemming back to 1734 by which the farmer and crofter were bound to the estate on which they were born.[8] Other reforms improved the situation of the farming community, notably through limiting the scope of 'hoveri'.

Initiatives in the area of education were to have great significance to the social, and in the long perspective, political development. In 1814 a new Education Act made primary schooling for all children compulsory. With amendments these statutes were in force until 1937. This landmark in Danish educational history was strongly influenced by pietism and substantiated the close link between civil and religious education.[9] Thus the Act laid down the following:

> The teaching of the children will in general be aimed at educating them to become good and righteous human beings, in accordance with the Evangelical-Christian teaching, and should confer on

---

6 S. Lagoutte and E.M. Lassen, 'Menneskerettigheder i forfatningen: billeder af fransk og dansk forfatningshistorie' in M. Kjærum, K. Slavensky and J. Vedsted-Hansen (eds.), *Grundloven og menneskerettigheder i et dansk og europæisk perspektiv*, Jurist- og Økonomforbundets Forlag, København 1997, p. 71.

7 But see T. Kjærgaard, *Den danske revolution 1500–1800: En økohistorisk tolkning*, Gyldendal, København 1992, p. 221, for the view that the agrarian reforms resulted in economic stagnation in the agrarian sector.

8 Lagoutte and Lassen, *supra* note 6, p. 71.

9 A. Faye Jacobsen, 'Children's rights: Snapshots into the history of education and child protection in Denmark (1700–1900)' in R. Aasgaard, M. Bunge and M. Roos (eds.), *Nordic Childhoods 1700–1960: Interdisciplinary Perspectives* (forthcoming) pp. 8–14.

> them the knowledge and skills necessary to become useful citizens of the State.[10]

The Education Act of 1814 should also be seen in connection with the agricultural reforms. Education of the peasants was seen as an instrument to strengthen society and state. At the end of primary schooling, a religious test took place, the passing of which was a rite of passage by which the young person gained civil rights and duties, and, for instance, was able to marry and enter an apprenticeship.

As the Education Act of 1814 illustrates, freedom of religion did not exist in the era of absolutism: the majority of the population had to belong to the state church. However, Jews were by a decree of 1814 given equal rights with other Danes, and they were allowed to have their own schools. The Jewish school aimed at integrating Jewish children into Danish society, and, in parallel to the religious test mentioned above, a religious test held at the synagogue had to be passed before the young person was able to enjoy rights and duties similar to those of other Danes.

Another important rights document of the early nineteenth century is the Poor-relief Regulations of 1803, which entitled individuals who could not sustain themselves (due to, for instance, age, severe disability, illness or orphanage) to receive help from the state.[11]

In the second half of the eighteenth century, public debates had centred on social and economic conditions of in particular agricultural society. In the first half of the nineteenth century, the political development of the state became the centre of attention.[12] This development was strongly influenced by events in Europe and in Schleswig-Holstein; the Danish king was duke of Holstein, which was part of the German Confederation. This link to Germany meant that the demands for increased political participation south of the border reached Denmark. In the 1840s the farmers and the National Liberals (who had their basis in Copenhagen and other towns) worked together for abolition of the absolutist regime and for a 'free' democratic constitution.

In March 1848 reports of the February Revolution in France and the turmoil in Germany reached Copenhagen, and strengthened the endeavours of those eager for political reforms. On 21 March representatives of the National Liberals and the farmers presented a demand for a free constitution to the King. The King gave in: the era of absolutism was over.

---

10 Faye Jacobsen, *supra* note 9, p. 9.
11 Lagoutte and Lassen, *supra* note 6, p. 72.
12 *Ibid.*, pp. 72–73.

A new government was established with support from the farmers and the National Liberals. At the same time a Constitutional Assembly (two thirds of its members were elected by means of 'common suffrage' whereas one third was appointed by the King) was established with a view to the creation of a free constitution.

3. THE CONSTITUTION OF 1849

At the first meeting of the Constitutional Assembly a draft for a new constitution was presented. The man responsible for the draft was the statesman D.G. Monrad. He was inspired by the so-called free constitutions in Europe, in particular the Belgian Constitution of 1831 and, to a lesser degree, the Norwegian Constitution of 1814. In 1848 a book was published containing a selection of European free constitutions. The book was meant to serve 'as a basis for discussions of constitutional questions', and was no doubt read by Monrad.[13] In some ways his draft was more democratic than other constitutions of the time, notably in the relation to rules of voting and eligibility to stand for Parliament.

After months of debate, the Constitutional Assembly agreed to the draft's central principles.

Danmarks Riges Grundlov came into force 5 June 1849, replacing the Danish Royal Law of 1660 and applying to the kingdom of Denmark and Schleswig (because of the war of 1848 and the ensuing conflicts in the Duchies, the Constitution was never implemented in Schleswig). Denmark had become a constitutional monarchy with responsible ministers and a popularly elected legislative assembly.

The debates of the Constitutional Assembly had in particular focussed on the electoral rules to Parliament's two chambers: Folketinget and Landstinget. The final constitution was a victory for the National Liberals and the farmers. The Folketing was constituted by 'equal and free election', which meant that men over 30 years of age had voting rights. However, there were exceptions: amongst others, individuals who received poor relief from the authorities and servants could not vote (1849, section 35). Women were also excluded from political participation.

In line with other free European constitutions, the Danish constitution contained predominantly political and civil rights, but the Constitution did also include several social and economic rights, namely property rights (1849, section 87), the right to poor relief (1849, section 89), right to trade (1849, section 88), and children's right to free education (1849, section 90). The latter right had already

[13] LAGOUTTE and LASSEN, *supra* note 6, p. 79.

been established in the Education Act of 1814. Monrad had originally suggested that the constitution should include provisions about the structure of agricultural society, including the abolition of tithes and 'hoveri', and a transfer from tenant farms to owner-occupied farms. However, neither the government nor the Constitutional Assembly were of the opinion that social reforms belonged in a constitution. This point of view, in alignment with European constitutional traditions, prevailed in Denmark, where economic and social reforms, as we have seen, had already started before 1848, independently from constitutional developments.

Outside the walls of the Constitutional Assembly, however, the pressure for social reforms was high. News about the political conflicts in a number of European countries reached Denmark, and added fuel to social discontent, as dramatically expressed in an article in the magazine *Almuevellet* ('The welfare of the peasant'):

> From several sides we have been told that the well-founded displeasure among crofters with their civil and economic position in this country is more pronounced and open at the moment, after the French rebirth, to equality and the recognition of human rights, has come to their attention.[14]

The events in Europe and their echoes in Denmark, combined with precarious conditions for large segments of agricultural society, appear to have created a fear of social unrest in political circles,[15] and a number of initiatives were taken — not by means of constitutional amendments but by statute law. In 1849, the Commission for Agricultural Reforms was established. The Commission prepared important legislative initiatives, and in 1850 'hoveri' for crofters was abolished. The right of the farmer to discipline adult servants and crofters in his service was abolished as well.[16]

Compared with other 'free' constitutions of the time, the Constitution of 1849 — the so-called First June Constitution — included rather democratic electoral rules. However, in 1866 this situation changed by means of a constitutional amendment. From then on until 1915 the propertied classes were able to monopolise the Landsting and put a halt to initiatives of the more democratically elected Folketing.[17]

---

14 Quoted from C. Bjørn, *Frygten fra 1848: Bonde- og husmandsuroen på Sjælland i foråret 1848*, Landbohistorisk Selskab, Odens 1985, p. 24.

15 *Ibid.*, p. 145.

16 Faye Jacobsen, *supra* note 5, pp. 311–342.

17 Lagoutte and Lassen, *supra* note 6, p. 82.

This constitutional setback added force to a particular political situation which developed in the last decades of the nineteenth century: the Constitution made it possible for the government to issue provisional laws in particularly pressing situations, without these laws having been passed in Parliament. This loophole was exploited by *Højre* ('The Right'), the political party in power and dominated by the biggest landowners. Thus the government issued a series of 'provisional laws' in the period from 1877 to 1895. This created an intense political struggle which only came to an end in 1901 with a victory of the principle of Cabinet responsibility.

4. THE SECOND JUNE CONSTITUTION OF 1915: SOCIAL AND ECONOMIC PROGRESS FACILITATED

The year 1901 marked a watershed in Danish political history. *Venstre* ('The Left'), the political party dominated by farmers, came into power. This created a momentum for democratisation of the electoral rules for Parliament's two chambers as well as for the initiation of social and economic reforms. The Constitution of 1915, the Second June Constitution, reflected the recent political drama. The new constitution reverted to more democratic electoral rules with 'free and universal suffrage', but in a much more inclusive sense than the Constitution of 1849. Most importantly, women and servants were granted suffrage. The right to vote in elections to the first chamber was lowered to 25 years of age. As for the second chamber, election and eligibility rules were democratised.

No new economic or social rights were added to the Constitution of 1915,[18] but in the following decades extensive legislation on economic and social rights was enacted. In this way the tradition of 1849, namely that social and economic reforms should evolve independently of the constitution and be regulated by statute law, was consolidated. Most notably, the so-called Steincke's Social Reform Act of 1933 contained social regulations on a large scale, for instance extending the scope of support during illness, help in old age, and child welfare. The statutes also laid down that such support, with certain exceptions, was not to be accompanied by repercussions in relation to other rights, such as voting rights.

[18] One constitutional novelty was the rule that parents are free to choose other ways of schooling of their children than the state schools (Constitution 1915, section 83). See also LAGOUTTE and LASSEN, *supra* note 6, pp. 82–83.

5. INTENTIONAL CONTINUITY: THE THIRD JUNE CONSTITUTION OF 1953

After an unsuccessful attempt at amending the Constitution in 1939, a new Constitution finally saw the light of day in 1953, the so-called Third June Constitution. The new Constitution contained a radical modernisation of the political system, namely the principle of Cabinet responsibility (already practised since 1901) and the abolishment of the upper chamber Landstinget. But the politicians endeavoured not to stray too much away from the Constitutions of 1849 and 1915. As stated by the prime minister in his presentation of the draft constitution:

> The Constitution of 1849 — and to a lesser degree — the Constitution of 1915 — were milestones in the history of the people. It is a much more modest stone-post we are now facing. The proposal which today is presented to Parliament does not mark a disruption from the past.[19]

And indeed, most sections of the Constitution of 1953 are identical to those of the 1849 Constitution. And as in previous constitutions, the Constitution of 1953 contains only a limited catalogue of rights, excluding most economic, social and cultural rights. There is thus a fundamental continuity from the first June Constitution of 1849 to the third June Constitution of 1953. This is contrary to many other modern European constitutions, which reflect both continuity and discontinuity (for instance the French Constitution).[20]

The Danish Constitution has not been amended since 1953. The limited rights catalogue in the Danish Constitution, the fact that the Constitution has not been amended since 1953, and its firm basis in the more than 150-year-old Constitution of 1849 — these factors contribute to give the present Constitution a somewhat old-fashioned image when seen in the context of modern society. This is accentuated by the fact that Denmark does not have a constitutional court (the Danish Supreme Court is reluctant to play this role and has only done so a few times).

It is unlikely that the Constitution will be amended in the near future. This is partly to do with the fact that the constitution can only be amended with great difficulty. Another reason is that, as public debates frequently illustrate, there is a pronounced hesitancy to change tradition as laid down in the Constitution. It follows that important developments in society which make a break with the past

19 Translation quoted from S. EIGAARD, *idealer og Politik: Historien om grundloven af 1953*, Odense Universitetsforlag, Odense 1993, p. 275.

20 LAGOUTTE and LASSEN, *supra* note 6, p. 82.

are not being reflected in the Constitution. One example of such a development relates to the area of religion.

Over the last 40 years the Danish demographic landscape has changed primarily due to immigration. As a result a considerable religious diversity has replaced an almost total religious homogeneity, which had its roots in the days of autocracy. At that time the king was responsible for ensuring that the population adhered to the Evangelical Lutheran faith, the theological foundation of the State Church (the Jewish Community, however, was officially established in Denmark in 1684, and in 1814 Danish Jews obtained rights and duties on an equal footing with other Danes).

The Constitution of 1849 made a clear break with the era of absolute monarchy in the sense that freedom of religion or belief was proclaimed: 'Citizens shall be at liberty to form congregations for the worship of God in a manner which is in accordance with their convictions, provided that nothing contrary to good morals or public order shall be taught or done' (The Danish Constitution 1849, section 81; identical to section 67 in the current Constitution of 1953). The Constitution of 1849 also laid down that 'No one shall be liable to make personal contributions to any denomination other than the one to which he adheres' (1849, section 82; 1953, section 68). The Constitution of 1849 moreover states that 'No person shall because of his faith be deprived of access to the full enjoyment of civic and political rights, nor shall he escape compliance with any common civic duty for such reasons' (1849, section 84). In the present Constitution of 1953, 'descent' was added to this section, as was the following: 'Personal liberty shall be inviolable. No Danish subject shall, in any manner whatsoever, be deprived of his liberty because of his political or religious convictions or because of his descent' (1953 Constitution, section 71). These amendments were caused by the experiences of wartime Nazi occupation, during which Jewish citizens were arrested.

In another and very fundamental way, the Constitution of 1849 (and subsequently those of 1915 and 1953) preserved the intimate connection between the state and the Evangelic Lutheran Church, a key characteristic of the autocratic regime. In fact, this bond was cemented in the Constitution, according to which 'The Evangelical Lutheran Church shall be the Danish Folkekirke [the Established Church of Denmark], and as such shall be supported by the State' (1849 section 3; 1953 section 4). Equality between religions, then, is not part of the constitutional make-up in Denmark. Nor is there today a political will to create a constitutionally based equality between religions vis-à-vis the state.

Within this constitutional framework, the Parliament and the Minister of Ecclesiastical Affairs constitute the highest decision-making body of the Folkekirke. An initiative of the Minister of Ecclesiastical Affairs in 2013 to address the issue of modernisation of the Folkekirke, including the decision-making processes in regard to the internal affairs of the Church, resulted in very modest proposals for changes; there seemed to be no pronounced wish on the part of the Folkekirke or politicians to loosen the bond to the state, including transferring power over internal affairs from Parliament to the Church.

In the area of organising state and religion, Denmark is unique amongst present-day Western European democracies, including Norway, which used to have a similar constitutionally based organisation of religions as in Denmark but which today has a constitution that reflects the modern landscape of religion and belief. By means of a constitutional amendment in 2014, the Norwegian Evangelical Lutheran Church was reaffirmed as Norway's Folkekirke and as such supported by the state, and by the same token it was also established that other associations of religion or belief would be supported on an equal footing (The Norwegian Constitution, amended 2014, section 16).

6. CONCLUDING REMARKS

As far as its content is concerned, the Coronation Charter of 1282 makes up a Danish parallel to Magna Carta. But it is the agrarian reform period starting in the late eighteenth century under the auspices of the autocratic government which is traditionally seen as the forerunner of the democratic state in Denmark. The most famous of these reforms is the abolition of adscription by the Act of 20 June 1788. Other reforms improved the situation of the farming community, notably through limiting the scope of 'hoveri'. In addition, a progressive educational act as well as poverty relief saw the day in the beginning of the nineteenth century.

Following the creation of the first 'free' Danish constitution of 1849, in which political and civil rights were laid down, social and economic reforms, expressed in statute law, continued in the late nineteenth and early twentieth century. The tradition of initiating social and economic reforms outside the constitutional framework together with the tradition of celebrating continuity in constitutional law may help to explain why even today most Danish policy-makers do not see a need for the Danish Constitution to be a fully-fledged rights document referring to the entire range of fundamental rights and reflecting societal developments.

Taking leave of the Liberty Monument the visitor to Copenhagen may walk a few hundred meters to the seat of the Danish Parliament. A large equestrian statue depicting King Fredrik VII stands in the middle of the parliamentary square. The inscription on the statue reads, in old-fashioned Danish: 'The giver of the Constitution'. In fact, the king was a reluctant and passive spectator to the abolition of the absolutist monarchy and the introduction of constitutional monarchy. If the inscription is not an accurate description of the situation at the time, it may nonetheless be illustrative of a prevailing fondness for tradition.

18. GERMANY: FUNDAMENTAL RIGHTS AS AN INSTRUMENT TOWARDS THE *RECHTSSTAAT*

Anja MIHR

1. INTRODUCTION

Germany has a short but steady tradition of fundamental rights. The first fundamental rights catalogue was established in 1849 as part of the *Paulskirche-Reichsverfassung* in Frankfurt. It only lasted for a short time and was never executed, as it lacked support from those responsible to implement it, the dukes and kings of the German confederation at that time. They refused to share the privileges they had over ordinary citizens. Nevertheless, similar to Magna Carta, this first catalogue needed another 60–70 years before entering into force with the Weimar Constitution in 1919. But already in the nineteenth century, the fundamental rights catalogue of the Paulskirche triggered major legal and political reform in the different German states in the Reich. In a way, its fate is reminiscent of Magna Carta 700 years earlier; but it took another 100 years before the enactment of the current and widely known German Basic Law, the *Grundgesetz* in 1949.[1] Hence, the first fundamental rights document from 1849 paved the way for what is today known as the *Rechtsstaat* in Germany and beyond.

2. PATHWAYS TO A FUNDAMENTAL RIGHTS CATALOGUE

The message and spirit of Magna Carta soon spread across Europe and in Germany the wind blew from the North. With the Swedish invasions and wars in the most northern part of Germany in the fourteenth century the ideas of freedom and liberty for those suppressed in servitude after hundreds of years of serfdom and peonage caught fire. Inspired by the changes in Sweden, farmers held in peonage opposed their nobles, claiming more freedom rights on the German island of Rügen in the Baltic Sea. They called their freedom claims 'little Magna

---

1 The original text of the Basic Law from 1949, see: <http://www.gesetze-im-internet.de/englisch_gg/basic_law_for_the_federal_republic_of_germany.pdf>.

Carta liberatum' in 1325, claiming more rights and freedom of self-determination against the feudalist order at that time. Their attempt remained a footnote in the history books, but nevertheless showed that the spirit of 1215 had already swept over to the continent.[2]

A more serious attempt to copy and paste Magna Carta from 1215 and transform it into a fundamental rights catalogue for Germany came around 1441, at the beginning of the Reformist wars, the uprisings of the farmers against the feudalism and arbitrariness that had lasted for centuries throughout the continent. In the fifteenth century, from Scandinavia to Switzerland, these reformist movements sought equal rights for people (depending on their social status, of course), similar to the barons' movements in England prior to Magna Carta 250 years earlier. Thus the spirit of Magna Carta, the idea of being equal and being treated equally and free from fear before the law, seemed to have also conquered the continent.

The emperor Friedrich III (1415–1493) of the Holy Roman-German Empire in response to massive pressure and the wars taking place in his empire initiated reformist ideas that engendered dramatic legal shifts throughout the empire's jurisdiction. It was he who coined the term the 'German Nation'[3] *Teutsche Nation* (sic!), followed by his attempts to draft a first 'Magna Carta' for the people of this German nation and his vast empire. This fundamental rights document aimed to reorganize the rights, entitlements, duties and relationships between the king and the nobles and the overall administration of the Reich. During a Reichs Assembly in Mainz 1441, he introduced the document in an attempt to appease the claims of admittedly only some lords and nobles for more independence from a divine and invisible law mostly executed by the church. Friedrich wanted to replace the traditional Roman law with a new public civic empire (*Reichs*) law. In his attempts for legal reforms he deliberately mentioned the idea of 'fundamental rights for the Reich', *Reichsgrundgesetze*, to emphasise the importance of laws and rights for people but without, of course, challenging his authority over these rights, vis-as-vis the existing order mandated by the Catholic church.[4] His attempt to separate state and church power was nothing more than an artefact for a nation that did not even exist and with which hardly anyone identified her or himself. His proposal for a Magna Carta was doomed to fail and thus remained but a noble idea. Albeit that there was some support, there were not enough adherents among the many kingdoms, dukes and nobles unwilling to join the reformist cause against the church during the decades of

---

2 P. BLICKLE, *Von der Leibeigenschaft zu den Menschenrechten: Eine Geschichte der Freiheit in Deutschland*, C.H. Beck, München 2006, p. 132.

3 The use of the term German Nation as in *'als ir uns, dem heiligen reich, euch selbst und teutscher nation zu stunde schuldig seid'* around 1475.

4 G.W. BÖHMER, *Kaiser Friedrich's III: Entwurf Einer Magna Charta Für Deutschland, Oder Die Reformation Dieses Kaisers Vom Jahr 1441*, Ullan Press, first print 1818 and 1923; 2012, pp. 50–51.

massive uprisings and discontent.[5] However, through the centuries of emancipation and liberation from feudalism, the intriguing idea of the rule of law persisted.

Although historians still dispute the authenticity of the document because it was never executed, Friedrich's Magna Carta showed the shift in times and mentality that had spread from England over the continent. Catholic Roman law slowly began to lose its functionality due to the pressure of reformism within the church at that time.

These early attempts illustrate that it was the struggle by nobles against the medieval religious and holy order at that time that provoked initiatives similar to the English Magna Carta, yet it took another 400 years until the first fundamental rights calatogue for citizens in relation to the German state came about. Even then, in 1848/49, the first catalogue *Made in Germany* had a more symbolic than legal character. It mirrored the desire of many German intellectuals and reformers to finally become what other European states had claimed for much longer, one nation. Overall, this constitution launched the idea of *Rechtsstaat* and for the first time equality before the law was constituted. But still absent were explicit and independent state institutions that would monitor and balance the interests of individuals *vis-à-vis* society.

3. FUNDAMENTAL RIGHTS FOR THE GERMAN PEOPLE

After decades of wars and political shifts between nationalists and liberals, delegates from various German confederation states declared the basic or fundamental rights of the German peoples *Grundrechte des deutsches Volkes* on 27 December 1848. A few months later in March 1849 it became the first constitution for all confederation states and thus for those that constituted Germany at that time. But no joint nation or Reich did exist at that time, despite the desire of the delegates in Frankfurt to establish a unified Germany under one Reich. The delgates in the Paulskirche in Frankfurt could not know that it would take another 22 years until the second German Reich would be established under Reichschancelor Otto von Bismarck and later Emperor Wilhelm I. The first constitution in 1849, the so-called *Reichsverfassung,* encompassed fundamental rights based on the idea of division of powers between nobles and citizens, administrative law, and significant liberties and freedoms for everyone. The terms 'fundamental' or 'basic' rights were explicitly mentioned to emphasise that these were the rights of people against state powers, and not rights given by kings or sovereigns to the people.[6] The delegate Jacob Venedey coined the term

---

[5] BÖHMER, *supra* note 4, p. 278.

[6] J. CARPENTIER (ed.), *The Emergence of Human Rights in Europe: An Anthology*, Council of Europe Publishing, Strasbourg 2002, pp. 77–84.

fundamental rights, the *Grundrechte*, in German. In making his proposal for the *Grundrechte und Forderungen des deutschen Volkes,* he had been influenced by the processes and declarations in France and the USA, as well as the English Magna Carta. The idea was the same; namely that citizens could make claims towards or against those who govern, in case of the abuse of these rights. The idea of the *Rechtsstaat* was born. Although the term *Rechtsstaat* was never explicitly mentioned in any of the constitutions or laws, its general concepts have greatly influenced public international and human rights law and its jurisdiction. For example: (1) the principle of proportionality of state power versus necessities of public interest; (2) the freedom to claim or defend fundamental rights through an independent judiciary (i.e. access to justice) regardless of the status or background of the individual; and (3) the guarantee of citizens' rights and justice. Since the beginning, the issue of proportionality has been the main legacy of the original idea of the *Rechtsstaat.*

Yet, the 1849 constitution also broke another taboo in Germany. At the center of state sovereignty was no longer the king but the people and their entitlements.[7] To highlight but a few rights from this first attempt, it included freedom of religion and of the press, and privacy. However, most importantly and highly innovative for its time in Germany, were those rights that allowed political organization (assembly) and participation in decision-making. Not surprisingly, this led to much opposition from among the monarchies at that time, and the first fundamental rights act was soon abolished. The parliamentarians during the first National Assembly in the Paulskirche in Frankfurt declared the urgency for all people to have at least a minimum of basic or fundamental freedom rights.[8] Even the abolishment of the death penalty and the idea of a constitutional court was born at that time, but never implemented. Women's rights, however, had not been explicitly mentioned in any of the nineteenth century constitutions and democracy was still a century off. Although never realised, many of the reformist ideas had a fundamental impact on civic law in Germany later on. The constitution as such lasted only a short while — less than two years — as it did not suit all states of the German confederation at that time. Consequently, during the Reich's Assembly in 1951 the *Grundrechte* catalogue was officially dissolved — even though it had never been enforced in the first place. And in the upcoming decades of uprisings, power games and wars among the kingdoms and the European nations, it was unlikely that this constitution would have had any successful revival. The Reich's subsequent constitutions of 1867 and 1871 carried little of its legacy. The opposite was true of the patriarchal and hierarchical legal and political traditions of German civic law, which were

7 B. Bublies-Godau, 'Jakob Venedey - Henriette Obermüller-Venedey: Der Held des Parlaments und die Heckerin' in S. Freitag (Hrsg), *Die Achtundvierziger: Lebensbilder aus der deutschen Revolution 1848/49*, C.H. Beck, München 1998.

8 N. Johnston, Daily German, published in June 1849, 'The Frankfurt Parliament', available at: <http://files.campus.edublogs.org/blogs.yis.ac.jp/dist/6/103/files/2011/09/Frankfurt-Parliament-history-1j5jd1a.pdf> accessed 10.05.2015.

reinforced. It continued to be the kings or later the emperor who 'granted' rights to citizen out of gratitude and not because of natural entitlement to fundamental freedoms. This concept of *Rechtsstaat* was far from the rule of law.

After World War II in 1948/49 when the allied powers asked for new governing bodies and a constitution, the delegates from West Germany who composed the basic law, drew connections to the fundamental rights act and the *Reichsverfassung* from 1849, and the 1919 Constitution from Weimar. The Weimar Constitution lasted only a few years longer than the *Reichsverfassung*. It was dissolved in 1933 when Hitler came to power and with the rise of the Nazi regime. In the 1919 Constitution, for the first time, fundamental rights and freedom rights, including women's rights, were manifested. The republican idea succeeded over that of the traditional German empire and the Reich, which had lasted for over 1,000 years. Despite the dramatic will for reform and a new start, the title of the constitution still carried the *Deutsches Reich* as a reference entity and, thus, sees a continuation of the second Reich that had existed since 1871. However, the Weimar Constitution from 19 August 1919 was the first with a functioning civil law protecting fundamental rights that deserved recognition. It perpetuated some of the major legacies of the 1849 consitution when it aimed to combine the best of the emancipatory civil rights movements.[9] It dedicated the entire chapter II to the Fundamental Rights and Duties of Germans, *Grundrechte und Grundpflichten der Deutschen*, and in total 181 articles and 54 titles to be adhered to and obeyed.[10] The duties emphasised that this was still a document of state powers for citizens, and not the other way around. Fundamental rights were always subject to scrutiny and only to be granted in the larger public interest. Although the individual character of rights enshrined in the constitution was a novelty, the superior character of the state versus citizens, that is core to the *Rechtsstaat*, was inherent. Equality among women and men (article 109), privacy (article 117), freedom of expression and assembly (articles 118 and 124), fundamental rights for children (article 122), and the right to education (article 145) were among those rights indicating that the constitution was one of the most progressive in Europe at that time — on paper. One of the major differences between Weimar and Frankfurt was just these social rights such as the right and duty to work, the right to education and the rights of sick and elderly people. They only became part of the *Rechtsstaat* in 1919.

However, it was difficult for German citizens to claim their fundamental rights, because a constitutional court did not exist. Hence the idea that these were entitlements given by a superior power to inferior citizens was not yet entirely resolved. Individual responsibility — which the Germans have struggled with throughout the twentieth century up until today — was not yet fully embraced.

---

9 H. PREUSS, *Politik und Verfassung in der Weimarer Republik*, Mohr Siebeck, Tübingen 2008.

10 Weimar Constitution, original text 11 August 1919, <http://www.documentarchiv.de/wr/wrv.html#ERSTER_ABSCHNITT02> accessed 11.05.2015.

The duty aspect and the stronghold of the state were more powerful. Consequently, these laws allowed for many restrictions that later gave leeway for the National Socialist Party to get into power. Yet, even if the Weimar Constitution was progressive compared to that of Frankfurt, what was missing and what later made the third attempt at a fundamental rights catalogue in 1949 in Bonn a success, was an independent monitoring body where people can claim their rights: the constitutional court.[11] This court has been the foundation of the modern *Rechtsstaat* ever since.

Hence, the story of fundamental rights in modern Germany is such that there was a first attempt in 1849 that lasted only for a short time and which was based on civil and political rights only; the second attempt in 1919 lasted 14 years and already included social and economic rights; but only the third attempt in 1949, which was largely imposed by external powers, turned the idea of fundamental rights and *Rechtsstaat* into a longer-lasting reality persisting until the present time. It is nevertheless different from the Anglo-Saxon concept of rule of law, which is much broader and less state-centric than the German concept of *Rechtsstaat*.

4. THE BASIC LAW IN 1949 AND THE *RECHTSSTAAT*

The *Rechtsstaat* in Germany was realised for the first time with the *Grundgesetz* in 1949 and with the establishment of the constitutional court in 1951. The *Rechtsstaat* differs from the concept of the rule of law, which Magna Carta claims to have created. This is because the *Rechtsstaat* explicitly emphasises the role of the state and state institutions to guarantee, monitor and judge the rights granted in the constitution. That makes it somewhat problematic if a state constitution does not enshrine the full spectrum of fundamental rights or has no independent monitoring body, as was the case in Weimar and during the Nazi period. This was also the case with the East German socialist constitution from 1949, which was never executed through a *Rechtsstaat* and never claimed to be.

Thus, in 1949 German ambivalence towards fundamental rights continued, on both sides of the Iron Curtain. Yet, after the war, Germany had a third chance to convert the idea of fundamental rights into a lasting constitution and civic law. Under Allied supervision and to some extent imposed, the German Basic Law, the *Grundgesetz*, was created during various assemblies at Chiemsee and Bonn. This law reflected much of the earlier fundamental rights catalogue from 1849, the Weimar Constitution from 1919, and the Universal Declaration of Human Rights (UDHR) from 1948. The aim was to improve upon previous attempts and

[11] The Weimar Repbulic had a Reichs court and a court of state affairs (*Staatsgericht*) which dealt with issues of the constitutions, but only if there was a dispute among the Reichs states (confederation) and the central government in Berlin.

to introduce a constitutional court to safeguard the principles of the (as yet provisional) *Grundgesetz,* which was announced in parliament on 23 May 1949 a few months prior to the establishment of the Federal Republic of Germany. The first 19 articles had been almost exactly copied from the UDHR. Fundamental rights were enshrined not based on duty but (finally) on a concept of rights. This was a novelty in German history. Article 93 manifests how this can look in practice. Citizens can individually claim their fundamental rights before the constitutional court and, inspired by the century-long efforts in Anglo-Saxon jurisprudence to guarantee fundamental rights through another legal instance, an independent court. This *Grundgesetz* also differs slightly from the 1849 *Rechtsstaat* concept because in the earlier *Reichsverfassung* the strong paternalistic notion of a state being the bestower of the rights and the law dominated.

Thus, three years after the end of World War II, there was a push for one of the most progressive constitutional designs at that time in Europe caused by the division of post-war Germany into the socialist East and the democratic West. It was the communist East, under the leadership of the newly established Socialist Unity Party (SED) and under strong surveillance of the Moscow Politburo that pushed for a two-state solution and two constitutions. But unlike west of the Iron Curtain, the new socialist constitution in the East, the *Sozialistische Verfassung der DDR,* which came into effect on 7 October 1949, did not anticipate a constitutional court or the principle of *Rechtsstaat* at all. Instead, the occupying power of East Germany, the Soviet Union, sought a two-state solution with very different constitutional arrangements and fundamental rights, symbolic of the emerging Cold War and its subsequent division of the continent and world for the next 40 years. Other than the *Paulskirchenverfassung* and the Weimar Constitution, the East German parliamentary assembly broke with the tradition of fundamental rights. Instead it highlighted the role of the state and government to 'shape' and form the socialist individual. Under communist leadership the constitution drafters in East Berlin claimed to build a new, social and just Germany under socialist doctrine. Yet, the socialist constitution also inherited some aspects of the legacy of Weimar, too. It included a catalogue of fundamental social rights whilst jettisoning freedom rights with the aim of being governed under communist and socialist doctrine. Nevertheless, because East Germany did not see itself as a provisional or divided state, as West Germany did, the Politburo simply claimed this constitution only to be valid for East Germany.

Whereas in the West, the delegates claimed to establish a *Grundgesetz* in continuation of Weimar and the first *Reichsverfassung* from 1849 and to be valid for both Germanys, the East did not make such references. In the West, to strengthen the fundamental rights character the parliamentarian assembly referred to a 'Lex fundamentalist'. The *Grundgesetz* was intended as a normative order that would bind people and empower them individually to claim their fundamental rights. Regardless of their nationality, those fundamental rights were to be granted to those living in the territory of Germany. Once passed in the parliamentarian assembly the *Grundgesetz* was never intended to be launched by a festive, emotional, let alone national ceremony. The semi-sovereign status of West Germany and the wish to unify both Germanys before calling for a new constitution did not allow for national patriotism. However, it was different in the East. The SED-Politburo in East Berlin was far from even recognising the urge for reunification let alone to adhere to the *Grundgesetz* or the *Rechtsstaat* and called its constitution what it was, a *Verfassung*.

In the Basic Law, the fundamental rights are meant as an instrument of the protection of citizens against an arbitrary state. On the other hand, the 'state' idea of the *Rechtsstaat* emphasises the notion that the law or rights are only guaranteed and executed by state institutions. If there is no state or an abusive one, such as the Third Reich or the GDR, what could be done? The concept of *Rechtsstaat* is grounded in the trust and use of a state court to enforce people's rights. This is not identical to the rule of law that requires, generally speaking, formal or informal measures to ensure adherence to the principles of supremacy of the law, equality before the law, separation of powers, participation in decision-making, legal certainty and legal transparency — to mention but a few characteristics.[12] There is a slight but relevant difference, because the concept of rule of law does not mention the state and its institutions as being the explicit point of reference, whereas the German *Rechtsstaat* does. Interestingly, the idea of *Rechtsstaat* has worldwide appeal/influence, in particular among the European institutions and the new EU member state-inspired constitutions and institution building, for example when looking at the jurisprudence of the European Court of Justice.

The German concept of *Rechtsstaat* differs from the Anglo-Saxon tradition of rule of law. In the Anglo-Saxon tradition fundamental rights are the rights belonging to individuals and not granted to them out of mercy by states or powerful kings with a certain ideology. There ought to be no superiority over citizens by those who govern. However, for the Germans that mentality shift has come a long way particularly in 1949. Obedience to the law, to harsh duties instead of responsibilities and to submit oneself to the judgments of a constitutional court is not the exeption but the rule. It determines much of the present understanding and interpretation of the *Grundgesetz*. Even though the Basic Law instilled the idea of the leadership of citizens and the people, it is the state, governments and institutions that govern, but are not superior to the citizens' will. This was often criticized as a fundamental lack of basic rights and democracy in Germany. To understand what democracy and fundamental rights are has been a major mind shift for all European countries. These were also enshrined in another major fundamental rights document of that time, the European Convention for the Protection of Human Rights and Fundamental Freedoms, from 1950.

---

12 T. BINGHAM, *The Rule fo Law*, Penguin Books, London 2011, p. 111.

In that respect, what really made the *Grundgesetz* a lasting 'constitution' by and for the citizens, was its court. The judges of the constitutional court have far too often had to remind the government and parliament repeatedly of article 20, paragraph 2, which provides that the power of the state is in the hands of the citizens and not of the government. Thus, governments cannot rule by law 'over' the people, but only with the people. However, practice has often been different and the paternalistic mentality remains well into present times. The German government has jeopardized the character of the Basic Law more than once, for example when it launched a decree against radical (mainly communist) parties and their supporters (*Radikalenerlasse*), or anti-terrorist laws in the 1960s and 1970s. These examples revoked many fundamental freedom rights of assembly, political participation, expression and so on.[13] Governing by decree in the name of public interest of security was the justification. Later, these practices were revisited after the constitutional court's intervention. The court took up complaints by citizens and decided that these laws were unconstitutional. But for many the court's decisions and calls for reform were too often needed to remind parliamentarians and citizens alike that democracy means that citizens have to take responsibility for their governments and not *vice versa*. Not surprisingly, the *Rechtsstaat* idea is not explicitly mentioned in the *Grundgesetz,* nor in the law for the court. What instead is described in it is the way to work *towards* a *Rechtsstaat*, namely through decisions that respect proportionality between the individual's claim and the interests of society as a whole.[14]

The dramatic restrictions on, for example, freedom of the press, the right to work and free movement challenged the fundamental rights of the people. Although the emergency laws had been revoked by the constitutional court, parliamentarians were slow to learn the qualitative difference between fundamental rights and laws. Thus, the court has emerged for some people at the level of a guarantor for rights and democracy in Germany. Judges have been called the ‚teachers for the Germans' because they were often the last resort in 'teaching' the Germans democracy by upholding fundamental freedoms. The fact that the constitutional court has overruled more anti-constitutional laws and decrees than ever anticipated in 1949, may come as a surprise but it also illustrates the existing different understandings of the concepts of rule of law and the *Rechtsstaat.*[15] Although according to its own laws, the court should not interfere with political interpretations and actions, it often did — and did so reluctantly (article 68, 1 Law of the German Constitutional Court).[16] When first

---

13 M. Steinbeis, M. Detjen and S. Detjen, *Die Deutschen und das Grundgesetz: Geschichte und Grenzen unserer Verfassung*, BpB, Bonn 2013, p. 205ff.

14 J. Detjen, *Verfassungswerte: Welche Werte betimmen das Grundgestz*, BpB, Bonn 2012, pp. 139–141.

15 C. Tomuschat, 'Die Karlsruher Republik', *Die Zeit*, 13 May 2010, <http://www.zeit.de/2010/20/P-oped-Verfassungsgericht> accessed 10.05.2015.

16 R. Graf von Westphalen (ed.), *Deutsches Regierungssystem*, Oldenburg Verlag, München 2001, p. 377.

established the court was intended to be a provisional court named after a constitution that did not yet exist. Hence, the German ambivalence between fundamental rights and constitutionalism is hard to better.

5. NEW CONSTITUTIONAL 'PATRIOTISM'

Finally, after the many attempts in 1441, 1849, 1919 and 1949, the reunification of Germany in 1990 gave hope for the first time that fundamental rights would be enshrined in a constitution for Germany. After reunification of the two Germanys in 1990 the debate about whether or not to shift from the Basic Law to a constitution became heated. It also opened up the cleavages that existed between the culture of a *Rechtsstaat* and that of the rule of law.[17] The debate continued right through the negotiation of the 1992 Maastricht Treaty that established the idea of a European Union with its own supranational constitution. Some German observers simply sought to preclude any constitutional act in their own state and instead wait for one on the European level, as a 'Magna Carta for Europe' in a way. In fact, when the constitutional process turned out to be more complicated than anticipated, and in 2000 when 'only' the EU Fundamental Rights Charter was launched; it fueled the opinion of those who claimed that the times for nationalistic or supranationalistic ceremonial constitutional orders and events are over. The anti-nationalist had won. A fundamental rights document with a court is everything that a modern state, the member state and the Union itself, might need. Hence, what turned out to be the European Fundamental Rights Charter and later the Lisbon Treaty was already dormant in the earlier heated and controversial discussions after German reunification — parallel to the (re)unification of Europe.

Citizens' referendums had never happened in post-war or post-unified Germany. Instead, the most effective way to guarantee more public participation and sovereignty of the law has been and still is through the constitutional court. That was not what Magna Carta and the concept of rule of law was key to. Rather, the German *Rechtsstaat* mainly existed because of the court and its increasing influence over democratic powers and peoples' sovereignty. Its role increased over the years rather than decreasing, as indicated by the number of claims filed which has increased dramatically over the decades to 6,000 per year. In 1999 there were around 4,880 claims, and in 2013 there were over 6,680 per annum.[18] Since its inauguration in 1951, the court has dealt with over 200,000 claims in total. They represent individuals or parties who believed their fundamental rights were jeopardized and could not otherwise be upheld politically. In the times of

---

17 STEINBEIS, DETJEN and DETJEN, *supra* note 13, p. 11.

18 Statistic of Bundesverfassunggericht (constitutional court) <http://www.bundesverfassungsgericht.de/DE/Verfahren/Jahresstatistiken/2013/gb2013/A-II-1.html; jsessionid=1CF85ED45ADF16AB636B 67F848E75197.2_cid393> accessed 10.05.2015.

Magna Carta that would have meant 200,000 people complaining about the incapacity and/or arbitrary mercy of a lord, baron or king to settle their disputes over fundamental rights. Parallel to this the 'constitutional patriotism', *Verfassungspatriotismus*, steadily grew. It has nothing in common with national patriotism, rather the opposite. It expresses the trust that people have in the *Grundgesetz* and thus in the *Rechtsstaat*. In 2011 the World Justice Project ranked Germany second in rule of law (behind Norway) out of 69 states, because of the institutional level of adherence and transparency, the execution of and access to justice and, thus the practice of *Rechtsstaatlichkeit*.[19] Although the evaluators call it the Rule of Law Index, they evaluate *Rechtsstaat*, meaning the level of transparency, access and responsiveness of state institutions when implementing and enforcing civic law. Thus, they were assessing the effectiveness of state institutions, but not whether people have fundamentally understood their rights.[20]

This links to the new 'constitutional' patriotism in Germany and the confidence by citizens in the Basic Law which remains extraordinary high. In 2012 over 80 per cent of the population supported and trusted the *Grundgesetz* and thought it was good for the citizens.[21] This is a blow to those who still see the *Grundgesetz* as a provisional constitution and lament its lack of democractic legitimacy and transmission of power to the people instead of its institutions.[22]

To what extent there should be an institution to monitor fundamental rights, rather than a simple executor of law is still very much in dispute. But *Verfassungspatriotismus* has given the constitutional court a second name *Praeceptor Germainae*: the master or again 'teacher' of the Germans and their legislative powers. Parliaments do not seem to handle legislative power well.[23] Tomuschat articulated what many feared, that the democratically legitimate legislative powers are too weak to establish laws in accordance with fundamental rights and too often fail in their implementation. Instead of asking democratically elected parliamentarians to guarantee and enforce fundamental rights which is their core business, citizens address themselves to the court to resolve any minor queries about how to interpret fundamental rights. The impression given is that

---

19 THE WORLD JUSTICE PROJECT, Rule of Law Index Report, 2011 <http://worldjusticeproject.org/sites/default/files/WJP_Rule_of_Law_Index_2011_Report.pdf> accessed 15.04.2015.

20 Sternberger and Habermas coined the term *Verfassungspatriotismus*. With this term they were aiming to explain why Germans do not miss a national constitution, based on emotional ceremonies or nationalism combined with excessive unhealthy patriotism as seen elsewhere. Instead, in their opinion, 'Germans adhere to their laws and institutions', and although *Verfassungspatriotismus* talks about constitutionalism, what they mean is adherence to the law not to a nationalistic binding idea. J-W. MUELLER, 'Verfassungspatriotismus, Eine systematische Verteidigung' (2010) 2 *Vorgänge* 111–118.

21 DETJEN, *supra* note 14, p. 7.

22 A. BRODOCZ, *Die Macht der Judikative*,Verlag für Sozialwissenschaften, Wiesbaden 2009, p. 179.

23 TOMUSCHAT, *supra* note 15.

Germans consider the judges as their 'teachers', telling them right from wrong. This is very much against the spirit of Magna Carta. But the reality remains that a number of non-elected (but appointed) judges are doing the job of those in parliament far too often.

Meanwhile, in 1992, article 23 of the *Grundgesetz* (which had allowed for the accession of East Germany to West Germany and thus reunification), also allows subsidiarity to EU institutions and later the EU Fundamental Rights Charter and the Lisbon Treaty. As a consequence, in the following years the German constitutional court had to deal with various claims asking the court to determine the democratic legitimacy of this article and the subordination of German institutions and citizens to a European law or treaty that was not authorised let alone legitimated through elections by people.[24]

6. CONCLUDING REMARKS: THE LEGACY OF MAGNA CARTA

Fifteen years after the EU Fundamental Rights Charter and 800 years after Magna Carta, Germany's constitutional and administrative laws have dramatically shifted. There are some curious and interesting parallels over the past two centuries concerning the two major anniversarial documents and German fundamental rights. From Magna Carta to the fundamental rights catalogue in the *Reichsverfassung*, to the *Grundgesetz* and the EU Fundamental Rights Charter, they all have in common that they were declared with little or no ceremonial pathos and under enormous pressure of time. These treaties were signed and sealed on short notice and sometimes failed to be implemented, but they slowly started to affect people's consciousness and behaviour.

Coincidently or not, it was Roman Herzog, the former president of the German constitutional court and former president of Germany who led the drafting convention for the EU Fundamental Rights Charter until 1999. Thus, it may not be such a coincidence that the EU Charter resembles an enhanced version of the German *Grundgesetz*, with more extended and elaborated articles on privacy, data protection, education, rights of children and the elderly, social protection for workers and their work place — all the necessary civil, social and economic rights that enrich and complement the fundamental rights catalogues of past centuries. It also enhances the rights and freedoms of individuals; the main legacy of Magna Carta.

Individual property rights, fair trial rights and free expression in Magna Carta (articles 20, 39 and 60) have continuously inspired similar efforts over the centuries including the *Grundgesetz*. If we look at the normative disputes at the court in Karlsruhe in recent years, most of them deal with issues of

[24] Steinbeis, Detjen and Detjen, *supra* note 13, p. 279ff.

proportionality over property/financial questions; family/same-sex partnerships or data protection/privacy security issues, and thus the *Rechtsstaat* idea develops further. Curiously enough these were the same normative issues (notwithstanding different terminology) hotly debated during the scenes at the royal court in Runnymede during the negotiations in 1215. Furthermore, these are the normative questions that the EU Fundamental Rights Charter aims to tackle in its current form and which consequently also affect the culture of the rule of law in Germany.

19. THE CZECH REPUBLIC: ON THE ROAD TO RIGHTS AND FREEDOMS

Jan HOLZER
Hubert SMEKAL

1. INTRODUCTION

The manner in which respect for the catalogue of fundamental rights has evolved is a fascinating historical topic whose roots reach far back through time (*longue durée*). Its evolution is fascinating both as regards the abstract argumentation that has formed the human rights agenda — or more precisely, in the historical context, the agenda of *rights and freedoms* — and as regards the practical efforts that have been undertaken to meet this agenda. These two aspects have been apparent throughout the lifetimes of two developmental types of state. The first of these types is the medieval state, the *regnum* or *imperium*; the second, the modern national state. Both types are key terms of reference in the topic area, and each has naturally been represented by the institutions, actors, social and economic characteristics, and types of conflict and resolution peculiar to it. But this has meant that the key spheres of analysis that belong to the topic — the *legal* and the *political* spheres — have not always proceeded in parallel, but rather in a contradictory, conflictual manner.[1]

The concise introductory notes given here aspire to general validity. But they also logically reflect the facts of Czech legal history, more particularly, the country's political history, which forms the core data of the text. Within Czech history, there is no extraordinary historical act comparable to *Magna Carta Libertatum*, not factually and not symbolically — no document whose anniversary may be celebrated by this collective monograph. This does not mean, however, that the topic of rights and freedoms is absent from Czech history, and this makes the question of why the Czechs never produced any similar document to Magna Carta that much more interesting. It is for this reason that the *processual* aspect outlined in the introductory paragraph is so important:

[1] Another extraordinarily interesting analytical level — and also a source of conflict — consists in clashes between the theoretical (intellectual) consideration of the topics treated here and their manifestations in the public life of political communities.

the appearance and disappearance of rights and freedoms as a topic and the success or lack thereof in gradually trying to anchor these concepts institutionally must, in the Czech case, be studied as they unfold over time.

What is written here therefore does not focus on a single moment in Czech history that is somehow exceptional, even if it does include a micro-study the authors considered typical for the same. The basic objective is rather to identify and describe the chief *cleavages* which have played a role in Czech history during the process of forming a competitive model of the state that offers institutionalised mechanisms and procedures to define and guarantee rights and freedoms to a gradually expanding group of actors. To describe these cleavages, the study refers to key documents in Czech legal history. The micro-study included serves as a concrete example of the difficulties faced by the actors who have shaped Czech historical processes and, at least to an extent, meets the objectives of the editors. These objectives may be addressed using tools from a variety of social science sources. The authors have opted to work from a political science standpoint, and the terminology employed therefore derives its primary vocabulary from that discipline and from historiography.

Conventional conceptions of Czech legal and political history set 1848 as the starting-point for the constitutional development of the Czech state.[2] This is no surprise. Most research speaks of the celebrated Spring of Nations as the moment at which politics 'invaded' European space, including Central Europe with the Austrian monarchy governed by the House of Habsburg (from 1780, the House of Habsburg-Lorraine) and the Czech Lands that had been under the monarchy since 1526. It is an approach fully in accord with the historical fact that, beginning in the late eighteenth and nineteenth centuries, the model under which Czechs formed a modern national community fit into a species of development towards a national state in which the nation creates a national community before the state itself. This community stands in opposition to the existing state — in the Czech case, opposition to the Austrian state. Under this model, the elites formulate the particular requirements for the system of government only after the fact.[3]

But what should be said about the period prior to 1848? Did the Medieval and Early Modern eras really represent apolitical periods without the presence of rights? To answer this question would require a freewheeling debate that exceeds the space available here. Having said that, this study does, of course, work with a concept that answers the question in the negative, that maintains it is indeed possible and sensible to apply terms such as 'politics' and 'law' to the historical

---

2 J. ZIMEK, *Ústavní vývoj českého státu*, Masarykova univerzita, Brno 1997.

3 Broadly see M. HROCH, *In the National Interest: Demands and Goals of European National Movements of the Nineteenth Century. A Comparative Perspective*, Charles University, Prague 2000.

events of the Medieval and Early Modern eras. We may illustrate the issue at hand in terms of the tension between the Anglo-Saxon doctrine of *checks and balances* and the Continental doctrine of the *separation of powers*.

The authors will use the term *checks and balances* to (surely simplistically)[4] designate the Anglo-Saxon practice of dividing the power of governance among several institutions, with the practical goal of protecting freedoms by having each group of individual power holders maintain supervision over the others. Or we may join Walter Bagehot in using the term to refer to all means that may be used to forestall the absolutisation of power.[5] In contrast, the doctrine of *separation of powers*, formulated by Charles Louis Montesquieu with practically the same ambition of limiting the danger of power being abused or usurped, identified precisely three types of power: the legislative, the executive, and judicial. These he strictly separated. As a side note, he formulated the doctrine in the mistaken belief that he was encoding a principle contained in the English constitution.[6] The doctrine of checks and balances thus reflects the openness of the Anglo-Saxon political situation of the era and does not incline toward a positive codification of the law; on the Continent at that time, the doctrine of separation of powers found its expected expression in the form of modern, positively stated constitutional documents.

This article presumes that recourse must be had to both doctrines to understand the Czech situation prior to the start of the modern constitutional age. The relevance of the doctrine of checks and balances lies in a realistic (critics might even say Machiavellian), open approach to the identification of the two actors that battled for position in the Medieval and Early Modern eras and the tools and strategies they employed in the struggle. At the same time, this approach does not presume the existence of any universal (human rights) framework that would embody a desired outcome. Rather, under this doctrine, all rights and freedoms have been formed in conflicts that escalated in the quest for power. Czech history nevertheless testifies to the intensive involvement of theorists in the consideration of concrete rights and freedoms, and it was the written or spoken *word* concerning these rights and freedoms that gave rise to the impulse to *act*. The formulation of abstract claims and the search for ways to codify them is thus a theme of relevance identical to that of power conflicts.

---

4 At this point the authors are not interested in obtaining an exact explanation with commentaries concerning this term (an example would be *Notes on the State of Virginia* by Thomas Jefferson) or polemics (for example, the theory stating that the three social classes, those of the king, the nobility and commoners, should be perceived as actors representing different political approaches and principles, disproved by Jeremy Bentham).

5 W. BAGEHOT, *The English Constitution*, Chapman & Hall, London 1867.

6 Once again, we simplify the topic somewhat by entirely discounting the prior theories of Aristotle, James Harrington, John Locke and many others who have focused on this topic.

Let us now step back into history several steps to meet our basic objective: to identify and describe key *cleavages*. These are the points around which significant tensions arose in Czech history during the search for a competitive model of the state. Among the characteristics that this competitive state should evidence were an ability to offer institutionalised mechanisms and procedures that define and guarantee rights and freedoms.

2. THE 'STATE-TERRITORIAL' CLEAVAGE: THE EMPIRE VERSUS THE CZECH LANDS

The process of building the medieval Czech regnum started in the first half of the tenth century. From the outset, the emerging Czech statehood took its shape from conflicts that arose by virtue of its *westward* power gravitation.[7] As an example, the first justified need for mutual contact among family clans in the future Czech state came in the tenth century when the Carolingian tribute was collected. The meeting point was Prague. In the early eleventh century, this western 'geopolitical vector' was clearly evident when the Czech Lands became part of the Holy Roman Empire (the *Sacrum Romanum Imperium*; from the fifteenth century, the Holy Roman Empire of the German Nation – *Sacrum Romanum Imperium Nationis Germanicae).*[8] The empire created an uneasy dependency, a source of discord that gave rise to continuous clashes, and it was here that the initial milestones of Czech statehood were sculpted:

- in 1085, Prince Vratislav II received a (non-hereditary) crown (as king Vratislav I.) from Emperor Henry IV as the first proof of the easing ties between Czech and German rulers;
- in 1158, Prince Vladislav II (as King Vladislav I) was granted a hereditary royal crown from Emperor Frederick Barbarossa at the Imperial Diet in Regensburg;
- in 1212, the Golden Bull of Sicily confirmed the hereditary royalty and other privileges of the Bohemian Kingdom to Premysl Otakar I, in particular relieving the Czech ruler of all obligations to the Holy Roman Empire except for participating in the Imperial Diet.

---

7 But this should not and must not mean that the other constitutive line — the *eastern* — is to be neglected. The eastern line was present in the tradition of the Great Moravian Empire, which places any attempt at statehood in the Czech basin back to the ninth century. This tradition serves as the medium for the second constitutive source, present even today, that the future Czech state would employ: the Byzantine mediation of the Christianising impulse. From the point of view of the Middle Ages and Early Modern era, this tradition was a 'dormant' source of the future modern Czech political identity.

8 For more details see K. HERBERS and H. NEUHAUS, *Das Heilige Römische Reich – Schauplätze einer tausendjährigen Geschichte (843–1806)*, Böhlau-Verlag, Köln, Weimar 2005.

The tension between the Imperial and the provincial thus clearly represented the first historical or geopolitical constant in Czech political and legal history. Futile efforts to overcome this tension make up the most recurrent theme not only of Czech medieval and early modern history but also in the modern era. If we replace the empire with the West, then it continues to be felt to the present day. Even the first King of Bohemia and the eleventh Czech king Charles IV (1346–78), the standout figure in Czech history, son of the Premyslid heiress Elizabeth of Bohemia and the Czech king John the Blind, a man who became Roman Emperor (1355–78) and ruler of all the kingdoms of the Holy Roman Empire, could not ignore it.[9] Although in the Golden Bull he confirmed the exceptional, independent position of the lands held by the Czech crown within the empire, this amounted to only a temporary success. Or it might be stated that the reign of Charles IV set a personal and power ideal which was never again achieved by anyone seeking out the status of the Czech Lands within the empire.

The reign of Emperor Charles IV is also interesting because it saw a remarkable attempt to codify existing legal customs in the Czech Lands into a codex. For this reason, his reign is worth exploring.

2.1. MICROSTUDY — MAIESTAS CAROLINA

Even the grand Premyslid predecessors of Charles IV considered the fragmentation of Czech legal customs in evidence at that time to be a key practical barrier to efficient governance. They tried, however much in vain, to create a written codex for the Czech kingdom. The steps taken by Charles IV to prepare and adopt the *Maiestas Carolina*, the legal code he proposed, did not therefore represent the first attempt at codification.[10] But their timing was clearly favourable because they were undertaken by an actor with extraordinary power — Emperor Charles IV. The story of its failure to be adopted thus serves all the more as an ideal model or outline of the *political-power* potential and the limits that confront efforts to realise such documents. Work on the codex started shortly after Charles IV acceded to the throne, probably as early as around 1348, with the declared goal of having validity in all countries under the Czech crown. The codex originated in several phases, with the most intensive work taking place between 1351 and 1353. First, Charles had the provisions of his

[9] In addition, Charles IV was King of Germany (Roman-German) (1346–1378), Italian (Lombard) King (1355–1378), King of Burgundy (1365–1378; incidentally, the last), Moravian Margrave (1333–1349) and Count of Luxembourg (1346–1353).

[10] The draft code to govern the Czech Lands was called *Maiestas Carolina* only from 1617 when it was published in a manuscript missing today. Originally, the document was known as *Codex Carolinus*. See K. MALÝ et al., *Dějiny českého a československého práva da roku 1945*, 3rd ed., Linda Praha a.s., Praha 2005, p. 100; L. BOBKOVÁ, *Velké dějiny zemí Koruny české. Svazek IV.a 1310–1402*, Paseka, Praha 2003, pp. 311–312.

predecessors collected, corrected, amended, and had signatures affixed.[11] But the codex was to be more than just a collection of written and unrecorded customs and norms. It also aspired to introduce new legal norms, and in this respect it drew on the canon law of that time, on the codex of Roman Emperor Frederick II, and to a limited extent, on Roman law. To describe all this in modern terms, it approached the form of a relatively comprehensive constitutional document that defines the basic power relationships in the country.

Conceptually, the *Maiestas Carolina* was built upon a doctrine of supreme governance by a sovereign ruler as the sole source of law. In this sense, Charles IV undoubtedly wished to rely on his own capacity for power deriving from his title as Emperor and his success in foreign policy, something evident in the preamble to the codex, which includes open argumentation that the right of the royal sovereign to establish laws is sanctified by God. Other points that reinforce royal power and limit the rights of the nobility over their subjects included the right of escheat — the king insisted that subjects who died without issue should pass their property to him, rather than to the nobility as current custom called for. At the same time, the codex seemed to simultaneously maintain that even the king was bound by the law and specified that petitions could be made against his decisions and actions. But in actuality, only against the officials responsible and not against the king himself could actions be called into question. Still other provisions mandated that royal power not be subject to the law (article 77) and that the sovereign stood above the law and judged all the people (article 41).[12]

For his part, Charles IV could not ignore reliance upon the estate-based character of his rule over the Czech Lands nor the requirement to present the document to the Czech princes and lords for an oath. It is for this reason that the *Maiestas Carolina* was not to take the form of a royal decree but was rather to be a symbolic agreement between the sovereign and the Czech estates. But in spite of this, the Czech nobility did not wish to be bound by written rules; it feared the potential weakening of its status.[13] In the end, the classic opposition of the estates rejected the codex, which they saw as reinforcing the sovereign's power, weakening their own position in the Bohemian Diet and restricting their right to 'freely seek the law in the Bohemian courts'.[14]

---

[11] Its internal layout suggests that the draft did not undergo a final editing process because the preface is located only after the first group of articles. Cf. M. NODL, 'Maiestas Carolina. Kritické postřehy k pramenům, vyhlášení a "odvolání" Karlova zákoníku' (2009) 1 *Studia mediaevalia Bohemica* 21, 24, 26.

[12] NODL, *supra note* 11, pp. 21, 27.

[13] R. ANTONÍN, 'Pater et filius iustitiae. The Ideal of Sovereign's Rule in Processes of Cultural Transfer by the End of the Thirteenth Century' in V. ČAPSKÁ (ed.), *Processes of Cultural Exchange in Central Europe, 1200–1800*, European Social Fund, Silesian University, Opava 2014, p. 300.

[14] BOBKOVÁ, *supra* note 10, pp. 313–314; MALÝ et al., *supra* note 10, p. 38.

The source of discord between the sovereign's vision and the opinions of the estates is therefore clear, but even so a number of disagreements among historians about the *Maiestas Carolina* have arisen. Particularly lively is the discussion of Charles's strategy for obtaining the nobility's consent to the codex. This is because no legal customs were in existence to govern the declaration and adoption of the codex in the Czech Lands. Some studies have it that the Czech nobility was to agree to preparation of the codex at the 1348 Diet; others disagree.[15] The codex, which gathered old acts to which the Czech princes and lords had agreed, was also to include seals (presumably of the princes and lords). And it was after these were symbolically attached — an act Charles IV probably considered evidence of agreement to the still incomplete codex — that the Czech nobility began to resist. As a result, the oath on adopting and maintaining the codex was never taken and the codex was therefore never declared or made public. While Charles IV had obtained at least formal preliminary agreement to the first version of the codex, as expressed by the attaching of the seals, the Czech princes and lords did not approve the second version. When Charles IV realised this, and that there would be no collective oath, he declared the first version of the codex 'burnt'. He did so in a document dated 6 October 1355, in which he explained the *Maiestas Carolina* had never been duly adopted and declared, and therefore had never entered into force. This manoeuvre allowed him to avoid rescinding the codex, something which might have been interpreted as a key political failure on his part. But by admitting he needed the Czech nobility's approval, in real terms Charles had given up the doctrine of absolute sovereignty. This did not prevent him from acting once again as God's chosen, consecrated sovereign, able to reign without the support of a written codex or of the nobility during the remainder of his era.[16]

What is important for our discussion is that a Czech translation of the text of the draft codex, originally written in Latin, has been preserved. In particular, two summaries, the so-called *summas*, were made to support the explication of Czech law, thereby functioning as an unofficial listing of legal norms and an aid in searching the law in the Czech Lands.[17] Thanks to these, we may comment on the text from a contemporary human-rights viewpoint. Most of its provisions concerned property, criminal, and religious law. Contemporary readers will find fascination in provisions prohibiting trials using hot irons and cold water (the so-called trial by ordeal), as well as physical punishment of subjects that would lead to their disfigurement. These provisions were inspired by religious thinkers. Not even lords were to be allowed to gouge the eyes or cut off the noses of their subjects, under threat of confiscation of their property. A fine could be imposed

15 NODL, *supra* note 11, pp. 21, 22, 25.

16 *Ibid.*, pp. 21, 25–35.

17 MALÝ et al., *supra* note 10, pp. 100–101, 114; *Návrh zákoníku Karla IV., tzv. Majestas Carolina*, <www.ucl.cas.cz/edicee/data/antologie/zliteratury/VZCL3/145.pdf> accessed 15.03.2015.

for cutting off arms or legs.[18] Top governmental officials were not to be appointed on a lifetime basis. Interesting sections of the *Maiestes Carolina* focus on the administration of justice.[19] To ensure the right of a just trial (articles 19 and 20), courts were to consist of three persons none of whom could be brothers. To be able to judge others, the judges had to speak Czech, and they had to be honest, moral, and free of transgression, all of which they pledged as part of their vows upon entering office. As noted above, the king himself could not be judged, but disputes against him could be addressed to responsible officials. Promises made under duress were vitiated.[20]

The draft codex also contained elements which would not be approved by contemporary defenders of human rights. These include proclamations made against infidels and heretics. Although the punishment of subjects who worked for the nobility was humanised to an extent, Charles IV had no hesitation about protecting his own assets, even using the law. A typical provision speaks of forest protection. The draft codex was based upon the principle of retribution, of sentencing the culprit to the same suffering he or she had inflicted. The penalties were truly intimidating: cutting down trees in the forest was to be punished by cutting off the culprit's right-hand; starting fires in the forest or encouraging others to arson was to be punished by burning, and so on.[21]

To summarise, the *Maiestas Carolina* as a whole was to represent a balanced collection of old customs and new laws. Its importance stemmed both from its provisions corresponding to basic rights, and for what it said about the sovereign's power. The story of the failure to adopt the codex is instructive above all because it outlines the possibilities and limitations of the practice of power in that era. If even a sovereign as powerful as Charles IV was forced to bow before the potential of the estates in their opposition to the written codex, this must be a significant characteristic of the political model in force in the Czech Lands during the High Middle Ages. By this we mean the existence of the nobility as a strong actor problematising the opportunity to wield absolute sovereign power in real terms. Not even the Roman Emperor and the Czech king Charles IV could simply implement his entire 'program', no matter what it said.

---

18 'Majestas Carolina' in F. PALACKÝ (ed.), *Archiv český čili staré písemné památky české i morawske. Díl třetí, svazek 1.*, Praha 1844, pp. 9–180 <http://147.231.53.91/src/index.php?s=v&cat=10&bookid=136&page=67> accessed 08.03.2015.

19 R. SCHNEIDER, 'Karls IV. Auffassung vom Herrscheramt' (1973) 2 *Historische Zeitschrift. Beihefte* 143–145.

20 'Majestas Carolina' in PALACKÝ, *supra* note 18, pp. 9–180.

21 M. CEMPÍREK, '"Lesní právo" ve středověku' in L. VOJÁČEK and J. TAUCHEN (eds.), *Sborníky z doktorandského semináře katedry Dějin státu a práva Právnické fakulty MU č. 2*, KEY Publishing, Ostrava 2012, pp. 9–11.

3. THE 'RELIGIOUS' CLEAVAGE: CATHOLICISM VERSUS PROTESTANTISM (THE HUSSITE MOVEMENT)

The subsequent period saw a gradual loss in the power held by the Czech Lands in the politics of the Empire, and an effort to insulate the rights of the Czech Lands from pressure abroad characterised the celebrated Hussite era of the first half of the fifteenth century. The well-known interpretation of this era, which sees in the Hussite movement a revolutionary phenomenon with ramifications across Europe, is completely in keeping with the central thesis of this article on the existence of internal *cleavages* around which key power tensions have formed throughout Czech history.[22] Among other things, then, the Hussite era brought an expansion of the state-territorial dimension to take in an entirely new theme, that of *religious rights*. How did this occur?

As early as in the fourteenth century, Reformation preachers were active in the Czech Lands. They included Jan Milíč of Kroměříž (between 1320 and 1325–1374) and Matthias of Janov (between 1350 and 1355–1393) who, with greater or lesser degrees of originality, engaged in both theological criticism of the contemporary church and social criticism of contemporary society. As part of this tradition of reform, intensive debates broke out at Prague University in the early fifteenth century over the teachings of John Wycliffe, the English thinker. In 1408, these disputes prompted Zbyněk Zajíc, the Archbishop of Prague and the university chancellor, to demand that, under threat of anathema, manuscripts containing Wycliffe's heretical views be turned in and his teachings no longer disseminated. This move caused a latent crisis that led to a cleavage that deeply, even fatefully, split the Czech Lands.[23]

Wenceslaus IV (1361–1419), firstborn son of Charles IV, Czech king from 1378 to 1419 and Roman Emperor between 1376 and 1400, decided to support the group of professors at Prague University who were in favour of the Reformation. Although most students at the university were of German origin, he issued a mandate in January 1409 inaccurately labelled the *Decree of Kuttenberg* in which he changed the ratio of voting at the university to 3:1 in favour of the Czech nation, replacing the prior 1:1 ratio. In reaction, approximately 700 to 800 German teachers and students decided to leave for other European universities, initiating a decline in the reputation of Prague University.[24] The Decree of Kuttenberg aroused hope in Reformation circles that secular authority would be placed over spiritual authority, and this would help put the church to rights.[25] In

22 M. MALIA, *History's Locomotive. Revolutions and the Making of the Modern World*, Yale University Press, New Haven, Conn. 2006, pp. 37–59.

23 Cf. F. ŠMAHEL, *Jan Hus. Život a dílo*, Argo, Praha 2013.

24 German in the sense of those whose mother tongue was German.

25 These events unfolded against the backdrop of the Council of Pisa, which was to end the Papal Schism and resolve the general ecclesiastical crisis. Wenceslaus IV hoped the Council would

this way, what had started out as a theological dispute turned into a central issue of power.

The extraordinarily popular preacher and Rector of Prague University in 1409–10, Jan Hus (ca. 1370–1415), became the most significant figure in the Reformation community. In parallel theses calling for the church to be reformed and the position of laymen to be changed, he radicalised the theological concept of truth, stating that it should not be monopolised by the church council because it is a clear spiritual principle, and he urged that the truth be confronted that all people, regardless of origin, regardless of position, are equal. Because of these ideas, provocative for the time, Master Jan Hus was called before the Council of Constance, where he was found guilty of heresy and burned at the stake. This only provoked his martyrdom to become a constituting symbol of the Czech identity.

The historical period we have just detailed, starting with the Decree of Kuttenberg and lasting until the burning at the stake of Master Jan Hus represented the opening phase of the Hussite era. It lasted two decades, and wrought a permanent cleavage in the Czech Lands based upon preferred faith — the Roman Catholic versus the Czech Calixtine (Hussite). This began a drawn-out historical process which, on a latent level, interconnected several planes of conflict: the primordial 'academic' dispute between religious reformists (Wycliffists) and their opponents, the 'ethnic' conflict between the German and Czech elements over influence at the university, the conflict between 'heretical' Bohemia and 'Christian' Europe over religious rights and their practical exercise, and the European-wide confrontation that had arisen from the papal schism and from personal claims on the Holy Roman title, in which the Czech king was deeply involved.[26] In any event, the Czech Hussite movement became the source of a significant — and for the Czech identity, constitutive — *political* tradition.

At the same time, the Hussite movement provided an extraordinary spiritual stimulus. In 1462, for instance, George of Podiebrad (1420–71), the Czech 'Chalice' king, proposed the creation of a *union of European nations* to ensure the maintenance of peace and justice, and to move towards relinquishing warfare as a tool for resolving disputes. This act was a reaction to the diminishing power of both the Pope and the German Emperor, accompanied by increasing parallel pressure from the Ottoman Empire. The proposition was based upon the principle of equal participation by sovereign Christian states, united in the fight

restore the his royal title as King of the Holy Roman empire, which he had lost to Ruprecht III of the Palatinate in 1400. Cf. P. Čornej, *Velké dějiny zemí Koruny české. Svazek V 1402–1437*, Paseka, Praha 2000, pp. 116–124; F. Šmahel and M. Nodl, 'Kutnohorský dekret po 600 letech. Bilance dosavadního bádání.' (2009) 107 *Český časopis historický* 1–45.

[26] In a footnote at least, we should note that Marxist historiographers and Marxist ideological propaganda emphasised the social issue as the central theme of the Hussite 'revolutionary' movement.

against the Turkish threat. Disputes between member states were to be resolved by peaceful means before a Conciliation Commission, or an international court. The use of military force by individual members had to be approved by the union itself; the proposal even called for collective aid if a member of the union should be attacked. But George came up against the power interests of other actors in the European political scene in that era. On the one hand, he obtained support for negotiations on the peace project from King Casimir of Poland and King Matthias of Hungary, but negotiations on this ambitious multilateral agreement with the French monarch, Louis XI, were halted by a lack of agreement from the Papal Curia.[27] In any event, for its time, the project offered a remarkably modern outlook on the potentialities of international law.

Another individual whose work stretched far beyond the borders of the Czech Lands was Peter Chelcicky (ca. 1390–1460). Chelcicky was a lay religious and social thinker who developed the notion of equality and engaged in social criticism of power in his treatises.[28] As the 'first pacifist Renaissance writer', he anticipated the ideas of Erasmus of Rotterdam by a good one hundred years.[29] And above all there is the work of the early Enlightenment Czech philosopher John Amos Comenius (Iohannes Amos Comenius; 1592–1670), including his philosophical and educational writings.[30] Both these names belong in the pantheon of Czech history. Their common denominator was the idea of *religious rights, freedoms, and tolerance*, and it was in the Czech Lands in the post-Hussite era, from the late fifteenth to the early seventeenth centuries, that this idea was 'discovered' for Europe.

On this level, interpreting the Czech Hussite movement as the initial phase of the Reformation, which was a Europe-wide phenomenon, is logical. But for the Czech Lands, or a significant portion of the Czech estates, the theme formed an important, even critical dimension from its very beginnings. This was further reinforced after what had historically been the Czech Lands was included in the Central European Habsburghaus Confederation (1526), which bore a strongly Catholic identity.

---

27 This is because Pope Pius II was bothered by the fact that two churches were in existence — the Roman Catholic and the Czech Calixtine (Hussite) in the Czech Lands. George of Podiebrad thus signed 'only' a bilateral alliance. Cf. P. Čornej and M. Bartlová, *Velké dějiny zemí Koruny české. Svazek VI. 1437–1526*, Paseka, Praha 2007, pp. 207–215; Malý et al., *supra* note 10, pp. 56–58.

28 J.S. Trojan, 'Idea lidských práv v české tradici' in A. Havlíček (ed.), *Lidská a přirozená práva v dějinách*, FF UJEP, Ústí nad Labem 2014, pp. 67–72.

29 The treaties of Peter Chelcicky had a significant impact on e.g., Leo Tolstoy, the Russian writer and philosopher and, indirectly, on Gandhi, Martin Luther King and Nelson Mandela.

30 Trojan, *supra* note 28, pp. 72–75.

4. THE 'REGIME' CLEAVAGE: THE ESTATES VERSUS THE ABSOLUTE MONARCHY

The inclusion of the historical Czech Lands in the Habsburg monarchy gave rise to the third constitutive conflict in Czech history: *the tension between the open estate*, on the one side, and *absolutism* on the other. This line of conflict became naturally established not only in the Czech-Habsburg context, but on the European level as well. Its presence makes clear what a historical milestone the year 1609 was, when Rudolf II of the House of Habsburg (1552–1612; King of Bohemia, Hungary, and Croatia) issued the Letter of Majesty (the so-called Rudolf's Majesty) under pressure from Czech non-Catholic estates. It ensured Christian denominations would have freedom of religion and freedom to organise church life.[31] In spite of this, the theme of religious tolerance or respect for the Calixtine denomination as a significant identitarian variable of the Czech estates gave rise to a military conflict. The Bohemian Revolt ended in 1620 in defeat, after which Ferdinand II, Holy Roman Emperor (1578–1637), abolished the Majesty and made Catholicism the only lawful religion.[32] By this time, Europe was already in the early years of the continent-wide Thirty Years' War which in the end, after the Peace of Westphalia in 1648 following the principle *cuius regio, eius religio*, confirmed the relevance of the European-wide religious cleavage.

For the Czech Lands, this principle meant the interconnection of the religious and regime cleavages; the liquidation of non-Catholic estates went hand-in-hand with the persecution of non-Catholic inhabitants. It was not until the reign of Emperor Joseph II (1741–90), who issued the Patent of Tolerance in October 1781, that the Augsburg (Lutheran), Helvetic (Calvinist), and Greek Orthodox confessions were recognised in addition to Catholicism.[33] This document, or rather a series of patents and regulations grouped under the name, placed Catholics and non-Catholics on equal footing, particularly in secular affairs, where non-Catholics were no longer forbidden from taking up clerical and bureaucratic positions, enrolling in schools, holding trade licenses, or acquiring property. By contrast, when it came to liturgy and religious life, many restrictions persisted.[34] Emperor Joseph II thus fulfilled his programme, which had been influenced by the Enlightenment: steps towards religious tolerance paradoxically also represented proof of the potential of absolutist governance in

---

31 See J. JUST, *9.7.1609. Rudolfův majestát. Světla a stíny náboženské svobody,* Havran, Praha 2009.

32 In the so-called Battle of White Mountain, fought on 08.11.1620. White Mountain thus became a symbol of the humiliation of the Czech Lands.

33 The principles of tolerance were applied to the Jews gradually over succeeding years, see P. BĚLINA and J. KAŠE and J.P. KUČERA, *Velké dějiny zemí Koruny české. Svazek X. 1740–1792*, Paseka, Praha 2001, p. 98.

34 MALY et al., *supra* note 10, p. 179.

the Hapsburg countries and the marginalisation of actors who preferred a more open, more pluralistic model of government — the estates.[35]

5. THE STRATEGIC CLEAVAGE: CONSTITUTIONAL-LEGAL-POLITICAL VERSUS GOVERNANCE SYSTEM-NATIONAL

In spite of the favourable nature of the climate, in the late eighteenth and early nineteenth centuries, the core of the so-called Czech National Revival began to form around the Reformation tradition (Hussite, Calixtine, and Brethren). Its motivation was the search for an identitary element that could represent a reasonable alternative to the publicly declared Catholic identity of the Habsburg Confederation. This element was also part of the Czech National Movement, which became a real factor in Austrian politics in the late nineteenth century. This movement gave rise to the fourth tension, the discrepancy between the *constitutional-legal-political* dimension and the *system of governance-national* dimension in building modern Czech politics. It sprang from the open period following the revolutions of 1848 that saw many constitutions come into existence, a period in which the first dimension of the building process of modern Czech politics also came into being, the *constitutional-legal-political* dimension. The basic prerequisite was the end of the absolute governance model in the Austrian monarchy and entry into the era of constitutional monarchy. The trend included the first attempts to apply the theory of the separation of powers (see the Pillersdorf Constitution dated April 1848, or the draft text of the constitution presented at the Reichstag in Kroměříž in winter 1848–49). It was later codified as part of a gradual process that saw the monarchy transformed into a constitutional state (starting with the 1860 October Diploma and Schmerling's Constitution of February 1861), tentatively aimed at guaranteeing human and civil rights, as well as other features present in modern democracies.

But the process of building modern Czech politics had another dimension, one we have labelled *system of governance-national*. Within this dimension, the Czech historical programme was to culminate in the confirmation or renewal of the land rights held by the Czech Lands historically, that is by Bohemia, Moravia, and Silesia.[36] In other words, there was a point contained in the Czech system of governance that was on the one hand historical but was still central for the modern era: recognition of the Czechs as a state-forming nation, regardless of

---

[35] From a purely quantitative point of view, the Czech non-Catholic element in the late phase of Joseph II's government seemed to be only a marginal actor practically condemned to extinction: at that time within the territory of the Czech Crown, only about 80,000 people were not Catholic, approximately 2% of the population. Cf. BĚLINA et al., *supra* note 33, pp. 89–95.

[36] We neglect historical changes within the Czech Lands and the frequent imperial conflicts and battles with neighbours over territory.

any differences among the estates or in social standing, a nation that bore the renowned banner of the Kingdom of the Czech Crown.

It was thus the national-liberal doctrine which combined the fight for a liberal conceptualisation of rights and freedoms within a nation-based framework. It can be seen in the so-called 'question of women' which emerged in the second half of the nineteenth century (until that time, the issue had not appeared in the Czech milieu). Strategies for obtaining guarantees of political and civil rights gradually also included women as welcome actors. The most important personalities at the turn of the twentieth century, such as Františka Plamínková and Alice Masaryková, particularly supported women's suffrage.[37]

Against the backdrop of this tension, the late nineteenth century saw the celebrated dispute over the meaning of Czech history, a dispute which functioned as an intellectual tool of the time in the search for the Czech national identity, particularly in contrast to Germany and the West in general, and in determining what tasks should be undertaken by the Czech national movement. A philosophical, *idealistic-teleological* approach to Czech history (represented by T.G. Masaryk) clashed with a historiographical, *empirical-positivist* concept (represented by J. Pekar). But from the standpoint of our theme particularly, there was once again the *Protestant* (Protestant-Socialist) position contrasted to the *Catholic* position.

This dispute produced no winners, but on a practical level, the Protestant interpretation undoubtedly won the day, and this was fully reflected in the notion of building an independent Czechoslovak state after the collapse of the Austro-Hungarian Empire at the end of World War I. Masaryk (1850–1937) became the first president of Czechoslovakia. He had already made use of the interpretation detailed above during his political exile at the time of World War I, in an effort to convince Western political elites that the intention to dissolve Austria-Hungary (an obscurantist medieval relic) made sense, and that a new, progressive Central Europe of national states should be built in its place. Concretely, this was supposed to mean that the Hussite movement would be considered the high point of Czech history and its heroes would be Master Jan Hus, Peter Chelcicky, and Comenius. Under their particularist claim to national emancipation, the Czechs were supposed to be the bearers of universal values of humanity and democracy since, in their permanent 'contact and struggle' with the German element, they had always stood on the side of historical progress and aimed at democracy and brotherhood, and these things represented Czech national characteristics.

---

37 So-called February Czechoslovak Constitution of 1920 stipulated that women are politically, socially and culturally equal to men and that they have voting right.

Thus equipped did the Czech political community enter the twentieth century. On the one hand, it possessed a plurality of viewpoints in its philosophical explanations of its own history; on the other, it expressed a clearly defined ideological preference that was consciously reflected in the building of the independent state. Due to the political turbulence of the twentieth century, the Czech political community was to face a number of challenges — disagreements with the German minority that led to the Munich agreement of 1938, the annexation of the Sudetenland to the Third Reich, and later the military occupation and establishment of the Protectorate of Bohemia and Moravia during World War II. Other challenges included the reluctance of Slovak politicians to accept the doctrine of a single Czechoslovak nation as preferred by Prague, twice leading to the declaration of an independent Slovak state — in 1939 and again in 1992 – and finally, after World War II, the Communist wave, and with it the establishment of a totalitarian communist regime and absorption of the state into the Soviet sphere.

6. CONCLUDING REMARKS

The authors have focused on the theme of early human rights documents as an opportunity to present a somewhat ambitious historical outline whose goal is to identify the key cleavages involved in the formation of the Czech state. We see these cleavages as the fundamental fractures dividing Czech actors of the era, based upon gradually emerging claims to the formulation and guarantee of basic rights and freedoms within the Czech environment. By means of the *Maiestas Carolina* microstudy and in other ways, this text participates in the intensifying debate over the historiography of human rights,[38] provoked in particular by Samuel Moyn in *The Last Utopia*.[39] The authors' approach emphasises the importance of the historical context and the power constellations of the time. That various historical documents speak of the same objects protected by contemporary human rights documents need not mean that humanitarian motives have the power to motivate *political* change; efforts to clothe a historical document in the garb of human rights simply because it contains mention of rights that today we understand as human seems to the authors counterproductive.[40]

Using the example of the *Maiestas Carolina*, a document 140 years younger than Magna Carta, we have shown that provisions which, on the surface, appear to

38 For a detailed description, see J-P. Lehners, 'Pleading for a New History of Human Rights' in A. Mihr and M. Gibney (eds.), *The SAGE Handbook of Human Rights*, SAGE Publications, London 2014, pp. 22–38.

39 S. Moyn, *The Last Utopia. Human Rights in History*, Harvard University Press, Cambridge, MA 2010. For a critical reaction to Moyn's approach, see C. McCrudden, 'Human Rights Histories' (2015) 35 *Oxford Journal of Legal Studies* 1, 179–212.

40 Compare S. Moyn, *Human Rights and the Uses of History*, Verso, London, New York 2014.

contemporary readers to speak to a flowering of human rights in fact were based upon a different logic than is currently employed in a constitutional and international agreement context. The events of Czech history indicate that the accent must be placed upon political conflict that naturally reflects discrepancies in the outlook on gradually formulated *rights and freedoms*. From a political science standpoint, it seems simply that rights and freedoms without a corresponding power base, and absent the willingness of specific political actors to protect them, may remain only social constructs. Their emergence in Czech history gave rise to four cleavages that are the subject of this paper: the state-territorial cleavage, the religious cleavage, the regime cleavage, and the strategic cleavage. All of these form interconnections between the plane of political, civil, economic, social, cultural or gender rights and freedoms and the plane of concrete political actions. The social sciences should reflect these interconnections as it ponders current political reality.

20. ROMANIA: THE BIRTH OF FUNDAMENTAL RIGHTS AS A FORM OF POLITICAL CONTENTION

Liana Andreea IONIȚĂ[1]

1. INTRODUCTION

The story of fundamental rights in Romania goes back in time to the early seventeenth century. The territory of today's Romania was divided into three separate Principalities — Wallachia, Moldavia and Transylvania — which, at that time, were tributary states under the suzerainty of the Ottoman Empire and were organised and governed in the political and social framework of a domestic feudal authoritarianism. Even though independently constituted, the three Romanian States were invariably connected to one another through cultural and economic relations and cooperation, which encouraged the emergence of a common ideal of unity and cohesive action[2] against external threats.

The first fundamental rights document was the modern charter of liberty established in Wallachia in 1631, named the Freedom Charter from Bucharest (*'Charta de libertăți' de la București*). Considering the nature of this agreement and the specific political circumstances of its time, this Charter may represent, according to Romanian scholars and historians, the possible foundation document of fundamental rights in Romania. The proclamation of this document was an expression of the will of Romanian society to create particular civil rights and freedoms for individuals, describing basic rights to be free from unequal treatment. The Freedom Charter from Bucharest makes reference to the right not to be killed without trial in front of judicial bodies and respect for all procedural safeguards. With an identical meaning to Article 39 of Magna Carta Libertatum (1215), these rights stipulated in the Freedom Charter from Bucharest are

1 This chapter is supported by the Sectoral Operational Programme Human Resources Development (SOP HRD), financed from the European Social Fund and by the Romanian Government under the contract number POSDRU/159/1.5/133675.

2 For a comprehensive analysis of the common ideal of unity within the three Romanian Principalities, see L. BOIA, *Istorie şi mit în conştiinţa românească* [History and Myth in Romanian Consciousness], Humanitas, Bucureşti 1997; N. DJUVARA, *Între Orient şi Occident. Ţările Române la începutul epocii moderne* [Between East and West. The Romanian Lands at the Beginning of the Modern Era], Humanitas, Bucureşti 1995.

considered innovative for seventeenth-century Romania in the sense of an early writ of *habeas corpus*. Even though this principle *talis qualis* is not included in the text of the Charter, it emanates from the nature of the provisions themselves. The early conceptualization of fundamental rights and freedoms can be traced to several documents issued in the three Principalities. Nonetheless, the formal institution of fundamental rights was first introduced in Romanian territory in the first modern Constitution of 1866. Inspired by the liberal ideas of the Belgian Constitution of 1831, considered at that time the most liberal constitution in Europe, the Romanian Constitution of 1866 incorporated the values, principles and practices of Western liberal democracies, such as the democratic principle of separation of powers, the principle of representative government, the principle of national sovereignty and the recognition of fundamental rights and liberties.

This study aims to reveal two emblematic moments in the history of fundamental rights in Romania, namely the first fundamental document and the first constitutional documents, by providing a thorough analysis of the nature of the granted rights in the context of the social and political evolution of Romanian society. Noting the essential role that women have played in enhancing modern societies and the universal recognition of the ideals of human rights and liberties, it is cross-culturally relevant to examine the gender discourse as it is reflected in the first fundamental rights documents and evolving attitudes towards equality between men and women. Throughout this fundamental rights narrative, the gender perspective will also be assessed in the light of changes and developments in Romanian society.

2. EARLY FUNDAMENTAL RIGHTS DOCUMENTS

One of the earliest Romanian fundamental rights documents was the feudal Freedom Charter from Bucharest, adopted within the area of the Romanian state of Wallachia in 1631. It was issued in the form of a chrysobull (*hrisov*) on 15 July 1631, by Leon Tomşa, the ruler of Wallachia (1629–1632). Even though a 'forgotten' document, it sheds light on the early history of fundamental rights in Romania. Romanian scholars even consider it a real 'Charter of Romanian Freedoms'[3] and a 'possible founding document of the Romanian modern constitutionalism', claiming that 'the constitutional potential'[4] of the fundamental rights stipulated in this Freedom Charter is similar to the English

---

3 V.A. Georgescu, 'Hrisovul din 15 iulie 1931 al lui Leon Vodă Tomşa în ŢaraRomânească şi problema "Cărţilor de libertăţi"' [The Charter of 15 July 1931 on Leon Tomşa, in Wallachia and the problem of 'Freedom Charters'] (1976) 29 *Revista de istorie* [The Journal of History] No.7, 1013–1031.

4 L.S. Stănescu, 'A Comparison between the Magna Carta Libertatum and the Freedom Charta from Bucharest in 1631 and the problem of a possible founding document of the Romanian Modern Constitutionalism' (2013) 13 *The USV ANNALS of Economics and Public Administration* No. 2.

Magna Carta Libertatum of 1215 and other *Chartae libertates* of European societies.

The Charter of Leon Tomşa makes reference to a set of civil rights and freedoms that can be divided into two categories. On the one hand, there are ecclesiastical freedoms for the monasteries and the Church leaders, and the right of succession and fiscal freedoms for the nobility; on the other hand, there are provisions regarding individual liberty in its earliest and most modest form of *habeas corpus*.[5] This second category is relevant for the present study. For the sake of an accurate exposition of the genesis of the first fundamental rights document, I will first outline the social and political realities of the modern Romanian society around 1631, then I will engage in a comprehensive examination of the document *per se* and the nature of the granted rights. Finally, I will assess the Charter's legal and symbolic value for the Romanian collective memory.

Within a hostile political and social environment,[6] characterised by solid opposition and regular uprisings of the nobles (*boieri*) against the politics of the sovereign (*domn*) aiming to consolidate the domination of the Ottoman Empire, the Freedom Charter was constituted as a pact between the *domn* and the *boieri*. It was signed by the *domn* under his oath, in front of the National Assembly.[7] The spread of Ottoman domination over Romanian lands in general and in Wallachia in particular[8] had been gradually consolidated through the growth of merchant elites of Greek origin, which were given land properties, noble titles and high state functions.[9] The Greek community had substantially grown on Romanian territory under the rule of Leon Tomşa (who was a ruler of Greek origin appointed by the High Porte), and its infiltration into the political and economic life of the state caused vigorous reactions on the part of the domestic

---

5 GEORGESCU, *supra* note 3, p. 1022.

6 The hostile environment of the seventeenth century is defined by socio-political crises, intensified by the Wallachia's international status as an Ottoman vassal state. In the early fifteenth century, Wallachia accepted the suzerainty of the Ottoman Empire, which lasted *grosso modo* until the nineteenth century, except for the short periods of Russian occupation. See C. REZACHEVICI, 'Fenomene de criză social-politică în Ţara Românească în veacul al XVII-lea' [Phenomena of socio-political crises in Wallachia in the seventeenth century] (1978) 9 *Revista Studii şi Materiale de Istorie Medie* [The Journal of Studies and Sources of Medieval History], Romanian Academy, 73–77.

7 The National Assemby (*Adunarea Naţională*) was the legislative institution of the Principality of Wallachia. Led by a Chancellor, the Assembly used to meet on a regular basis in order to vote laws and decide on the most important issues.

8 F. CONSTANTINIU, *O istorie sinceră a poporului român* [A Sincere History of the Romanian People], 2nd ed., Univers Enciclopedic, Bucharest 2002, pp. 140–142. In the Middle Ages and before their independence, the three principalities were *de iure* vassal states, which used to pay a certain tribute to the Porte, but *de facto*, they had a special status of autonomy, which permitted them to keep their own political, administrative and military structures, due to the numerous anti-Ottoman rebellions.

9 A. FALANGAS, 'Post-Byzantine Greek Merchants of the Fifteenth-Seventeenth Centuries' (2007) 33 *Journal of the Hellenic Diaspora* No. 1–2, 7.

nobility, on the basis that the Greeks were considered a major challenge in terms of trade and estates, and regarding the status of the officials at the court. The conflict between the nobles and the sovereign had given rise to a common hostility of the Romanian nobility towards the Greek ruler of state[10] and, as a result, anti-Greek uprisings had attained a critical point.

Being under pressure from the domestic nobility, the ruler of Wallachia, Leon Tomşa, was forced by the National Assembly to issue a *hrisov*. The liberties proclaimed in the Freedom Charter from Bucharest[11] represented the consensus of the 'whole country', as is mentioned in the document, but in fact, this formula was referring only to major and minor nobles and landowners, nobles removed from their jobs, nobles composing the body of cavalry and the royal servants.[12] Under the form of an oath, Leon Tomşa declared in the preamble of the document: 'I give you this most honourable [...] which is above all honourable gifts, this present *hrisov* of mine, so to be of great faith to the nobles of my country [...] for the things and bad habits that have been brought by foreign people to my country', which have 'greatly damaged the country'.[13] The *hrisov* embodied anti-Greek sentiment and imposed a new regime on foreigners in Wallachia, demanding the expulsion of Greek people who were not married with local women or did not have any land properties, on the grounds that 'all the needs and the poverty of the country start from the Greek foreigners'.[14] In the context of these anti-Greek measures, such as the expulsion under the conditions mentioned above and the expulsion of Greek monks, in order 'to be only Romanian monks, as they were for centuries',[15] two categories of freedoms were nevertheless provided.

The first category includes ecclesiastical freedoms, namely the autonomy of the Romanian Church and the election of Church Leaders by a local synod and only with the blessing of the patriarch.[16] The rights of succession or inheritance rights are mentioned as well and in this regard, the Charter stipulates that in the event of 'the death of a noble or every man',[17] the right of succession belongs to the

---

10 See P. TEODOR, 'Monarhia feudală' [Medieval Monarchy] in M. BĂRBULESCU, D. DELETANT, K. HITCHINS, Ş. PAPACOSTEA and P. TEODOR (eds.), *Istoria României* [The History of Romania], Corint, Bucureşti 2007, pp. 196–230.

11 For the original version of the Freedom Charta (*'Charta de libertăţi' de la Bucureşti*), see D. MIOC, *Documenta Romaniae Historica (DRH), B.Ţara Românească*, vol. XIII (1630–1632), no. 255, Academia Republicii Socialiste România, Bucureşti 1969, pp. 406–409. This study is part of a broader collection of DRH documents, issued under the patronage of the Romanian Academy. All translations from Romanian archaic language into English are my own unless otherwise noted.

12 *Ibid.*

13 *Ibid.*

14 *Ibid.*, article 2.

15 *Ibid.*, article 3.

16 *Ibid.*, articles 3, 12 and 13.

17 *Ibid.*, article 4.

heir-of-law or to whomever the deceased may decide. Moreover, the nobility enjoyed a number of exemptions from taxes in an endeavour to strengthen their control over their lands.[18]

The second category consisting of a series of individual freedoms provides the justification for classifying this Charter as one of the earliest Romanian fundamental rights documents. The *hrisov* makes references to 'measures of judicial safeguards of individual liberty',[19] stating that

> no one shall be killed without trial in front of the *Divan*, but the person in question shall be imprisoned first, and then shall be judged by the members of the *Divan* and his fault shall be publicly recognised; only then, shall be punished according to the laws and his guilt.[20]

The *Divan* was a political institution in Wallachia, constituted of approximately 10 to 15 nobles, which played an extremely important role in providing assistance to the ruler of the country on political, fiscal and judicial matters regarding internal and external policies. Besides this responsibility, it was also tasked with ensuring that the ruler was governing the country in the best interests of the nobility — the ruling class of the feudal state. Under these conditions, the ruler of the country could not judge anybody without the *Divan*.[21] According to Article 9 of the Charter, everyone had the right to an effective remedy and to a fair trial and moreover, capital punishment was not to be imposed if guilt was not proved in front of the *Divan*. Furthermore, the Charter stated that each judgment shall serve justice, after the Christian rules, and no longer serve the will of the nobility, so that abuses, duplicity and bribes could be prevented.[22]

Romanian scholars have suggested that the Freedom Charter from Bucharest can be put on an equal footing with other *Chartae Libertatum* from different countries, which highlights the integration of the Romanian Principalities within the general evolution of the European societies.[23] Article 9 of the Freedom Charter of 1631 looks directly back to Article 39 of Magna Carta Libertatum of 1215, which mentions that

---

18 The Freedom Charta, *supra* note 11, article 1.

19 V. OPRICĂ, 'Gender Equality and Conflicting Attitudes Toward Women in Post-Communist Romania' (2008) 9 *Human Rights Review*, no. 1, 292.

20 The Freedom Charta, *supra* note 11, article 9.

21 N. STOICESCU, *Sfatul domnesc şi marii dregători din Ţara Românească şi Moldova (Sec. XIV–XVII)* [The National Assembly and the landowners nobles from Wallachia and Moldavia (XIV–XVII)] Editura Acad. Republicii Socialiste România, Bucharest 1968.

22 The Freedom Charta, *supra* note 11, article 8.

23 R. ECONOMU, '1631 - O chartă a libertăţilor' (1986) 20 *Magazin Istoric* [Historical Journal], no. 10, 9.

> No free man shall be seized or imprisoned, or stripped of his rights or possessions, or outlawed or exiled, or deprived of his standing in any way, nor will we proceed with force against him, or send others to do so, except by the lawful judgment of his equals or by the law of the land.[24]

Therefore, it seems that the ideas and provisions included in the Freedom Charter from Bucharest are directly traceable to the English Great Charter. In addition, the hostile historical context is similar in both cases: the threats of civil war in England and the civil uprising, rebellions and anti-Greek movements in Wallachia. Beyond a shadow of a doubt, one can observe in the *hrisov* from 1631 the central contextual elements characterising the emergence of any fundamental rights document: firstly, 'the profound, long-lasting and intensified conflict between the dynamic nobility and the weak but authoritarian sovereign' and secondly, the Charter's regulatory character over a series of serious basic problems,[25] which were caused in this case by the Greek migrants who had been encouraged by the High Porte to come and settle in Wallachia and eventually had become favoured by the sovereign, to the dissatisfaction of the domestic nobility. When pleading for the expulsion of Greek migrants and invoking the need for restitution to the initial social and political framework, which existed before their arrival in Wallachia, it is understood that these regulations encapsulate the principles of *restitutio in integrum* and *reformatio*, even though not explicitly mentioned in the *hrisov*.

To conclude, the Freedom Charter from Bucharest remains, therefore, in the Romanian collective memory due to its innovative character when it comes to asserting the earliest origins of fundamental rights in modern Romanian society, in the context of the social and political framework of the seventeenth century. However, the precarious continuity of its legal regulations has transformed it into a somewhat 'forgotten' document, as a result of the fact that 'what characterizes the history of the Romanian law is that the activity of the law is not imposed'[26] by all of the subsequent rulers of Wallachia. Leon Tomşa's oath included the need for future commitment, on the part of his successors, to this moral and legal behaviour, by stating that:

> these wills of the country, of the National Assembly, all mentioned above, I swear with great oath, to keep them all during my reign. [...] And after my reign, the following ruler of Wallachia, chosen by the will of God, shall respect this *hrisov*, as

24 Magna Carta Libertatum, article 39 <http://www.orbilat.com/Languages/Latin/Texts/06_Medieval _period/Legal_Documents/Magna_Carta.html> accessed 11.03.2015.

25 GEORGESCU, *supra* note 3, pp. 1021–1022.

26 OPRICĂ, *supra* note 19, p. 290.

mentioned above. If not, he shall be punished and damned by the Jesus Christ [...] forever, amen.[27]

In Romanian society, the oath was seen as a judicial procedure, so it was supposed to 'transform the state of fact into a fact of law'.[28] Although this final part of the Charter also engages successors, the oath of the sovereign does not have the power to establish real legal obligations for the subsequent ruler of Wallachia.

Besides the Freedom Charter from Bucharest of 1631, several other early fundamental rights documents with legal significance were issued on Romanian land, among which it is worth mentioning the Tudor Vladimirescu's Proclamation from Padeş[29] of 1821, from Wallachia, the Carbonari's Constitution of 1822[30] from Moldavia and the Supplex Libellus Valachorum Transsilvaniae[31] of 1791–1792, from Transylvania. An important moment for Romanian fundamental rights history is the Romanian Revolution of 1848, which had its roots in the French revolutionary ideals of the same year. It was the first modern revolution, which took place almost concomitantly in the three Romanian states under the domination of great powers (the Ottoman Empire, the

---

27 The Freedom Charta, *supra* note 11.

28 D. BARBU, *O Arheologie Constituţională românească* [A Romanian Constitutional Archaeology], Editura Universităţii, Bucharest 2000, p. 47.

29 In 1821, the three Romanian Principalities were making progress towards unification and independence and therefore, several social and national movements took place. The Wallachian Revolution in 1821 was a peasants' uprising, conducted by Tudor Vladimirescu and his army of pandours, against the Ottoman Empire. Inspired from the Enlightenment principles and the French Revolution of 1789, their claims were included in two documents, The Proclamation from Padeş and The Demands of Romanian People, which contained basic principles of social order: the appropriation of peasants with land, the abolition of the peasants' economic obligations to the nobles (the boyards), the proclamation of the principles of liberty and equality, along with a series of reforms in all the sectors of the society. See A. OŢEŢEA, *Tudor Vladimirescu şi revoluţia din 1821* [Tudor Vladimirescu and the Revolution of 1821], Editura Ştiinţifică, Bucharest 1971 and N. DJUVARA, *Între Orient şi Occident. Ţările Române la începutul epocii moderne* [Between East and West.The Romanian Principalities at the Beginning of the Modern Age], Humanitas, Bucharest 1995.

30 The so-called Carbonari's Constitution of 1822 was a constitutional project which made reference to the Italian Carbonari, the secret revolutionary society from the early nineteenth century. Inspired by the French Revolution of 1789, it was claiming the respect for the property, the liberty of the individual, the equality before the law and the constitutional principle of 'the rule of law', in the sense that the authority of the sovereign must be limited and subordinated to the representative body. A part of it was not approved by the nobility at that time, so it was rejected. See T.L. POP, *Constituţiile României* [The constitutions of Romania], Editura Ştiinţifică şi enciclopedică, Bucharest 1984.

31 The Supplex Libellus Valachorum Transsilvaniae was a petition of the Romanians (Vlachs) from Transylvania, who represented approximately 60% of the population. Inspired by the French Declaration of the Rights of Man and of the Citizen of 1789, it demanded equal political rights between them and the Hungarians and the other ethnicities of Transylvania. However, the Petition was rejected and therefore, the status of the Romanians was not changed. See CONSTANTINIU, *supra* note 8, pp. 182–183.

Tsarist Empire and the Austro-Hungarian Empire).The three separate documents, namely the Proclamation from Islaz, in Walachia, the National Petition from Blaj, in Transylvania and the Petition-Proclamation in Moldavia, encapsulated the unitary will for liberty and equality, the common goal of building a national unitary state, as well as several social and political demands, such as freedom for gipsy slaves from Romanian lands, freedom of expression, the abolition of nobles' privileges, peasants' rights to land and so on.[32]

The absence of any explicit reference to the legal status of women in the first fundamental rights documents and especially the uncertain development of women's conditions, from the seventeenth-century Romanian Principalities until the beginning of modern times, are based on several social and political aspects. First of all, the context of a 'rigid feudal structure of Romanian society impeded until very modern times the emergence of a local bourgeoisie and made it simple to exploit the local peasantry'.[33] Secondly, the society was dominated by masculine universalism, so any reform or revolutionary project was considered a conservative project, which belonged mainly to the masculine elites — 'the only ones who had necessary social, economic and intellectual capital in order to envision the reform of the society'.[34] For these reasons, it is difficult to discuss women's rights in the early stages of the Romanian Principalities. The uprising of 1821 and the previously mentioned revolution of 1848 represented a breaking-point: among the revolutionary demands, 'individual liberty and human rights [...] are the main themes of reflection'.[35] In this respect, women's education was perceived as an essential condition for 'the success of the social and political revolution'.[36] This was the main important moment which generated the emancipation of women in Romanian society and has defined their social importance. It is worth mentioning that the leaders of the revolutionary movement of 1848 initiated in their programmes (and especially in the Proclamation from Islaz), which have carried the ideological marks of equality, fraternity and citizenship, an innovative provision regarding equal educational rights for both sexes, which was implemented by the government-in-office.[37] 'It was the first breach in the system of laws and practices that had consecrated the prevalence and privileges of men in social and political life.'[38] Access to equal

32 For a comprehensive perspective on the Romanian Revolution of 1848, see D. Berindei, *1848 în Țările Române* [1848 in the Romanian], Editura Științifică și Enciclopedică, Bucharest 1984 and Constantiniu, *supra* note 8, pp. 209–216.

33 Falangas, *supra* note 9, p. 14.

34 I. Băluță, *La Bourgeoise Respectable. Réflexion sur la construction d'une nouvelle identité féminine dans la seconde moitié du XIXe siècle roumain*, Editura Universității din București, Bucharest 2008, p. 39.

35 *Ibid.*, p. 35.

36 *Ibid.*, p. 55.

37 *Ibid.*, p. 43.

38 I. Moroianu Zlătescu, *A Culture of Peace, Democracy and Tolerance in Romania*, UNESCO, Bucharest 2002, p. 96.

education was the first step towards the emancipation of women and towards women's rights in Romania.

3. EARLIEST DOCUMENTS OF A CONSTITUTIONAL NATURE

Once the ideal of the Union of the Romanian Principalities had been partially achieved in 1859[39] between Wallachia and Moldavia, a wide array of issues related to fundamental rights took on even greater importance, especially in terms of freedom and national unity. This 'Small Union' was perceived in the collective memory as the first *fait accompli*,[40] according to the known Romanian historian Nicolae Iorga, which generated the foundations of the modern Romanian state. As stated by Keith Hitchins, 'the independence of Romania, as the Romanians now called their country, was all but assured.'[41] In these conditions, the individual citizen's fundamental rights were constitutionally guaranteed for the first time in the Constitution of 1866,[42] exclusively designed by the Romanian political elite[43] and promulgated by Prince Carol of Hohenzollern – Sigmaringen.[44] Being inspired by the Belgian Constitution of 1831 and French constitutional ideals (such as the liberties and fundamental rights of citizens and the separation of powers), it was considered 'the first modern Romanian Constitution',[45] which was in essence a liberal document.

---

39 The Union of the Principalities of 1859 was called the 'The Small Union' between Wallachia and Moldovia, under the name of 'Romania', and the Union of 1918 was declared 'The Great Union' of Transylvania with Romania.

40 N. IORGA, *Istoria românilor. Unificatorii* [The Romanians' History.The Unifiers], vol.9, Editura Enciclopedică, Bucharest 2010 [1938], p. 214.

41 K. HITCHINS, *Românii, 1774–1866* [The Romanians, 1774–1866], translated by Delia Rădulescu and George G. Potra, EdituraHumanitas, Bucharest 1998, pp. 386–387.

42 The Constitution of 1866, *Monitorul Oficial al României* [The Official Gazette of Romania], no. 142/ 1–13.06.1866.

43 Before the Constitution of 1866, which has a domestic constitutional origin, even though inspired by the Western constitutional projects at its time, the Romanian Principalities ware ruled on quasi-constitutional organic law, called Organic Regulations, promulgated in 1831 in Wallachia and 1832 in Moldavia, in the context of the Russian occupation (stipulated in the Treaty of Adrianople of 1829). These Organic Regulations were abolished in 1858, when the Convention of Paris entered into force. This document established the Union of the Principalities and their international recognition, in the framework of the Treaty of Paris of 1856, ending the Crimean War. In 1864, the Developing Statute of the Paris Convention of 1858 was proclaimed as the new 'Constitution'. However, there are no stipulations regarding the status of fundamental rights in these documents, besides the only provisions from the Convention of Paris, indicating the equality before the law of the Wallachian and Moldavian population and their right to private property.

44 Carol of Hohenzollern – Sigmaringen (or Carol I of Romania) was the Ruling Prince of Romania (1866–1881) and later on, the King of Romania (1881–1914). After the Russo-Turkish war (1877–1878), also called the Independence War by the Romanians, Carol I declared that Romania was a sovereign state, with full rights in international relations.

45 R.E. IORDACHE, 'Church and State in Romania' in S. FERRARI, W.C. DURHAM and E.A. SEWELL (eds.), *Law and Religion in Post-communist Europe*, Peeters Publishers, Leuven 2003, p. 240.

While fundamental rights had 'been rather promoted as aristocratic rights'[46] until the mid-nineteenth century, the constitutional moment of 1866 can, therefore, be assessed as a turning-point and one can easily observe the similarity between the development of fundamental rights and liberties in the Romanian Constitution and the Western European political and judicial conception of those times. This first constitution is considered 'a genuine progress towards consolidation of the institution of civil rights'.[47]

Citizens' rights and liberties were established in detail in Title II of the constitution, 'On the Romanians' Rights' (articles 5–30). The first stipulated right is referring to freedom of conscience,[48] education,[49] oral and written press,[50] the freedom to organize meetings[51] and freedom of association.[52] Freedom of conscience was regarded as 'an absolute freedom' and 'the freedom of all religions is guaranteed as long as their ceremonies are not in conflict with the public order and morals'.[53] The constitution guaranteed to all land owners the absolute right of possession, claiming that private property, of whatever nature it may be, was 'sacred and inviolable', while expropriation was possible only for reasons regarding public utility.[54] All individuals were granted equality before the law, regardless of class (as there was no class differentiation), and had the obligation to contribute to public taxes and tasks.[55] 'Individual liberty is guaranteed' and nobody could be prosecuted or arrested without a judicial warrant or beyond the conditions provided for in law,[56] while capital punishment was abolished in peacetime.[57] The inviolability and privacy of the home was proclaimed in the constitution, meaning that a citizen's home 'may be entered only in instances provided by the law'.[58]

Besides these explicitly addressed freedoms, there are also other fundamental rights that triggered intense debate and would be developed in further documents of a constitutional nature. For example, the problem of citizenship was a controversial and long-debated issue in 1866 and Article 7 stated that citizenship was granted only to Christian people; thus, bearing in mind that the Romanian

---

46 M. Guțan, 'The Challenges of the Romanian Constitutional Tradition. Between Ideological Transplant and Institutional Metamorphoses' (2013) *Giornale di Storia Costituzionale* [Journal of Constitutional History], no. 25, Semester I, 227.
47 Moroianu Zlătescu, *supra* note 38, p. 133.
48 The Constitution of 1866, *supra* note 42, articles 5 and 21.
49 *Ibid.*, articles 5 and 23.
50 *Ibid,*, articles 5 and 24.
51 *Ibid.*, article 5.
52 *Ibid.*, article 27.
53 *Ibid.*, article 21.
54 *Ibid.*, articles 19 and 20.
55 *Ibid.*, article 10.
56 *Ibid.*, article 13.
57 *Ibid.*, article 18.
58 *Ibid.*, article 14.

Orthodox Church was declared the 'dominant religion of the Romanian state',[59] non-Christians could not become citizens.[60] Even though this article was excluded in 1879, the freedom and protection of all religions was stipulated only in the Constitution of 1923,[61] along with the reiteration that citizenship was no longer conditioned by religious affiliation.

Another sensitive problem was political rights, namely voting rights, which were attributed only to men in 1866 and even in 1923. Women are not even mentioned in the Romanian electoral acts and consequently they are excluded from the sphere of political power; thus, before 1923, they were considered 'the outsiders of democracy'.[62] However, the Constitution of 1923 constituted a major step towards the improvement of the status of women in Romania and proclaimed, on the one hand, that 'women's civil rights shall be established on the basis of full equality between the sexes' and on the other hand, that 'special laws, passed with a 2/3 majority, shall establish the conditions under which women could enjoy the exercise of their political rights'.[63] Women's suffrage was first established in 1929, on the basis of the Electoral Act of 1926, which granted electoral rights only with regard to local elections.[64] Absolute electoral rights for women were proclaimed in the Electoral Act of 1946,[65] which declared genuine direct and universal suffrage.[66]

Even though the emancipation of women and the feminist movement acquired more visibility in the early decades of the twentieth century, in fact, it was only after the Second World War that the gender perspective became relevant in almost any field of legislation. During the communist regime, the emancipation of women and the principle of equality were perceived as a goal, 'at least at declarative level', which in fact, 'was rather the correspondent of some slogans that were trying to give legitimacy to the specific totalitarianism'.[67] One could note, for example, the legislation that advanced the principle of equality of both spouses regarding the ownership of assets acquired during the marriage, in the

59 The Constitution of 1866, *supra* note 42, article 21.

60 *Ibid.*, article 7.

61 The Constitution of 1923, *Monitorul Oficial al României*, no. 282/ 29.03.1923, Tit. II, article 22.

62 BĂLUTĂ, *supra* note 34, p. 105.

63 The Constitution of 1923, *supra* note 61, article 6.

64 The Electoral Act of 1926, *Monitorul Oficial al României*, no. 71/ 27.03.1926, article 1.

65 The Electoral Act of 1946, *Monitorul Oficial al României*, no. 161/ 15.07.1946, article 3.

66 See M.N. TURLIUC and C. TURLIUC, 'The Struggle for Women's Political Rights in Modern Romania. The Crystallisation of Feminist Movement and the Constitutional Debates' in I. SULKUNEN, S-L. NEVALA-NURMI and P. MARKKOLA (eds.) *Suffrage, Gender and Citizenship: International Perspectives on Parliamentary Reforms*, Cambridge Scholars Publishing, Cambridge 2009, pp. 259–278.

67 S.I. MIHAIU, 'Aspects of Gender Inequality in Romania. A Study on Sexual Violence' (2013) 5 *Contemporary Readings in Law and Social Justice*, No. 2, 1006.

Family Code of 1954[68] and also the policies regarding equal working conditions for both sexes and, thus, equal remuneration for equal work. In reality, all these measures coincided with the communist doctrine of planned economy in order to solve all social inequalities. The inequality between the sexes was subsumed to social inequalities. Thus, women's political rights were just formal rights and the equality between the sexes was just a formal equality. Even though signs have been identified of progress towards the improvement of the status of women and their independence, in terms of access to education and legal standing, the communist gender policies were institutionalised in the context of totalitarian ideology and therefore they could not be considered 'representative for our social reality'.[69]

Absolute gender equality was expressly recognized in the Constitution of 1991. Established immediately after the fall of the communist regime in Romania, gender equality was strongly influenced by the challenging and long-lasting transition to democracy and a market economy. In line with Western European realities, the Constitution of 1991 promotes respect for fundamental rights and liberties in conformity with the Universal Declaration of Human Rights and the conventions to which Romania became a party in the last decade of the twentieth century, by implicitly and explicitly proclaiming non-discrimination, dignity and fundamental rights and liberties on grounds of gender, as well as the equality of citizens before the law:

> Article 1
> (3) Romania is a democratic and social state, governed by the rule of law, in which human dignity, the citizens' rights and freedoms, the free development of human personality, justice and political pluralism represent supreme values, in the spirit of the democratic traditions of the Romanian people and the ideals of the Revolution of December 1989, and shall be guaranteed.
> Article 4
> (2) Romania is the common and indivisible land of all citizens, without any discrimination on account of race, nationality, ethnic origin, language, religion, sex, opinion, political adherence, property or social origin.
> Article 16
> (1) Citizens are equal before the law and public authorities, without any privilege or discrimination.[70]

---

68 The Family Code of 1954, *Buletinul Oficial* [The Official Bulletin], No. 9/ 31.01.1954, article 35. This Family Code was meanwhile modified by the new Family Code of 2011, but the ideas covered in article 35 remained the same.

69 MIHAIU, *supra* note 67, p. 1007.

70 The Constitution of 1991, *Monitorul Oficial al României*, no. 233, 21.11.1991, Tit. I, articles 1(3), 4(2) and 16(1).

Achievements in fostering equality between women and men have progressively advanced the development of a gender discourse in Romania. However, it is difficult to speak about gender mainstreaming due to the fact that 'there is no legal provision for gender impact assessment in Romania, nor is it mentioned in any national or ministerial strategy or other plan of action'.[71] Even if the equal treatment legislation has been properly applied, the gender perspective is not yet fully embodied and public policies and specific measures aiming for advancement of women have not been adopted. During the process of European Union accession, Romania has translated the *acquis communautaire* into national legislation and thus has complied with all the European Union's standards and criteria, among which gender equality was regarded as a founding value. Thus, given such European pressures, the rights of women have entered a new era.[72] Adapting to the European conditionality, Romania has expanded the legal framework for equality between the sexes by adopting an anti-discrimination law in 2000, that is the Government Ordinance regarding the prevention and sanctioning of all forms of discrimination[73] and in 2002 the Law 202/2002 on Equal Opportunities and Treatment for Women and Men.[74] The latter refers, on the one hand, to equal opportunities between the sexes, and on the other hand, to different kinds of discrimination, leading to the prohibition of 'direct and indirect gender-based discrimination'[75] in all fields of society, discriminatory workplace behaviour and attitudes, discrimination based on maternity[76] and sexual harassment.[77] Besides these particular stipulations, the term gender equality is not mentioned at all, which fact leads Romanian scholars to consider that 'the clear aim of the law is to combat discrimination, rather than promote any policy favouring gender equality'.[78] A positive aspect is the fact that a recent amendment to this law, in 2013, has been made integrating the 'gender perspective in national policies'.79 It is also argued that the trajectory of improvement of the status of women in the entire territory of Romania has been similar to the post-communist societies in general and not to countries with a

71 I. BĂLUȚĂ, 'Gender Impact Assessment in Romania', 2014, Comments Paper - Romania, *Exchange of good practices on gender equality,* European Commission, p. 3 <http://ec.europa.eu/justice/gender-equality/files/exchange_of_good_practices_at/ro_comments_paper_ at_2014_en.pdf> accessed 18.03.2015.

72 I. IONESCU, 'Romania' in S. BURRI and H. VAN EIJKENGENDER (eds.), *Equality Law in 33 European Countries: How are EU rules transposed into national law in 2013?*, European Commission, 2014, pp. 193–201 <http://ec.europa.eu/justice/gender-equality/files/your_rights/gender_equality_law_33_countries_how_transposed_2013_en.pdf> accessed 15.03.2015.

73 Government Ordinance 137/2000, *Monitorul Oficial al României,* no. 431, 02.09.2000. It was modified in 2002.

74 Law 202/2002, *Monitorul Oficial al României*, no. 301, 08.05.2002. It was amended several times with the aim to create and eventually dissolve The National Agency for Equal Opportunities between Women and Men.

75 *Ibid.*, article 5(1).

76 *Ibid.*, article 9(1).

77 *Ibid.*, articles 10 and 11.

78 BĂLUȚĂ, *supra* note 71, pp. 3–4.

79 Law 202/2002, republished in *Monitorul Oficial al României*, no. 326/ 5.06.2013, Chapter V.

long democratic tradition. Romanian society has 'not yet reached the stage of having a meaningful feminist movement'.80An explanatory reasoning is that gender assessment in Romania may be attributed to fifty years' communist legacy and it is going through a very complex social process of reinforcement of representations and socially constructed sexual and gender roles,81 in order to reach a consensus on gender equality policy and make gender equality a real political objective.

4. CONCLUDING REMARKS

The perspectives discussed in this chapter indicate that conceptions regarding fundamental rights and their protection mechanisms in the Romanian tradition vary in terms of different principles and values which Romanian society has placed on individual rights and liberties throughout history. The genesis of fundamental rights in Romania started back in the Middle Ages and the first written evidence in the early seventeenth century, the Freedom Charter from Bucharest of 1631, represents a valuable source of certain moral standards of human behaviour. These were institutionalised, later on, alongside the modern evolution of Romanian society, in documents of a constitutional nature, i.e. the Constitution of 1866, which enshrines for the first time the rights and freedoms which are internationally respected and protected.

It was only after the Second World War that the doctrine of fundamental rights acquired a final shape, similar to the Western European modern conception. The communist legacy has inevitably left its mark on Romanian society and the transition from an authoritarian regime to a democratic one has generated a slow evolution in the sense of the development of specific legislation and efficient mechanisms regulating the protection of fundamental rights and freedoms. Nevertheless, the integration of Romania into European and international structures and its actions as a member and party of various organizations and conventions have advanced the conceptualization of fundamental rights according to internationally recognised standards. Romania has been making efforts in the last decade to increasingly align its legal and institutional framework with current European and international standards of democracy, freedom, good governance, respect and protection of human rights and gender equality.

---

[80] M. MIROIU and L. POPESCU, 'Post-Totalitarian Pre-Feminism' in H.F. CAREY (ed.), *Romania since 1989 – Politics, Economics, and Society*, Lexington Books, Lanham 2004, p. 298.

[81] I. BĂLUŢĂ, '(Re)Construire la démocratie sans les femmes. Genre et politique dans la Roumanie postcommuniste', *Clio,* no. 41 (forthcoming in 2015).

The turning-point on the issue of egalitarian attitudes in civil society and the gender-sensitive approach in legislation took place in Romania only in the late twentieth century. The major legislative changes in the political and social status of women and their rights occurred after the fall of the communist regime in 1989 and especially in the early 2000s. Thus, the legal framework addressing gender equality was introduced for the first time in the Romanian Constitution of 1991, but progress, although slow, towards raising awareness of gender issues and fighting gender inequalities was made in the context of European Union accession. The dynamics of Europeanization in the first decade of the twenty-first century have accelerated this process and reshaped the discourse of fundamental rights in general, and gender equality in particular. For these reasons, gender equality, as constructed in Western European discourse, has been perceived in Romanian society and culture, at least from the point of view of legislative initiative, as an 'exogenous concept'.[82]

[82] OPRICĂ, *supra* note 19, p. 29.

21. BULGARIA: THE LIBERAL TARNOVO CONSTITUTION

Nikolay NATOV

1. INTRODUCTION

The scientific and practical aim of this narrative is to review and explain the rules of the first fundamental rights document adopted in the area of Bulgaria. These will be compared with the respective norms of the Charter of Fundamental Rights of the European Union (CFREU).[1] The intention is to identify a such historical document that shows that the fundamental rights dimension was not limited to England in the seventeenth and France in the eighteenth century but touched Bulgaria too.

It is appropriate to begin with some words about the history of Bulgaria. The country's historical heritage is related to the culture of Ancient Thrace. After the collapse of the Western Roman Empire, Bulgarian land became an integral part of the Eastern Roman (Byzantine) Empire. During the second half of the seventh century, the northeastern part of today's Bulgaria was gradually inhabited by Proto-Bulgarians or Bulgars. In alliance with the Slavonic tribes they formed the Bulgarian State on the river Danube which was recognised by the Byzantine Empire in 681 AD. The head of the new state was Khan Asparouh and the town of Pliska was the first capital. Under Khan Kroum (803–814 AD) Bulgaria bordered the Empire of Charles the Great (the Holy Roman Empire of the king Charlemagne) to the west and to the east the Eastern Roman (Byzantine) Empire. Christianity was adopted as official religion of the nation in 864 AD, the main result of which was the building of a unified Bulgarian nation.

In the late ninth century the brothers Cyril (Constantine the Philosopher) and Methodius created and began disseminating the Cyrillic alphabet. Bulgaria started developing its culture based on the new alphabet and religion. The Cyrillic alphabet was gradually spread to other Slavonic countries and as it is known today, it is used in Russia, Ukraine, Belarus, Serbia and Macedonia.

---

1 Charter of Fundamental Rights of the European Union [2000] OJ C 364/01.

The reign of Czar Simeon I (893–927 AD) was named the 'Golden Age of Bulgarian Culture', and the territory of the state reached the Black Sea and the Aegean Sea. However, in 1018, after several wars, Bulgaria was conquered by the Byzantine Empire. From the very first years of Byzantine rule, the Bulgarians fought for their freedom and in 1186, an uprising led by two boyars, the brothers Assen and Peter, overthrew the Byzantines and the Bulgarian state was re-established with Turnovo as its capital. The earlier power of Bulgaria was restored during the reign of their youngest brother, Kaloyan (1197–1207). During the reign of Czar Ivan Assen II (1218–1241) the Second Bulgarian Kingdom reached its greatest upsurge: political hegemony was established in Southeastern Europe, the territory of the country spread to the Black Sea, the Aegean Sea and the Adriatic Sea, and the economy and culture flourished quickly.

In 1235, the Head of the Bulgarian Church was given the title of Patriarch. After years of political and economic decay the country was conquered by the Ottoman Empire in 1396 and for the next 482 years Bulgaria was under Ottoman rule. The people fighters, the 'haydouts', were the first to oppose the new rulers. Several uprisings in the North-Western and central parts of the country marked the early attempts towards freedom. In the seventeenth century the first modern history of Bulgaria, 'Istoria Slaviano-Bolgarskaia', was written by the Bulgarian Paisii, a monk in Hilandar monastery in Greece.

The start of the organised revolutionary movement for liberation from Ottoman rule is associated with the name and work of Georgi Rakovski (1821–1867), writer and journalist, founder and ideologist of the national liberation movement. The main figures in this movement were Vassil Levski (1837–1873), strategist and ideologist of the movement and national hero; Lyuben Karavelov (1834–1879), writer and journalist, leader and ideologist of the movement and Hristo Botev (1848–1876), poet and journalist, revolutionary, democrat and national hero.

In 1876 the April Uprising broke out. It was the most significant and organised attempt at liberation from Ottoman rule. The uprising was brutally crushed but it drew the attention of the European countries to the Bulgarian national question. The Russian Empire decided to settle the question by the use of military force. As a result in 1878, after the Russian-Turkish War of Liberation (1877–1878) the modern Bulgarian State emerged again on the Balkan Peninsula.

In 1879, the first Constitution of Bulgaria was adopted and was considered advanced for its time.[2] It is known as the Tarnovo Constitution of 1879. The Tarnovo Constitution (in Bulgarian Търновска конституция – Tarnovska

---

2 H. CHISHOLM (ed.), 'Bulgaria/History', *Encyclopædia Britannica,* 11th ed., Cambridge University Press, Cambridge 1911.

Constititsia) was a modern legal act of bourgeois-liberal character.[3] It was enacted on 16 April 1879 (O.S.) by the Constituent National Assembly held in Veliko Tarnovo as part of the establishment of the Principality of Bulgaria.[4] It remained the fundamental law of Bulgaria until the communist regime came to power in the country at which point the Tamovo Constitution was abolished. On 4 December 1947 it was replaced by the so-called Dimitrov Constitution.

2. THE LIBERAL-DEMOCRATIC IDEAS BEHIND THE TARNOVO CONSTITUTION

2.1. RELIGIOUS FREEDOMS, RELIGIOUS EQUALITY AND DIVERSITY, PROHIBITION OF DISCRIMINATION BASED ON RELIGION OF BELIEF

The Tarnovo Constitution formally established Bulgarian Orthodox Christianity as the official religion of the nation, but at the same time it proclaimed that people of the non-Orthodox Christian faith as well as of other religions were considered equal to those who followed the official faith. In conformity with article 40, freedom of religion is granted not only to Bulgarian citizens but also to foreign nationals who live permanently or temporarily in Bulgaria. The single requirement for all of them is to follow their religious traditions and to perform their rites in accordance with the rules of law. These rights and duties are comparable to Article10 of the Charter of Fundamental Rights of the European Union. Clearly article 40 of the Tarnovo Constitution is based on the idea that everyone has the right to freedom of thought, conscience and religion as well as that this right includes freedom in public or in private, to manifest religion or belief, in worship, teaching, practice and observance, on which idea Article 10 CFREU is also established. The constitutional rule in question is an expression of religious tolerance.

The same rule also evidences that the Bulgarian state respected religious diversity. This corresponds to Article 22 CFREU entitled 'Cultural, religious and linguistic diversity' under which "The Union shall respect ... religious ...

---

3 E. HERTSLET (1891), 'Constitution of the Principality of Bulgaria', The Map of Europe by Treaty; which have taken place since the general peace of 1814. With numerous maps and notes, IV (1875–1891), 1st ed., Her Majesty's Stationery Office, London, pp. 2866–2776, retrieved 25.12.2012.

4 The text of Tarnovo Constitution was officially published in Bulgarian as Конституция на българското княжество (законъ от 16 априлий 1879), Сборник на действующите съдебни закони на княжеството (1878–1906), Официално издание на Министерството на Правосъдието, София 1906 (Constitution of the Bulgarian Principality; Law of 16 April 1879; Collection of the laws in operation in the Principality – 1878–1906, Official issue of the Ministry of Justice, Sofia 1906).

diversity'. The Bulgarian legislature of the time when drafting the first constitution of the new state followed principles that are actual nowadays, amongst them respect for religious diversity.

Equally, article 40 of the Tarnovo Constitution is an expression of another democratic idea namely the prohibition of discrimination based on religion or belief. The drafters clearly proclaimed that people of non-Orthodox Christianity as well as of other religions, i.e. Muslims, Jews etc. were equal to those who followed the official faith in the state. In this sense foreign nationals regardless of their religion were also equal to Bulgarian nationals.

2.2. SUPREMACY OF THE RULE OF LAW

Article 46 of the Tarnovo Constitution provides for the principle of supremacy of the rule of law. Under this provision the Bulgarian Principality is ruled in precise conformity with the law. The latter is drafted and published as regulated by the Constitution.

2.3. EQUALITY OF ALL PEOPLE BEFORE THE LAW

In accordance with article 57 of the Tarnovo Constitution, Bulgaria promulgated equality for all its citizens. The first indent of this article reads: 'All Bulgarian nationals are equal before the law'.

Despite being a monarchy, Bulgarian legislators prohibited the promotion of any kind of aristocratic titles. In this aspect the second indent of article 57 added the idea of equality by declaring that the separation of citizens based on aristocratic titles or classes is forbidden.

The above rule also equalises men and women and excludes gender discrimination. This is in conformity with the principle well established by Article 23 CFREU which proclaims equality between men and women and requires it to be ensured in all areas, including employment, work and pay.

Comparing article 57 of the Tarnovo Constitution with Article 20 CFREU entitled 'Equality before the law' which declares that everyone is equal before the law it can be concluded that the Constitution was close to this modern principle of democracy. The same could be said as regards the idea behind article 57 of the Constitution and that behind Article 21 CFREU entitled 'Non-discrimination'.[5] Obviously the Constitution is not as detailed and does not cover

---

5 The text reads: '1. Any discrimination based on any ground such as sex, race, colour, ethnic or social origin, genetic features, language, religion or belief, political or any other opinion, membership of a national minority, property, birth, disability, age or sexual orientation shall be prohibited. 2. Within the scope of application of the Treaty establishing the European

all the grounds for non-discrimination listed in Article 21 CFREU but what is more important is that the non-discrimination principle is a basic one for a Constitution which dates back to the year 1879.

2.4. PROHIBITION OF SLAVERY AND OF TRADE IN HUMAN BEINGS, RIGHT TO LIBERTY

Article 61, which dealt with slavery and human trafficking, was one of the reasons why the Tarnovo Constitution was considered to be liberal and ahead of its time. It reads: 'Nobody in the Principality of Bulgaria is permitted to buy or sell human beings. Each and every enslaved human being, regardless of his/her gender, faith or ethnicity is declared free at the moment he/she sets foot in our land'.

Comparing the above article of the Constitution with Article 5 CFREU entitled 'Prohibition of slavery and forced labour' one could infer that except the prohibition of forced or compulsory labour the other basic rights namely the prohibition of slavery and of human beings trafficking were protected in Bulgaria in 1879.

By declaring that each and every enslaved human being, regardless of his/her gender, faith or ethnicity shall be free at the moment he/she sets foot on Bulgarian land, the Tarnovo Constitution corresponds to some extent to the right to liberty and security proclaimed in Article 6 CFREU that expressly provides for the right to liberty and security of person for everyone.

2.5. RIGHT TO PROPERTY

The Constitution declared property rights to be sacrosanct (article 67). Forcible deprivation of property was in principle prohibited. An exception was allowed only in a situation of state or municipal (public) need and after prior fair compensation. The procedure for deprivation was regulated by a law enacted specifically to this end (article 68). Article 75 excludes confiscation of property as a penal measure regardless of the nature of the accusation.

When comparing the above rules of the Tarnovo Constitution with Article 17 CFREU entitled 'Right to property' it can be concluded that the Bulgarian drafters also had the vision that everyone has the right to own, use, dispose of and bequeath his or her lawfully acquired possessions as well as that no one may be deprived of his or her possessions, except in the public interest and in the

---

Community and of the Treaty on European Union, and without prejudice to the special provisions of those Treaties, any discrimination on grounds of nationality shall be prohibited.'

cases and under the conditions provided for by law, subject to fair compensation being paid in good time for their loss. The use of property may be regulated by law in so far as is necessary in the general interest.

2.6. FREEDOM OF ASSEMBLY AND FREEDOM OF COMPANIES

All Bulgarian citizens were allowed the freedom to gather in meetings and assemblies to discuss any question without the need for prior permission. The only requirement for the above events was to be peaceful and with no weapons. If the event was held in the open it fell under the laws of the police article 82 of the Tarnovo Constitution).

In conformity with article 83 of the Constitution Bulgarian citizens were free to form their own companies if the company did not contradict state and public order, religion or morality.

In the light of Article 12 CFREU which declares freedom of assembly and of association it is clear that the Bulgarian drafters aimed at establishing freedom of peaceful assembly and freedom of association at all levels. It was not expressly proclaimed by the Constitution but could be inferred that these freedoms covered in particular political, trade union and civic matters and imply the right of everyone to form and to join trade unions for the protection of his or her interests.

2.7. INVIOLABILITY OF PERSON, DWELLING AND CORRESPONDENCE

In articles 73 to 77 personal inviolability, inviolability of dwellings as well as of correspondence were proclaimed. All these rules apply *erga omnes* regardless of nationality, gender or religion.

Article 73 prohibits punishment of any citizen whose case had not been examined by a court or whose sentence had not entered into force under the law. In other words it granted personal inviolability to all. By this the Tarnovo Constitution introduced the spirit of respect and protection of human dignity. It corresponds to Article 1 CFREU which declares human dignity inviolable and requires its respect and protection.

The Constitution completely proscribes torture regardless the nature of the accusation (article 75). This corresponds to the prohibition of torture, inhuman or degrading treatment or punishment proclaimed by Article 4 CFREU.

Under article 74 imprisonment and searches of dwellings are allowed only in conformity with the laws in operation. Article 75 of the Constitution also prohibits any punishment that is not provided by law. These principles formulated in the Tarnovo Constitution developed and are detailed nowadays in Article 49 CFREU which provides for legality and proportionality of criminal offences and penalties.[6]

The Constitution provides for some exceptions as regards the application of articles 73 and 74 but only under strict conditions. Such exceptions can be imposed only for public security reasons and only by the Prince, in the whole territory of the country or in part of it. They must also be approved during the first session of Parliament following the imposition of the exception. The conditions establish strong and narrow limits for the application of the exceptions thus providing a guarantee that they will not turn into ordinary, routine practice.

Article 77 declares that private letters (correspondence) as well as private telegraph communications are inviolable. It also introduces legal responsibility of all officials for breach of privacy of correspondence.

2.8. OTHER CIVIL AND POLITICAL RIGHTS

The Tarnovo Constitution grants political rights to Bulgarian citizens only (article 60). Without dividing men from women this rule equalises the genders in Bulgaria as regards their political rights. The same rule declares that all nationals who live in the Principality of Bulgaria, regardless of citizenship enjoy civic rights in conformity with the law. On one hand this means equalization of everyone before the law and on the other, that the national regime is applicable to all foreign nationals who live in the country. As has been stated Article 20 CFREU provides for equality of people before the law. It states that everyone is equal before the law. The same idea inspired Bulgarian legislators when drafting the above rules of the Constitution. The similarity of the instruments is clear.

Under article 62 of the Constitution police statutes as well as administrative statutes on public services are applicable to everybody, i.e. they are applicable *erga omnes*. This means that if foreign nationals live in Bulgaria they have not only rights but duties too. In this case the rights and duties stem from the

[6] Article 49
Principles of legality and proportionality of criminal offences and penalties
'1. No one shall be held guilty of any criminal offence on account of any act or omission which did not constitute a criminal offence under national law or international law at the time when it was committed. Nor shall a heavier penalty be imposed than that which was applicable at the time the criminal offence was committed. If, subsequent to the commission of a criminal offence, the law provides for a lighter penalty, that penalty shall be applicable.
2. This Article shall not prejudice the trial and punishment of any person for any act or omission which, at the time when it was committed, was criminal according to the general principles recognised by the community of nations.
3. The severity of penalties must not be disproportionate to the criminal offence.'

national administrative legislation (generally speaking the police statutes have administrative character).

Article 78 declares that primary education is compulsory for all Bulgarian citizens. This education is free of charge in conformity with the Constitution which imposes on every Bulgarian national an obligation to graduate from primary education. The text is in line with Article 14 CFREU under which 'Everyone has the right to education ...' (paragraph 1) 'This right includes the possibility to receive free compulsory education' (paragraph 2).

Under article 79 the press in Bulgaria is free and any kind of censorship is prohibited. The prohibition of censorship establishes a real constitutional guarantee of freedom of the press. Article 11 CFREU entitled 'Freedom of expression and information' is a more detailed expression of same principle. It declares that everyone has the right to freedom of expression. This right shall include freedom to hold opinions and to receive and impart information and ideas without interference by public authority and regardless of frontiers (paragraph1). Paragraph 2 adds that the freedom and pluralism of the media shall be respected.

In consequence of article 84 of the Tarnovo Constitution every Bulgarian citizen had the right of petition which could be exercised individually or collectively. The same right is granted to institutions legally established within the country; their representatives can also submit petitions. The similarity of this rule to Article 44 CFREU is clear. The latter reads: 'Any citizen of the Union and any natural or legal person residing or having its registered office in a Member State have the right to petition the European Parliament'.

The Tarnovo Constitution was far from ensuring equal opportunities for participation of women in all spheres of public life. Nevertheless it encompassed rules a result of which was the equalization of men and women as well as the prohibition of discrimination against women. Firstly here article 86, which proclaimed equal voting rights for men and women, should be mentioned. Every Bulgarian citizen above the age of 21 had the right to vote. No gender discrimination for suffrage was allowed.[7]

The Constitution also provided for the right of every Bulgarian citizen to be elected to Parliament without gender discrimination. The requirements for those who wished to stand as candidates for Parliament were that they must be over the age of 30 and literate. The rule reveals some similarities with Articles 39 and 40

---

[7] In fact due to various reasons mainly old fashioned ones the equal voting rights of men and women have not been applied for decades after the entering into operation of the Constitution and women have not been encouraged to vote.

of the CFREU.[8] The most important fact here is that in 1879 men and women were equalised for suffrage and no gender discrimination in this field was allowed by the Tarnovo Constitution.

3. CONCLUDING REMARKS

The Referendum of 1946 led to the transition from a constitutional monarchy to a people's republic in Bulgaria. Till the changes in 1989 the official name of the country was The People's Republic of Bulgaria. From a strictly normative point of view this referendum was illegal since the Tarnovo Constitution did not provide for a change in the type of government. On the other hand Bulgaria was under Soviet military occupation at the time of the referendum. The Tarnovo Constitution was permanently abolished in 1947 when another one, bearing the name of the communist party leader Georgi Dimitrov, came into effect. The Dimitrov Constitution was less liberal and democratic than the Tarnovo Constitution, as it allowed censorship and abolished political pluralism and the multiparty system by establishing of a one-party regime while depriving citizens of certain fundamental rights including the right to private property.

In the light of the above facts regarding the communist constitution which forcibly replaced the Tarnovo Constitution it should be concluded that the Tarnovo Constitution was a legal act that was ahead of its time in being liberal-democratic and proclaiming some fundamental rights that are now part of the modern legal system of the European Union. Today the democratic ideas behind the Constitution are standards of society not only in Bulgaria and the rest of the EU but in many other countries. This underlines the importance of the instrument in question and its role as a legal basis of the first fundamental rights in Bulgaria at the end of nineteenth century.

---

[8] Article 39
Right to vote and to stand as a candidate at elections to the European Parliament
1. Every citizen of the Union has the right to vote and to stand as a candidate at elections to the European Parliament in the Member State in which he or she resides, under the same conditions as nationals of that State.
2. Members of the European Parliament shall be elected by direct universal suffrage in a free and secret ballot.
Article 40
Right to vote and to stand as a candidate at municipal elections
Every citizen of the Union has the right to vote and to stand as a candidate at municipal elections in the Member State in which he or she resides under the same conditions as nationals of that State.

22. FINLAND: RIGHTS TO FACILITATE PARTICIPATION

Markku SUKSI

1. INTRODUCTION

Participation appears to be the main objective in the rights discourse of Finnish constitutional history. Participatory rights in the broad sense were present as early as 1766, in the Freedom of the Press (Constitution) Ordinance, issued at a point of time when territories currently forming Finland were an integral part of the Kingdom of Sweden. Participation through elections, together with complementary rights necessary for meaningful participation (freedoms of speech and the press, of association, and of assembly), were in focus in 1906 when electoral reform introduced a unicameral parliament based on proportional elections in what was then an autonomous part of the Russian Empire.

At these two junctures, Finland did not exist as an independent state: independence occurred only in 1917. Until separation from the Kingdom of Sweden in 1808–1809, areas that today make up Finland were included in the regular Swedish legal order. This was significant from the point of view of constitutionally established fundamental rights, because during the eighteenth century the Swedish legal order started to make a distinction between constitutional laws or fundamental laws on the one hand, and ordinary laws on the other. Upon the separation from the Kingdom of Sweden in 1808–1809 this understanding was carried over to the separate Finnish jurisdiction: in a pledge of the Czar of Russia on 27–29 March 1809 (the legal effects of which are debatable), it was said that Finland would be ruled under the law that had previously been in force in Finland. In the area of constitutional law, this meant that the 1772 Form of Government (Constitution) Act of Sweden and the 1789 Act of Union and Guarantee of Sweden were considered to be in force.[1] Consequently, while being an autocratic ruler in the rest of the Russian Empire, in Finland the Czar was, at least in the minds of Finnish lawyers of the time, a constitutional monarch under the title of the Grand Duke of Finland.

---

1 In fact, an early formulation of a general rule of law can be discerned in section 2 of the 1772 Form of Government (Constitution) Act.

Therefore, two sets of first documents of a fundamental rights nature are identified here. On the one hand, reference will be made to the 1766 rules on freedom of the press and access to government-held documents, because these rules appear to have their political and intellectual root in what is today Finland, and, on the other hand, the presentation will also encompass the 1906 electoral rights and accompanying political rights. The first set of rights celebrates its 250th anniversary in 2016, while the second set of rights celebrated its 100th anniversary in 2006. The two sets are related to each other through the distinction between two norm-hierarchical levels of the law, constitutional law and ordinary law, first conceived in the Kingdom of Sweden during the eighteenth century and applied in Finland during the nineteenth and the twentieth century.

2. FREEDOM OF THE PRESS AND ACCESS TO DOCUMENTS

2.1. WRITTEN RULES ON FREEDOM OF THE PRESS AND ACCESS TO DOCUMENTS

The first legal rules of a constitutional nature concerning freedom of the press and access to public documents were enacted in 1766 by the Estates of the Realm of the Kingdom of Sweden in a document the overall title of which is His Majesty's Gracious Ordinance Relating to Freedom of Writing and of the Press. The rules concerning freedom of press and access to information and documents were promulgated on 2 December 1766 in a document enacted by the Diet of Sweden identified as a fundamental law, but nonetheless entitled 'Ordinance' by the King of Sweden, Adolphus Frederick. He was at the time a figurehead king over a state encompassing, *inter alia*, areas that today are identified as the states of Finland and Sweden. The main focus of the ordinance was on freedom of the press and the right to express in writing anything one wished, but already at that time the organic relationship to access to public documents and information was a key component of the rules: in order to have something to write about and to publish in print matters concerning state affairs, it was necessary to have recourse to the sources of information held by the courts, public authorities and the Diet.

In the Preamble to the 1766 Ordinance, the reasons for passing the Ordinance were based on arguments supporting freedom of the press. However, the Ordinance referred to freedom of the press as one of the best means of improving morality and promoting obedience to the laws 'when abuses and illegalities are revealed to the public through the press'.[2] This implies that the content that was

---

[2] Quotes from His Majesty's Gracious Ordinance Relating to Freedom of Writing and of the Press (1766) originate from a translation by Peter Hogg published in J. MUSTONEN (ed.), *The World's*

intended to be published on the basis of freedom of the press contained materials or was based on materials retrieved from the courts and public authorities, possibly containing information about abuses and illegalities. This idea is reinforced in section 11 of the Ordinance, where freedom of the press and probably also access to public documents is advanced so 'that all Our loyal subjects may be persuaded of the honourable conduct of their delegates during the sessions of Parliament'. Hence there is a connection to the accountability of government in the Ordinance.

The 1766 Ordinance was enacted by three of the Estates in the Diet during the fall of 1766 and promulgated by the King of Sweden on 2 December 1766. The decision of the Diet was, of course, a remarkable political decision at that time. The main person credited with advancing the idea of freedom of the press, including access to public documents, and drafting the Ordinance during the Diet of 1765–1766 was Mr. Anders Chydenius, a priest and a (junior) member of the Clergy in the Diet, appointed from the coastal region of Ostrobothnia, today a part of Finland.[3] He was originally a curate in the parish of Nedervetil, or in Finnish Alaveteli, and later became the pastor of Gamlakarleby or in Finnish Kokkola. Influenced by the ideals of the Enlightenment, Chydenius was active in numerous fields, such as freedom of trade and the free market economy, as well as the working conditions of labourers, and the promotion of agriculture, and he assisted — during the Diet of 1789–1790 — the King in enhancing freedom of religion. During those times, various thinkers in addition to Chydenius were propagating progressive ideas, the most theoretically influential of whom was Mr. Peter Forsskål from Helsingfors or in Finnish Helsinki, which at that point was a tiny provincial town. This thinking can be understood as a Nordic variant of or parallel to the ideas of the Enlightenment elsewhere in Europe. Because these thoughts were expressed in Swedish, the thinking was hardly known, and much less recognised, in other parts of Europe.

It would be incorrect to attribute the ideas about free press and access to public documents and freedom of the press to Chydenius. He was the political *primus motor* and leading member during the Diet of 1765–1766 in relation to these issues; however, the ideas had existed prior to his engagement in political issues, presented, for instance, by Forsskål in his writings.[4] In his early political

First Freedom of Information Act: Anders Chydenius' Legacy Today. Anders Chydenius Foundation's Publications 2, Anders Chydenius Foundation, Kokkola 2006, available at: <http://www.chydenius.net/pdf/worlds_first_foia.pdf> accessed 27.02.2014, pp. 8–17.

3 For a thorough historical analysis of Chydenius as a democratically minded politician during the Enlightenment, see P. Virrankoski, *Anders Chydenius: Demokratisk politiker i upplysningens tid*, Timbro, Stockholm 1995.

4 Forsskål published in 1759 an essay entitled *Tankar om borgerliga friheten* (Thoughts on Civil Liberty; see <http://www.peterforsskal.com/thetext.html#top> accessed 03.03.2015), in which he advocated, *inter alia*, freedom of speech and freedom of the press. While para. 21 of the piece is mainly about the right to speak and publish freely on societal issues, there is also a reference to the possibility of society's affairs becoming known to everyone and indications of substantive

reflections, Chydenius had been opposed to the sovereignty of the Diet subject to a prohibition of the imperative mandate, established in 1747.[5] Chydenius wished to see the introduction of the imperative mandate so that the electors of the members of the various Estates could influence by binding instructions their representatives at the Diet. The reason for introducing an imperative mandate would have been to enable the electors of the members of the Diet to receive information about the discussions in the Diet as well as about the grounds for its decisions, which were mostly considered secret.[6] Access to documents was therefore primarily directed towards parliamentary documents, the need for which was revealed when the political party of the Hats felt compelled to disclose certain disturbing facts to the Diet concerning state finances.

When Chydenius understood that access to parliamentary documents could produce accountability similar to the imperative mandate of a delegate, he switched his political attention to access to public documents and dropped his claim of the imperative mandate. Increasing the political accountability of members of the Diet was probably a cornerstone of Chydenius' activities during the Diet. The combination of freedom of the press and the abolition of censorship with access to public documents was included in a report of the special Committee on the Freedom of the Press, of which Chydenius was a member and later also the unofficial secretary, in which capacity he directed the Committee's activities. The Committee on the Freedom of the Press included documents of the Diet amongst those public documents to which everyone should have access.[7] Although the debates in the various committees of the Diet regarding general access to public documents were lively, the assemblies of three Estates (Clergy, Burghers and land-owning Peasants[8]) accepted the report of the Committee without objections, while the Nobility disagreed in part and requested some changes.[9]

The role of Chydenius in passing the text of the Ordinance has been characterised by one source as follows: 'It would seem that no single ingredient

---

areas where access to public information and documents could be useful. On Forsskål, see J. Manninen, 'Anders Chydenius and the Origins of World's First Freedom of Information Act' in J. Mustonen (ed.), *The World's First Freedom of Information Act: Anders Chydenius' Legacy Today*. Anders Chydenius Foundation's Publications 2, Anders Chydenius Foundation, Kokkola 2006, available at: <http://www.chydenius.net/pdf/worlds_first_foia.pdf> accessed 27.02.2014, pp. 29–31.

5 On the issue of whether the elected members of the Diet should take instructions from their principals, see M. Roberts, *The Age of Liberty: Sweden 1719–1772*, Cambridge University Press, Cambridge 1986, pp. 68 f., 146.

6 See Virrankoski, *supra* note 3, p. 182. See also Manninen, *supra* note 4, pp. 32, 34, 38, 45 f.

7 Virrankoski, *supra* note 3, p. 184.

8 Land-owning peasants were individuals who owned their property, such as the farm-land they cultivated, in contrast to tenants of various kinds. Because of formal ownership, they were taxed, and their presence in the Diet was required, *inter alia*, in order to participate in taxation decisions.

9 Virrankoski, *supra* note 3, p. 193.

of the [Ordinance –MS] was especially invented by Chydenius, but his mode and zeal in combining the different ingredients produced something unprecedented.'[10] Chydenius' great historical achievement was to serve as the pioneer of the political thinking leading to the adoption of the Ordinance.

2.2. PRINCIPLES OF A CONSTITUTIONAL NATURE

As such, the term 'Ordinance' indicates rules that exist at the level of a decree, that is, below the level of an act. However, the Ordinance was enacted during the so-called Era of Liberty under the sovereignty of the Diet, which was undisputable, and therefore, the Ordinance is, in fact, an Act of the Diet. In addition, section 14 of the Ordinance defines itself as an irrevocable fundamental law. On the basis of section 14, it is clear that the material object of the regulation was freedom of writing and of the press, that is, a general right of citizens. Such a general right of citizens could only be conceived at the level of the constitution or at the level of an ordinary act of parliament, the reference to 'irrevocable fundamental law' implying the former: the material contents of the Ordinance established a constitutional right for the citizens.

In order to understand the meaning of 'irrevocable fundamental law', it is necessary to know that ordinary acts passed by the Estates required the majority of three of the four estates in the Diet (Nobility, Clergy, Burghers and land-owning Peasants). This principle was established on the basis of the 1720 Instrument of Government Act and the 1723 Rules of Procedure of the Diet Act. Both of these Acts were considered fundamental laws, and the 1766 Ordinance can be understood as a complementary fundamental law in relation to them.[11] Because neither freedom of the press nor access to public documents was part of these two earlier constitutional acts and because no absolutely clear distinction between a formal constitutional act and an ordinary act existed concerning the procedure of adopting constitutional acts, the 1766 Ordinance was not antithetical to the material constitution (in particular, the privileges of any of the Estates) and could therefore be adopted by three Estates as a fundamental law in spite of the fact that the Nobility was opposed to some parts of it.[12] Thus, the Ordinance could be understood as a fundamental law of the same order as the constitutional acts of 1720 and 1723. In fact, the Nobility had also supported

---

10 MANNINEN, *supra* note 4, p. 52. See also VIRRANKOSKI, *supra* note 3, pp. 194–195.

11 The preamble to the 1720 Instrument of Government Act identifies the Act as a fundamental law enacted by the unanimous decision of the four Estates. The 1723 Rules of Procedure Act was also considered to be a constitutional act. The distinction between ordinary law and fundamental law was at least partly based on the notion of privileges of the Estates, the amendment of which on the basis of section XIX of the 1723 Rules of Procedure Act required the unanimous decision of the four Estates, while other legislation was decided by the majority of three out of four Estates. On the understanding of the fundamental laws of 1720 and 1723 as constitutional documents of a superior nature in relation to previous documents, see ROBERTS, *supra* note 5, p. 61 f.

12 VIRRANKOSKI, *supra* note 3, p. 193.

freedom of the press and the Ordinance, although it preferred a slightly altered version of it, so at the end of the day, it was possible for the King to promulgate the Ordinance as a fundamental law. Therefore, and in spite of opposition from the Nobility to some provisions of the Ordinance, it was defined from this point on as a fundamental law comparable to the fundamental laws of 1720 and 1723.[13] The Ordinance was an effective legal norm with direct applicability in concrete situations: the various constitutional and public bodies (governmental authorities and courts) started to act accordingly, with a great variety of printed matter being published and with the right of access to public documents being enforced.[14] It is therefore clearly apposite to talk about constitutional and concrete legal significance for the Ordinance.

However, the nature of the Ordinance as a fundamental law could not withstand the *coup d'état* performed by the king, together with the military in 1772. At that point, young king Gustav III had grown weary of his role as a figurehead and longed for a restoration of royal powers, staging a swift campaign that ended with a wholesale revocation of all those fundamental laws that had been enacted after 1680, including the Ordinance of 1766. Nevertheless, the Ordinance was re-introduced as soon as 1774, although not as a fundamental law, but as a royal decree, which made it possible for the government to interfere with the freedom by means of its own decisions. Another ordinance on freedom of the press was issued in 1792 after the death of Gustav III, which again re-introduced this general freedom (and, in particular, abolished censorship). However, no specific mention was made of access to public documents. Therefore, it can be assumed that access to public documents was in that situation an integral part of the general freedom of the press. This Ordinance, too, was issued only as a royal decree. Thus, access to public documents, first established in the Ordinance of 1766 as a fundamental law, suffered a normative downgrading in 1772 and in the subsequent Ordinances of 1774 and 1792. From 1766 until 1809, the survival of freedom of press and the right to access to public documents was uncertain.

This was the legal situation that existed during the period when the eastern part of the Kingdom, that is, more or less the area that is currently Finland, was separated from Sweden and made part of the Russian Empire as an autonomous Grand Duchy within the Russian Empire. According to the Czar of Russia, Alexander I, the Grand Duchy of Finland would be governed under Swedish laws, which in Finland was interpreted as covering the constitutional acts of 1772 and 1789 as well as the general code of laws of 1734 and other acts. Therefore, the 1792 Freedom of the Press Ordinance, which had been issued as a decree, was not amongst those Swedish Acts that would have been carried over

---

[13] See the decision of the Diet of 15 October 1766, para. 6, in which the process of enacting constitutional acts is outlined. See also ROBERTS, *supra* note 5, pp. 68, 168–170.

[14] For some examples of enforcement, see J. HIRSCHFELDT, '1766 års tryckfrihetsförordning och offentlighetsprincipens utveckling' (1998) *Förvaltningsrättslig tidskrift* 1, 7.

to or applied in the Grand Duchy of Finland. In fact, censorship of the press and of mail was practiced in Finland after 1809, in part because Russia wanted to prevent the spread of Swedish revanchism in Finland. Therefore, it is likely that freedom of the press and access to public documents was not part of the Finnish legal order after 1809.

In the 1865 Freedom of the Press Ordinance of Finland, free press and access to public documents was re-introduced and specified in a manner more or less in line with provisions that had existed in Sweden since 1809, and while an Ordinance of 1867 again limited the freedom of the press in Finland, it maintained access to public documents materially almost as provided for in the 1865 Ordinance. The 1891 amendments to the Freedom of the Press Ordinance considerably limited the freedom of the press and access to public documents. Therefore, for the greater part of the history of the autonomous Grand Duchy of Finland, freedom of the press and access to public documents were in the hands of the executive power, much in the same way as in Sweden between 1772 and 1809. Hence there was not much legal continuity in this field: the situation in Finland during the nineteenth century appears to have differed dramatically from that of Sweden.

3. INTRODUCTION OF MODERN UNICAMERALISM

3.1. CONSTITUTIONAL AND POLITICAL BACKGROUND

Between 1809 and 1917, Finland was an autonomous part of the Russian Empire and therefore had a legal order of its own. In 1869, a new Diet (Constitution) Act was passed, but at that time, this body, which had a share in the exercise of legislative powers, was still based on the four Estates. Towards the end of the nineteenth century, Russian authorities became more negative towards the autonomy of Finland and grew also more repressive.[15] At the same time, there were proposals developed in Finland for the enactment of a new Form of Government (Constitution) Act. Additionally, political parties started to emerge, such as the Finnish Party in 1863, the Swedish Party in 1870, the Liberal Party in 1880, the Young Finns in 1894, and the Social Democratic Party in 1899. The Russian political situation became very difficult in 1905 as a consequence of the defeat of Russia by the Japanese, which marked the first time a non-European country prevailed in war over a European power. Internal disturbances turned into a general strike both in Russia and in Finland, and the widespread unrest forced the Czar of Russia to undertake constitutional reforms.[16] Originally, the main grievance in Finland had been the unconstitutionality of unilateral

---

15 On the constitutional conflict between Finland and Russia in 1899–1905, see A. JYRÄNKI, *Lakien laki*, Lakimiesliiton kustannus, Helsinki 1989, pp. 449–456.

16 JYRÄNKI, *supra* note 15, pp. 456–458.

measures by the Russian authorities within the jurisdiction of Finland, but the initial aim of restoring constitutional order was overtaken by the greater aim of reforming the constitution altogether, in particular electoral rights.[17]

At this juncture, Russia instituted its first written constitution, the so-called 1906 Constitution of the Duma Monarchy. It recognised the supreme autocratic power of the Czar, but that power was no longer unlimited in quite the same way it had been during past centuries. The 1906 Russian Constitution contained in its Chapter II a list of rights and obligations of the Russian subjects, in most cases formulated so that their exercise required specifications in law. However, these rights did not apply in the territory of Finland, because according to section 2 of the 1906 Russian Constitution, '[t]he Grand Duchy of Finland, while comprising an inseparable part of the Russian state, is governed in its internal affairs by special decrees based on special legislation'.[18] Therefore, the process of constitutional reform in Finland during that turbulent time was a 'domestic' one and resulted in the adoption of two constitutional acts, the 1906 Parliament (Constitution) Act, which replaced the 1869 Diet (Constitution) Act, and the 1906 Freedom of the Press, Assembly and Association (Constitution) Act, which was a new piece of law at the level of constitutional law. What remained in force was the 1772 Form of Government (Constitution) Act and the 1789 Act of Union and Guarantee. The constitution of the autonomous Grand Duchy of Finland was thus multi-documentary and to a great extent of Swedish provenance. What was of particular importance in the context was the continued distinction between constitutional acts and ordinary legislation, first introduced in the eighteenth century Kingdom of Sweden.

3.2. PARLIAMENTARY REFORM: HIS IMPERIAL MAJESTY'S PROPOSAL

From the beginning of parliamentary affairs in the Kingdom of Sweden, the entire population, including those living in the Eastern part of the Kingdom, in what is today Finland, had participated in the Diet through the Estates, which were composed of the Nobility, the Clergy, the Burghers, and the land-owning Peasants. The right to vote and the right to stand as candidate were not open to everyone, but only to the members of the relevant Estate. This meant that only around 20–25% of the entire population could feel represented in the Diet, which, depending on the prevailing relationship to the King and the Council of the State, was more or less involved in the adoption of general legislation, in granting new taxes for various purposes of the state, and in deciding on matters of war and peace. This system of government continued in principle after 1809

17 *Ibid.*, p. 458.

18 *Ibid.*, p. 469; M. Szeftel, *The Russian Constitution of April 23, 1906: Political Institutions of the Duma Monarchy*, Les éditions de la librairie encyclopédique, Bruxelles 1976, p. 84.

in the autonomous Finland, but the practice of convening Diets was discontinued until 1864, when a more regular schedule of meetings was re-introduced.

In the political pressure created in 1905, one clear aim of those demanding constitutional reform was to re-make the institution of representation. The Government of Russia including the Czar, but also the Government of Finland with the Grand Duke (who was the Czar of Russia), had no option but to comply with these demands. As a consequence, His Imperial Majesty issued a manifesto on 4 November 1905 according to which a modernization of the organization of the Finnish people's representative body would be implemented along the lines of the principles of universal and equal suffrage.

These election elements were incorporated in His Imperial Majesty's Gracious Proposal to the Estates of Finland concerning a new Parliament (Constitution) Act and an Election Act for the Grand Duchy of Finland (Proposal No. 11/1906), given to the Extraordinary Diet of 1905–1906.[19] The relatively short proposal that originated in the Government of Finland began by concluding that representation through a Diet based on the Estates was no longer in harmony with the social conditions which had evolved during the past decades of economic and social development. Therefore, and for the implementation of universal and equal suffrage, it was felt necessary to create an entirely new form of representation for the country. The proposal also concluded, together with a brief consideration of a bicameral system, that a unicameral system of representation would be more trusted by the people. In addition, it was stated in the proposal that a proportional system of representation would, without doubt, be of great importance in such a unicameral setting, because the various political opinions would be represented in proportion to their numerical strength.[20]

The Grand Duke also proposed that the political right to elect would be recognised for women. The point was made that in a country with relatively few inhabitants, it is important that all those members of society who are capable of doing so are offered the opportunity to contribute to the development of the society through creating a representative body for the people. In this respect, according to the proposal, experiences in Finland of women's participation in general activities had given rise to no doubts that would speak against including women in those with the right to vote.

---

[19] Hans Kejserliga Majestäts Nådiga proposition till Finlands Ständer angående ny landtdagsordning samt vallag för Storfurstendömet Finland, No. 11. *Handlingar tillkomna vid urtima landtdagen i Helsingfors åren 1905–1906*, andra delen, Helsingfors 1906.

[20] However, some guarantees for political minorities were built in the proposal, such as the possibility to leave legislative proposals in abeyance and preparation of proposals in a Grand Committee. The proposal expressed some doubts about the rationality of the voters when making the point that the voting age and the age requirement for candidacy should be 24 years, which was higher than the general age of legal maturity at that time, which was 21.

The proposal concerning a Parliament (Constitution) Act was accompanied by a proposal concerning an Election Act. The reason for this was that most provisions about elections were too detailed to be incorporated in the Parliament (Constitution) Act and should preferably not be given the attributes of a constitutional law. The main forum for material deliberations in the Diet was the Constitutional Law Committee, which gave a lengthy opinion (Opinion No. 1/1906) concerning the proposal.[21]

3.3. THE CONTENTS OF THE REFORM

The Diet passed for its part the Parliament (Constitution) Act by unanimity of the four Estates. In its reply to the proposal of His Imperial Majesty, the Diet, including the Nobility, explained that with his approval, the new system of representation with a unicameral parliament based on the principles of universal and equal suffrage would cause a sudden disruption in historical continuity. However, the Estates felt that such a consequence was completely justified under the circumstances that prevailed at the material time.

The Parliament (Constitution) Act (No. 26/1906) entered into force on 1 October 1906. In the Preamble to this constitutional act, the Emperor of Russia and Grand Duke of Finland declared that it had become necessary to develop the organization of the Finnish people's representation through a new constitution, which in itself indicated that this act should be regarded as a constitutional act at a higher normative level than ordinary acts. This is made explicit in section 80(1) of the Parliament (Constitution) Act, which repeals the 1869 Diet (Constitution) Act and the manifestos of 1879, 1886, and 1897, which were repressive in nature. Of great importance in this respect is the reference in the section according to which the 1906 Parliament (Constitution) Act shall in all its parts apply as an unamendable constitutional act, until amended or repealed by joint decisions of the Regent of Finland and the Parliament. Here, the distinction between constitutional acts and ordinary acts, dating back to the so-called Swedish Era, manifests itself in a manner that reproduces the idea of continuity. The principal provisions concerning the main election elements were included in sections 4, 5 and 6 of the Parliament (Constitution) Act of 1906.

Section 5(1) of the Parliament (Constitution) Act provided the following: 'The right to participate in elections of the members of parliament is held by each citizen of Finland, both man and woman, who has become 24 years old before the year of elections.' Universal suffrage amongst men was never an issue, but it is remarkable that there was also very little discussion about women's right to vote in 1906, at least in the official documentation. The Constitutional Law

[21] Grundlagsutskottets betänkande No. 1 i anledning av Hans Kejserliga Majestäts nådiga proposition till Finlands Ständer angående ny landtdagsordning samt vallag för Storfurstendömet Finland.

Committee reiterated the contents of the proposal in this respect and concluded that this issue had not been the subject of any remarks in the Committee. The Committee pointed out that the reform finds strong support in the conditions prevailing in Finland and that in their youth, women in Finland receive the same upbringing and experience as men. Thus this part of the matter was very straightforward. However, there is, in the provision, a reference to both sexes, which would seem to indicate that it was felt necessary to underline *expressis verbis* that also women would have the right to vote.[22]

What is perhaps more remarkable is that there seems to have been no discussion on whether the political rights of women should be limited to the right to vote, without extending them to the right to stand as a candidate: universal suffrage implied both the right to vote and the right to stand as a candidate. Section 6 stated this as follows: 'Eligible as a member of parliament is, without prejudice to the place of residence, any person who has the right to vote.' Finland is often referred to as the first country in the world where women gained both the right to vote and the right to stand as a candidate. However, this happened in 1906, when Finland was not yet an independent country. Independence came more than a decade later, in 1917, while in 1906, the correct reference group would be other sub-state entities, such as other territorial autonomies or states in federations. This would allow the comparison with New Zealand, where independence from Great Britain started to evolve only during the decades after World War I but where women got the right to vote in 1893 and the right to stand as a candidate in 1919. A similar development occurred in a part of the self-governing territory of Australia. In the United States of America, states in the Western part of the federation were frontrunners in this matter, giving women political rights about at the same time as in Finland, although at the federal level, these rights were established only in 1920. The conclusion might be warranted that political systems peripheral to the centre could allow themselves to be more progressive concerning political rights than the main political forum of the state. Anyway, by the time of Finnish independence in 1917, universal suffrage for both women and men was still quite rare in Europe. Certainly in 1906, there were no countries in Europe where this would have been the case.[23]

Section 5(2) excluded some categories of persons from the right to vote, *inter alia*, in paragraph 5 'the one who is receiving support from the services for the poor, if the support is not only temporary'. The Committee did not react to this in its Opinion, but two members of the Committee felt that a provision that excludes the poorest from the act of voting constitutes a violation of human rights and of human dignity. Therefore, they filed a dissenting opinion according

[22] However, at the level of local government, women got the right to vote only in 1917, after independence.

[23] Undoubtedly, the introduction of the right to vote for women in Finland was also linked to the suffragette ideas promoted around Europe at that time.

to which the problematic provision should be deleted, but this did not find support amongst other members of the Committee. However, amongst those who had the right to vote, the vote was, according to section 4(3) of the Parliament (Constitution) Act, equal: 'In the elections, all those who have the right to vote have an equal vote.'[24]

Under section 4, the elections would be proportional: 'The members of parliament are elected by means of direct and proportional elections; and for such elections, the country shall be divided into at least twelve and at the most eighteen electoral districts.' Although it seems on the basis of the *travaux preparatoires* that the choice of proportional elections was self-evident, some comparisons of the benefits of the proportional system of elections over the majoritarian system were carried out by the Constitutional Law Committee. The calculations considering the two alternatives convinced the Committee that the former was superior to the latter. In this context, the Committee made reference to elections in the Grand Duchy of Baden, where a party that had collected close to one third of the votes did not get any representatives in the parliament, while a numerically weaker party gained more than half of all seats (evidently, this was a majoritarian electoral system). It also made reference to some election results from Belgium and the United Kingdom indicating a similar bias in the majoritarian system. While recognising the fact that there was some suspicion in the country against proportional elections, the Committee nonetheless supported the principle of proportional elections, because it would result in a parliament which would be varied and representative as to its composition. Therefore, in commenting on the proposal concerning the Election Act and giving examples concerning the calculation of the election result, the Committee put forward the d'Hondt method for the distribution of seats in the electoral districts.

On the first page of the Parliament (Constitution) Act, a note has been appended according to which the Act should be read out from the pulpit. This means that the text, consisting of altogether 80 sections, was read out for the people in the churches by the priests. In this manner, new legislation, in this case parliamentary reform, was brought to the attention of everyone.

In the first parliamentary elections on 16–17 March 1907, where turnout was 70,7%, altogether six political parties gained mandates in the Parliament, the largest one being the Social Democratic Party with 80 seats out of 200 (40%). Already in these first elections, 62 women out of a total of 762 candidates stood as candidates, and 19 women were elected as MPs in 1907: altogether 8% female candidates resulted, without quotas, in a share of 9.5% female MPs. In this way,

---

24 In fact, in the beginning of the history of parliamentary elections in Finland, each voter had three votes, resulting in a more complicated electoral system than currently practiced. On this issue and the history of election legislation, see L. Tarasti and H. Taponen, *Suomen vaalilainsäädäntö*, Edita, Helsinki 1996, pp. 32–39.

an ancient form of representation, the Diet consisting of four Estates, was replaced by a representative organ that was amongst the most progressive of the time, a unicameral parliament elected through proportional election.

However, the reform of the representative system was limited to the law-making body only, while the other parts of the constitutional system continued to operate under the 1772 Form of Government (Constitution) Act, which gave the autocratic monarch wide powers. For instance, the principle of parliamentary accountability was not practiced between the Senate (that is, the Government) and the Parliament until after independence in 1917, which meant that the Senate (that is, the Government of Finland), appointed by the autocratic monarch, did not reflect the composition of the Parliament. The monarch also had the right to dissolve Parliament, which happened as early as 6 April 1908, although the normal term of mandate according to section 3 of the Parliament (Constitution) Act would be three years. New elections were, due to dissolutions, held in 1908, 1909, 1910, 1911, 1913, 1916, and 1917.[25] This reflects a dissolution praxis that effectively hampered the functioning of Parliament. The contribution of the Parliament of Finland to legislation was therefore marginal before independence in 1917, with only a few pieces of law or none at all enacted on an annual basis. Norms of a general application were issued on a regular basis, but they were either Decrees of the Grand Duke or Decisions of the Senate (that is, the Government) of Finland. This is, in part, explained by the exceptional circumstances caused by World War I which started in 1914. The legislative impact of a directly elected parliament was, thus, very limited under the circumstances that prevailed towards the end of the Era of Autonomy.[26] This did not, however, prevent the Parliament from becoming a body where heated political discussions took place.

---

25 For election results by party in these elections, including turnout figures, see <http://yle.fi/vintti/yle.fi/satavuottaeduskuntavaaleja/ vaalitilastot.htm#v1909> accessed 07.03.2015.

26 In 1910, the applicability of some all-Russian legislation in the jurisdiction of Finland was enacted by the Russian State Council and State Duma and ratified by the Czar, understood as measures that on the part of Finland were understood as very unconstitutional and repressive designed to undermine the autonomy of Finland. See Af Riksrådet och Riksduman antigen samt Nådigt fastställd lag 1097 angående ordningen för utfärdande af Finland berörande lagar och författningar af allmän riksbetydelse (No. 45/1910). According to V-P. VILJANEN, *Kansalaisten yleiset oikeudet*, Turun yliopisto, Turku 1986, p. 163 f., this all-Russian Act transferred law-making powers concerning freedoms of speech, press, assembly and association from the competence of the Parliament of Finland to the Russian law-maker. According to JYRÄNKI, *supra* note 15, pp. 469–471, the Act created a supremacy doctrine for all-Russian legislation in relation to Finnish legislation. In this Act, provisions were also made for the participation of the autonomous Finland in the constitutional bodies of the 1906 Duma Constitution. According to section II of this Act, the Parliament of Finland would appoint two Finnish citizens to be seated the State Council and four to be seated in the State Duma.

3.4. COMPLEMENTARY CIVIL LIBERTIES

It seems clear that the introduction of the universal and equal vote in proportional elections would not suffice to give effect to the reform of the system of political representation. The right to vote and the right to stand as a candidate had to be accompanied by complementary civil liberties, which provide for the infrastructure of political activities and political campaigning. In fact, the Grand Duke had already committed himself to proposing such civil liberties of a constitutional nature in the manifesto of 4 November 1905. Therefore, to the same Extraordinary Diet of 1906, the Grand Duke submitted His Imperial Majesty's gracious proposal to the Estates of Finland on an Act concerning the Freedoms of Speech, Assembly, and Association (Proposal No. 13/1906).

In the short motivations to the actual text of the proposed Act, it is stated that the constitutions of Finland do not contain provisions on rights of the citizens of Finland concerning freedom of speech or freedom of the press concerning pictorial expressions, nor about freedoms of assembly and association for citizens. The Constitutional Law Committee of the Diet reiterated the proposal, drafted by the Government of Finland, and added that such freedoms were in compliance with the perception of justice of the people of Finland and of extraordinary value for the guarantee and evolution of civic life and activities. In particular as concerns the freedom of speech and the press, some link to the normative ideas of 1766 can probably be discerned. However, more direct links at the textual level to other, more recent, constitutional provisions elsewhere in Europe have been found. As concerns free speech and press, the closest would have been the 1850 Prussian Constitution, but the formulations can also be traced back to the 1848/1849 Frankfurt Declaration and the 1867 Austrian Constitution on Civil Liberties and, ultimately, to the 1789 French Declaration. Hence, materially speaking, the Finnish Act was less of Swedish provenance, while the understanding of the Act as a constitutional act (see below) was in keeping with the Swedish tradition. As concerns the freedoms of assembly and association, the Finnish formulation being somewhat more liberal in tone, the closest model would seem to be the 1831 Constitution of Belgium, although not as clearly as the models for freedom of speech.[27]

The Freedom of Speech, Assembly and Association (Constitution) Act (No. 38/1906), also often referred to as the constitutional act on civil liberties, was enacted by the consent of all four Estates in conjunction with the right to vote in direct and proportional elections to the unicameral parliament. The Act was undersigned and promulgated by the Emperor and Grand Duke on 20 August 1906. On the first page of the Act, a note has been appended according to which the Act should be read out from the pulpit, which means that the text was read out for the people in the churches by the priests so that everyone would know

[27] VILJANEN, *supra* note 26, pp. 157–159.

about the new law. The Act contained the freedom of association and assembly and — importantly — the freedom of speech, including that of the press. However, unlike in Sweden, the freedom of the press had in this context no bearing on the access to public documents. The Act itself did not contain any ordinary sections numbered in a consecutive order, but was one coherent text in three paragraphs, preceded by a short Preamble.

The Preamble of the Act goes on to say the following: 'It is hereby provided, for the development and guarantee of the general rights of the citizens of Finland and with the force of a constitution: (...).' Here, we can again find the expression of the constitutional nature of the Act, which means that in the hierarchy of norms, this Act is higher than the ordinary acts. The implication of this is stated explicitly in the third paragraph, where a regulatory reservation is made, the effect of which is that this act of a constitutional nature was probably not intended to be directly enforceable, but required ordinary legislation for the freedom to take effect: 'Provisions for what should be taken into consideration in the exercise of these rights shall be passed in the order that is applied for general law.' This is a so-called 'requirement of an Act' (Ger.: *Gesetzesvorbehalt*), which means that provisions concerning the exercise of these freedoms could only be passed by the Parliament, not by executive authorities. This was understood as absolutely necessary under the prevailing circumstances, because governmental authorities and the Russian gendarmerie had, throughout the Era of Autonomy, limited these freedoms in an arbitrary manner, including by means of censorship established by the executive power.

The constitutional implication of the requirement of an Act was that the regulatory authority concerning these freedoms was elevated from the executive power to the legislative powers, that is, to the Parliament. It is at the same time important to understand that these constitutional freedoms were not primarily intended to be directly applicable in concrete situations. Instead, the applicability of these rights was to be created by means of Acts of Parliament: the constitutional provisions created the rights, but they would operate on the basis of provisions in ordinary legislation. In spite of this norm-hierarchical limitation, lower courts actually implemented the Act in practice at least as concerns the freedom of the press and enforced that freedom, although the highest instance was negative towards this praxis. In cases of freedom of association, the Government looked into the possible existence in the rules of the association of matters contrary to law or good morals, and if there were none, the Government declared that the association was free to carry out its functions. It has been remarked that it is of principal importance that in the absence of implementing legislation, courts and administrative authorities referred directly to this constitutional act on civil liberties.[28]

[28] VILJANEN, *supra* note 26, pp. 177–180.

The first paragraph of the Act states the following: 'A citizen of Finland has the freedom of speech and the right to publish in print writings or pictorial presentations, and there shall be no prior obstacle set for this.' The principle of free speech and the free press was thus established as a positive freedom, but more importantly, censorship was explicitly prohibited. This explicit prohibition of censorship would have meant that censorship could not be instituted even by means of an ordinary Act of Parliament, so the Act limited the regulatory options of Parliament to reactions *ex post facto*. In reality, however, no legislation concerning freedom of speech or of the press was enacted between 1906 and 1918, and only the 1919 Act on the Freedom of the Press (1/1919, p. 1) fulfilled the requirements of an Act under the constitutional act of 1906. According to Opinion 1/1918 of the Committee on Legislation, the Government had submitted a proposal to the Parliament of 1905–1906, but the Bill passed by the Parliament was not ratified by the Emperor — the Grand Duke. In 1908, there was another proposal to the following Parliament, but it lapsed because the Parliament was unable to finish the adoption procedure before it was dissolved. However, during the Era of Autonomy, newspapers and other print media existed, including for the purposes of political communication (several of the newspapers currently existing were established during the latter half of the nineteenth century), although a great number of newspapers were also closed down by the authorities.[29] Therefore, there was at least a relative freedom of the press under the executive rules concerning the exercise of this freedom, although at the same time censorship existed and other administrative measures could be taken against print media. Of course, freedom of the press (as other freedoms) was curtailed during World War I, often by means of administrative measures.[30] It is possible to conclude that the pledge of the constitutional act of 1906, whilst not altogether worthless, was not very effective with regard to freedom of speech.

The second paragraph of the Act establishes the following: 'Citizens of Finland have the right, without prior permission, to convene for deliberation of general matters or for other permissible purposes and to constitute associations for the pursuit of aims that are not in violation of law or good morals.' Here, the principles of free assembly and free association were established, and in principle permit regimes making it possible for authorities to exercise prior control of the exercise of these freedoms were banned. In that respect, the second paragraph was similarly constructed to the first paragraph. However, Parliament retained the possibility of regulating the range of permissible purposes by an act, while good morals obviously constituted a relatively open clause that could allow all sorts of limitations of the two freedoms, although praxis developed in a

[29] *Ibid.*, pp. 131–136. See also K.J. STÅHLBERG, 'Painovapaus Suomessa' (1913) 11 *Lakimies* 213, 225, where, after an historical account about the development of this freedom, the author concludes that the freedom of speech was in Finland around 1913 relatively well catered for, while the opposite was true about the freedom of the press.

[30] See Kejserliga Senatens för Finland beslut innefattande förbud att i tidningarna offentliggöra särskilda uppgifter angående krigs- och marinväsendet (No. 22/1914).

more positive direction. The first Parliament managed to enact the 1907 Act on Assemblies of a General Nature (No. 6/1907), but the Act opened up some leeway for public authorities to meddle with the actual exercise of the freedom.[31]

However, freedom of association suffered a similar fate to freedom of the press: the Government had submitted a proposal to the Parliament of 1905–1906, but the Bill passed by the Parliament was not ratified by the Emperor — the Grand Duke. In 1908, there was another proposal to the next Parliament, but it lapsed because the Parliament was unable to finish the process of legislation before it was dissolved. Therefore, in reality, there was no ordinary legislation concerning the freedom of association that would have fulfilled the 1906 requirement of an act until the 1919 Association Act (No. 1/1919, p. 19) was passed. This means that the pledge of the constitutional act of 1906 was not particularly effective during the latter part of the Era of Autonomy, although the Government tended to declare that no hurdles for the functioning of the association existed if the aims of the association were not found to be contrary to law or good morals.[32] Therefore, a number of parties were created around this time, prior to the first elections, such as the Swedish People's Party, the Christian Workers' Party of Finland, and the Agrarian Party. Several of these are still actively engaged in Finnish politics and currently seated in the Parliament.

4. CONCLUDING REMARKS

In the Finnish context, the first fundamental rights documents function in the area of participation and are focused on civil and, in particular, political rights. This is the case with freedom of the press and the rules on access to government-held documents, elaborated in 1766 in the Kingdom of Sweden on the basis of ideas stemming from cities which are today located in Finland. This is also the case with the political reforms of 1906, introduced in the autonomous Grand Duchy of Finland. The level of sophistication displayed by the drafters and decision-makers was at a high and surprisingly modern level. For instance, the

---

31 See K.J. STÅHLBERG, 'Kokoontumisvapaus Suomessa' (1913) 11 *Lakimies* 113, 117, where, after an historical account about the development of this freedom, the author gives an example of a court of appeals case where a governor and a chief of police were sentenced as public officials to pay fines for a breach of duty, because they had prevented a legitimate meeting contrary to the provisions in the 1906 constitutional act on civil liberties and the 1907 Act on Assemblies of a General Nature.

32 See K.J. STÅHLBERG, 'Yhdistymisvapaus Suomessa' (1912) 48 *Tidskrift, utgifven af Juridiska föreningen i Finland* 367, 374, where, after an historical account about the development of this freedom, the author points out that the Senate (i.e., the Government of Finland) made a decision in 1907, after a vote, that it could begin to ascertain whether, in the proposed rules of an association, there is anything contrary to the law or good morals. If nothing of the kind was noticed, the Senate gave a positive decision on the basis of the 1906 constitutional act of civil liberties. In spite of this, bureaucratic measures were taken to hamper the activities of associations, for instance, as concerns their local chapters.

consequences of the d'Hondt system of proportional distribution of seats in a unicameral parliament were correctly calculated, anticipated and assessed, including the existence of a so-called hidden threshold of votes in the electoral districts, a feature that grew to be a problem in Finland a century later.[33] The importance of access to government-held documents as a corollary right to freedom of the press is being generally recognised in the world only today, 250 years after its inception in Finland.

The early introductions of freedom of the press and access to government-held documents and of political rights, including complementary civil rights, were not immediately very effective. It took some time before these rights became completely established. For instance, the reform of the representative structures in 1906 resulted in an electorate that was ten times larger than previously, in a modern party structure, and in women taking up seats in the Parliament, but all of this became fully functional only after independence in 1917, after the demise of the autocratic Russian regime. The parallel liberties of the citizen were applied to some extent even where implementing acts had not been enacted and created an atmosphere of at least relative freedom in society. After independence, they were incorporated in the Form of Government (Constitution) Act of 1919 along with a number of other fundamental rights, but they continued to lack a self-executing character, depending for their applicability on ordinary legislation passed by the Parliament. The direct applicability of the fundamental rights provisions was further circumscribed by the interpretation that courts of law had no jurisdiction to review the constitutionality of legislation and by the fact that Finland had and still has no constitutional court. Today, of course, these fundamental rights constitute core provisions that define the relationship between the individual and the state, and the Constitution of Finland of the year 2000 makes it possible even for courts to set aside a provision in an ordinary law in situations where the application of the ordinary law is in evident conflict with the Constitution.

---

33 On the hidden threshold of votes, see M. SUKSI, 'Finland: Mergers of Municipalities, Linguistic Rights and Amendments to the Constitution' (2014) 20 *European Public Law*, no. 3, 369, 392 f.

23. ESTONIA: FIRST LANDMARKS OF FUNDAMENTAL RIGHTS

Hesi SIIMETS-GROSS
Marelle LEPPIK[1]

'Chapter II of the Constitution of the Republic of Estonia deals with fundamental rights of the citizens. This, as Prof. Dr. Berendts writes — "is precious treasure, which is granted and given to Estonian citizens, treasure, without which a human becomes physically, mentally and spiritually a slave." It is necessary to take care that this treasure does not remain only on paper as a dead letter, but must find just application in real life.'[2]

Meinhard Vasar, attorney at law, in 1932

1. INTRODUCTION

The question of exactly when the first signs of fundamental rights in the territory of the current Republic of Estonia were clearly established is not easy to answer. Would it be correct to begin with the Fundamental Laws of the Russian Empire from 23 April 1906,[3] or should we begin the story about fundamental rights in Estonia with the first Constitution of the Republic of Estonia which was passed by the Constituent Assembly (*Asutav Kogu*) on 15 June 1920 and entered into

1 This article is supported by Estonian Science Foundation Grant No. 9209 and IUT20-50. The authors are grateful to professor Marju Luts-Sootak for help and comments.

2 M. VASAR, 'Eesti Vabariigi Põhiseadus ja KAS § 380' (1932) 7 *Õigus*, 309, 312; E. BERENDTS, 'Eesti Vabariigiriigi kohus ja 1920. a. põhiseaduse printsiibid' (1920) 3 *Õigus* 56, 57. Original quote in Estonian: 'Eesti Vabariigi Põhiseaduse II peatükk käsitleb kodanikkude põhiõigusi. See, nagu kirjutab prof. dr. Berendts, — "on kallis varandus, mis Eestikodanikkudele kingitakse ja lubatakse, varandus, ilma millet inimene kehaliselt, vaimselt ja hingeliselt orjaks muutub." On tarvis kanda hoolt, et see varandus ei jääks ainult paberile surnud tähena, vaid leiaks õiglast kohaldamist tegelikus elus.'

3 *Основныезаконы Российской Империи*. In English available at <http://www.angelfire.com/pa/ImperialRussian/royalty/russia/rfl.html> accessed 07.03.2015.

force on 21 December 1920?[4] Estonian legal historian T. Anepaio takes one step further and suggests that the first acts establishing certain fundamental rights were introduced with the judicial reforms of 1889[5] by the Emperor of Russia, Alexander II. Thus, the question is: should we draw a line between the legal acts of the Russian Empire and Estonia's own national pre-constitutional and constitutional legal acts?

New problems and possibilities for subjective interpretation arise, however, even if we frame the discussion only in terms of national Estonian legal acts. In the theory of constitutional law there have been discussions concerning which documents are, *per se,* pre-constitutional. In the interwar period, the Estonian leading legal theorist and specialist in administrative law, A. T. Kliimann (1899–1941), based his theory on the basic formative steps of national independence.[6] According to Kliimann, the important pre-constitutional acts of Estonia were as follows: firstly, the decision of the Estonian National Council (*Maanõukogu otsus*);[7] secondly, the Manifesto to All the Peoples of Estonia, known as the Declaration of Independence, of 24 February 1918[8] under which Estonia was a democratic republic from 15 November 1917, followed thirdly by the Temporary Regime of Government of the Republic of Estonia passed by the Constituent Assembly on 4 July 1919.[9]

Legal scholar and politician, and the last prime minister during the interwar period, J. Uluots (1890–1945) added to Kliimann's list five other documents which had, in his opinion, pre-constitutional significance.[10] However, the Manifesto to All the Peoples of Estonia belongs, according to all prominent

---

4 'Eesti Vabariigi põhiseadus' (Constitution of the Republic of Estonia), RT (State Gazette) 1920, 113/114, 897. In English published as *The Constitutionof the Esthonian Republic (Passed by the Constituent Assembly on the 15th of June 1920),* Ühiselu Tallinn (Reval) 1924.

5 Sudebnye Ustavy 20.11.1864 s izlozheniem rasuzhdenii, na koikh oni osnovany. Vtoroe dopolnennoe izdanie. Ts. III. Utshrezhdenie sudebnyh ustanovlenii, Sankt-Peterburg 1867. In the territory of Estonian those laws were enforced with the special Act of 9 July 1889. See T. ANEPAIO, 'Justice Laws of 1889: A Step in Estonia's Constitutional Development' (2005) *Juridica International* 157, 159 (with further references and analysis). Available on the website <http://juridicainternational.eu/public/pdf/ji_2005_1_150.pdf> accessed 07.03.2015.

6 E-J. TRUUVÄLI, *Põhiseaduse teel,* Iloprint, Tallinn 2008, p. 14. A.T. KLIIMANN, 'Eesti iseseisvuse areng' (1935) 2 *Õigus,* 49, 54–66.

7 'Maanõukogu otsus kõrgemast wõimust' (decision of the Estonian National Council about higher power) from 15.11.1917. The original is available on website <https://www.riigiteataja.ee/viitedLeht.html?id=1> accessed 15.04.2015. See also TRUUVÄLI, *supra* note 6, p. 14.

8 'Manifest kõigile Eestimaa rahvastele' (Manifesto to all People of Estonia), RT (State Gazette) 1918, 1, 1. English translation available: <http://president.ee/en/republic-of-estonia/declaration-of-independence/index.html#sthash.9FqVRcc7.dpuf> accessed 10.03.2015.

9 'Eesti Vabariigi valitsemise ajutine kord' (Temporary Regime of Government of Republic of Estonia) 04.07.1919.RT (State Gazette) 1919, 44, 345.

10 J. ULUOTS; 'Eesti Vabariigi konstitutsioonilised aktid' in H. RUNNEL (ed.) *Seaduse sünd. Eesti õiguse lugu.* Ilmamaa, Tartu 2004, pp. 280–292 (first published in *Põhiseadus ja Rahvuskogu,* Tallinn 1937); TRUUVÄLI, *supra* note 6, pp. 14–15.

theories, indisputably in the list of pre-constitutional acts which essentially influenced the fundamental rights chapter within the first constitution.

Furthermore, there were documents written before the manifesto that had an important effect on its wording.[11] It is well known that at the end of 1917, before the manifesto, famous Estonian poet G. Suits (1883–1956) drafted the text of a memorandum entitled 'The Work Republic of Estonia' (*Eesti Töövabariik*) and that the National Council published an explanatory statement about the independent state of the people of Estonia (*Iseseisev Eesti rahvariik*).[12] Historians emphasise that all such documents were closely linked and built on one another.[13] The common aims of all these documents were to declare Estonia an independent republic in the near future and to provide cultural autonomy to all the minorities therein. Additionally, new aspects were addressed in the form of fundamental rights regarding the equality of citizens and their civil rights.[14]

As these examples illustrate, the legal texts which enact fundamental rights are not established from scratch, but refer back to predecessors. A subjective choice on the part of the authors is therefore necessary as to which legal documents and fundamental rights to analyse. It is considered that this chapter must first mention the judicial reform of 1889 in the Baltic provinces, as the formal equality of citizens before the court was heavily influenced by this reform established by the Russian Empire. Secondly, the Russian Fundamental Laws of 1906 will be analysed, as this legal document directly influenced freedom of speech in Estonia. Finally, the pre-constitutional acts of the Republic of Estonia from 1918 and the Constitution of the Republic of Estonia of 1920 will be examined alongside the practical example of the implementation of article 6 (equality rights) of the 1920 Constitution.

2. THE RUSSIAN JUDICIAL REFORM OF 1889 IN THE BALTIC PROVINCES

In a situation in which there is no legislation declaring and guaranteeing fundamental rights, another Act may substitute for a constitution. This function is often claimed for private law codifications,[15] but T. Anepaio suggests that in the territory of Estonia the judicial reform of 1889 was the first 'where several

[11] A. PAJUR, 'Iseseisvusmanifesti sünd' (2003) 2 *Tuna* 27, 30.
[12] A. PIIP, *Tormine aasta: Ülevaade Eesti välispoliitika esiajast 1917.–1918. aastal dokumentides ja mälestusis*, Akadeemiline Kooperatiiv, Tartu 1934, pp. 96–98.
[13] E. LAAMAN, *Eesti iseseisvuse sünd*, Vaba Eesti, Stockholm 1964, p. 234; PAJUR, *supra* note 11, 30.
[14] Among other issues, the need to create Estonia's own court system, to release political prisoners and to restore democratically elected government were emphasised. PAJUR, *supra* note 11, 30.
[15] D. GRIMM, *Recht und Staat der bürgerlichen Gesellschaft*, Suhrkamp, Frankfurt 1987, pp. 192–212.

principles of the rule of law (public administration of justice, separation of powers, formal equality of citizens [before the court]) were so extensively (of course not fully!) and complexly implemented. This allows to claim that the function of substituting for a constitution belonged to the procedural codes on which the 1889 judicial reform was based, together with the Courts Administration Act.'[16]

Of course, this argument holds only if the preconditions for implementation of these rights are also met. For example, 'a separation of administrative and judicial powers will have a modernising effect only if the activities of the administrative power can indeed be controlled by the justice.'[17]

Whether, when and to what extent the rights were implemented is not fully understood at the current stage of research. There is then a further question of whether the changes in procedural norms influenced material law to such an extent that we can accurately refer to fundamental rights. It is best simply to state, therefore, that the first ideas of fundamental rights, if greatly limited in extent, were introduced in Estonia with the judicial reforms of 1889.

3. FUNDAMENTAL LAWS OF 1906 OF THE RUSSIAN EMPIRE

It is characteristic of Estonian historiography that fundamental rights or, more precisely, research on fundamental rights, generally starts from the formation and adoption of the Constitution of the Republic of Estonia in 1920.[18] If we take into account that the turbulent period in which the enforcement of the Russian Constitution of 1906 took place was from an Estonian point of view just a transitional time providing conditions favourable to independence, this is understandable.

The Russian Fundamental Laws of 1906 nonetheless occupy an important place in the history of fundamental rights in the territory of Estonia. The Russian Emperor promised civil liberties and participation by the Duma (Parliament) in the legislation process, in his manifesto of 17 October 1905.[19] This manifesto and other legal acts were incorporated into the Fundamental Laws of 1906 on 23 April 1906 and were applicable in Estonia.[20]

---

16 ANEPAIO, *supra* note 5.

17 M. LUTS-SOOTAK, 'The Ambivalence of Reforms and their Absence: Baltic Lections of the 19th Century' (2006) *Juridica International* 68, 74.

18 ANEPAIO, *supra* note 5, 150.

19 *Polnoe Sobranie Zakonov Rossiiskoi Imperii.* Series III, v tipografii II Otdeleniia, St. Petersburg 1884–1916.

20 L. SCHULTZ, *Das Verfassungsrecht Russlands. – Russlands Aufbruch ins 20. Jahrhundert. Politik-Gesellschaft-Kultur*, Olten-Freiburg: Walter Verlag, Freiburg 1970, p. 47.

After the Emperor promised civil liberties on 17 October 1905 in an effort to calm down the strikes, many people started to demand the promised rights in practice in Estonia. The editor in chief of the leading newspaper, politician and later prime minister, foreign minister and head of state J. Tõnisson (1868–1941) wrote: 'Now, through the fundamental laws, i.e., the Constitution the field of activities is legally widened. [...] Options to use the remedies to fight have become wider'.[21]

If a civil servant of the empire closed a newspaper or prohibited a scheduled meeting, it was possible to claim in court that the restriction was in conflict with the fundamental laws. The employees and friends of J. Tõnisson's newspaper, *Postimees* (Postman), started actively to exercise their freedom of speech and their right to hold meetings. Since the liberties and rights promised in the text were somewhat declarative, Tõnisson was able to bluntly ask: 'What must we do, to completely enforce the new fundamental laws?'.[22]

The main focus of the Russian Fundamental Laws of 1906 was to determine the scope of the emperor's power. According to the Fundamental Laws, the emperor had to share legislative power with the Duma and the Council of State (Chapter I, article 7). S. Zetterberg sums up the general view by arguing that Russia adopted a partial constitutional monarchy, although in reality the emperor kept the position of an autocrat.[23] The low importance of fundamental rights is evidenced by their place in the constitution, that is in Chapter VIII. Nonetheless, some very important fundamental rights were enacted such as protection against unfair trial (article 72) and the right that infringement of personal freedoms could only occur in accordance with the law (article 73). The right of inviolability of the home (article 75) and personal property (article 77), the freedom to choose one's habitation and profession (article 76), freedom of speech, the right to hold meetings, freedom of association and freedom of religion (articles 78–81) were also laid down.

The general right of equality, however, was not guaranteed by the Russian Fundamental Laws of 1906, and, as always, the implementation of the principles depended on special regulations and administrative practice.[24]

---

21 J. TONISSON. *Postimees* 26.10.1905 (referred in: H. KALMO, 'Enesemääramise saatuslik tund' in T. TANNBERG and A. PAJUR (eds.), *Iseseisvusmanifest. Artikleid, dokumente ja mälestusi,* Greif, Tartu 2014, p. 169).

22 J. TONISSON. *Postimees* 31.10.1905 (referred in: H. KALMO, 'Enesemääramise saatuslik tund' in T. TANNBERG and A. PAJUR (eds.), *Iseseisvusmanifest. Artikleid, dokumente ja mälestusi,* Greif, Tartu 2014, p. 169).

23 S. ZETTERBERG, *Eesti ajalugu*, Kirjastus Tänapäev, Tallinn 2009, p. 356.

24 T. KARJAHÄRM, 'Isevalitsuselt duumamonarhiale' in S. VAHTRE (ed.), *Eestiajalugu V. Pärisorjuse kaotamisest Vabadussõjani*, Ilmamaa, Tartu 2010, p. 366.

The Fundamental Laws of 1906 repeated rights which had prior existence in various Acts. For example, censorship had already been tightened in 1905, due to the publication of revolutionary opinions in newspapers.[25] Therefore the rights had been withdrawn[26] and in Estonia some newspapers were closed. S. Zetterberg gives some illustrative examples: The Journal of Tallinn (*Tallinna Teataja*) was closed after the censor filed 15 accusations during the period from 19 October until 5 December 1905. The publisher of the journal (who was an Estonian politician, later to serve five times as the head of state, prime minister, in duties of state leadership and speaker of the parliament, and who became the first president of Estonia in 1938), K. Päts (1874–1956) was accused of inciting rebellion. After another publisher J. Tõnisson in his newspaper *Postimees,* criticised the new laws regulating Duma elections, the newspaper was shut down. Altogether, during the period from 1905 until 1908 over 20 newspapers were closed in Estonia. Some of them were, however, restarted later (e.g. *Postimees*).[27]

It is nevertheless possible to say that despite the censor's bureaucratic demands, the situation for Estonian newspapers was certainly better after 1905 and 1906. Last but not least, the growth in printed materials made the exercise of censorship quite complex, since it was difficult to thoroughly monitor all publications.[28]

The fundamental rights enacted in 1906 at least gave an opportunity to test their limits. After 1905, for example, the first political parties were formed in Estonia and during 1905–1906 the first political strikes and demonstrations were organised. It is notable that these developments took place before the enactment of the constitution.[29]

Article 83 stated that 'Specific laws define exceptions to the rules expounded in this chapter regarding localities under martial law or under exceptional circumstances'. A state of emergency which was imposed in 1881 endured until 1917 in Russia.[30] There are different views on the Russian Fundamental Laws of 1906 in Russia as well as in Western Europe. The German political theorist Max Weber, for instance, viewed the Act as a caricature of constitutionalism.[31] Critical analyses originate from the fact that the emperor still had, compared to

25 ZETTERBERG, *supra* note 23, p. 362.

26 KARJAHÄRM, *supra* note 24, p. 366.

27 ZETTERBERG, *supra* note 23, p. 362.

28 T. RAUN, 'Eesti lülitumine modernsusse: "Noor-Eesti" roll poliitilise ja sotsiaalse mõtte mitmekesistamisel', Tuna, 2/2009, 39-50, 49; B. RIGBERG, 'The Efficacy of Tsarist Censorship Operations, 1894–1917' (1966) *Jahrbücher für Geschichte Osteuropas* 14, lk. 327–328, 343.

29 ZETTERBERG, *supra* note 23, p. 359.

30 SCHULTZ, *supra* note 20, p. 55.

31 M. WEBER, 'Zur Lage der bürgerlichen demokratie in Russland' (1906) 22 *Archiv für Sozialwissenschaft und Sozialpolitik* 345.

other western constitutional monarchs, considerable power and political control.[32] Estonian lawyer H. Kalmo has made a critical remark in the context of self-determination of nations and the principle of autonomy for minorities that the 'emperor and administration did not care much [for] the constitution and even did not name the document enacted in 1906 the "constitution".'[33] On the other hand, in the opinion of L. Schultz, it is significant that fundamental rights were recognised as subjective public rights in the territories of the Russian Empire, although the rights were limited by special laws in a state of emergency.[34]

The state of emergency was imposed for different periods in various parts of Russia. According to T. Anepaio: 'an emergency situation in the form of a state of war (not an enhanced or emergency state of defence) was fully established on the Estonian territory only on 20 December 1905 and it was lifted on 15 September (26 August) 1908'.[35] In T. Karjahärm's opinion, an enhanced state of defence was thereafter established and it lasted until 4 September 1911, after which it was maintained only in Tallinn and Riga.[36]

It may be concluded that, although the Russian Fundamental Laws of 1906 had less impact than hoped and expected, they were valid in Estonia and influenced the practice of rights in Estonia.

Even in later case law of the Supreme Court of the Republic of Estonia, the court has examined how fundamental rights were guaranteed when Estonia was a part of Russia: 'During the temporary government of Russia females could freely enter the higher educational institutions and they had the right to become a civil servant if they ended the course, so all doubts disappear about that now, under the Constitution of the Republic of Estonia [...] article 6, that enacts as follows: "All Estonian citizens are equal in the eyes of law. There cannot be any public privileges or prejudices derived from birth, religion, sex, rank or nationality." Thus, harmonizing the rights of both genders'.[37] This court case from 1924 illustrates that later, in the Republic of Estonia, it was considered inappropriate for wider fundamental rights to be granted in Russia than in independent Estonia, at least with respect to gender equality.

---

32 SCHULTZ, *supra* note 20, p. 48.

33 H. KALMO, 'Enesemääramise saatuslik tund' in T. TANNBERG and A. PAJUR (eds.), *Iseseisvusmanifest. Artikleid, dokumente ja mälestusi,* Greif, Tartu 2014, p. 171.

34 SCHULTZ, *supra* note 20, p. 50.

35 ANEPAIO, *supra* note 5, 158.

36 T. KARJAHÄRM, *Ida ja Lääne vahel. Eesti-Vene suhted 1850–1917 (Between east and west. Estonian–Russian relation 1850–1917)*, Eesti Entsüklopeedia kirjastus, Tallinn 1998, p. 122.

37 The Grand Chamber of the Supreme Court, decision 01.09.1924 No. 44 in T. ANEPAIO (ed.), *Riigikohus. Otsuste valikkogumik 1920–1940*, Elmatar, Tartu 1999, p. 43.

4. PRE-CONSTITUTIONAL ACTS OF THE REPUBLIC OF ESTONIA, 1918–1920

Before the first Constitution of the Republic of Estonia was passed by the Constituent Assembly on 15 June 1920 (entering into force on 21 December 1920), other Acts were passed that filled the place of a missing constitution.

Estonian independence was declared by the Manifesto to All the Peoples of Estonia on 24 February 1918.[38] According to one author of the manifesto, F. Peterson, the purpose of the manifesto was as follows: 'Thus, the manifesto is at the moment a fundamental act of state governance. The manifesto has to include the fundamental rights of an independent Estonia; regulations about forming the Constituent Assembly; clarifications about the status of soldiers in the Estonian military, so that they cannot be stigmatised as deserters of the Russian military; and regulations about future actions of the government with respect to the security of citizens and property. The manifesto must give a clear promise of what citizens can expect from their own Estonian state'.[39] The idea was to give to the manifesto 'such a substance as if it were a reduced form of constitution'.[40] The manifesto was even called 'the cornerstone of the development of independence'.[41]

In the Declaration of Independence or Manifesto of 1918, the most important fundamental rights were compressed and listed in three points:

> 1. All citizens of the Republic of Estonia, irrespective of their religion, ethnic origin, and political views, shall enjoy equal protection under the law and courts of justice of the Republic.
> 2. All ethnic minorities, the Russians, Germans, Swedes, Jews, and others residing within the borders of the Republic, shall be guaranteed the right to their cultural autonomy.
> 3. All civic freedoms, such as the freedom of expression, of the press, of religion, of assembly, of association, and the freedom to strike as well as the inviolability of the individual and the home, shall be irrefutably effective within the territory of the Estonian

---

38 According to A. Pajur, the manifesto was probably already published and declared on 23.02. 1918. A. Pajur, 'Iseseisvusmanifesti sünnilugu' in T. Tannberg and A. Pajur (eds.), *Iseseisvusmanifest. Artikleid, dokumente ja mälestusi*, Greif, Tartu 2014, p. 127.

39 F. Peterson, *Mälestusi ja tähelepanekuid,* Tallinna Tehnikaülikooli Kirjastus, Tallinn 2001, pp. 161–163. Original quote in Estonian: 'See manifest on momendil põhiline riigi valitsemise akt. Manifest peab sisaldama iseseisva Eesti riigi maa-alalised ja õiguslikud põhialused, määruse Asutava Kogu kokkukutsumiseks, selgitama Eesti sõjaväelaste staatuse, et neid ei saaks tembeldada väejooksikuteks Vene sõjaväest, ja määrused riigi valitsuste edaspidise tegevuse kohta kõigi kodanike julgeoleku ja varanduse kindlustamiseks. Manifest peab andma selge tõotuse, mis on rahval oodata oma Eesti riigilt, kui asutakse seda verega kaitsma.'

40 Peterson, *supra* note 39, p. 279.

41 A. Piip, 'Vabariigi Aastapäevaks' (1938) 7 *Akadeemia* 1, 4.

> Republic and based on laws which the Government shall immediately work out.[42]

The manifesto was inspired by independence declarations (such as the Declaration of Independence of the United States and the French Declaration of the Rights of Man and of Citizen) that had their basis in the natural rights of every human being (*les droits naturels, inaliénables et sacrés de l'Homme*) which must be protected by every political association.[43]

In addition to the manifesto, fundamental rights were part of other pre-constitutional acts, such as the Temporary Regime of Government of the Republic of Estonia of 4 June 1919.[44] The general principles of the Temporary Regime of Government of the Republic of Estonia were later enacted in the first constitution of 1920. It was established in this document that Estonia is an independent, sovereign and democratic republic (§ 1).The document also determined the provisional borders of the state and named the parts of the land that belonged to the Republic of Estonia (§ 2). According to this document, the official language of the state should be Estonian; at the same time, minorities were granted the right to use their own language (§ 3), all Estonian citizens were declared equal before the law and there could be no prejudice or privileges[45] (§ 4). As the social and economic power of the estates, especially the German nobility, was very strong until that point, the abolition of estates was a significant change. Similarly to the manifesto of 1918, the Temporary Regime of Government included a chapter about fundamental rights (§§ 4–8). In addition to personal and political rights, social rights were guaranteed: free obligatory primary education in the native language (§ 5); the right to acquire land for agriculture and exploitation (§ 7); the right to an adequate standard of living (§ 7); the right to gain employment and labour protection (§ 7); and the right to state support for those who are old, young or unable to work (§ 7), etc. The highest power belonged to the people, in whose name the Constituent Assembly should act (§ 9). The important task of the Constituent Assembly was to pass the Constitution of the Republic of Estonia (§ 10).

---

42 'Manifest kõigile Eestimaa rahvastele' (Manifesto to All People of Estonia), RT (State Gazette) 1918, 1, 1. English translation available: <http://president.ee/en/republic-of-estonia/declaration-of-independence/index.html#sthash.9FqVRcc7.dpuf> accessed 10.03.2015. Published also in T. Tannberg and A. Pajur (eds.), *Iseseisvusmanifest. Artikleid, dokumente ja mälestusi,* Greif, Tartu 2014, pp. 11–15. There are some differences in Estonian wording in the various texts of the manifesto, pp. 237–239.

43 J. Undusk, 'Iseseisvusmanifesti intertekstuaalsus' in T. Tannberg and A. Pajur (eds.), *Iseseisvusmanifest. Artikleid, dokumente ja mälestusi,* Greif, Tartu 2014, p. 24.

44 'Eesti Vabariigi valitsemise ajutine kord' (Temporary regime of the government of the Republic of Estonia) 04.06.1919.RT (State Gazette) 1919, 44, 345.

45 Later the equality principle was confirmed by the Constituent Assembly on 09.06.1920, when assembly passed special law called Abolition of Estates Act. ('Seisuste kaotamise seadus'), RT (State Gazette), RT 1920, 129/130, 254.

5. FIRST CONSTITUTION OF THE REPUBLIC OF ESTONIA OF 1920

The Constituent Assembly enacted the first Constitution of the Republic of Estonia[46] on 15 June 1920, and it entered into force on 21 December 1920. As a result of the legislative process, the fundamental rights in the Constitution of 1920 were, in comparison with the Temporary Regime of Government of the Republic of Estonia, specified and widened, while not being changed in principle.

However, in drafting the Constitution it was first discussed whether fundamental rights should be included in the constitutional text in Estonia at all, as doing so was uncommon at that time, let alone earlier.[47] For example, most constitutions in German states after 1848 did not mention fundamental rights, for they were considered in legal theory to be self-evidently guaranteed. Nonetheless, it was decided in the Weimar Constitution that, to tie the Constitution with the one from 1848, an extended series of fundamental rights should be included.[48] The Latvian Constitution of 1922 did not address human rights.[49] After the question about the necessity of fundamental rights in the Estonian Constitution arose, there was demand for establishing fundamental rights in the Constitution on all sides, from the right wing and the left,[50] and consequently fundamental rights were enshrined there as legal guarantees.

In the opinion of an Estonian lawyer from that period, E. Laaman, the Estonian Constitution of 1920 was influenced by the French Declaration of the Rights of Man and of the Citizen, by extreme collectivism in Soviet Russia, and by the Weimar Constitution. The Weimar Constitution and the French Declaration were considered to be the best examples at that time. The French Declaration was an example for all constitutions developed after its adoption. The Weimar Constitution was held up as a model of a modern and democratic constitution of the twentieth century, and it was indeed one of the most advanced constitutions of its time.[51] So the best constitutional acts were chosen as the standard.

---

46 'Eesti Vabariigi põhiseadus' (Constitution of the Republic of Estonia), RT (State Gazette) 1920, 113/114, 897.

47 H. Siimets-Gross, 'Social and Economic Fundamental Rights in Estonian Constitutions Between World Wars I and II: A Vanguard or Rearguard of Europe?' (2005) *Juridica International* 135, 136.

48 F. Hartung, 'Die Entwicklung der Grundrechte seit 1776. – Die Entwicklung der Menschen- und Bürgerrechte von 1776 bis zur Gegenwart' in F. Hartung and G. Commichau (eds.), *Quellensammlung zur Kulturgeschichte*. Bd. I., Muster-Schmidt Verlag, Göttingen 1985, pp. 28–29.

49 J. Lazdiņš, 'Rechtspolitische Besonderheiten bei der Entstehung des lettischen Staates und seiner Verfassung' (2014) 7 *Juridiskā zinātne* 9, 16.

50 E. Laaman, 'Isik ja riik Eesti põhiseadustes' (1937) 3 *Õigus* 102, 106.

51 *Ibid.*

The fact that French Declaration of the Rights of Man and of the Citizen was taken as a model was certainly important for the self-esteem of the newly established state. When comparing the Constitution of 1920 with the French Declaration, some similarities can be seen. Both contained guarantees of personal rights (such as equality of the sexes), but there were no social rights in the Declaration, whereas these were provided in the Estonian Constitution of 1920. It can be said that the liberal spirit of the French human rights declaration was incorporated into the Constitution of 1920. In both the French document and the Estonian Constitution of 1920, the section containing the series of fundamental rights was the first to follow the introduction. Additionally, the title of the chapter on human rights, 'About Fundamental Rights', was very characteristic of the general aim and essence of the Constitution of 1920.[52]

As noted above, the Constitution of 1920 was also influenced by the Weimar Constitution. Although the Constitution of 1920 set itself apart from the German tradition — according to which the series of human rights, inclusive of social and economic human rights, was traditionally very thorough (the Weimar Constitution contained 56 sections) — the authors find some of the Weimar Constitution's social and economic fundamental rights similarly worded in the Estonian Constitution of 1920. Article 25 contains a translation from the Weimar Constitution — that the organisation of economic life must be in accordance with the principles of equity. However, this article was criticized during preparatory work on the Estonian constitution; the claim was 'that equality stays only on paper' since civic democracy is only a delusion.[53] In fact, from a legal point of view article 25 of the Estonian Constitution was more precise and clear: it gave guidelines for the legislator concerning the areas that needed regulation.

Although an influence over the Constitution of 1920 came, in the opinion of the authors, from the Weimar Constitution of 1919, there are some clear differences as well. The fundamental difference lies in the title of the chapter, which in the Weimar Constitution was 'Concerning the rights and duties of Germans' (*Grundrechte und Grundpflichten der Deutschen*[54]). As J. Rückert has formulated, 'when the right and duty each applies, will be the principal question'.[55] As the chapter in the Estonian Constitution of 1920 was entitled 'On the Fundamental Rights of Estonian Citizens', this was not a problem for that constitution (though it was different later, e.g., in 1938). In the Constitution of 1920, individual rights and freedoms were in focus.

---

52 SIIMETS-GROSS, *supra* note 47, 137.

53 LAAMAN, *supra* note 50, 107.

54 Weimarer Reichsverfassung, 11 August 1919. Available on the website: <http://www.jura.uni-wuerzburg.de/fileadmin/02160100/Elektronische_Texte/Verfassungstexte/Die_Weimarer_Reichsverfassung.pdf> accessed 15.04.2015.

55 J. RÜCKERT, 'Weimars Verfassung zum Gedenken' (1999) 18 *Rechtshistorisches Journal* 215, 218.

Thus, in Chapter II of the Constitution of 1920 the obligations of the state in favour of the citizen were not in focus, but the obligation of the state to refrain from intervention in the freedoms of citizens was emphasised, according to one of the compilers of the constitution, J. Uluots.[56] The concept of the 1920 Constitution was based on individuality, rather than on collectivism, and beside the fundamental rights there were few obligations.

Because of the more than 20 fundamental rights in Chapter II, the 1920 Constitution is described as 'very democratic'. Some historians however think it has been described as more democratic than it deserves,[57] since its less democratic aspects have been left out from some analyses. Moreover, we still lack complete and systematic data on how fundamental rights were actually realised in everyday life and applied in legal practice and how fundamental rights were implemented and interpreted by the independent court system.

To illustrate this critical remark, let us take article 6 of the 1920 Constitution. According to article 6, all citizens were declared to be equal before the law, men and women alike: 'There cannot be any public privileges or prejudices derived from birth, religion, sex, rank, or nationality. In Estonia there are no legal class divisions or titles.' Compared to the usual wording of the equality principle, this norm contains the short addition 'public', which can lead to non-application in private law questions.[58]

Even in the public sphere where equality should prevail and was *expressis verbis* affirmed by the Supreme Court, the reality could be different. On 1 September 1924 the Grand Chamber of the Supreme Court issued an opinion on a complaint submitted by Mrs. Auguste Susi-Tannebaum, who challenged the decision that she — as a woman — was not suitable to be appointed to the position of judge candidate. Lower court instances had interpreted a special law, the Judicial Institution Act of 1917, and reached the conclusion that it was not permitted for a woman to enter the judge's profession, because of her gender. The Grand Chamber of the Supreme Court explained that the interpretation of the court of lower instance was not in accordance with article 6 of the 1920 Constitution, since there may be no privileges dependant on gender. Additionally, the Supreme

---

56 J. ULUOTS, 'Rahvas ja ta funktsioneerimine Eesti põhiseaduse järgi' in H. RUNNEL (ed.), *Seaduse sünd. Eesti õiguse lugu: Jüri Uluots*, Ilmamaa, Tartu 2004 (first published in 1932), p. 263.

57 K. ARJAKAS, 'Eesti Vabariigi põhiseadustest' in E. PÄRNASTE and Ü. AASKIVI (eds.), *Põhiseaduse tulek*, Tallinna Raamatutrükikoda, Tallinn 2002, p. 35.

58 In two cases concerning testaments, which according to valid private law norms required male witnesses, the Civil Chamber of the Supreme Court found that the restrictions based on gender were violating the equality principle (article 6 of Constitution of 1920). The Civil Chamber of the Supreme Court, judgement of 31.05.1928 No. 3, in Estonian State Archive No. 1356.3.76 and judgement of 28.04.1932 No. 375, in Estonian State Archive 1356.3.92. See also M. LUTS-SOOTAK and M. LEPPIK, 'Die Verfassungsgerichtsbarkeit nach Estlands Grundgesetz von 1920 und in der höchstrichterlichen Rechtsprechung' (2014) 7 *Juridiskā zinātne* 21, 28–29.

Court drew attention to the fact that women were allowed to receive higher education in 1924, and that women were allowed to work as civil servants.[59]

Thus, the right to become a candidate justice, regardless of gender, was according to the Supreme Court the only solution that was constitutionally consistent and in support of gender equality. We can see this from the judgment of the Grand Chamber of the Supreme Court from 1924, which may be the first court case concerning gender equality in Estonia. However, it is an historical fact that there were no women working as justices in ordinary courts during the period 1918–1940 in the Republic of Estonia.[60]

On the other hand, even in 1925 the legal scholar and politician, and first head of state during the interwar period, A. Piip (1884–1942) commented on how gender equality was not, in his opinion, always objectively implemented: 'It is interesting to note that despite this provision many laws exist which protect women in industry, thereby discriminating favourably against men.'[61]

This, together with the non-equality of gender in the private sphere and the restriction of freedom of movement such that it applies only within one's home country, shows a restrictive approach in the interpretation of fundamental rights which are widely formulated.[62]

6. CONCLUDING REMARKS

Taking account of the traditions and history of the Republic of Estonia, it is not hard to understand why research on fundamental rights in Estonia generally starts with the Declaration of Independence (Manifesto to All the Peoples of Estonia) of 24 February 1918, and why the debate about fundamental rights in Estonia begins with analysis of the historical context of the first Constitution of the Republic of Estonia of 1920. However, if the question is when the first fundamental rights in Estonian territory were enacted, it is necessary to expand the investigation to earlier legal acts. At the same time, it cannot be said that all fundamental rights that are considered important today were laid down concurrently.

The judicial reform of 1889 in the Baltic Provinces can be viewed as the first attempt to establish some fundamental rights in a certain area of law in the Russian Empire. As often happens, the Russian Fundamental Laws of 1906

---

59 The Grand Chamber of the Supreme Court, decision 01.09.1924 No. 44 in T. ANEPAIO (ed.), *Riigikohus. Otsuste valikkogumik 1920–1940*, Elmatar, Tartu 1999, pp. 41–44.

60 T. ANEPEIO, *Eesti Vabariigi kohtunikekorpus (1918–1940),* master thesis, Tartu 1993 (manuskript in the Library of University of Tartu).

61 A. PIIP, 'The Constitution of the Republic of Esthonia' (1925) 9 *Constitutional Review* 3, 7.

62 SIIMETS-GROSS, *supra* note 47, 140.

followed massive civil disorder. This did not mean that all of the important fundamental rights were guaranteed, or that full use of them was allowed. For example, freedom of speech and publishing, as well as the right to hold meetings, were guaranteed and restricted before the Fundamental Laws entered into force. Thus, the Constitution of 1906 did not greatly change some aspects of fundamental rights from the *status quo*. The recognition of fundamental rights as subjective public rights in the territory of the Russian Empire was still important, despite restrictions in the special laws and the fact that the equality principle was not yet laid down.

The idea of an independent state, the Republic of Estonia, included the wish that it should be a state with the rule of law in which fundamental rights were followed. For this reason, both pre-constitutional acts stressed fundamental rights.

Despite certain doubts about including the fundamental rights catalogue in the first Constitution of the Republic of Estonia of 1920, those rights were laid down in the second chapter of that Act. How necessary this was, and that the presence of rights was not as self-evident as it was claimed to be during discussions in the Constituent Assembly, was demonstrated by the various interpretations of the text in theory and practice. Our example concerning gender equality shows different views and practices in the courts and society. However, the catalogue of fundamental rights in Chapter II of the 1920 Constitution with the possibility of a constitutional review by the Supreme Court[63] was predominantly liberal and modern.

[63] See M. LUTS-SOOTAK and M. LEPPIK, 'Die Verfassungsgerichtsbarkeit nach Estlands Grundgesetz von 1920 und in der höchstrichterlichen Rechtsprechung' (2014) 7 *Juridiskā zinātne* 21, 21–31.

24. SLOVAKIA: THE RIGHT OF A NATION

Tomáš GÁBRIŠ
Mária PATAKYOVÁ

1. INTRODUCTION

When searching for the first fundamental rights documents in Slovakian history we must admit that these emerged relatively late in comparison with other European countries — in the mid-nineteenth century. Additionally, they are marked by a specific feature of being aimed at collective rights rather than individual rights. Individual rights (mostly political ones) were only to serve the execution of the most important fundamental right — the right of a nation to equality, which has later turned into the right of a nation to self-determination. This was the main goal strived at by the small nations of Central Europe, and in case of Slovakia, it took almost two centuries until the right to self-determination of the Slovakian nation was fully executed. That is what makes this right of special interest in Slovakia, and hopefully of importance also for the purposes of this book.

At the very beginning of our treatment of the documents related to Slovakia, we must note that we shall not discuss one sole document, but rather a series of documents, which are additionally mostly of political rather than of legal nature. This was caused by the fact that Slovakia did not have any independent legislature until recently. The Slovak Republic is one of the youngest states on the map of Europe, gaining its independence only on 1 January 1993. The history of fundamental rights in the territory of Slovakia before 1993 is therefore strongly linked to the history of the Hungarian Kingdom (until 1918) and Czechoslovakia (until 1992). Still, Slovak national leaders independently authored several political declarations and projects in the nineteenth century (mainly in 1848, 1849, and 1861), specifically aimed at the rights of the nation, hand in hand with requests for individual political rights. The fact that these were political declarations rather than laws was perhaps the reason why these documents of the nineteenth century were more radical than the reforms introduced by the actual laws of the conservative multi-national Hungarian Kingdom.

The idea of a nation being a legal person, carrying specific collective fundamental rights, is the main feature of all these documents. The arguments that were used to support the idea of collective rights originated both in history and in natural law, and whilst at first they were aimed at the equality of nations within the Hungarian Kingdom, finally they reached their peak in national self-determination (of a fictitious Czechoslovak nation) outside the platform of the Hungarian Kingdom (in various political documents from 1914–1918).

After 1918, it took some further decades until the right to national self-determination of the Slovak nation was fully executed in the context of the unitary Czechoslovak Republic. Unfortunately, Slovak independence was reached in 1939 under direct influence of Nazi Germany, which caused the Slovak wartime state of 1939–1945 to be considered null and void from a legal point of view. After 1945 it was nevertheless recognised that there are two nations living in Czechoslovakia, and in 1968 the Slovak nation was attributed the status of a legal (constitutional) personality and gained the form of a National Republic within the Czechoslovak federation. This member state with its supreme authorities was the direct predecessor to the current Slovak Republic, established in 1993 after peaceful negotiations on the dissolution of Czechoslovakia.

There is a main difference when comparing the 1992/93 situation with the dissolution of the Hungarian Kingdom in 1918, though. While the first attempt at self-determination in 1918 was opposed by the elites of the Hungarian Kingdom which was not providing equality of nations, the 1992 dissolution of Czechoslovakia was marked by mutual agreement on dissolution without any negative resentment. The experience of the Slovak nation of the right to self-determination hence includes both the situation of an oppressed nation as well as the situation of a recognised nation striving for its formal independence. While in the Hungarian Kingdom the Slovaks lacked any relevant collective rights and were possessed of only limited individual rights providing for a very restricted share in the administration and government of the country, in the Czechoslovak federation the position of the Slovak nation was much more satisfactory in this respect. Nevertheless, the nation made use of its legitimate right to self-determination in 1992/93 in spite of this.

From the doctrinal legal point of view, it is obvious that the right to self-determination of a nation presupposes a legal person — a nation, being a subject of the right. In our contribution, we are going to explain the route to the idea of personality of nations and of collective rights of nations before the right to self-determination was internationally recognised in 1917/1918. In this context, we shall explain the formation of the Slovak nation in Central Europe, and the specific circumstances which led to the execution of its right to self-determination.

The basic documents of a quasi-constitutional nature that we are going to devote our attention to in this respect, are mainly the following: the Demands of the Slovak Nation (1848), the March Petition (1849), the 1861 Memorandum, the 1914 US Memorandum, and the 1918 Washington and Martin Declarations.

While the former three paved the way to collective rights of a nation and to the equality of nations, the latter three paved the way to, and explicitly invoked, the right to national self-determination proper.

2. THE COLLECTIVE RIGHT TO SELF-DETERMINATION

The current worldwide discourse on the right to national self-determination notwithstanding historical borders clearly shows that the idea of a nation-state and of the fundamental right of a nation to self-determination is still not obsolete even in the twenty-first century. This fundamental right, recognised mainly during World War I and especially in 1917/1918 is used as a legal basis for various political ambitions nowadays.

While fundamental rights are mostly individual rights, the right of a nation to self-determination has the nature of a collective right, instead of an individual human right. It is therefore a fundamental right of a nation, and not of individual natural persons.[1] This principle applies both at the level of international law, and at the level of national legal systems. For example, in the present-day Slovak Republic, it is recognised explicitly that the right to self-determination is a collective right of a nation. The Constitution of the Slovak Republic, however, only speaks of the right to self-determination in its preamble,[2] the legal nature of which is an issue of discussion. In practice, the Constitutional Court disregards the wording of the preamble and according to prevailing opinion the preamble has merely symbolic and ceremonial significance.[3]

In the actual wording of the Constitution of Slovakia proper, the right to self-determination is not expressly referred to, nor do collective rights otherwise have

---

1 J. VALUCH, *Medzinárodné právo verejné*, EUROKÓDEX, Bratislava 2012, pp. 209–210.

2 I. CIBULKA et al., *Ústavné právo : Ústavný systém Slovenskej republiky*, Univerzita Komenského v Bratislave, Právnická fakulta, Bratislava 2014, p. 62.
We, the Slovak nation,
bearing in mind the political and cultural heritage of our ancestors and the centuries of experience from the struggles for national existence and our own statehood,
mindful of the spiritual heritage of Cyril and Methodius and the historical legacy of Great Moravia,
recognizing the natural right of nations to self-determination,
together with members of national minorities and ethnic groups living on the territory of the Slovak Republic,
in the interest of lasting peaceful cooperation with other democratic states,
seeking the application of the democratic form of government, guarantees of a free life, development of spiritual culture and economic prosperity,
that is, we, the citizens of the Slovak Republic,
adopt
through our representatives
this Constitution...

3 *Ibid.*, p. 65.

a place in the Constitution of the Slovak Republic. Although some political rights, such as petition rights or assembly rights, are obviously implemented collectively, in fact these are only individual rights exercised collectively.[4] Even in the case of minorities, Slovakia does not recognise any collective rights of minorities; only the minorities' representatives carry certain individual rights.

The collective right to self-determination was in fact exercised first, within the establishment of the Slovak Republic, before its declaration in the preamble to the Constitution. The sovereign of the newly created Slovak Republic is not the collective Slovak nation, but rather all the citizens of the Slovak Republic, who share equal individual rights.

Despite the fact that the actual wording of the Constitution (besides the preamble) does not recognise the collective right to self-determination, nonetheless, with respect to the historical experience of the Slovak strife for self-determination and its practical implementation in the establishment of today's Slovak Republic, as well as with respect to international recognition of the right to self-determination, it certainly cannot be argued that the Slovak Republic does not recognise this right. It might be inferred that the collective right to self-determination was exercised when creating the Slovak Republic, and is currently in a state of deep sleep, with the possibility of use again in the future, for example in case of threats to national unity and sovereignty of the Slovak Republic.

3. THE INTERNATIONAL RECOGNITION OF THE RIGHT TO SELF-DETERMINATION

The right of a nation to self-determination is not, of course, a 'Slovak invention'. The origin of this right can be found in the context of the US Declaration of Independence (1776)[5] and in the French Declaration of the Rights of Man and of the Citizen (1789).[6] In practice, however, it was exercised in Europe only in the nineteenth century, especially in the context of unification efforts in Italy and Germany.[7] The first official and practical application of the right of a nation to self-determination in the form of creating a national state occurred in 1830, when

---

4 CIBULKA et al., *supra* note 2, p. 87.

5 In the very first sentence: 'it becomes necessary for one people to dissolve the political bands which have connected them with another, and to assume among the powers of the earth, the separate and equal station to which the Laws of Nature and of Nature's God entitle them'.

6 Article 3 reads: 'The principle of all sovereignty resides essentially in the nation. No body nor individual may exercise any authority which does not proceed directly from the nation'.

7 J. JANKUV, 'Právo národov na sebaurčenie v kontexte judikatúry Výboru pre ľudské práva' in *Právo národov na sebaurčenie v kontexte moderného medzinárodného práva*, Trnavská univerzita v Trnave, Trnava 2012, pp. 47–48. See also M. POTOČNÝ, 'Zásada sebeurčení národů' (1968) *Mezinárodní vztahy* 2, 23 ff.

the world powers — Britain, France and Russia — recognised Greece, fighting for liberation from Ottoman rule, as an independent state.[8] Subsequently, since the 1840s, the ideas of collective rights of nations were also present in the Habsburg Empire, but still mostly respecting the traditional historical borders.

The concept of the right to self-determination in the meaning of crossing traditional borders' *status quo*, i.e. the right to self-determination including the right to 'tear-apart', emerges specifically at the end of World War I. Vladimir Ilyich Ulyanov (Lenin) was devoted to this topic already in his works from the years 1915 and 1916, and subsequently he presented this right formally and in a legally binding way in the Russian Decree on Peace of 26 October 1917 (8 November 1917). This decree suggested in one of its provisions that nations forcibly restrained in another state should have the right to freely decide on the form of their national existence.[9] (It should be emphasised that this principally concerned violently oppressed nations, which will be of importance here.) At the same time, the US president, Woodrow Wilson expressly recognised the right to self-determination in his 14 points on 8 January 1918.[10] The Transatlantic world was thus inclined to the possibility of the collapse of centuries-old monarchies, according to the will of their nations, which actually took place in 1918, in the form of the collapse of the Austro-Hungarian monarchy.

Nevertheless, in the interwar period of the twentieth century, the right of nations to self-determination was not enshrined in any international legal instrument. The Covenant of the League of Nations did not expressly provide for this right.[11] A further milestone in establishing the right of nations to self-determination at the international level was only reached much later in the so-called Atlantic Charter, adopted in 1941, by US President Roosevelt and British Prime Minister Churchill, where both declared their intention to respect the right of nations to choose their form of government and to execute their sovereign rights, which had been forcibly restricted during World War II.[12]

The most important documents of international law which addressed the issue of the right of nations to self-determination subsequently became the UN Charter of 1945. Already in article 1(2) there was included among the objectives and aims of the UN the development of friendly relations among nations based on respect

---

8 D. LANTAJOVÁ, 'Otázka sukcesie vo vzťahu k uplatneniu práva národov na sebaurčenie' in *Právo národov na sebaurčenie v kontexte moderného medzinárodného práva*, Trnavská univerzita v Trnave, Trnava 2012, p. 90.

9 JANKUV, *supra* note 7, p. 48.

10 Article X: 'The peoples of Austria-Hungary, whose place among the nations we wish to see safeguarded and assured, should be accorded the freest opportunity to autonomous development'.

11 The International Court of Justice in the Namibia case in 1971 stated that the true meaning of Article 22 of the Covenant of the League of Nations, albeit not explicitly invoked, was the right to self-determination. JANKUV, *supra* note 7, p. 49.

12 *Ibid.*, p. 50.

for the principle of equal rights and self-determination of nations. From at least the time of the adoption of the UN Charter, the right of nations to self-determination has thus become an explicit integral part of international law, being one of its fundamental principles.[13] Some authors even consider this right to be *ius cogens*, although this is not universally accepted.[14]

Further development of this right and its expression in normative and policy texts took place again particularly at the United Nations level. The UN General Assembly Resolution of 16 December 1952 emphasised that the right to self-determination is a prerequisite for the full exercise of fundamental human rights. The right of nations to self-determination was then further enshrined in the International Covenant on Civil and Political Rights (1966),[15] and in the International Covenant on Economic, Social and Cultural Rights (1966). The concept of the right of nations to self-determination was also specifically emphasised in UN Resolution 1514 (XV) of 1970, where this right was extended to colonial and non-independent nations. UN Resolution 1541 (XV) in turn referred to the obligations of the mother country, in particular the obligation to ensure a full degree of autonomy for non-independent nations. Finally, UN General Assembly Resolution 2625 (XXV) of 1970 contains the Declaration of Principles of International Law concerning Friendly Relations and Cooperation among States in accordance with the UN Charter, whereby the Declaration stated as one of its principles the principle of equal rights and self-determination of nations. This may also serve as evidence of the general acceptance of the right to self-determination as a fundamental right.

According to the last-mentioned Resolution, a nation can exercise its right to self-determination by either creating a sovereign and independent state, or through free association with another sovereign state, or by integration with an independent state, or through any other political arrangement that a nation freely chooses. The Resolution prohibits any violent actions that would prevent a nation from enjoying the right to self-determination. It even enshrines the right of a nation to resist such violent action.[16] The right to self-determination is however not to be construed so as to justify or encourage conduct that would distort the territorial integrity or political unity of sovereign and independent states that behave in accordance with the principle of equal rights and self-determination of nations, and whose governments are representing all nations pertaining to their territory without distinction as to race, creed or colour.[17]

---

13 I. BROWNLIE, *Principles of Public International Law*, Clarendon Press, Oxford 1990, p. 596.

14 A. GIERTI, 'Štát in statu nascendi' in *Právo národov na sebaurčenie v kontexte moderného medzinárodného práva*, Trnavská univerzita v Trnave, Trnava 2012, p. 19.

15 International Covenant on Civil and Political Rights. Article 1(1): All peoples have the right of self-determination. By virtue of that right they freely determine their political status and freely pursue their economic, social and cultural development.

16 GIERTI, *supra* note 14, p. 22.

17 GIERTI, *supra* note 14, p. 24.

From today's point of view, somewhat anachronistically, it might be stated that the principles which apply currently to the right to self-determination of a nation (an obligation to respect the rights of minorities and nations in multinational states, otherwise they may exercise their right to self-determination), precisely fit the situation and the circumstances under which the Slovak nation in the nineteenth century demanded, and finally in 1918 exercised its right to self-determination. The historical experience of the Slovak nation in the period until 1918 was marked by a very minor and limited possibility to participate in the government, or to take part in the administration of the Kingdom of Hungary. This was the primary reason why the Slovaks demanded, first, the equality of nations within Hungary, and then, later, the right to self-determination notwithstanding the borders of Hungary.

4. THE EMERGENCE OF MODERN NATIONS IN THE EIGHTEENTH AND NINETEENTH CENTURIES

In order to further discuss the exercise of the right of the Slovak nation to self-determination in its historical context, a definition of the Slovak nation is necessary (which is a multidimensional issue, and for the purposes of this brief contribution has to be simplified[18]) as well as an explanation of the emergence of modern nations in Central Europe. In this respect, the Czech author Miroslav Hroch is an important expert on nationalism, national movements, and modern nations in Central Europe and his views will be referred to. According to Hroch, at the beginning of every national revival in Central Europe there was interest by a few individuals, usually intellectuals devoted to the study of the language, culture, and history of the repressed ethnicity. These individuals, however, remained without any significant social impact, and usually never attempted a patriotic revolution. Their interest was solely motivated by enlightened patriotism, i.e. feelings of a certain affection for the country. Only the subsequent phases of national revival were associated with patriotic movement and finally with mass national movements. Hroch has thus discerned three phases of national revival of small nations of Central Europe — scholarly interest, patriotic movement, and mass national movement.[19]

The Slovaks experienced the first phase of their national revival as early as the eighteenth century. From the early eighteenth century, new forms of patriotism began to be disseminated mainly in the territory of what is now Germany, which influenced the non-noble university students from Upper Hungary (today's

[18] On the notion of nation see, e.g. A. FINDOR, *Začiatky národných dejín*, Kalligram, Bratislava 2011, p. 22 ff.

[19] M. HROCH, *Evropská národní hnutí v 19. století*, Svoboda, Praha 1986, pp. 63–65, 359.

Slovakia).[20] In addition to 'love for the country', the core of this patriotism was mainly an attempt by commoners to reformulate the traditional concept of the noble nation so that this term was no longer reserved exclusively for the nobility, but would also encompass non-noble intellectuals. These were not, therefore, primarily the efforts of 'oppressed ethnicities', but rather the efforts of somewhat neglected social strata, non-noble intellectuals, attempting to strengthen their role in the contemporaneous concept of the 'nation'.

In this intellectual environment of former students returning from Germany, a new national concept was formed in Hungary, named as *Hungarus*. This was an alternative to the noble nation known as *Natio Hungarica*, which included only the noble population. The new idea of *Hungarus* nation was thus to also include commoners who rightly felt inferior as they did not fall within the noble *Natio Hungarica*. Similarly, under the influence of German scholarship, namely the Göttingen school of statistics, a categorization of populations of the Hungarian Kingdom was introduced — into the so-called major and minor nations of Hungary, whereby the criterion was the number of their nationals. In the case of the Hungarian Kingdom, the population was hence statistically classified into four major nations — Hungarians, respectively true Hungarians (*Magyaren / wahre Ungarn*), Slavs, Germans and Vlachs, and varying number of minor nations.

Slovaks identified themselves with the major nation of 'Slavs', which earned a generally positive assessment in the works of German philosophers (such as Johann Gottfried Herder, Johann Gottlieb Fichte, Friedrich Ludwig Jahn, Carl Wilhelm Friedrich Schlegel, Karl Gottlob Anton, etc.). These philosophical ideas were disseminated in Hungary mainly also due to the activity of students who studied in Germany. Under this philosophical and literary influence, intellectuals in Hungary began to assert the need for cultivation of the numerous national languages in the Hungarian Kingdom.[21] The language, culture and ethnic Slavic basis hence became the decisive factors in determining membership in the 'Slavic', and respectively later the 'Slovak' nation. This is where one must seek the origin of the concept of the ethnic nation, which in Central Europe (including in Slovakia) prevails until this day. This concept of an ethnic nation is to be distinguished from other concepts of nations prevalent in historically older states, which instead recognise the political concept of the nation, considering all inhabitants of a historical state to represent one single nation.[22]

---

[20] P. ŠOLTÉS, 'Národnopolitické koncepcie slovenských evanjelikov v prvej polovici "dlhého" 19. storočia' in D. KOVÁČ et al. (eds.), *Sondy do slovenských dejín v dlhom 19. storočí*, Historický ústav SAV, Bratislava 2013, p. 58.

[21] *Ibid.*, p. 62.

[22] M. GIBA, 'Ústavný a politický vývoj Slovenska' in Ľ. CIBULKA et al. (eds.), *Ústavné právo: Ústavný systém Slovenskej republiky*, Univerzita Komenského v Bratislave, Právnická fakulta, Bratislava 2014, p. 30.

A combination of the ethnic and political nation began to be preferred by Hungarian political (not necessarily intellectual) elites at the end of the eighteenth century. In fact, from the late eighteenth century two contradictory ideas crystallised in Hungary — that of state (political) nationalism predominantly preferred by the Hungarian (ethnically mostly Magyar) nobility, and ethnic nationalism of non-Magyar intellectual elites.[23] Initially, it seemed that the idea of a single Hungarian political nation would also be embraced by the Slovaks. Juraj Papánek (1738–1802) and Juraj Sklenár (1744–1790), for example, expressed their view that the Slovak 'ethnic group' should be considered equal with other Hungarian ethnicities within the *Natio Hungarica*, and that the idea of *Natio Hungarica* should therefore be supra-ethnic in the form of a political nation. Therefore, they never contended there was a separate *Natio Slovaca*, and never even mentioned the Slovak nation in today's sense of the word. Neither did Anton Bernolák (1762–1813), who was the first to codify the Slovak language, ever claim that there was a separate *Natio Slovaca*. He was loyal to the *Natio Hungarica*, and his country (*patria*), the Hungarian Kingdom.[24]

This approach had been sustainable while the Hungarian nationalism of the Hungarian political elites was primarily political, connected with the Hungarian state, and not with the Magyar language and ethnicity. However, the Hungarian parliament in 1792 approved the first of a series of legislative measures which attributed a privileged position to the Magyar language instead of the previously official language, Latin, at the expense of other languages of the Hungarian Kingdom. Political Hungarian nationalism thus began to be identified with ethnic Magyar nationalism. In 1844, the Hungarian parliament completely replaced Latin as the official language with the Magyar language, which was newly labelled as a 'national language', and the only language of state administration.[25]

Observing this trend, Slovaks, especially Ján Kollár (1793–1852) and his peers, within the second phase of national revival (phase of patriotic agitation), ceased to recognise the idea of a political *Natio Hungarica* and preferred instead the idea of a Czechoslovak ethnic tribe. This idea was already at that time widespread among Slovak protestant intellectuals due to their previous traditionally close religious and cultural relations with the Czechs (forming a part of the western half of the Habsburg Empire).

In the 1840s, Ľudovít Štúr (1815–1856) and his associates, acting within the Hoch's third phase — of mass national movement — took a further step; they ceased to perceive Slovaks as a part of the Hungarian political nation, but rather

---

[23] P. Brock, *Slovenské národné obrodenie 1787–1847: K vzniku modernej slovenskej identity*, Kalligram, Bratislava 2002, p. 14.

[24] *Ibid.*, pp. 26, 37.

[25] *Ibid.*, pp. 76–78.

as a part of the Czechoslovak cultural entity.[26] Štúr began to regard Slovaks as an independent nation with its own language and with the right to a certain political autonomy, the idea of which was publicly presented in 1848 for the first time.[27] In the Demands of the Slovak Nation of May 1848, there was formulated for the first time the idea of the *Slovak national personality*. At the same time, a specific constitutional concept of Slovak national equality within the proposed Hungarian Federation was raised,[28] leaning on various natural law and historical law arguments. Upon the rejection of these 1848 Demands, the Slovaks went even further — abandoning the platform of a Hungarian homeland completely, and turning to Vienna, requesting the creation of a Slovak state outside Hungary, potentially as a part of the federal Habsburg Empire (Austria).[29]

5. THE DEMANDS OF EQUAL RIGHTS BY THE SLOVAK NATION

In the situation of the progressive strengthening of the Magyar language at the expense of Latin and other languages in Hungary starting in 1792, the Hungarian Kingdom ceased to be a supra-ethnic Kingdom and the *Natio Hungarica* was gradually transformed into the *Natio Magyarica*. Under the changing situation, Slovaks responded in the1840s by formulating their national demands,[30] but in the period up to 1848 these were mainly aimed at linguistic and cultural rights and did not contain any constitutional program for solving the status of the Slovak nation.[31] Their goal was just to establish the balance between languages within Hungary.[32]

Constitutional requirements of Slovaks were only voiced in relation to the developments starting in 1848. The revolutionary year was marked in Hungary by the enactment of a series of laws which meant a break with the period of feudal law and feudal society and a transition to the modern (bourgeois) state. However, Slovaks and other non-Magyar nations of Hungary saw the absolute omission of national issues as a major problem of these revolutionary laws. The newly introduced individual political rights in fact favoured the Magyar ethnic

---

26 J. Chovanec and F. Červeňanský, *Názory Ľudovíta Štúra na štát a právo*, Procom, Bratislava 2005, p. 52.

27 Brock, *supra* note 23, p. 100.

28 Chovanec and Červeňanský, *supra* note 26, p. 119.

29 *Ibid.*, p. 122.

30 The texts of the documents are published in: *Dokumenty slovenskej národnej identity a štátnosti I, II*, Národné literárne centrum, Bratislava 1998. See also F. Bokes, *Dokumenty k slovenskému národnému hnutiu v rokoch 1848–1914*, SAV, Bratislava 1962 (vol. 1, 473 pp.), 1965 (vol. 2, 496 pp.).

31 On an exceptional private initiative in this respect see R. Jáger, 'Jozef Hložanský a jeho štátoprávna koncepcia Bieleho Uhorska', in *Stát a právo v letech 1848–1918 ve středoevropském kontextu*, Bratislavská vysoká škola práva, Bratislava 2007, pp. 115–121.

32 Brock, *supra* note 23, p. 85 ff.

group through the introduction of various conditions for taking part in the exercise of political rights (property, education, knowledge of Magyar language), to the disadvantage of non-Magyar nations, including Slovaks.

Still, under the revolutionary atmosphere, the non-Magyar nations of Hungary for the first time dared to formulate their own constitutional, i.e. other than simply cultural and language, requirements. They formulated these primarily as demands for collective as well as individual fundamental rights that would allow the nation (a collective) and its members (individually) free national development and a share in the administration of state power within Hungary. One might thereby infer that even the demands of individual rights were in fact primarily intended here to reach the equality of nations, i.e. the collective rights of a nation. We shall try to prove this hypothesis below, on the basis of selected documents, which we consider the most representative from among the numerous projects submitted by Slovak leaders between 1848 and 1918.

The first of the Slovak quasi-constitutional programmatic documents (it was not a legally binding text) was the previously mentioned *Demands of the Slovak Nation of 1848*. They were adopted by the Slovak representatives summoned by Ľ. Štúr on 10 May 1848,[33] and were presented in the name of the 'nation' — a special legal personality demanding its rights. The Demands confidently proclaimed the Slovak nation to be an 'antique nation in the country', by way of historical legal argumentation. On the basis of the natural law argument of equality of nations the authors sought to establish a common general representative body (parliament) for Hungary, as well as numerous 'special national parliaments'. This requirement thus included the demand to transform the Hungarian Kingdom made up of many 'Hungarian nations' into a federation. It seems the nations were hence seen as collective personalities and holders of collective rights — foremost the right to national equality as a possible embryonic element of the later internationally recognised right of a nation to self-determination.

Furthermore, the demanded list of individual rights of citizens, which would allow for the share of individual citizens in the administration of the country, also seems to have served here only as a guarantee for the *collective right of a nation to equality*. This is manifested in our view primarily by the demand of universal suffrage for men. Neither the Austrian, let alone Magyar political leadership had by then even come close to such an understanding of the idea of

[33] J. HUČKO, 'Žiadosti slovenského národa ako reakcia na neriešenie slovenskej otázky v marcových zákonoch roku 1848' (1994) 42 *Historický časopis* 4, 672–680; *150. výročie Žiadostí slovenského národa*, Matica slovenská, Martin 1998; M. OTČENÁŠ, 'Slovenský revolučný program na jar 1848. K významu Žjadostí slovenskjeho národu' in *Národnostná otázka v strednej Európe v rokoch 1848–1938*, Universum, Prešov 2005, pp. 45–51.

sovereignty of the people.[34] This requirement, if fulfilled, would certainly guarantee the possibility for the Slovak nation to take part in government and in the administration of the country, which otherwise suffrage reserved for approximately 6% of citizens (mainly well-off and ethnically non-Slovak) could never allow for. Suffrage as an *individual right should* thus in our opinion *be seen* in this context *as a means of ensuring collective national rights*, especially the right to equality of nations, and the share of the nations in state power, which is also currently required as a sign of fair treatment of a nation within any multinational state.

Effective implementation of the collective rights of the Slovak nation (its equality) can similarly be found hidden under other demands of individual rights and freedoms listed in the Demands of the Slovak Nation of 1848 — freedom of the press, of assembly and of association. In the case of these freedoms and rights there is again no doubt that these were primarily perceived as tools that would allow, in the event of full implementation, the fulfilment of the objective of free national development of the Slovak nation.

After the Demands were rejected by the Magyar elites, Slovaks and other Slavic nations living in the Habsburg monarchy attempted a closer mutual cooperation in order to reach enforcement of their very similar national demands. With this goal in mind, the so-called Slavic Congress was organised in Prague (in June 1848), where a policy of redesigning the Habsburg Empire into a federation with a predominance of Slavs was the prevailing stance. Austria (Austro-Slavia) as a constitutional federal monarchy, was to consist of eight member units, based on the eight major nations of the empire. One of the units was to be the 'Czechoslavs' (Czechs, Moravians, and Slovaks), leaning on the idea of a single Czechoslovak nation, which was, however, strictly refused by Štúr and his associates.

Although the Slavic Congress was terminated forcibly by the imperial army, Slovaks still believed that the Emperor in Vienna would provide Slovaks with greater concessions than the Magyar elites. With this in mind, the Slovaks created the Slovak National Council in Vienna in September 1848, as a revolutionary body of the Slovak nation, and on its behalf Ľ. Štúr declared Slovakia's independence from the Hungarian government on 19 September 1848.[35] Despite initial sympathy from the Emperor and his counsellors with respect to constitutional reform in Hungary, ultimately, conservative views and efforts to maintain the *status quo* in Hungary prevailed.

---

[34] J. BEŇA and T. GÁBRIŠ, *Dejiny práva na území Slovenska I*, VOPraFUK, Bratislava 2008, pp. 146–147.

[35] D. ŠKVARNA, 'Slovenská národná rada z roku 1848 a jej inšpiračná rola' in D. KOVÁČ et al. (eds.), *Sondy do slovenských dejín v dlhom 19. storočí*, Historický ústav SAV, Bratislava 2013, p. 94.

The Slovak politicians, however, again moved a bit further forward in the meantime — by the end of January 1849, they were promoting the radical idea of the Slovak crown country as an independent state separate from Hungary, but still falling within the broader framework of the crown countries of the Austrian Empire (Habsburg Empire). This demand was formulated in March 1849 in the so-called *March Petition of 1849*. Again, the argument of equality of nations (probably as being specific legal personalities) is being used here, as well as the argument that the goals of nations could not be met under the conditions current in Hungary. Therefore, calls for the allocation of a special status for Slovakia outside Hungary, where the equality of the Slovak nation (as a separate collective entity) could be realised, were voiced. However, this movement was not successful.

The subsequent project, constituting the pinnacle and the long-term policy agenda of Slovaks, was — due to the internal political situation in the Habsburg Empire — only formulated after several years, in 1861, and it is known as the *Memorandum of the Slovak Nation*.[36] The Memorandum requested the allocation to the Slovaks of an autonomous territory within Hungary, along with representation of Slovaks in the Hungarian Diet (parliament), including its upper chamber. The natural law argument of national equality was employed here again, but it is interesting to note that for the first time there was explicit use of the concept of '*national personality*', which should probably be understood as a collective legal entity, holder of collective national rights, particularly the right to equality. Historical reasoning was also used, explaining the roots of the right of nations to equality by claiming that original historical 'ethnicities' in Hungary turned into 'nations', and just as the ethnicities were once equal, the nations should be considered equal as well, particularly those which have had hitherto been oppressed.

The Magyar governmental officials nevertheless refused the demands voiced in the Memorandum, claiming that the Hungarian constitution with its civil liberties guaranteed freedom and equality to everybody notwithstanding ethnicity. Individual rights were hence seen by Magyar elites as guarantees to the rights of nations, without the need for any special rules on collective rights of nations. This would be perfectly acceptable, of course, provided the legislation allowed for effective implementation of the individual rights of members of the various nations and nationalities living in the Hungarian Kingdom. In fact, however, such effective implementation was not provided for under the contemporaneous legal situation. The Slovaks did not exert any impact on, or have a share in, the government or in the exercise of state power in Hungary, not even in the territory which they inhabited concentratedly. Not only could they not make use of the right to vote (due to strict conditions imposed on the right to vote), but also their individual language and cultural rights could not be fully utilised because of the

---

36 M. KOVAČKA (ed.), *Memorandum národa slovenského*, Matica slovenská, Martin 1991.

absence of legislation concerning the use of minority languages.[37] The status of nations (nationalities) and rules on use of their languages within Hungary were only regulated in detail by the Act of 1868. This Act voiced the principle of *only one political nation*, and the idea of *only individual rights*. Contrary to the demands of the Slovaks formulated in the individual documents described above, the Act did not recognise various Hungarian nations as separate legal entities, but only one Hungarian nation, which overlapped linguistically and ethnically with the Magyar nation. Other (ethnic) nations in Hungary were considered only nationalities. Languages of nationalities were allowed to be used — as an individual right of members of nationalities — before the courts and before the local authorities only on the condition that the use of the minority language was requested by one-fifth (20%) of citizens, i.e. of persons with voting rights. However, since the right to vote was subject to a relatively high financial status, this condition could rarely be met by inhabitants of Slovak nationality and consequently municipalities in which they lived, often employed the Magyar language instead of Slovak. The 1868 Act on nationalities thus did not provide Slovaks with any guarantees of their collective or individual national development. Such guarantees would have been granted only if the Slovak demands of general political rights for all men (gender equality was still unknown to Slovaks at this stage) irrespective of property had been realised. *Without the full implementation of individual political rights*, it remains true that *the status of non-Magyar nations did not meet the basic standards of fair national development and treatment in the multinational Kingdom*. Neither the non-Magyar nations collectively, nor their members individually, had any relevant share in the exercise of state power, or any real possibility to exercise their basic political, economic or cultural rights.

6. THE EXECUTION OF THE RIGHT TO SELF-DETERMINATION

The position of the Slovak nation in Hungary was characterised by a lack of guarantees for freedom of national development. The *collective rights of nations did not exist legally, and the individual rights of members of the nations were not effectively implemented* due to various legal obstacles. In such a situation, during the Great War (World War I), Slovak patriots did not hesitate to cooperate — especially in the circles of Czech and Slovak emigres abroad — with the Czech national movement which was experiencing similar national resistance against the (Austrian) attempts to restrict Czech national equality. Ever since early modern times, due to Protestant cooperation between Czechs and Slovaks, there existed the idea of common Czecho-Slovak national unity, which was also

[37] P. MOSNÝ and R. JÁGER, 'Dôsledky rakúsko-uhorského vyrovnania na slovenský národný pohyb' in *Rakousko-uherské vyrovnání1867 a jeho státoprávní důsledky v českých zemích a na Slovensku. Sborník příspěvků ke 140. výročí rakousko-uherského vyrovnání*, KEY Publishing, Ostrava 2007, p. 74.

manifested at the Slavic Congress in 1848. It is therefore not surprising that the Czech and Slovak politically active emigrants found common ground in efforts to improve the situation of their nations.

In the *Memorandum of the Slovak League of America of 10 September 1914*, however, emigrant Slovaks still strived for Slovak national independence without the Czech nation, requesting for '*the Slovak nation full autonomy and freedom of self-determination both political as well as in cultural and economic fields*'.[38] Fundamentally, they refused any form of political union with the Hungarians.[39] The innovation here is the use of the term '*self-determination*', which replaced the previously established concept of 'equality of nations of Hungary' invoked in the previous Slovak policy documents. Employment of this new legal concept is to be the subject of further research; however, it appears to be influenced by contemporaneous theories on the right of nations to self-determination, which ultimately came into real existence when Lenin and Wilson invoked the right in the years 1917/1918.

The Agreements of 1915, and 1918, concluded between the Czech and Slovak immigrants in the USA, subsequently abandoned the idea of an independent Slovak state and the idea of execution of the right to self-determination of the 'Slovak nation', and instead called for establishment of a common state of Czechs and Slovaks. The same objectives had also been followed since 1915 by the Czech and Slovak emigrants in Europe. In particular, the Czechoslovak National Council in Paris had played an essential role in the establishment of the new Czechoslovak state and respectively, in its international recognition. The Council was recognised by the Allied powers as the representative of an allied nation, and as the future government of Czechoslovakia — also due to the organization of allied military forces consisting of Czechs and Slovaks under the name 'Czechoslovak legions'.

The idea of a common state began to take priority also on domestic ground — the Czech deputies in the Vienna Parliament publicly called for federalization of the monarchy on 30 May 1917, whereby the Czech Lands and Slovakia would form a common state; a member of the Habsburg federation.

Subsequently, in the 14 points of President Wilson, declared in January 1918, the US president recognised openly the right of the peoples of Austria-Hungary to self-determination, with a free opportunity for the nations to decide on their future, regardless of the integrity of the empire. This was a clear confirmation of the international fundamental right of nations to self-determination. Following this evolution, the culmination of the Czechoslovak fight for independence

---

[38] BEŇA and GÁBRIŠ, *supra* note 34, p. 204.

[39] See excerpts from letters by Matúš Jankola on the Slovak issue and Slovako-Czech orientation (Bridgeport, Connecticut 11. And 15.12.1914). BEŇA and GÁBRIŠ, *supra* note 34, p. 204.

peaked in the Washington Declaration of Independence of the Czechoslovak Nation, also known as the *Washington Declaration of 18 October 1918*, declared in the situation of existing recognition of the Czechoslovak National Council as the government of the future Czechoslovak state by France (the French Governmental Declaration of 29 June 1918 recognised the right of the Czechoslovak nation to independence), as well as by the United Kingdom (in August 1918), and the USA (in September 1918). The Washington Declaration invoked the argument of historical natural law (which is a non-existent concept, combining the historical rights of nations to statehood, which Czechs could rely on, and a natural law right to self-determination, which Slovaks could rely on) and requested the joining of Czechs and Slovaks into a common state, the state of a 'Czechoslovak nation'.

In response to these documents, Slovak national representatives in the territory of Hungary could no longer passively await the creation of Czechoslovakia. First on 19 October 1918 Ferdinand Juriga, Member of the Hungarian Parliament of Slovak nationality proclaimed that the Slovak nation was invoking the right to self-determination, and a few days later, when Austria-Hungary surrendered, on 28 October 1918 the Czechoslovak state was spontaneously declared in Prague, supported additionally by Slovaks at their national meeting convened on 30 October 1918 in Martin. The *Martin Declaration* adopted in this meeting of Slovaks stated that the Slovak nation is a part of a historically and culturally single Czechoslovak nation and for this nation it demanded the *unrestricted right to self-determination based on complete independence*. The Slovaks thus proclaimed their will to become a part of the Czechoslovak State as a state of one nation — the Czechoslovak nation.

7. THE SLOVAK NATION IN CZECHOSLOVAKIA

Albeit that the Slovaks volunteered to be a part of the single Czechoslovak nation, and of a unitary Czechoslovak state, those convinced of a single ethnic Czechoslovak nation were in a minority among the Slovaks, and the connection with the Czechs was instead perceived as a strategic move for the period of time until the Slovak nation had developed capacity for the exercise of the right to its own self-determination. According to the representatives of these ideas, the basic problem in the constitutional law of Czechoslovakia was the absence of any constitutional regulation of the position of Slovakia. A number of proposals of legal solutions, pursuing the objective of the autonomous status of Slovakia, were thus prepared and submitted to the Czechoslovak parliament, but all of them were unsuccessful.[40] Only in the context of weakened Czechoslovakia after the surrender of the territory given away to Nazi Germany in 1938, did Slovak

[40] See J. Rychlík, *Češi a Slováci ve 20. století: Česko-slovenské vztahy 1914–1945*, Academic Electronic Press, Bratislava 1997, pp. 104–106, 121, 138.

autonomists manage to utilise the situation and autonomy was finally granted to Slovakia by the Constitutional Act of 1938.

Subsequently, on 14 March 1939, the autonomous Slovak parliament declared an independent Slovak state under direct pressure from Hitler, and Czechoslovakia dissipated. Strangely, however, the right to self-determination was not invoked in this process by Slovak politicians at all, since the Slovak political leaders understood what the actual circumstances of the establishment of the Slovak state were at this juncture.[41] The circumstances of its creation also affected the duration of this state. Its authoritarian political regime led to its rejection and the Slovak nation was subsequently willing to sacrifice 'its own' state in order to return to the democratic regime of Czechoslovakia in 1945.

The experience of Slovak statehood was, however, indelible. It was not possible to simply return to the pre-war Czechoslovakia. The new Czechoslovak government, formed in 1945, was forced to recognise the equality of Czechs and Slovaks as two brotherly nations. The Slovak nation enjoyed from that time a kind of autonomy within Czechoslovakia — albeit distorted by the political centralism of the Communist Party of Czechoslovakia, which ruled Czechoslovakia from 1948 to 1989.[42]

After a breaking-point in the democratization process in Czechoslovakia, brought about by the invasion of Soviet troops in 1968, the Communist Party decided to calm down the situation by transforming Czechoslovakia from a unitary state into a federation. According to the preamble to the Act on *Czechoslovak Federation*, this evolution was based on an agreement between the Slovak and the Czech nations, as an agreement of *two constitutional legal personalities, leaning on the collective right of nations to self-determination.* The Slovak nation was thus attributed a status of a national republic within the federation.

It was only after the fall of Communist Party dominance in 1989, that the crisis of the relationship between the two nations in the federation was revealed. Division of competences within the federation, the pursuit of visibility by Slovaks in international fora, as well as disputes concerning the official name of the state led to the weakening of the bond between the two nations. In this atmosphere, on 17 July 1992, the Slovak Republic approved the *Declaration of Sovereignty of the Slovak Republic. It proclaimed the inherent right to self-*

---

41 V. BYSTRICKÝ and T. GÁBRIŠ, 'Kontinuita a diskontinuita v dejinách: Slovenská republika 1939 a Slovenská republika 1993' in M. LONDÁK and S. MICHÁLEK (eds.), *20 rokov samostatnej Slovenskej republiky: Jedinečnosť a diskontinuita historického vývoja*, VEDA, Bratislava 2013, p. 49.

42 J. BEŇA, *Vývoj slovenského právneho poriadku*, Univerzita Mateja Bela, Banská Bystrica 2001, pp. 343–346, 353.

determination of the Slovak nation.[43] From then, the route to the division of Czechoslovakia was direct. On 1 September 1992 the Slovak Constitution was adopted. On 25 November 1992, at the federal level, an agreement between political leaders of Czechs and Slovaks on the adoption of the Act on the dissolution of the Czech and Slovak Federal Republic was reached, according to which '*upon the expiry of 31 December 1992, the Czech and Slovak Federal Republic shall cease to exist. Successor states of the Czech and Slovak Federal Republic shall be the Czech Republic and the Slovak Republic*'. The *expiry of 31 December 1992 hence witnessed the final execution of the right of the Slovak nation to self-determination.*

8. CONCLUDING REMARKS

One can but agree with a partially modified argument by Lehners that fundamental rights '*are the result of a learning process and they respond to experiences of injustice and suffering*'.[44] The unequal status of the Slovak nation within the Kingdom of Hungary, together with the absence of guarantees of individual rights allowing for a share in state power, had been the reason why from the mid-nineteenth century the representatives of the Slovak nation supported the idea of collective national rights, specifically the right to equality of nations in Hungary, and actively fought for both collective and individual rights (the latter seen mainly as tools to enforce collective rights). During World War I, the Slovak *demands for the collective right to equality were transformed into the modern right of a nation to self-determination*, which represents a different quality of the idea of equality of nations — it encompasses even the possibility of changing the international *status quo,* by way of a change in state borders.

Hence, when the concept of the right to self-determination gained general international recognition in 1917/1918, the Slovaks used this collective right in conjunction with the Czechs and formed a unitary Czechoslovak Republic of a single Czechoslovak nation. This conjunction, however, took place mostly due to the weakness of the Slovak nation, which was still in 1918 at a developmental stage that did not allow Slovaks to create their own statehood. Their right to self-determination was fully executed (apart from a short adventure under pressure from Hitler in 1939–1945) only in 1993, with the emergence of today's Slovak Republic.

---

43 See E. Stein, *Česko-Slovensko: konflikt roztržka rozpad*, Academia, Praha 2000, pp. 164, 167, 179, 211–212.

44 J-P. Lehners, 'Pleading for a New History of Human Rights' in A. Mihr and M. Gibney (eds.), *The SAGE Handbook of Human Rights,* SAGE Publications, London 2014, p. 34.

To conclude, the history of the Slovak nation is definitely not the cause, nor the author, but nevertheless reflects the evolution of the right of a nation to equality, and subsequently of the right of a nation to self-determination. After the recognition of this fundamental right by representatives of Bolshevik Russia and by the President of the USA in 1917/1918, there was a unique situation favourable to a substantial transformation of the European continent based on this right that Slovaks and Czechs have used. The achieved *status quo* is, however, not definite. The collective right to self-determination as a fundamental right always allows for subsequent changes in the internal constitutional arrangements of states, as well as allowing for international changes in state borders. The *conditions for* such changes in terms of *legality are currently twofold* — the *oppression of a nation* in the previous constitutional arrangement, or a *mutual agreement* by nations sharing a common statehood. The Slovak nation as a collective entity making use of the right to self-determination went through both of these experiences during the twentieth century.

25. LATVIA: SECOND PART OF THE CONSTITUTION AS A PROJECT FOR NEXT GENERATIONS

Artūrs KUČS
Jānis PLEPS

1. INTRODUCTION

The Republic of Latvia, which proclaimed independence on 18 November 1918, is still a young state with a relatively short history of national statehood and constitutional traditions. However, the historical development of Latvian statehood makes its constitutional system unique and interesting in a European context.

The foundation of Latvia's constitutional system is formed by the Constitution of the Republic of Latvia of 15 February 1922 (hereinafter the Constitution or the *Satversme*).[1] Currently the *Satversme* can be considered to be one of the oldest constitutions in force in Europe. The fact that the Republic of Latvia after restoration of independence at the beginning of the 1990s did not draft a new constitution, but renewed the *Satversme*, is unique.[2] This decision meant that a constitution, the operation and application of which had been stayed more than 50 years previously, was returned into force. No other state has conducted a constitutional experiment of this kind.

In this context it is quite strange that only on 15 October 1998, did the 6th *Saeima* (Parliament) of the Republic of Latvia adopt the amendments in the Constitution of the Republic of Latvia, which supplemented the Constitution with a new, chapter 8, entitled 'Fundamental Human Rights'.[3]

The aim of this discussion is to analyse the first expanded catalogue of fundamental rights — the second part of the Constitution — in the constitutional

---

1 Latvijas Republikas Satversme. *Valdības Vēstnesis*, 30.06.1922., Nr. 141. The text of the Constitution of the Republic of Latvia in English available at <http://saeima.lv/en/legislation/constitution>.

2 C. TAUBE, *Constitutionalism in Estonia, Latvia and Lithuania. A study in comparative constitutional law*, Iustus Förlag, Upsala 2001, pp. 46–55.

3 Grozījumi Latvijas Republikas Satversmē. *Latvijas Vēstnesis*, 23.10.1998., Nr. 308/312.

system of Latvian Republic. The chapter begins with a brief characterisation of provisional constitutions that contained some norms of fundamental rights and continues with an analysis of the content of the second part of the Constitution and the Latvian Constitutional Assembly debate on this project.

2. PROVISIONAL REGULATION OF FUNDAMENTAL RIGHTS

2.1. FIRST PROVISIONAL CONSTITUTION (1918–1920)

On 17 November 1918, the representatives of Latvian political parties, when deciding on the establishment of the state, announced themselves to be the People's Council of Latvia, which until the convening of the Constitutional Assembly possessed sovereign state power. The People's Council also adopted the Political Platform of the Latvian National Council.[4] This Political Platform was intended to establish the core principles of the provisional constitution and identify the main political direction of the provisional government. The Political Platform of the People's Council consists of a partial regulation of the basic issues of a political system, while paying extensive attention to the political objectives of the interim government before the election of the Constitutional Assembly.

The importance of fundamental rights is illustrated by the fact that out of eight sections of the declaration two were devoted to fundamental rights. Section IV[5] of the Political Platform set forth the rights of national minorities, while Section V[6] prescribed civic freedoms. When commenting on the Political Platform, professor Kārlis Dišlers has indicated in this respect the following: 'At first, the rights of the national minorities to participate in the People's Council and the provisional government have been recognised — as can be seen, with the intention to involve also the national minorities already from the very beginning in the very difficult and important work of organising the state. The national minorities are granted recognised political rights (general, equal, direct, proportional elections by secret ballot) and they are promised assurance of their

---

4 Latvijas Tautas padomes politiskā platforma. *Pagaidu Valdības Vēstnesis*, 14.12.1918, Nr. 1.

5 IV. Rights of national minorities
1) National minorities delegate their representatives in the Constitutional Assembly and legislative institutions on the basis of proportional election rights (see paragraph 2 of section I).
2) National minorities, which are included in the Latvian National Council, participate in the Provisional Government on the grounds of the paragraph 3 of section III.
3) The cultural and national rights of the national groups are to be ensured in the fundamental laws.'

6 V. Civic Rights
1) The freedoms of press, speech, meeting, and assembling are to be ensured with the regulations of the Provisional Government.
2) Amnesty in all cases excluding crime.
3) Possibility for the citizens of the Republic of Latvia to return to homeland.'

cultural and national interests in the fundamental laws. The latter promise, of course, could not bind the Constitutional Assembly, and in the adopted Constitution, we cannot find any guarantees of rights for the national minorities, which, naturally, does not imply that these rights are denied or restricted. The fifth section contains a promise to ensure freedom of speech, meetings, and assembly subject to statutory conditions'.[7]

Parallel to the norms included in the provisional constitution regarding fundamental rights, the founders of the Latvian state pronounced on the subject also in the 18 November 1918 Proclamation Act of the Republic of Latvia. The Prime Minister Kārlis Ulmanis concluded his speech with the following utterance: 'All citizens, without distinguishing between nationality, are invited to assist, because the rights of all nationalities in Latvia will be ensured. It will be a country of democratic justice, where there can be no place for suppression or injustice'.[8] It has been recognised in the modern times that the speech of the Prime Minister portrays the political choice of the provisional government — to create Latvia as a democratic, socially oriented country, where justice would prevail.[9] Such a country, without a doubt, recognises and ensures both the rights of national minorities and the fundamental rights of the person. As has been written by professor Aivars Endziņš, the values of a democratic state and the rule of law were written in the red-white-and-red flag of Latvia that November of the year 1918. 'Also in those times, the idea of rule of law was a self-evident and necessary element in the dream about statehood of Latvia'.[10]

2.2. SECOND PROVISIONAL CONSTITUTION (1920–1922)

The Latvian Constitutional Assembly adopted a second provisional constitution: the 27 May 1920 Declaration on the State of Latvia[11] and the 1 June 1920 Provisional Regulations on the Latvian State System.[12]

The task of the Provisional Regulations, as implied by the name of the deed itself, was regulation of the provisional administration.[13] It was not intended to maintain these regulations as effective for an extended period of time.

---

7 K. DIŠLERS, 'Latvijas Republikas Satversmes attīstība' in M. ĀRONS (ed.), *Latvija desmit gados. Latvijas valsts nodibināšanas un viņas pirmo 10 gadu darbības vēsture*, Jubilejas komisijas izdevums, Rīga 1928, 73–74.

8 K. ULMANIS, 'Ministru prezidenta runa' in *Latvijas valsts pasludināšana 18. novembrī 1918. g. Rakstu vainags H. J. sakopots*, Apgādniecība 'Astra', Rīga 1918, 19..

9 J. STRADIŅŠ, '18. novembra Ulmanis (Latvijas Republikas pirmais Ministru prezidents)' in *Kārlim Ulmanim 125*, Latvijas Vēstures institūta apgāds, Rīga 2003, 25.

10 A. ENDZIŅŠ, 'Tiesu sistēmas un politikas saskarsme un dinamika', *Jurista Vārds*, 2002, Nr. 9 (242).

11 Deklarācija par Latvijas valsti. *Likumu un valdības rīkojumu krājums*, 31.08.1920, Nr. 4.

12 Latvijas valsts iekārtas pagaidu noteikumi. *Likumu un valdības rīkojumu krājums*, 31.08.1920, Nr. 4.

The Provisional Regulations on the Latvian State System consisted of 12 articles, where in a concise form the tasks and the term of office of the Latvian Constitutional Assembly were stipulated, and the reciprocal relations of the state authorities were regulated. By comparison with the Political Platform of the People's Council, the Regulation was much more specifically elaborated and reminiscent of a characteristic constitutional text.

Within the transitional regulations of the Latvian political system, article 9[14] is devoted to fundamental rights. Professor Kārlis Dišlers when commenting on this norm, has succinctly indicated: 'In this concise deed, we find the guarantee of the most recognisable civic freedoms'.[15] He has also written: 'Article 9 of the transitional regulations is of declarative character: it declares the so-called civic freedoms: immunity of a person, residence, and correspondence, freedom of press, speech, cognition, strikes, meetings, and assembly, which are to be ensured with relevant legislation. Following the example of the "Human and civic rights declaration" of the Great Revolution of France, similar declarative articles or even whole sections of declarative character can be found in nearly all constitutions. In transitional times, when the said civic freedoms still have not been ensured through relevant legislation, the practical importance of such declarative articles is insignificant, however the key value thereof is still preserved in the fact that the principles established therein are binding for the legislator. Likewise, the permanent significance of article 9 of the Provisional constitution of Latvia, implying that it is binding for the successive legislators, whose responsibility will be "to set forth and ensure" the said civic freedoms, but who under no circumstances will be allowed to infringe or restrict any of the principles of the civic freedoms as declared by the Constitutional Assembly'.[16]

3. SECOND PART OF THE CONSTITUTION

3.1. CONTENT OF THE FUNDAMENTAL RIGHTS PART OF THE CONSTITUTION AND DEBATES WITHIN THE CONSTITUTIONAL ASSEMBLY

The main purpose of the Latvian Constitutional Assembly was to draft the Constitution of the Republic of Latvia. It was intended that the constitution would have two parts. The first part of the Constitution defined the new state as a parliamentary republic, it prescribed the powers of the President, the legislature,

13 K. DIŠLERS, 'Latvijas pagaidu konstitūcija. Vispārīgas piezīmes' *Tieslietu Ministrijas Vēstnesis*, 1920, No.2/3, 52.

14 '9. In Latvia, there is the immunity of a persona and residence, freedom of press, speech, cognition, strike, meeting, and assembling, immunity of correspondence, which are to be ensured and established with the relevant laws.'

15 DIŠLERS, *supra* note 7, 74.

16 DIŠLERS, *supra* note 13, 51.

the executive and the courts as well as containing rules about the election of Parliament. The second part of the constitution was intended to formulate citizen's rights and obligations. As one of the deputies in charge of the drafting this part of the constitution, A. Kuršinskis stated in the debates of assembly, this part of the constitution would regulate the relations between the citizen and the state. He further added that it would fulfil the democratic content of the first part of *Satversme* because citizens deprived of rights would not be able to develop and maintain the democratic state institutions which the first part of the *Satversme* establishes.[17]

The general climate of 'constitutional romanticism'[18] prevailing after World War I, the foundation of the League of Nations and the fact that fundamental rights were embedded in the constitutions of many European states influenced both the attitude of the deputies towards the necessity to include a fundamental rights chapter in the constitution of the newly established state and the debates on its content. The idea that fundamental rights should be inserted in the constitution seemed natural in the context of developments at the international level and in other states. Debates at the Constitutional Assembly demonstrate that the majority of the deputies of the assembly were in favour of including the fundamental rights chapter in the constitution. For instance on 7 February 1922 when the Constitutional Assembly voted on the first draft of the fundamental rights chapter it was supported unanimously by the deputies.[19]

However, opinions about the content and importance of this part of the *Satversme* differed markedly among various political groups and deputies.

Many of the members of the assembly, such as for instance A. Bergs and A. Petrevics, criticised the draft text of this part of the *Satversme* as too abstract. They emphasised that the *Satversme* only declares but does not grant substantial rights to citizens and allows the parliament (the *Saeima*) and in certain conditions also the government to specify and limit most of the fundamental rights by adopting subsequent laws.[20] A. Bergs also referred to other states like the United Kingdom and France where fundamental rights are not granted in the constitution but, despite this, citizens are free in these states. The representative of the social democrats F. Cielēns and the above-mentioned A. Kuršinskis partly agreed to claims to formulate the rights in the constitution more concretely. However, they both also stressed the ideological and symbolic role of this part of the *Satversme*. F. Cielēns emphasised that there is no democratic culture or tradition in a new republic compared to western European democracies, where

---

17 Ā. ŠILDE, *Latvijas vēsture (1914–1940)*, Daugava, Stokholma 1976, 363

18 J. PLEPS, 'Pamattiesību katalogs starpkaru periodā' (2008) *Jurista Vārds* Nr. 48 (543).

19 ŠILDE, *supra* note 17, 363.

20 Latvijas Satversmes sapulces V sesijas 1. sēdes 1922. gada 17. janvāra stenogramma, in *Latvijas Satversmes sapulces stenogrammas*, Satversmes sapulces izdevums, Rīga 1922.

citizens would organise themselves and protect their rights and freedoms despite the absence of constitutional guarantees. He considered the constitutional protection of citizen's rights and obligations to be an important tool to eliminate the psychological and political remains of the Czarist Russia's monarchy.[21]

Similarly, A. Kuršinskis agreed that this was a crucial period in the development of the state and also felt that so-called declaratory norms have their importance in the political development of the state and a role in citizens' education about and awareness of their rights. Lastly, F. Trasūns, representing Latgale's Christian Peasant's Union, criticised the second part of the *Satversme* for formulating many rights, but not establishing the obligations of citizens. He insisted on the need to protect the young generation against harmful information and to strengthen citizen's obligations versus the state.[22]

The content of which fundamental rights should be granted was largely influenced by the catalogue in the 1919 Weimar Constitution (*Weimarer Verfassung*)[23] and the 1789 French Declaration of the Rights of Man and of the Citizen.[24] The elements of direct democracy and extensive powers of citizens to organise referenda on many issues were inspired by the constitution of Switzerland. During the debates members of the assembly referred also to the Magna Carta of 1215, the British Bill of Rights of 1689 and the Bill of Rights of the United States. Professor Kārlis Dišlers clearly indicates the Weimar Constitution as the source of inspiration for the second part of the Constitution.[25] Fēlikss Cielēns, who in general adamantly refused the idea that the Constitution of Latvia should be 'copied' from the Weimar Constitution,[26] nonetheless with respect to the second part of Constitution clearly indicated that it 'was elaborated by the commission under influence of the German constitution',[27] and the draft 'was basically formed of the relevant parts of the Weimar Constitution'.[28]

The draft fundamental rights part of the *Satversme* guaranteed major civil and political rights and freedoms: freedom of speech and religion, freedom of assembly and association, inviolability of the home and of correspondence. The *Satversme* also prescribed certain social and economic rights: the right to property, the right to strike, free access to compulsory education until the age of 18 and the provision to low income families of support as regards children's

---

21 Latvijas Satversmes sapulces V sesijas 1. sēdes 1922. gada 17. janvāra stenogramma, in *Latvijas Satversmes sapulces stenogrammas*, Satversmes sapulces izdevums, Rīga 1922.

22 *Ibid.*

23 ŠILDE, *supra* note 17, 363.

24 Latvijas Satversmes sapulces V sesijas 1. sēdes 1922. gada 17. janvāra stenogramma, in *Latvijas Satversmes sapulces stenogrammas*, Satversmes sapulces izdevums, Rīga 1922.

25 K. DIŠLERS, *Demokrātiskas valsts iekārtas pamati*, A. Gulbis, Rīga 1931, 179.

26 F. CIELĒNS, *Laikmetu maiņā. Atmiņas un atziņas*, 3.grāmata, Apgāds Memento, Stokholma 1998, 113.

27 *Ibid.*

28 *Ibid*, 107.

dress, food and educational equipment. As far as cultural rights are concerned access to art and science were guaranteed. While the Latvian language was proclaimed as the official state language, the rights of national minorities and free use of minority languages were recognised. Furthermore, in line with the policy of the new republic to bring to an end the privileges which Baltic Germans and nobility had enjoyed for centuries, the *Satversme* stated that all ranks and titles should be abolished.

The draft constitution also included a number of rights, which at the beginning of the twentieth century were recognised in only a few European democracies: for instance equality between men and women, including equality in marriage, equal rights to vote and stand for elections. The constitution prohibited the death penalty, except in emergency and war situations when such penalty could be applied by martial courts. In order to fight corruption among civil servants, the constitution also directly established the responsibility of civil servants for illegal acts. The second part of the constitution also dealt with social matters, prescribing that 'a strike is a legal means for economic battle' and 'the physical and mental work of Latvian citizens and their production are under the protection of the state'.

Serious debates within the Constitutional Assembly took place around the principle of separation of church and state and its insertion in the text of the *Satversme*. The deputies from the eastern part of Latvia, Latgale, the region which in the seventeenth century was under Polish-Lithuanian rule, and is predominantly inhabited by members of the Catholic Church, raised objections against this principle. However, the majority of deputies decided to declare that there is no state church in Latvia and to include the principle of separation of church and state in the final draft of the fundamental rights part of the *Satversme*. Furthermore, as in the Constitutions of Switzerland, Norway, the Republic of Estonia and other European states, the draft of the fundamental rights section specifically included a ban on another religious congregation — the Jesuits. However, after debates the members of the assembly decided to remove this article from the *Satversme*. Deputies from Latgale's Christian Peasant's Union and Latgale's People Party, including F. Trasūns and F. Kemps, supported the idea that Jesuits should be allowed to perform their religious services and that there was no evidence that they would act against the Latvian state. They stressed the historic contribution of Jesuits to the development of Catholic churches and the education of priests in Latgale.[29] Other deputies, like J. Goldmanis representing the Latvian Peasants Party, considered it unnecessary specifically to single out Jesuits in the *Satversme*. They preferred the option to

29 Latvijas Satversmes sapulces V sesijas 1. sēdes 1922. gada 17. janvāra stenogramma, in *Latvijas Satversmes sapulces stenogrammas*, Satversmes sapulces izdevums, Rīga 1922.

ban by ordinary law the activities of Jesuits and any other group if they act against the interests of the state.[30]

Besides the regulation of fundamental rights in the draft version, it was planned to establish a prohibition against the citizens of Latvia receiving awards from other countries, as well as a prohibition against the state of Latvia granting awards. The draft also included a condition that the mail service and telegraph were subject to state monopoly, as well as the principle that the state owned the railroads, waterways, and other transportation routes of general importance.

Despite the rather progressive catalogue of fundamental rights and general support of the members of the Constitutional Assembly to include a fundamental rights section in the constitution, the final text of the fundamental rights chapter failed to be adopted in the assembly. The principal reason for this lies in the disagreements between various political groups about the content of the final text of the chapter. The social democrats argued for stronger guarantees for employee protection and recognition of the right to strike not only in cases of protest against economic difficulties but also as a form of political protest. Similarly, the deputies from the eastern part of Latvia (the Latgale region) insisted on the need to refer in the text to the autonomy of Latgale and to abandon the principle of separation between the church and state. These disputes finally led to a negative vote on the inclusion of fundamental rights in the *Satversme*. As the deputies from Latgale and the social democrats[31] abstained in the vote as a protest against non-inclusion of their claims in the final text of the constitution, there were not enough votes to approve the second part of the *Satversme*: 62 deputies voted in favour of the final draft of the fundamental rights chapter, six voted against and 62 abstained.

3.2. IMPLICATIONS OF NON-INCLUSION OF FUNDAMENTAL RIGHTS IN THE CONSTITUTION FOR THE PROTECTION OF FUNDAMENTAL RIGHTS

The non-inclusion of a fundamental rights chapter was certainly unfortunate, because apart from its legal importance, this part of the constitution would have had symbolic meaning and would have raised awareness of citizens about their rights and freedoms. According to the famous Latvian historian Ādolfs Šilde, rejection of the fundamental regulations regarding civic rights and freedoms was a significant loss in the constitutional operation of the Constitutional Assembly. Even though these same rights later in some laws were assured for Latvian citizens, yet establishment of the said rights in the fundamental law would have

30 Latvijas Satversmes sapulces V sesijas 1. sēdes 1922. gada 17. janvāra stenogramma, in *Latvijas Satversmes sapulces stenogrammas*, Satversmes sapulces izdevums, Rīga 1922.

31 V. Cielava, 'Latvijas Satversme: vēsture un mūsdienas' *Cīņa*, 01.04.1989.; V. Blūzma, 'Tiesiskas valsts pirmsākumi Latvijā' (1999) *Latvijas Vēsture* Nr. 1, 47.

had an important significance in establishing principles of a democratic mode of social life in the nation. 'With the adoption of part II of the Constitution, a favour would have been done for the legal structure of Latvia both formally judicially and psychologically/ideologically. The Latvian awareness of rights would have had gained useful impulses'.[32]

The supreme court of Latvia — the Senate of Latvia — has however applied article 9 of the Provisional Regulations on the Latvian State System as a valid legal norm. The Senate of Latvia, in a case on registration of trade unions,[33] began the list of valid legal norms with a norm of constitutional rank — article 9 of the Provisional Regulations on the Latvian State System which provided for freedom of association. The Senate also indicated that 'the slogan of a deductive nature' included in article 9 of the Provisional Rules 'can only be interpreted in the sense that manifestation of this freedom cannot come into conflict with existing laws'.[34]

This formal gap in the constitution was partly filled by separate laws on political parties, minority rights, press freedom and regulations concerning the implementation of other fundamental rights. There were debates and repeated attempts to adopt the fundamental rights chapter in subsequent years. However, the economic crisis at the end of the 1920s gradually led to social unrest and a transition from democracy to authoritarian regimes in almost the whole of Central and Eastern Europe. The Republic of Latvia was no exception. On 15 May 1934 following the transition to authoritarianism in other Baltic States, the head of government Kārlis Ulmanis dismissed the parliament and proclaimed himself the head of state. While the coup did not provoke any violent clashes, this change of political system was accompanied by restrictions on fundamental rights, most notably the censoring of free speech, banning of political parties, cancellation of elections and restriction of the rights of minorities.[35] The inclusion of fundamental rights in the Constitution and their application in practice became even more problematic and even impossible after the occupation of the Republic of Latvia by the Soviet Union on 17 June 1940. Therefore, fundamental rights found their way in the Constitution only after the restoration of independence in Latvia.

---

32 ŠILDE, *supra* note 17, 363.

33 Judgment No. 64, 20 November 1929

34 *Latvijas Senāta spriedumi (1918–1940). 3. sējums. Senāta Administratīvā departamenta spriedumi (1926–1930)*, Latvijas Republikas Augstākā tiesa, Senatora Augusta Lēbera fonds, Rīga 1997, 1200.

35 *Ibid.*, 589–593.

3.3. THE EVOLUTION OF THE FUNDAMENTAL RIGHTS CHAPTER OF THE CONSTITUTION AFTER THE RESTORATION OF INDEPENDENCE

The human rights of free speech, free press and freedom of assembly played a crucial role at the end of the 1980s in the transformation from the authoritarian Soviet system to democracy. This period coincided with the attempts to re-establish the independence of the Republic of Latvia and the struggle against the authoritarian regime, migration and suppression of the Latvian language. Even prior to the restoration of independence the first democratically elected parliament adhered to core human rights documents as a way to illustrate the democratic nature of the new political regime and acquire international recognition for the re-established Republic of Latvia. This is evidenced by the fact that on 4 May 1990 when the Supreme Soviet of the Latvia SSR adopted a *Declaration of the Renewal of the Independence of the Republic of Latvia* it also issued a *Declaration on the Accession of the Republic of Latvia to International Instruments Relating to Human Rights.*[36] According to this document the Republic of Latvia ascribed to 51 UN and OSCE human rights instruments. Moreover, direct reference to the state's obligation to guarantee fundamental rights to all citizens and permanent residents of Latvia is found in the *Declaration of the Renewal of the Independence of the Republic of Latvia.* According to article 8 of the Declaration, the Supreme Soviet of the Latvia SSR decided: 'To guarantee citizens of the Republic of Latvia and those of other states permanently residing in Latvia social, economic and cultural rights, as well as those political rights and freedoms which comply with the universally recognised international human rights instruments. To apply these rights in full extent also to those citizens of the USSR who express the desire to continue residing in the territory of Latvia without accepting its citizenship'.[37]

Contrary to the neighbouring Baltic States, Estonia and Lithuania, the Latvian parliament did not adopt a new constitution, but restored the pre-war Constitution of the Republic of Latvia, which did not contain a fundamental rights chapter. Therefore, initially, fundamental rights were granted in the constitutional law 'The Rights and Obligations of a Citizen and a Person', which was adopted on 10 December 1991. According to article 1 of the constitutional law: 'A person, his/her existence, liberty, honour and rights are the highest

---

[36] Par Latvijas Republikas pievienošanos starptautisko tiesību dokumentiem cilvēktiesību jautājumos, *Latvijas Republikas Augstākās Padomes un Valdības Ziņotājs*, 17.05.1990., Nr. 20. The text of the Declaration in English available at <http://www.humanrights.lv/doc/latlik/dokdekl.htm>.

[37] Par Latvijas Republikas Neatkarības atjaunošanu, *Latvijas Republikas Augstākās Padomes un Valdības Ziņotājs*, 17.05.1990, Nr.,20. The text of the Declaration in English available at <http://www.humanrights.lv/doc/latlik/neatkdek.htm>.

fundamental values of the State of Latvia'.[38] This law guaranteed core civil and political as well as social and economic rights. It is interesting to note that apart from rights the law also emphasised the obligations of each citizen. For instance it referred to such obligations of citizens as to be loyal to and defend the independence and democratic parliamentary system of the state, to pay taxes and to protect the environment.[39] This law played the central role in safeguarding human rights protection at national level until the inclusion of fundamental rights in the Constitution of the Republic of Latvia in 1998. Among other important human rights laws the Law on Press, adopted in 1990, and the Law on Ethnic Minorities, adopted in 1991, are worth mentioning.

However, internal discussions and international recommendations gradually led to the incorporation of fundamental rights in the Constitution itself. On 15 November 1998 chapter 8 or the so-called Fundamental Rights Chapter was adopted and integrated within the pre-war constitution of the Republic of Latvia. The chapter was inspired both by the pre-war draft of the second part of the Constitution and by the development of fundamental rights at the universal and regional level during the 50 years of Soviet occupation. This is evidenced by the first clause of the fundamental rights chapter, article 89 of the Constitution, which lays down what is known as the principle of openness of the Constitution to international human rights law. It states: 'The State shall recognise and protect fundamental human rights in accordance with this Constitution, laws and international agreements binding upon Latvia'.[40] The Constitutional Court of the Republic of Latvia, which has extensively referred to international human rights sources to interpret the scope of the fundamental rights protected by the constitution,[41] in its case-law has emphasised that: 'In cases, where there is doubt about the contents of the norms of human rights included in the *Satversme*, they should be interpreted as far as possible in compliance with the practice of application of international norms of human rights'.[42] The words 'as far as possible' mean that in situations where the Constitution guarantees higher protection of fundamental rights than international human rights treaties, the constitutional guarantees should prevail.

The fundamental rights chapter of the Constitution, similarly to the pre-war draft, contains most civil and political rights as well as social and economic rights. It is

---

[38] Konstitucionālais likums 'Cilvēka un pilsoņa tiesības un pienākumi', *Latvijas Republikas Augstākās padomes un valdības ziņotājs*, 30.01.1992, Nr. 4.

[39] *Ibid.*

[40] Latvijas Republikas Satversme. *Valdības Vēstnesis*, 30.06.1922., Nr. 141. The text of the Constitution of the Republic of Latvia in English available at <http://saeima.lv/en/legislation/constitution>.

[41] J. PLEPS, *Satversmes iztulkošana*, Latvijas Vēstnesis, Rīga 2012, 236–247.

[42] The judgment of the Constitutional Court of the Republic of Latvia, Case No. 2000-03-01, 30.08.2000, para. 5. The text of the judgment in English available at <http://www.satv.tiesa.gov.lv/upload/2000-03-01E.rtf>.

essential to note that in contrast to many states, where social and economic rights are only formulated as principles, in the *Satversme* these are individual rights which individuals can claim before the courts. In a decision on the compliance of certain provisions of the 'Law on State Social Allowances' with the *Satversme*, the Constitutional Court has made clear that: 'If some social rights are included in the Constitution then the State cannot refuse from them. These rights do not have only a declarative nature. These rights have become the rights of an individual. A person may require realization of these rights from the State, as well as may defend the above rights in a court'.[43]

In addition to the human rights catalogue established in the Universal Declaration of Human Rights the *Satversme* also includes rights of minorities. Article 114 of the *Satversme* states: 'Persons belonging to ethnic minorities have the right to preserve and develop their language and their ethnic and cultural identity'.[44] This was an important step to demonstrate that in a similar way to in the pre-war republic the rights of minorities to use their language and develop their culture are protected. A relatively new and progressive phenomenon is also the recognition in the *Satversme* of third-generation rights, such as the right to live in a favourable environment. Article 115 of the *Satversme* declares: 'The State shall protect the right of everyone to live in a benevolent environment by providing information about environmental conditions and by promoting the preservation and improvement of the environment'.[45] On the basis of this clause individuals have successfully challenged in the Constitutional Court the decisions of a municipality to build a waste utilisation factory next to their houses[46] or municipal development plans which provide for extensive building in an area despite objections by the local population.[47]

As noted above the fundamental rights chapter was adopted eight years after the restoration of the independence of Latvia. Nevertheless, the legacy of the Soviet past as well as values which played an essential role during the struggle for independence found their way into the text of the new chapter of the *Satversme*. For instance, chapter 8 starts with article 90 which guarantees that everybody should be informed about his/her rights. Furthermore, article 100 of the Constitution in addition to guaranteeing freedom of expression, specifically

---

43 The judgment of the Constitutional Court of the Republic of Latvia, Case No. 2007-15-01, 12.02.2008., para. 5. The text of the judgment in English available at <http://www.satv.tiesa.gov.lv/upload/judg_2007_17_05.htm>.

44 Latvijas Republikas Satversme. *Valdības Vēstnesis*, 30.06.1922., Nr. 141. The text of the Constitution of the Republic of Latvia in English available at <http://saeima.lv/en/legislation/constitution>.

45 *Ibid.*

46 The judgment of the Constitutional Court of the Republic of Latvia, Case No. 2002-14-04, 14.02.2003. The text of the judgement in English available at <http://www.satv.tiesa.gov.lv/upload/2002-14-04E.rtf>.

47 The judgement of the Constitutional Court of the Republic of Latvia, Case No. 2008-38-03, 06.07.2009.

emphasises that all censorship is prohibited. In view of 50 years of the Russification policy during the Soviet occupation, a number of articles of the Constitution emphasise the protection of and the role of Latvian as an official language in citizens' interaction with the authorities.

Lastly, development of fundamental rights in the constitution did not end with the adoption of chapter 8 of the *Satversme*. First of all, interpretation of the fundamental rights has been influenced by Latvia's accession to a number of human rights treaties of the Council of Europe and the jurisprudence of the European Court of Human Rights. Secondly, the fundamental rights in the *Satversme* have subsequently been shaped by Latvia's membership in the European Union and the conclusion of bilateral agreements with other states, which limit certain rights and freedoms, for instance the prohibition of extradition of citizens to a foreign country. Thirdly, an essential difference from the pre-war period is the establishment of the Constitutional Court in 1996 and the introduction of the individual petition procedure in 2001. The Court has played an enormous role in the evolution of the fundamental rights set out in the *Satversme* and has developed significant jurisprudence interpreting and giving substance to the fundamental rights in the *Satversme*, making them a 'reality for citizens'.

4. CONCLUDING REMARKS

The intention of the Constitutional Assembly of Latvia was that the Constitution should have two parts. Hence, the Constitutional Committee of the Constitutional Assembly prepared a project on organisation of state authority and a declaration of civil rights and duties. However, the second part of the Constitution was dismissed in the third reading on 5 April 1922 and the Constitution came into force on 7 November 1922 without any fundamental rights chapter.

The second part of the Constitution was thus an unsuccessful attempt by the Latvian constitutional legislator to formulate a catalogue of fundamental rights. But the second part of the Constitution, cannot be considered only as a monument of legal history. After the entry into force of the Constitution politicians and lawyers returned several times to the issue of the constitutional regulation of fundamental rights. Only on 15 October 1998 did this discussion lead to success — the legislature adopted chapter 8 of the Constitution. This chapter is largely based on the earlier draft second part of the Constitution. The idea that the final chapter of the Constitution should consist of a catalogue of fundamental rights, the structure of the chapter and the wording of several of the norms are taken from the draft of the second part of the Constitution, modernised according to the development of human rights and Latvian international obligations. Consequently, the second part of the Constitution was as it turned out largely prepared as a catalogue of fundamental rights for the future — for the new century.

26. THE HISTORY OF FUNDAMENTAL RIGHTS IN EUROPE: A LONG AND WINDING ROAD

Kalliope AGAPIOU-JOSEPHIDES
Jean-Paul LEHNERS
Manfred NOWAK
Markku SUKSI

1. INTRODUCTION: AN IMPORTANT STEP IN THE NEW HISTORIOGRAPHY OF FUNDAMENTAL RIGHTS

To produce a volume about the first fundamental rights documents in the Member States of the European Union was a real challenge. It was clear from the beginning that it would be difficult to find a common methodology, common definitions and a common understanding of fundamental rights. The result is nonetheless convincing, although we have many different approaches, or perhaps the result is convincing precisely because we have these different approaches. The quality of the volume is indeed a consequence of the variety that can be found in the fundamental rights documents

This volume is not only an interesting overview of the early history of fundamental rights in Europe, providing new insights based on little studied documents or on new interpretations of well-known documents, but also a contribution to the discussion about the development of fundamental rights insofar as some ideas expressed in the early documents can still inspire us today. At the outset of the project, the risk of retrospective teleology was identified. Fortunately, almost all the contributors have avoided this, even though they are writing about the predecessors of modern fundamental rights.

The result of the collated endeavours of the authors feels like an important contribution to a new historiography of fundamental rights that avoids, as much as possible, the above-mentioned retrospective teleology, identifies new cleavages, and reflects on the (mis)use of history and memory for current political and ideological aims.

2. GENERAL OBSERVATIONS

It is possible to find 'first' fundamental rights documents across Europe. Each of the current Member States of the European Union included in this volume can refer to one or more documents of this kind in their constitutional or legal history. From this point of view, the review of the first fundamental rights documents in Europe has produced a definitive result by uncovering antecedent fundamental rights thinking that has not necessarily been generally known. The historical perspective of these documents is, however, very broad, because a good number of these first fundamental rights documents are ancient, while some of them are relatively recent. Whatever the specific point of time when these documents were granted or adopted, their significance for the individual who lived in that specific historical context was similar and implied recognition of at least some intrinsic value for the human being. When thinking about the fundamental rights document(s) in the various contributions of this volume, please take into consideration that you might find the text of the original document and perhaps even a translation of it into English on the internet at http://www.eiuc.org/first-fundamental-right-documents.

It is evident on the basis of the various fundamental rights documents reviewed in this volume that their emergence and evolution display many differences. It is possible to distinguish several documents on the basis of a number of dimensions. These include: fundamental rights as recognition of the individual in relation to the 'state' or the powers-that-be; fundamental rights evolving from privileges of some groups to general rights implying equality; fundamental rights moving from particularism to universalism in the relevant jurisdiction; fundamental rights in the vertical dimension and in the horizontal dimension; fundamental rights embedded in ordinary law or established in constitutional law and fundamental rights in nation-building. On the basis of these dimensions, it is also easy to detect links to international human rights, although these were not in focus in this volume.

A number of the documents reviewed here focus on fundamental rights as recognition of the individual in relation to the 'state' or to the powers-that-be. This is the case with, for instance, Magna Carta (UK) and the Golden Bull (Hungary), and this aspect becomes very tangible in the fundamental rights documents adopted in the aftermath of the important year of 1848, when Europe was re-invigorating the rights-thinking of the 1789 French Revolution. The vertical aspect of fundamental rights is thus clearly present in the history of fundamental rights, but the materials reviewed in this volume also indicate a large number of instances where relationships in the horizontal dimension have, early on, been regulated in a manner that can be understood as fundamental, such as marriage between free persons and slaves (Greece), right of inheritance for women (Greece, Ireland), the legal position of the indigenous (Spain), and the right to use the forest (Austria, UK), as well as the early nineteenth century understanding of fundamental rights as negative freedoms. Of course, at the material time, hundreds of years ago, the law-makers and regulators were not aware of the nature of these legal relationships as fundamental rights; they appear as such for the modern reader, but might not have been perceived so when they first emerged, and at a point when their existence perhaps was discontinued due to changes in society, beneficiaries of such rights might not have protested the loss of their fundamental rights. It is nonetheless possible to detect an equality component of some sort in many of the examples put forward in this volume, and in the modern reader, this would summon to mind fundamental rights.

It is also possible to make the general observation that around the time of the adoption of Magna Carta in England, similar thoughts were written down in normative language elsewhere in Europe. Potentially (and highly speculatively), increases in population numbers resulted in such a density of people that there arose a need to consider legal relationships between the rulers and the ruled and also between members of society in a manner that went beyond the traditional horizontal relationships between individuals (as is indicated in the Austrian contribution). In some instances, fundamental rights evolved from privileges of some groups to general rights implying equality between individuals. The most salient example of this is Magna Carta (UK), but other ones exist, too, across Europe (for instance, the Czech Republic, Lithuania, Hungary, and Poland). In this sense, the Nordic understanding of privileges implies the opposite: the privileges granted at different points of time and for different reasons to the nobility, the clergy, the bourgeoisie, and the land-owning farmers were not perceived as fundamental rights of everyone and never developed such a quality (Denmark, Finland, Sweden). Instead, rights of a fundamental nature applicable to everyone started to evolve in the eighteenth century on the basis of an understanding that such rights would be general and independent from belonging to a particular social group that enjoyed some privileges established by the ruler (France). The general trend, however, seems to have been one where the rights thinking has evolved from particularism (rights of specific social groups) to universalism (rights of everyone) within the relevant jurisdiction, achieved by way of evolution (as with Magna Carta), by way of revolution (as with the 1789 French Declaration or the German *Paulskirchenverfassung* of 1848) or by way of normative developments that can be placed between these two extremes.

From the normative point of view, the emergence of constitutionally entrenched fundamental rights was not actually possible before the normative separation between constitutional law and ordinary law. This development, which is a broader phenomenon not only limited to fundamental rights and which encompasses the separation of powers, internal organisation of the state and other typical constitutional issues, grew stronger during the eighteenth century and resulted around the mid-nineteenth century in a multitude of constitutions in Europe which were furnished with a bill of rights. Therefore, many of the fundamental rights documents established before the eighteenth century formulated rights of a fundamental nature in the horizontal dimension in what we would today identify as ordinary law (see, for instance, the Irish contribution). A formal understanding of fundamental rights is thus also dependent on an evolution of normative thinking and on ideas that revolve around the ways in which the state can limit its own actions by means of positive legal norms. This distinction is at least in part reflected in the organisation of the book, with the first part devoted to contributions on first fundamental rights documents before the eighteenth century laid down in ordinary laws and the second part containing contributions on first fundamental rights documents from the eighteenth century on, laid down in constitutions. In the first part of this volume, fundamental rights are discussed from a more material perspective, while in the second part, fundamental rights are treated from a more formal perspective, i.e. from the point of view of their constitutional nature. The second part of this volume therefore also brings in fundamental rights in the processes of nation-building, a process that at least at times subordinated fundamental rights to the ideology of nationalism and — in some instances — still continues to do so today, as pointed out in the Slovakian and Hungarian contributions. Whether this is 'good' or 'bad' depends on the circumstances and on the political context.

Fundamental rights are, from this perspective, at the top of the hierarchy of rights, because an Act of a constitutional nature is superior to ordinary Acts. This means that fundamental rights are often formulated in a more or less abstract form in the constitution of the country. It also means that before they are implemented in practical situations involving individuals, they must often be made more concrete by means of provisions in ordinary law. As a consequence, they become applicable by administrative authorities and also controlled by a judicial authority, such as supreme courts or constitutional courts, or by extra-judicial mechanisms.

Much has been discussed in more recent controversies between historians about the continuity or discontinuity of the historical evolution of contemporary human rights, as we find them in a variety of international and regional treaties adopted after the end of World War II. Some authors seem to advance discontinuities rather than continuities in the relationship between fundamental rights in national constitutions and the normative universal human rights framework of today. The contributions to this volume indeed show that there is little continuity between the early freedom charters and other ancient and medieval documents covered in the first part and later developments of fundamental rights in the respective countries and territories or — even less so — human rights at the international level. Some authors of these historical contributions explicitly emphasise that they have doubts whether these documents should be called 'fundamental rights' documents at all, because they have very little in common with later fundamental rights thinking and documents. As privileges granted to a particular group of human beings, as a result of a particular historical power-struggle, these documents lack even the aspiration of granting rights to human beings for the simple reason that they are human beings. The element of equality may be totally missing from these early documents.

On the other hand, the contributions to the second part of this book indicate a certain continuity between the evolution of fundamental (constitutional) rights at the domestic level since the late eighteenth and nineteenth centuries and the codification of international human rights after World War II, although this link was not a focus of our joint endeavour. As with contemporary international human rights, the idea that all human beings are born free and equal, and therefore (should) enjoy equal and inalienable rights as human beings, plays an important role in the philosophical origins as well in the normative manifestation of fundamental (human) rights since the French Declarations of the Rights of Man and of the Citizen of 1789 and 1793. It is true, of course, that the concept of 'man' (*l'homme*) at that time was understood in the narrow sense of the male members of the bourgeois class, thus excluding in reality women, children, slaves, servants, landless peasants and wage-workers, but at least in theory, the concept of equality was established, and women, slaves, peasants and the working class could base their struggle for equal rights on the idea that all human beings are born with equal and inalienable rights. The fact that Olympe de Gouges was executed during the French Revolution in part for having published a French Declaration of the Rights of Woman and the Female Citizen does not take away the fact that women could later successfully claim equal rights with men on the basis of the same French documents, which were later incorporated without any changes in contemporary French constitutions. Similarly, the Universal Declaration of Human Rights of 1948 and later human rights treaties adopted within the framework of the United Nations and a growing number of regional and sub-regional organisations use the same wording as the old fundamental rights documents and are based on the same concept of equal and inalienable rights of all human beings.

Fundamental rights, according to their philosophical foundation in natural law theories, were originally aimed at protecting human beings against violations by other human beings, and the State derived its main legitimacy from the protection of these natural rights through its monopoly of power. However, from the late nineteenth century fundamental rights came to be seen as defining primarily the relationship between the individual and the state. In the bourgeois concept of fundamental rights, which was further developed by legal positivism, civil rights were defined as granting liberal freedom from State interference, and political rights as empowering citizens with political freedom, i.e. the freedom to participate in the political decision-making process. In the early documents discussed in the first part of our book, we find concepts such as liberties, privileges, and freedoms. Today we use concepts such as values, rights and constitutional principles without always making the necessary distinctions.

These issues are at the heart of this volume. 'Fundamental rights' encompass both rights and duties/responsibilities.

We have been interested in who it is that might be placed under a duty to fulfil the rights to a lesser extent, but this volume does also provide some reflections on that topic. Additional questions present in the volume are plentiful. Who issues fundamental rights? The monarch, the government, the parliament, or local authorities? Who is concerned or identified as the beneficiary? The whole population living and/or working on a territory, residents, only citizens, or only specific categories of society such as nobles, clergy or the bourgeoisie? Only men? Are the rights acquired or perhaps declared as inherent? Who influenced the drafting of texts: poets or thinkers preparing the terrain by sermons, pamphlets, a memorandum, or by a book published in Denmark containing a selection of European constitutions? This is important especially if it is not the document which is the main focus, but the conditions, situations and contexts in which the document has been produced. We must also not forget the texts of philosophers, for example, the influence of personalism in Poland that added a moral perspective as far as the obligations of the State are concerned.

We also have to consider the influence of documents between different countries in Europe. A good example of this is the liberal Belgian Constitution of 1831 that inspired drafters of constitutions in many other European countries during the nineteenth century, such as Austria, Bulgaria, Denmark, Finland, Germany, and Romania. In Denmark, the king was also the Duke of Holstein. This 'link to Germany meant that the demands for increased political participation south of the border reached Denmark' (Denmark). In these cases we seek of course concrete indications of these influences and not a vague feeling that the spirit or the message of one text spread over the continent. At the same time, it is possible to detect, in the context of the nineteenth century and in the spread of the fundamental rights thinking, a certain delay caused by the Russian imperial influence in the North-Eastern parts of the current European Union (Estonia, Finland, Latvia, Lithuania, Poland) that started to wither away only with the constitutional reforms of 1906 in Russia.

3. METHODOLOGICAL OBSERVATIONS

When considering methodological issues, it is necessary to start by mentioning that the different chapters in this volume depend in part on previous studies that have been carried out on the history of fundamental rights in the various countries. When it is not possible to rely on historical studies new hypotheses can, of course, be developed, but these hypotheses must at some juncture be verified or checked against the documents. Sometimes it is also difficult to identify what has been published, as a number of territories of today have been part of other political entities during the past centuries. It is not self-evident that a Finnish scholar is aware of everything that has been published in Sweden, or that a historian in Luxembourg would know everything that has been published in Belgium or the Netherlands on relevant antecedents to their national constitutional history.

The personal national background of the contributors may influence their work. If one comes from a country that only recently became independent or became independent again after a long period of foreign rule or occupation, there might naturally be an interest in the right to self-determination, such that it is declared as the most important fundamental right (Slovakia). If the researchers come from a country that in recent years has not been considered a champion in the field of human rights, such as Hungary, the contribution may point out the political misuse of documents in justifying the politics of today.

A short remark about territorial background is also warranted. Territories and jurisdictions of today are different from territories and jurisdictions in the past. Not many countries in Europe have had their current borders for centuries, although this is the case for Portugal. Some situations are also very complicated: countries of today have been part of other territories and have depended on other political powers than those which prevail today. In some cases there have been specific laws for more or less autonomous regions (Austria, Finland, Italy, Greece, etc.). Situations of this sort have increased the complexity of our research.

There are authors who are convinced that they have clearly identified the first fundamental rights document on the territory of their actual country. These may have been established in ancient times (The Great Code of Gortyn in Crete adopted in the fifth century BC), hark back to ancient traditions formulated later (Senchas Már in Ireland compiled in the seventh century), or date back to medieval times (like England, Belgium, Germany) or the early modern history of the nineteenth century (such as the Freedom Charter of Bucharest in Romania). Other contributors are more hesitant and declare the first documents they have found as pre- or proto-constitutional. 'It would — lest there are new findings leading to new insights — not be legitimate to insist on constructing an early history of fundamental rights, in the modern sense, in the Austrian ancestral lands before the eighteenth century' (Austria). 'First references to individual rights of man do not appear in the Belgian tradition until the revolutionary period at the end of the eighteenth century' (Belgium).

We have chapters focusing on one document, as in Spain (Laws of Burgos), Denmark (the abolition of adscription), Sweden (the Freedom of Press Act), and Slovakia (self-determination). Others try to accomplish a more or less complete overview of all the documents known to date or compare a historical set of rights with documents currently in force, like the Charter of Fundamental Rights of the European Union (Bulgaria). In the contributions we find different types of documents: charters (Magna Carta, the Great Code of Gortyn), constitutions (around 1848), drafts of constitutions (Latvia), and reflections by individual persons and political thinkers (Finland, Greece). It is also clear that the simple mention of rights in a document does not mean that this is automatically considered as a fundamental rights document.

As is evident from what has been said above, the understanding of fundamental rights and of what it is that constitutes a first fundamental rights document is hinged on concepts that have evolved relatively recently, such as the normative separation between constitutional law and ordinary law and the rights of individuals in relation to the public powers. The persons who developed and codified provisions of this kind during the thirteenth century were doubtless unaware of how those stipulations would be viewed several centuries later. In spite of that, provisions dealt with here were probably highly important for the individuals of the material time in a manner that warrants a modern characterisation of those provisions as fundamental. At the very least, they give evidence of rights-thinking of an early kind. Thus, the different chapters tell us not only something about the development of fundamental rights in the past, but also about our conception of fundamental rights today. An even clearer invention of modernity is the discussion around different categorisation of rights within international human rights, namely civil, cultural, economic, political and social rights. However, the modern nature of the exercise should not prevent us from trying to use categorisation as a tool to describe fundamental rights in the first fundamental rights documents, because such a profile of historical fundamental rights can be very helpful in structuring our discussion and analysis.

The contributions in this volume do not, however, yield much basis for any systematic analysis, but warrant only a very general and superficial intimation of such a profile. It appears that so-called civil and also political rights have been in focus in the fundamental rights documents dealt with here and that some surprising formulations of rights of an economic and social rights nature can also be spotted in the materials, while cultural rights are not featured in the contributions, except in one instance of early mention of rights of national minorities (Estonia). The same is true in relation to norms concerning women: the position of women is only sporadically regulated in the early fundamental rights documents. However, there are interesting examples in the Code of Gortyn and in the Senchas Már of rules that apply to women. These norms appear to regulate rights in the realm of the family, such as inheritance and marriage. A more political dimension with regard to women emerges only in the turmoils of the French Revolution through the above-mentioned French Declaration of the Rights of Woman and the Female Citizen and gains further footholds in the beginning of the twentieth century when the right to vote and to stand as a candidate is extended to women (e.g., Finland 1906).

4. FUNDAMENTAL RIGHTS HISTORY IN CONTEXT

It is necessary to ask a general question right at the beginning of this review of results: Do we start with the drafting of constitutions and then ask if they have a chapter on fundamental rights, or do we try to find out when fundamental rights have been declared independently of the drafting of a constitution? In this book we can identify both approaches. We also have examples of fundamental rights in political declarations instead of laws (Slovakia in the nineteenth century).

Which is the oldest fundamental rights document in Europe? We should recall that this volume is published on the occasion of the 800th anniversary of the English Magna Carta, but Magna Carta is not the only document in the historiography of fundamental rights in Europe. It is not even the oldest (even in England, see the Charter of Liberties in 1115). Several authors are very affirmative as far as the role of fundamental rights in European historiography is concerned. Latvia has one of the oldest constitutions that are in force in Europe (1922), if the interregnum during the Soviet rule is not taken into account (but see Luxembourg 1868). Poland had the first written constitution in Europe drafted and adopted in a democratic way (1791), while in Greece during the fifth century BC, one of the earliest code of laws and the first European one was produced in Crete. Identifying early documents on fundamental rights depends *inter alia* on the definition of such rights (see above, section 2).

If it is important to discover why the documents were produced, it may also be interesting to analyse why in certain territories such documents were never issued, why declarations appear and disappear, why there are successes or failures, and what the main cleavages are (state-territorial, religions, regimes, strategies and the interconnections between these aspects) (see, *inter alia*, the Czech Republic). If fundamental rights are not mentioned in a text, it may be possible to infer that they had been considered as self-evident (which seems to be the situation in France, where the Constitutional Council introduced the Declaration of 1789 through its decision-making practice into the Constitution of 1958). There are disagreements among historians about the interpretation of a number of documents (such as the Maiestas Carolina in the Czech territory, or the Laws of Burgos in Spain).

Almost all of the early documents were, at least originally, intended for a specific segment of society and not for the entire population. In these documents we can identify a certain reciprocity: the sovereign provides protection of the law, and in exchange, the nobles etc. give him loyalty and service. Besides written texts we have oral traditions, such as in Belgium where 'The unwritten basis of constitutional guarantees for the Flemish Estates against the Count of Flanders turned out to be much more effective in practice than the written documents in Brabant and Liège'. But at the same time, '[w]ritten documents had a considerable advantage in that they could be transmitted, remembered and interpreted extensively throughout the centuries' (Belgium).

Many, but not all, documents have been produced following a conflict situation of some sort. The others are similar to a contract between the sovereign and the people or a segment of society. Declarations have been signed after a rebellion of the nobles against the king (England), after new social categories asking for rights (for example Belgium), after situations of injustice (Spain), and following an increase in the role of one part of society (bourgeoisie) (e.g., Italy, France).

Some constitutions have been adopted but were never in force or were soon abolished or restricted depending on new political constellations (Portugal in 1822 after less than one year; the constitutions following the revolutions in 1848 in many countries in Europe). In Denmark 'the Constitution of 1849 [...] included rather democratic electoral rules. However in 1866 this situation changed by means of a constitutional amendment [...]. The tradition of 1849, namely that social and economic reforms should evolve independently of the constitution and be regulated by statute law, was consolidated'.

Some documents have elements of fundamental rights, but also contain articles that may be contrary to our actual understanding of fundamental rights: 'The maintenance of serfdom until 1781 and the only superficial attempts to contain the persecution of witches stand in stark contrast to any potential fundamental rights', (Austria) which nevertheless could not prevent the emergence of new rights thinking in Austria during the nineteenth century.

In the different documents we do not always have new rights, but sometimes guarantees of former rights (England). Many documents are reissued or updated (illustrating the fundamental rights document as a living document). That does not mean that we always have a continuous development of rights over centuries; interruptions may occur due to a change of political regimes, occupations, etc.

A certain number of constitutions are linked to national independence and identity. Several texts insist on this link between the appearance of fundamental rights and the shaping of a national identity: 'Even the demands of individual rights were in fact primarily intended to reach equality of nations, i.e. the collective rights of a nation' and here especially the right to self-determination (Slovakia).

In Italy the *Liber Paradisus* is not per se a fundamental rights document. It contains a list of slaves who are liberated, with one of its aims the increasing of tax revenues (an aim familiar in many other territories in Europe). However, the prologue of *Liber Paradisus* makes reference to universal values.

To make a deeper analysis of the documents we have to differentiate between the different segments of society. For example in Denmark after the abolition of adscription of peasants in 1788, 'crofters benefitted far less from the agrarian reforms than the farmers, legally and in social practice, and as for women, they gained even less'.

Are constitutions changed or abolished or kept after a change of regime such as the ones that took place in 1989/90? In Latvia, and this is probably unique, the pre-war constitution was restored, while fundamental rights were added only in 1998.

The discussion of the first fundamental rights document is often reduced to a consideration of the first constitutional mention of fundamental rights as we understand them today. If constitutions and other texts that refer to fundamental rights do not correspond to a willingness of political actors to protect them, these rights run the risk of remaining 'social constructs' (Czech Republic).

Some documents are not intrinsically of great importance, but became significant later on because others made reference to them (such as Sir Edward Coke in the seventeenth century with Magna Carta), established a genealogy of rights, or used them for ideological and political purposes. 'The resurrection [of fundamental rights documents] in subsequent times vested these texts with the authority they lacked at the time of their promulgation' (Belgium).

5. PROSPECTS FOR FURTHER RESEARCH

This book is a first step in a new historiography of fundamental rights in Europe. The research and analysis it contains should be continued, if possible, by developing interdisciplinary research projects bringing together researchers and academics from different disciplines: law, history, political sciences, philosophy etc., with the aim of trying to find a common language and departing from different perspectives (thoughts in this direction are expressed in the contribution of, for instance, Austria).

Ongoing research must make a clear distinction between memory and history. Some contributors have made very interesting and important reflections on this topic (Hungary and Italy). Documents can be interpreted in different ways. '[T]he document can be invoked as a point of reference both for extension of human rights and the restriction of equality depending on political will' (Hungary).

We must be aware that 'unified national history is a construction, an after-the-fact creation that is an important part of the national identity of states' (Hungary). Therefore, we have to develop counter-histories to, for example, the official history of the Holy Crown and the Golden Bull in Hungary. The role of fundamental rights in nation-building seems firmly established, but not in nation-keeping. In this context commemorations of anniversaries of historical documents may insist on one document but might not mention others with similar or even higher importance (e.g. the 1798 *Staatsregeling* in the Netherlands neglected when commemorating in 1998 the anniversary of the Constitution of 1848).

It will also be necessary to identify borderlines between medieval and modern periods that are among others characterised by the equality of rights (Hungary). We have to identify 'crucial junctures'. It is 'possible to find a point in history at which socio-political circumstances generally associated with the enactment of fundamental rights instruments at domestic or international level coincided, leading to the formulation of a normative act that enshrined something that, in that very moment, had the value of what nowadays we call a fundamental rights declaration or the declaration of a fundamental right' (Italy). We should explore whether there is a more or less direct link between early documents and current fundamental rights, albeit not necessarily a linearity.

Contextualisation of the documents is a key concept. In attempting to take further the research started in this book it will be necessary to go deeper into the historical context in which the documents have been produced. Findings must be harmonised, checking whether the same definition of fundamental rights has been used, and we should compare and establish analogies, similarities and divergences. This was not always possible in this volume, because some authors refer to documents from other countries that the authors working on these countries did not mention, for example a model for a constitution in another country that is not mentioned in the chapter for that country. But this does not help us with the more important task of contextualisation. Here micro studies could be very helpful. Of high importance is the question of the level of analysis: were the documents produced on a national, regional or local level? If so, how can we link the different levels?

In today's discussions, it should be possible to take advantage of the knowledge of ancient texts, for example the 'principles of community, hospitality, responsibility and justice' (Ireland), 'collective rights over water sources' (Ireland), specific rights, freedoms and privileges for specific segments of society that we find in medieval texts and also in the more current UN Conventions and Declarations. 'Will ancient traditions be our future solutions?' (Belgium).

We have in this volume shed light on some of the early history of the formalisation of fundamental rights in Europe. The exercise is, as has been explained above, incomplete. Nonetheless, the interpretation of historic documents remains our responsibility and we hope that in opening this original phase to scrutiny we have contributed to the process of understanding fundamental rights documents, both nationally and internationally, in such a manner that we might be fit to face the unknown challenges of the future.

INDEX

I

K

L

M

N

P

R

S

T

U

V

www.ingramcontent.com/pod-product-compliance
Ingram Content Group UK Ltd.
Pitfield, Milton Keynes, MK11 3LW, UK
UKHW051920100926
8556IPUK00021B/1274

9 781780 683607